NIGERIA: OPTIONS FOR LONG-TERM DEVELOPMENT

NIGERIA: OPTIONS FOR LONG-TERM DEVELOPMENT

Report of a mission sent to Nigeria
by the
World Bank

Chief of Mission and Coordinating Author
Wouter Tims

THE JOHNS HOPKINS UNIVERSITY PRESS
Baltimore and London

Library of Congress Catalog Card Number 73-19354
ISBN 0-8018-1602-5 (clothbound)
ISBN 0-8018-1603-3 (paperbound)

Library of Congress Cataloging in Publication data
will be found on the last printed page of this book.

FOREWORD

This is the fifth in the current series of World Bank country economic reports that are being made available for the use of scholars and practitioners in the field of economic and social development. It is the second to be published formally on behalf of the Bank, following "Economic Growth of Colombia: Problems and Prospects" in 1972. Others published less formally by the Bank itself in 1973 have been "Employment in Trinidad and Tobago," "The Current Economic Position and Prospects of Ecuador" and "The Current Economic Position and Prospects of Peru."

Such reports are prepared regularly by the Bank on all borrowing countries, in support of its own operations. They serve as a basis for decisions on Bank policy and operations, and for discussions with the governments. Many are used by the governments themselves as an aid to their economic planning, and by various consortia and consultative groups of governments and institutions providing development assistance. Several have been published by the governments concerned, on their own initiative.

Since there has been an expressed desire for wider access to these reports, the Bank's policy is to publish as many of them as possible, always subject to the affected government's approval, in order to encourage academic research and facilitate the interchange of knowledge and experience.

The present study results from the work of a mission to Nigeria in 1971 under the leadership of Mr. Wouter Tims. It was presented to the Bank's Executive Directors in June 1972. While many of the quantitative projections have been affected by intervening events, such as increases in petroleum production and prices, most of the basic analysis is still valid.

Hollis B. Chenery
Vice President for Development Policy
The World Bank

A World Bank Country Economic Report published under the general editorship of Ian Bowen. *Nigeria: Options for Long-Term Development* is based on the findings of an economic mission headed by Wouter Tims and including general economists T. K. Osgood, C. Wilkinson, E. Lim and D. C. Rao, industrial economist B. H. Decaux, fiscal economist V. P. Gandhi, employment economist M. Leiserson, population specialists J. E. Gholl and F. J. Rath, water supply specialists P. W. Whitford and V. Rajagopalan, loan officer D. Pearce, and statistical assistant C. D. Papavassiliou. This book also draws from the findings of 1971 reports by a World Bank Agricultural Sector Review Mission, a World Bank Transport Sector Review Mission, and a Unesco Project Identification Mission. The chief of mission and coordinating author is responsible for the scope and overall conclusions of the report.

Notes

AREA: 923,768 km^2

POPULATION: 68 million (1971)[a]

DENSITY: 74 per km^2

CURRENCY EQUIVALENTS

Unit: Nigerian pound [£N]

Prior to December 20, 1971:
U.S.$1: £N0.357
£N1: U.S.$2.80
£N1,000,000: U.S.$2,800,000

Since December 20, 1971:
U.S.$1: £N0.329
£N1: U.S.$3.04
£N1,000,000: U.S.$3,040,000

FISCAL YEAR: April 1 to March 31

WEIGHTS AND MEASURES

1 mile: 1.6093 km
1 acre: 0.4047 ha
1 sq. mile: 259 ha

1 lb: 453.59 gm
1 long ton: 1,016.05 kg

[a]Official estimate; other estimates are as much as ten million lower.

TABLE OF CONTENTS

TABLES

MAPS

CHARTS

NIGERIA: OPTIONS FOR LONG-TERM DEVELOPMENT

SUMMARY

Nigeria had a per capita income of about U.S.$100 in 1971 and a population of approximately 65 million. As in most countries at a similar income level, the main source of income and employment is agriculture, and future growth of income and employment opportunities for the majority of the population will continue to depend largely on development in the rural sector. The distinguishing feature of the economy in the short- and medium-term is the rapid development of its oil-producing sector, which is providing a considerable degree of relief from balance of payments pressures and resource mobilization difficulties. The direct impact of the oil sector is small, however, and the diffusion of the sector's growth-generating effects will be particularly difficult.

This report reviews briefly the major trends and policies that have characterized the country's economic development to date and examines in more detail the current position of the economy, its prospects during the remaining period of the Second National Development Plan (1972/73 - 1973/74) and the longer-term outlook through the early 1980s. The report also includes a detailed description of the petroleum industry (Chapter 6) and a brief discussion of education, agriculture, manufacturing and infrastructure (Chapter 7).

Recent Developments

Quite apart from the impact of the civil war, the second half of the 1960s was a turning point in Nigeria's economic development. Until then the vicissitudes of international markets for Nigerian produce had largely determined the pattern of income, investment and the balance of payments. Agricultural exports were primarily responsible for an average GDP growth rate of about 5 percent per annum during the 1950s and the early 1960s. Growth was provided mainly by the employment of surplus land and labor, and by the substitution of higher value export crops for subsistence crops, without significant reorganization of the society or the introduction of new production techniques. Technological changes were introduced in the form of new crops and in the concomitant development of modern transport and processing facilities. Economic growth thus took place within a fairly static framework with little intervention by the colonial administration before 1960 or the independent government thereafter.

A new development pattern emerged in the mid-1960s, as agricultural exports stagnated from 1962 onward. Rapidly growing industries, until then too small to be significant, began to exert considerable influence on the economy; even more dramatic was the emergence of petroleum mining as the leading growth sector. In 1966, however, these trends were largely obscured by the unrest and uncertainty preceding the civil war which resulted in a slackening of investment activity and a fall in the rate of GDP growth. The ensuing civil war caused major losses of production in the East and Mid-West, and serious damage to infrastructure, notably roads and other transport facilities, in other parts of the country as well as in the areas directly affected by the hostilities. The disturbances preceding the war and the war itself displaced a large number of people, many of whom were skilled workers and highly trained professionals.

The resilience and strength of the Nigerian economy was clearly demonstrated during the civil war. Production of food crops outside the war areas as well as exports of cocoa and groundnuts continued undisturbed except for internal transport difficulties. The loss of manufacturing industries in the East, coupled with the severe restriction of imports, led to sharp increases in manufacturing output in the rest of the country. Military expenditures of the federal government were financed almost entirely by domestic resources despite the sharp decline in foreign exchange earnings and government revenues attributable to the loss of all on-shore production of oil. The government effectively rationed the use of scarce foreign exchange during the war years with a series of increasingly stringent direct and indirect controls. Thus Nigeria emerged from the civil war with a sizable but manageable internal debt; a negligible increase in external public debt; an increased level of economic activities, particularly in the manufacturing and petroleum sectors; and most importantly, with considerably increased confidence in both the underlying strength of its economy and the ability of the government to manage the large and diverse economy.

Current Position

Since the end of the war in January 1970, the rapid reintegration of the three Eastern states into the economic, political and social life of the nation is evidence of a remarkable postwar atmosphere of reconciliation and of the government's ability to enforce its pledge of non-reprisals against the Ibos. The federal government has now established a strong central position in the twelve-state federation, although many questions relating to the future constitutional pattern of the nation remain to be resolved. Physical repair and rehabilitation of the country's infrastructure after the civil war has been pursued with energy and a good deal of imagination and self-help, particularly in the states most directly affected, and is now virtually complete. A national population census was scheduled for November 1973, and is underway. The very effective management of the economy both during and immediately following the war, in particular, augurs well for the future, when a public sector role in the development effort substantially larger than ever before will be called for.

The postwar increase of the national product and income has been considerably faster than the average maintained during the early 1960s, with growth originating mainly in the petroleum and manufacturing sectors. The recovery of agriculture was relatively slow, however, with current output per capita still below the prewar (1966) level. In contrast, output of the oil sector in 1971 was about three times the maximum prewar level and income from the sector was further augmented by the world-wide revision of petroleum price and tax arrangements early in the year. Outside the oil sector private investment activities were also being maintained at about double the average prewar level. In 1970/71 total investment was estimated at about 21 percent of GNP, compared with an average of 14 percent in the first half of the 1960s. Current trends indicate that GDP over the 4 years of the current Plan period (1970/71-1973/74) will grow by an average rate slightly over 10 percent per annum in real terms – about 4 percent higher than the rate envisaged in the Plan – despite agricultural growth only roughly in line with population growth rate.

In FY 1971/72, government revenues from the oil sector increased to about £N320 million (U.S.$920 million, or about $13 per capita) from slightly less than £N100 million in the previous year. Owing largely to further increases in revenues expected from the oil sector, the government's fiscal position is expected to be strong over the remainder of the current Plan period if defense expenditures, which now represent about 7 percent of GNP, do not exceed the current level substantially. The increase in foreign exchange earnings attributable to the oil sector has already enabled the government to liquidate the £N220 million of commercial arrears which had accumulated during and immediately after the war. During the next two years, the remaining import payment restrictions could probably be removed without difficulty. Imports, which increased rapidly over the last two years, have apparently stabilized recently and balance of payment prospects over the next few years appear to be favorable. Private and official capital inflows should be sufficient to meet the small current account deficit that is expected to persist.

The immediate postwar economic and financial crisis in Nigeria is now over. This report is therefore addressed primarily to the country's longer-term development problems and opportunities. The main findings and conclusions are summarized in the following paragraphs.

Investment Program

Nigeria's public investment program is being implemented within the broad framework of its Second National Development Plan (1970/71-1973/74) which is concerned primarily with the requirements of reconstruction and rehabilitation. Although the fiscal year immediately following the civil war (1970/71) was designated as the first year of the Plan, actual implementation of the Plan was not initiated until April 1971. The government's first progress report on Plan implementation in April 1972 indicated considerable slippage during the first 18 months, with an overall shortfall of about 35 percent in public investment. The scarcity of prepared projects and limited executive capacity have also contributed to the delay, particularly in agriculture, industry and education. The performance of the twelve states has also been uneven.

While there has been some strengthening of administrative arrangements for planning and implementing public investment programs, it will probably be difficult to expand executive capacity in the short term – especially in the states – sufficiently to take full advantage of the country's improved resources. The present Plan contemplates total nondefense public investment of £N726 million over the four year period and this is the maximum likely to be realized. During the following four years, however, a public investment program of the order of £N1,200 million – roughly 8 percent of GNP compared with 6 percent in the current four-year period – is clearly justified in terms of the country's economic and social needs. Project preparation on a very large scale is therefore an immediate priority.

While there are little data outside the oil sector, available evidence indicates that private investment has increased rapidly since the end of the war, probably exceeding Plan targets substantially. It is expected that private investment, of which approximately 25 percent is presently accounted for by the oil sector, can be maintained at about 15-16 percent of GNP throughout the present Plan period and thereafter, with expanding activities outside the oil sector offsetting the expected decline in petroleum exploration and development after the mid-1970s. An uncertainty regarding the expansion of private investment is government policy toward increasing indigenous equity participation and replacing expatriate managerial and technical staff. A February 1972 Nigerian Enterprises Promotion Decree provides that selected manufacturing, service and commercial activities be reserved entirely to Nigerian enterprises after 1974, with a second group of activities under certain sizes required to acquire or maintain minimum indigenous equity participation of 40 percent. The government policy also involves mandatory and progressive reductions in the quotas of expatriates employed in all enterprises. Although there is no evidence as yet that the Nigerianization policy has affected foreign investment activities, a balance between investment growth and increased indigenous ownership, and between efficient operation and rapid Nigerianization of management will be difficult to strike over the coming years.

Fiscal Prospects

Current fiscal concerns relate primarily to the efficient allocation of resources accruing to the public sector which are expected to rise by nearly 40 percent over the next two years and to continue growing at a rate of about 10 percent per year thereafter. Even assuming a fairly considerable rate of increase of current expenditure, the fiscal position of the government as a whole should remain favorable. Current budgetary surpluses equivalent to roughly 8 percent of GNP might be realized from 1973/74 through the end of the decade. While limited planning and implementation capacity may keep the public sector's investment program below this level, there is little doubt that, in addition to the traditional development activities now being undertaken, adequate programs to increase employment and income opportunities in the rural sector and to provide infrastructure for the rapidly growing urban areas would require more financial resources than these surpluses will provide.

Recent developments in Nigeria's public finances underline the need for early consideration of a wide range of policy options and for longer-range planning and institutional development. Increased recurrent and capital expenditures on economic and social services, greater incentives to private activities in the agricultural and/or industrial sectors, participation in new or existing industries, and accumulation of reserves are some of the available options for allocating public resources. The need for new or enlarged industrial and agricultural credit facilities, finance for the domestic construction industry and assistance to Nigerian investors and entrepreneurs may also justify transfers of revenues to the indigenous private sector.

Projections of public sector revenues and expenditures over the next several years highlight the fact that federal revenues, being largely a function of the petroleum profits tax, are likely to rise much faster than state revenues. Whereas the federal government can look forward to substantial surpluses, the states may face rising recurrent deficits by mid-decade. It may therefore be difficult for the states to make full use of existing infrastructure capacity and to establish the new facilities that are necessary to overcome some of the regional disparities that now exist. Moreover, if there is to be scope for flexible agricultural price policies, the states must be freed of their present heavy reliance on produce taxes, including marketing board surpluses.

Inflation

In the two years ending December 1971, the money supply (including savings deposits) in Nigeria increased by 52 percent. Some of this increase was accounted for by remonetization in the eastern states. Most of it, however, stemmed from the government's reliance on short-term borrowing from the banking system and contributed to the rapid rate of urban inflation. The urban, low-income consumer price index increased by 13.8 percent during 1970 and by a further 15 percent during 1971, mainly attributable to food prices which increased by 24 percent and 27 percent respectively. Import liberalization measures introduced in 1971 eased the excess demand pressure on manufactured goods considerably, but anti-inflationary efforts have had little effect so far on food prices; credit guidelines introduced to restrain effective demand have been seriously breached and price controls have had little success. Inflation will therefore continue to be a matter of concern in view of recent and projected wage increases, a rising level of government activity and distribution bottlenecks, all of which contributed to inflationary pressures in the urban areas.

Balance of Payments

The medium-term prospects for Nigeria's balance of payments appear to be very favorable. The country's external resource balance (net export of goods and non-factor services) showed a surplus of £N65 million in 1971 despite import payments some 120 percent higher than the level only two years earlier. As the economy returns to normal, import growth should decelerate substantially over the next few years. Exports, on the other hand, are projected to increase rapidly, at an average annual rate of 12 percent at least until the second half of the 1970s, attributable almost entirely to quantity and price increases in oil. As a consequence, the external resource surplus could increase to approximately £N250 million at the end of the current Plan period, with further growth thereafter. Correspondingly rapid increases in factor payments abroad by the oil sector are expected to result in small deficits in the current account balance which should, however, be more than offset by private and official capital inflows. The overall balance of payments position of the country is therefore expected to be strong through the current Plan period and probably for some years to follow.

After the middle of the decade, however, the growth rate of petroleum exports may decline to about 7 percent while imports are likely to maintain a rate well above this level. A substantial resource gap may therefore re-emerge in the early 1980s, again constraining economic growth and development. Balance of payments difficulties could recur considerably sooner if public consumption were to rise more rapidly than projected.

Petroleum

The prospects for Nigeria's balance of payments and fiscal position depend to a large extent on developments in the petroleum sector. The oil industry is expected to account for some 85 percent of total export earnings and over 50 percent of combined government revenues from 1975 onward, based on continued increases in crude oil production from the current level of 1.7 million barrels per day to about 3 million by the late 1970s. Exploration in Nigeria is still at an early stage, however, and there are considerable uncertainties regarding the extent of its potential oil reserves. Moreover, government revenues from petroleum in Nigeria, even under the most optimistic assumptions, are unlikely ever to approach those of, say, Iran or Venezuela on a per capita basis.

There are two central issues with respect to government policies toward the petroleum sector: the division of net income per unit output between the government and the producing companies and the time-phasing of the expected total flow of national income from the sector. The former is unlikely to be an urgent issue in Nigeria over the next four to five years since the government's take per barrel of crude oil produced is now governed by the May 1971 agreements with the producing companies. Increases in the share of net income accruing to Nigeria in the foreseeable future are likely to occur only as the result of parallel increases in other producing countries.

The second issue is more complex. The government of a petroleum producing country can increase future income accruing to the economy at the expense of current income either by limiting the rate of extraction, or by acquiring equity shares in the producing companies. Therefore it has a certain degree of freedom concerning the time-phasing of national income flows from given reserves of oil. Limiting output for purposes of "conservation of wasting assets" is not yet a real issue in Nigeria. As the petroleum industry is still at a relatively early stage of exploration, it seems unlikely that a policy of conserving an asset whose magnitude is still unknown would be pursued in a country with Nigeria's overall needs.

Participation is a far more urgent question. As the returns to investment in the producing companies are likely to be high, participation appears to be a financially attractive option for the investment of current resources which might otherwise be used for less productive purposes. An increased role for Nigerians in the country's major industry would also be politically and socially desirable and participation in the equity and control of petroleum companies is now the explicit policy of the major oil exporting countries, including Nigeria. Unlike most major oil producing countries, however, Nigeria's available resources from petroleum are not large compared with the needs of the population. Government policies towards the petroleum sector may need to be pursued quite independently from countries whose oil revenues and income per capita are far larger than Nigeria.

Agriculture

Despite the growing importance of other sectors, agriculture, including forestry and fishing, which accounted for about 50 percent of GDP at factor cost in 1970/71, will remain a key factor in Nigeria's economic development as the largest employer of labor (about 72 percent of the labor force in 1970/71), the principal source of food and raw materials for the increasing population and a significant, albeit relatively declining, earner of foreign exchange. The acceleration of agricultural growth and the provision of additional employment opportunities in the sector is, therefore, crucial to the country's future progress.

There are comparable opportunities for growth in the sector, based primarily on the existence of expanding foreign and, particularly, domestic markets for Nigeria's agricultural output; the abundance of land and human resources whose diverse productive capacities are presently under-utilized; and the availability of improved technology which, if exploited, could increase productivity substantially. The constraints, on the other hand, are several: low producer incentives; transport and distribution bottlenecks; inadequate machinery for planning, coordinating and implementing a national policy for rural and agricultural development; insufficient qualified manpower; and shortages of improved seeds, fertilizers, chemicals, credit and other farm inputs.

Manufacturing

Since independence, the manufacturing sector has expanded very rapidly: the growth of value added has averaged over 11 percent annually. In large-scale manufacturing alone, it has risen over 15 percent annually since 1960 and about 20 percent during each of the past two years. Development began from a small base, however, and manufacturing's contribution to GDP is still well below 10 percent. The surplus capacity of earlier years has disappeared in many industries and recent increases in output have not kept pace with the rapid growth of consumer demand. Vigorous investment activity and lively foreign interest in new ventures have resulted.

The largest manufacturing groups are predominantly foreign-owned and controlled. The industrial structure is not yet well diversified and there has been little increase in domestic value-added which amounted to only 26 percent of gross output in 1967. Backward and forward integration is not yet significant, although the government is promoting such development, particularly in textiles. Export processing industries have grown considerably slower than import-substitution industries and their share of manufacturing value-added declined from 50 percent in 1958 to 25 percent in 1967.

The government has provided tax and tariff incentives to industry — particularly to firms producing consumer goods and import substitutes — on a rather general and generous basis. The wide range of existing nominal and effective duty rates has developed over the past decade largely on the basis of revenue and protection considerations; major revision of the tariff structure might now be appropriate in order to relate incentive system more directly to government priorities for the development of the sector. Over the longer term, agricultural modernization and growth, higher farm incomes and some correction of the present imbalance between urban and rural incomes could play an important role in the growth of manufacturing.

Social and Economic Infrastructure

During the 1960s, primary and secondary school enrollment grew at estimated annual rates of 2.2 percent and 1.5 percent respectively, while population rose by about 2.5 percent per year. In 1970, the primary and secondary school enrollment ratios were about 34 percent and 4 percent respectively for the country as a whole. In that year, federal and state government expenditures on education amounted to only about 3 percent of GDP and a substantial increase appears to be desirable and well within the financial capability of the public sector. The states are primarily responsible for financing education which, in 1970/71, accounted for about 35 percent of their recurrent expenditures. Better statistics and improved planning at both federal and state levels are crucial to strengthening Nigeria's educational system. There is also an urgent need to develop estimates of future manpower requirements. Areas where immediate qualitative improvements appear to be feasible are industrial training, reform of general secondary education curriculum and adult education.

Transport and utilities, the main public investment sectors, were in a critical position at the end of the civil war, reflecting low investment, inadequate maintenance and war damage, particularly in the three eastern states. There has been substantial restoration of overhead services, but little, if any, new expansion of facilities. Nigeria's infrastructure suffers from problems of imbalance between areas and between the levels of service available within a particular area (e.g., trunk versus feeder roads); lack of adequate planning tools and, in turn, poor planning; excessive centralization of certain operational functions and responsibilities; financing, particularly in areas of state responsibility (e.g., water supply) and management, training and technical competence. The increasingly strong fiscal position of the federal government will provide the resources for easing some of these problems but the solution of others will require long-term efforts to improve institutions and upgrade planning, management and executive capacity within the government departments and the statutory corporations. Given the prospective demand for skilled and professionally qualified people for the economy as a whole, the absolute number of expatriates in the country may have to be increased temporarily, although Nigerians should be able to fill an increasing share of the posts involved.

Development Prospects and Policies

With a view toward a better understanding of the Nigerian economy and for the purpose of testing the implications of different assumptions regarding future developments, a model of the economy was prepared. The results of this exercise are drawn upon throughout this report and the model itself is described in Chapter 9. The long-range projections are presented in terms of point estimates for certain dates — generally 1978/79 and 1983/84, the presumed terminal years of successive five year plans. These should, of course, be treated as suggestive of possible developments toward the end of the current decade and in the first half of the next, rather than as projections (much less forecasts) of specific magnitudes at particular times. The conclusions presented here are therefore tentative and are intended primarily to suggest the dimensions of choice open to Nigerian policy makers and the implications of alternative growth patterns.

The potential of the Nigerian economy over the next 10-12 years as suggested by this exercise may be summarized as in the table on the following page.

These projections indicate that Nigeria may well have the resources to double per capita income within the next 12-15 years. A large proportion of the additions to national income over the next decade will accrue to the government and the achievement of the economy's growth potential will depend to a large extent on the government's ability to maintain a rate of growth of public consumption in line with reasonable needs and on its capacity to expand public sector investment over a broad range of sectors and geographical areas.

The rapid growth suggested will almost certainly require a continued infusion of technical, organization and managerial skills from abroad to help increase the level of public and private investment in the short run and ensure the continued growth of such investment in the long run. Some of these skills are perhaps most effectively applied in association with those types of capital

| | | Projected Range[b] | | |
| | Absolute Level 1978/79[a] | Growth Rate | | |
		1966/67-[c] 1973/74	1973/74- 1978/79	1978/79- 1983/84
Indicator				
£N million (1970 prices)				
GNP	4,200-4,400	6.0	7.0- 8.5	7.5- 9.0
Population (million)	85	2.6	2.65	2.7
GNP per capita (U.S. $)	150- 160	3.2	4.5- 6.0	4.5- 6.0
Investment	950-1,100	12.7	7.0-10.5	9.0-11.0
National saving	650- 800	11.2	6.5- 9.5	4.5- 6.0
£N million (current prices)				
Export of goods and NFS	1,565	18.6	9.0	6.5
of which: petroleum	1,325	35.0	10.5	7.0
Imports of goods and NFS	1,100-1,250	13.2	7.5-10.0	9.0-11.0
Net factor payments abroad	420- 450	19.8	8.5- 9.5	5.5- 6.0

[a]Fiscal year ending March 31.

[b]Projected range reflects alternative assumptions concerning government recurrent expenditures and incremental capital-output ratios.

[c]The last year before the civil war.

projects typically financed under external assistance programs. At the same time, incentives for private investment outside the oil sector will be required.

Employment and Distribution Implications

Future employment and income distribution patterns in Nigeria will be determined largely by developments in the rural sector. Although no reliable data on employment are available, it is clear that Nigeria's employment problems will not respond easily to short-run or narrowly conceived remedies and, in the short- and medium-term, improvement in income and employment for most workers, particularly for new entrants to the labor force, will depend largely on developments in the agricultural, small industry and service sectors, where detailed planning and administrative capacity present the most difficult problems.

Since the present growth impetus originates in sectors accounting for only a small proportion of national income and employing only a small fraction of the labor force, adjustment to structural changes in the economy will be difficult in terms of human dislocation and the infrastructure to be provided. Several conclusions emerge from an examination of the likely trends in this regard. First is the crucial importance of agricultural development and modernization as a means of increasing rural income; unless a major effort is initiated by the public sector, income growth in the next 10-15 years will be concentrated mainly in the urban areas, resulting in urban population growth two or three times the overall annual rate of 2.6 percent. Second is the inadequacy of existing transport, storage and marketing facilities, implying that investment in moving agricultural products from the producer to the consumer needs to be very large, not only to keep up with urban growth but also to meet present minimum needs. Most of this investment will be required in the rural sector, in the form of feeder and access roads, storage facilities etc., which will therefore provide not only better market outlets and improved urban supplies but also additional rural income opportunities. Third is that failure to accelerate rural development could adversely affect the direction of industrial development, leading to a concentration of urban-based industries processing largely luxury products. A broad-based development strategy, on the other hand, would stimulate the growth of wage-goods industries which would benefit from economies of scale to the fullest extent and generate in turn the growth of localized markets for small-scale industries. Fourth, in view of the inevitable growth of the cities, is the urgent need to organize and strengthen the urban institutions which must plan the substantial investments that will be required.

The overriding conclusion with respect to Nigeria's economic prospects is that the opportunity now exists to achieve a significant increase in per capita income within the relatively short time-span of 10-15 years. To translate the country's potential resources into a permanent improvement in the general standards of living, however, it is essential that policies and strategies be adopted during the coming years to improve the balance between urban and rural growth, between the development of agriculture and the modern sectors, and between the different regions of the country in terms of economic and social infrastructure. The distribution of increased government resources between uses and claims can have a major impact on each of these and can, in the process of planning and spending, contribute to the establishment of institutions capable of carrying the main responsibility for development during the 1970s and thereafter. Foreign aid in the public and private sectors, both in the form of capital and technial assistance, can be of great value in a period when the opportunities for development appear to be well in excess of the country's capacity, in terms of domestic organization and skills, to make full use of these opportunities. The efficient allocation and effective use of resources over the coming decade is also important because the longer-term balance of payments prospects appear at present to be considerably less favorable and, even under the most optimistic assumptions discussed in this report, per capita income in Nigeria would only be about U.S.$200 in the mid-1980s.

CHAPTER 1
ECONOMIC TRENDS AND DEVELOPMENT POLICIES

Macroeconomic Trends

The Nigerian economy traditionally was dominated by the trends and fluctuations of its major export crops. For a long time, the vicissitudes of international markets for its produce have largely determined the growth path of income, investment and the balance of payments. It is for that reason the economy was characterized by a prolonged period of stagnation for approximately 15 years before 1950, as agricultural exports increased by an average rate of less than 1 percent per annum during this period. Per capita income undoubtedly fell over the period since population grew by about 2 percent annually.

On this low base, economic growth has been sustained at an impressive level since 1950. The average growth rate of real GDP over the last two decades has never been below 4 percent per annum over a significantly long period. From 1950 to 1957, the average growth rate apparently accelerated in the two years immediately before independence in 1960. From 1958/59 to 1966/67, the average growth of real GDP was approximately 6 percent per annum.

Domestic production was seriously disrupted by the civil war from 1967 to 1970. However, provisional estimates of GDP over the period indicate an average annual growth rate of some 5.5 percent, attributable primarily to a remarkable recovery of economic activity in 1970/71. The average GNP growth rate over the last 12 years was about 5 percent per annum, slightly below the GDP growth rate estimated at about 2.5 percent, GNP per capita appears to have increased on the average by 2.5 percent per annum over the last decade.

Despite this impressive record of growth, Nigeria's GNP per capita in current prices was estimated at only about £N26 in 1966/67. Provisional estimates would indicate the level to be about 30 percent higher in 1970/71, at approximately £N32 (about U.S.$100).

Sectoral Development

Export agriculture was undoubtedly the engine of growth in the Nigerian economy from 1940 to about the mid-1960s. Dynamism in the sector was provided primarily by farmers' response to income incentives generated by the integration of the traditional agricultural economy into the world market. Output per head in the sector was increased mainly by the employment of surplus land and labor, and by the substitution of higher value export crops for subsistence crops, without significant reorganization of the society or the introduction of new production techniques. Within this fairly stable framework, technological change was introduced in the form of new crops, and in the concomitant development of modern transport and processing facilities. In the rest of the agricultural economy, production of traditional food crops evidently kept pace with the increased demand generated by higher income and the growing population, also without significant change in production techniques.

Concurrent with this sustained but relatively moderate growth in agriculture, the expansion of large-scale manufacturing industries was very rapid. Increased demands generated by this rapid growth of industrial production as well as export agriculture led to very substantial expansion in the public utilities, transport, and construction sectors. From 1950 to 1962, modern manufacturing output expanded fivefold, while vehicle registration increased tenfold, cement consumption threefold, and electricity consumption eightfold.

A threshold in the development of the Nigerian economy seems to have been reached in the years 1962 to 1964. Following more than a decade of sustained growth, export agriculture stagnated after 1963. On the other hand, manufacturing industries continued to maintain a rate of growth higher than 10 percent per annum and began to exert a considerable influence on the overall economy. Almost simultaneously, the petroleum mining sector emerged to become the leading growth sector in the economy.

The differential rates of sectoral growth since 1950 are clearly discernible in the national account series presented in Table 1-1. From 1950 to 1963, the growth rate of export agriculture was maintained at an average of over 5 percent per annum, but no real growth is perceptible in the sector since then. Most national account estimates assume a growth trend of food crop production

Chart 1-1: NIGERIA: MACROECONOMIC TRENDS, 1950 TO 1970 AND PROJECTIONS TO 1985

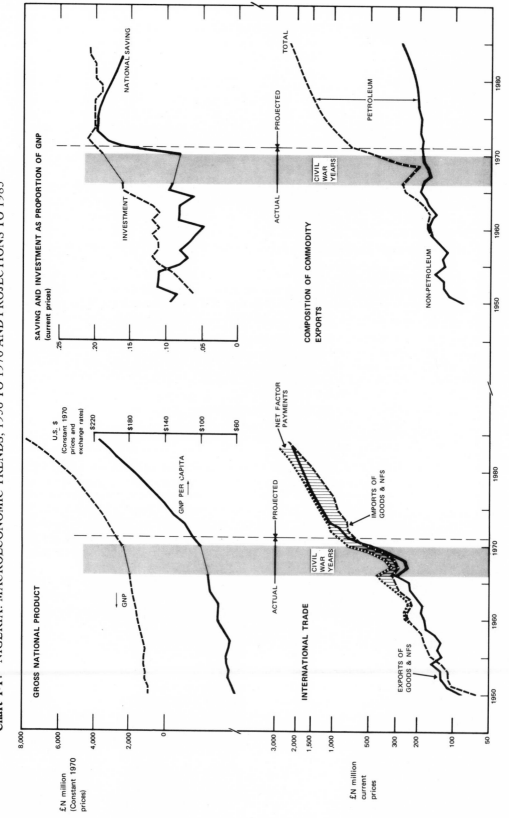

Chart 1-1:   NIGERIA: MACROECONOMIC TRENDS, 1950 TO 1970 AND PROJECTIONS TO 1985 (cont'd.)

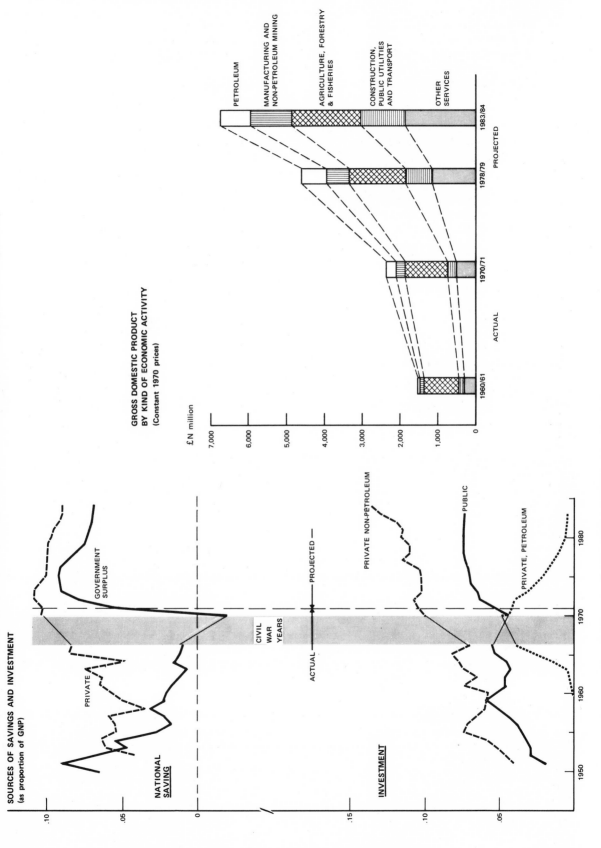

roughly equal to population, i.e. 2-2.5 percent per annum from 1950 to 1966. As there has been no apparent excess demand pressure for food over this period, this assumption seems reasonable although the growth of food production might have been even higher in view of the substantial increase in per capita income. Thus, the average annual growth rate of the agriculture sector as a whole from 1950 to 1966 is estimated at approximately 3 percent per annum, or about 1 percent higher than the rate of population growth. After 1967, the sector appears to have been affected considerably by the civil war and is only now recovering to the prewar level.

Value-added in the mining sector has been dominated by development of the petroleum industry since 1960. From a virtually negligible amount in 1960, value-added in petroleum mining increased sharply to represent about 5 percent of GDP in 1966. An average growth rate of over 25 percent was maintained in the sector after 1966/67 despite the sharp fall in petroleum production during part of the civil war period. Large-scale manufacturing also began to dominate the manufacturing and crafts sector after 1958. The overall sectoral growth rate since then averaged about 10 percent per annum. The infrastructure sectors — power, transport and construction — grew at a rate about 2-3 times that of GDP from 1950 to about the mid-1960s, although the growth rate has declined sharply in recent years.

Structural Change

Although the current official series of GDP estimates are not comparable to the pre-1958 estimates, the evidence is that economic growth in the 1950s was achieved without significant structural transformation of the economy. Agriculture, livestock and forestry, which accounted for 67 percent of GDP in 1950, continued to represent more than 60 percent of total domestic product at the end of that decade. At the same time, the more rapidly growing sectors such as large-scale manufacturing, power and transport services were initiating growth from a base too small to affect significantly the structure of the economy. From 1958/59 to 1970/71, however, the decelerated growth of agriculture, together with the rapid growth of manufacturing and

Table 1-1: SECTORAL GROWTH RATES

(Percent)

	Shares in 1962/63	Average annual over period, in real terms			
		1950-57	1958/59- 1962/63	1962/63- 1966/67	1966/67- 1970/71[a]
Gross domestic product	100.0	4.1	6.4	5.5	5.5
Agriculture	61.5	2.9	4.6	2.0	0.8
Mining (incl. petroleum)	2.1	3.1	27.0	44.0	26.5
Manufacturing	5.8	5.6	13.9	10.5	9.7
Power, transport and construction	9.6	15.1	12.1	5.5	3.8
Services	21.0	3.4	6.8	7.0	6.2

[a]Provisional estimates

Sources: 1950-57: Okigbo, *Nigerian National Accounts 1950-57.* 1958-70: Federal Office of Statistics, Nigeria.

mining, resulted in the decline of the share of agriculture from more than 65 percent to 50 percent. Mining and manufacturing in 1970/71 represented about one-fifth of total GDP, as compared to about 5 percent at the end of the 1950s. The share of the service sectors also expanded somewhat over this period. Table 1-2 gives the percentage distribution of GDP by type of activity from 1958/59 to 1970/71.

Investment

The long-term growth trend of gross fixed investment in Nigeria is appreciably higher than that of GDP. From 1950 to 1957, expenditure on fixed capital formation increased on the average by slightly more than 12 percent per annum in real terms mainly on the strength of a rapid increase in capital formation expenditure by the government and public corporations (Table 1-3). After 1958, the rate of expansion in the public sector declined substantially and did not exceed 3 percent per annum except for a brief period in 1966. On the other hand, the annual growth rate of private investment which averaged about 8 percent over the period 1950 to 1962, increased substantially to an average of about 16 percent from 1962/63 to 1970/71 despite some wide fluctua-

Table 1-2: GDP BY TYPE OF ECONOMIC ACTIVITY

(Percentage Distribution)

	1958/59	1962/63	1966/67	1970/71
Agriculture	68.4	61.5	54.4	50.0
Mining	0.8	2.1	5.0	11.6
Manufacturing	4.4	5.8	7.3	8.0
Power, transport and construction	7.3	9.6	9.8	8.3
Services	19.1	21.0	23.5	22.1

Source: Federal Office of Statistics, Nigeria.

Table 1-3: GROWTH RATES OF INVESTMENT EXPENDITURES
(Average Annual, in Constant Prices)

(Percent)

	1950-57	1958/59-1962/63	1962/63-1966/67	1966/67-1970/71
Gross fixed investment	12.5	6.0	13.2	8.8
Public	14.2	2.8	7.9	0.7
Private	7.6	8.5	16.5	15.9
Private, excluding petroleum	7.6	8.5	5.8	16.5

Sources: 1950-57 Okigbo, *Nigerian National Accounts, 1950-57.* 1958/59-70/71 Federal Office of Statistics, Nigeria.

tions during 1966-1970. Excluding the petroleum sector, the growth rate of private investment over the period averages about 10 percent per annum. Total investment expenditures around 1965 were at least double, in current prices, the levels in the early 1950s, and may now be as much as two and a half times higher.

This rapid growth of investment expenditure is reflected in the increasing share of fixed capital formation in GNP. Estimates of investment expenditure in the 1950s roughly comparable to the current official estimates would indicate the share of total fixed capital formation in GNP to be about 8 percent over the period 1952 to 1954, with a rapid increase to about 11 percent at the end of the decade. In subsequent years, the share increased moderately to reach a level of about 15 percent in 1966. Provisional estimates for 1970/71 indicate a level of investment at about 19 percent of GNP.

Public sector investment appears to have been maintained at around 5 percent of GNP from 1958/59 to 1970/71, with some minor year-to-year fluctuations. A trend calculation would even indicate a minor decline over the period. Private investment, appreciably more impressive, increased strongly from an average of 6 percent of GNP in the years 1958/59 to 1960/61 to 10 percent during the latter half of the 1960s, and apparently reached a high of 15 percent in 1970/71. The recent rise in private investment expenditure is attributable in large part to activities in the oil sector and to the completion of delayed projects and rehabilitation expenditure; the share of private non-oil investment in GNP has risen consistently since 1958/59 except for a moderate decline during the civil war (Table 1-4).

A comparison of time series data on output growth and investment expenditure indicate an incremental capital output ratio (ICOR) in Nigeria roughly comparable to the experience of other economies at similar stages of development. From the low base in 1950, the gross ICOR for the following decade is estimated at approximately 2.5. The ratio is also about 2.5 for the period 1960 to 1970, but increases to 3.0 outside the oil sector. The higher ICOR for the non-oil sector in the last decade seems to be reasonable in view of the increasingly capital-intensive nature of the more recent growth sectors. However, any conclusions drawn from estimated levels of capital formation

Table 1-4: GROSS FIXED CAPITAL FORMATION

(Annual Average, in Current £N Million)

	1958/59-1960/61	1961/62-1963/64	1964/65-1966/67	1967/68-1969/70	1970/71[a]
Gross fixed investment	120	165	250	244	450
Public	58	63	81	86	100
Private, non-petroleum	62	98	126	111	235
petroleum	–	4	43	47	115
(percent of GNP)					
Gross fixed investment	11	12	15	15	19
Public	5	5	5	5	4
Private, non-petroleum	6	7	8	7	10
petroleum	–	–	2	3	5

[a]Provisional estimates.

Sources: 1958/59-1968/69: Federal Office of Statistics, Nigeria. 1969/70-1970/71: Federal Ministry of Economic Development, Nigeria, version estimates.

in Nigeria must be extremely tenuous in view of the problems in estimating rural investment expenditure. The available time series data also indicate considerable fluctuations in the implicit ICOR, but, again, the quality of the data involved does not allow any conclusions on these short-term movements.

Savings and Consumption

Investment and saving ratios derived from the national account identity of *ex-post* savings and investments and from balance of payments estimates of foreign capital inflow, are presented in Table 1-5. As evident from the table, the expanding share of capital formation in Nigeria's GNP over the last two decades was financed increasingly by external savings. In the early 1950s, gross national savings in Nigeria were considerably larger than the economy's ability to invest, thus allowing surplus funds in the form of government and marketing board surpluses to accumulate as external reserves. Increases in investment expenditure, however, quickly outstripped national savings. By the latter half of the decade, external finance accounted for about one-fourth of total investment expenditure. This ratio has steadily increased over the last decade to a level of about 50 percent (Table 1-5).

During this twenty-year period, private foreign direct investment excluding the enclave type activities in the oil sector has been steady at a level of about 2 percent of GNP, except for a temporary decline during 1966-70. Inclusion of investment expenditure by the petroleum companies would increase the ratio to about 4 percent of GNP from 1964 to 1968, reaching an

Table 1-5: INVESTMENT AND SAVINGS RATIOS

(Percent of GNP in Current Prices)

	1952-54	1955-57	1958/59-1960/61	1961/62-1963/64	1964/65-1966/67	1967/68-1969/70[a]	1970/71[b]
Gross fixed investments	8	11	11	12	15	15	19
Financed through national savings	10	8	6	8	9	8	10
Governments, recurrent surplus	5	2	2	1	1	-3	-2
Private	5	6	4	7	8	11	12
External finance	-2	3	5	4	6	7	9
Direct private investment[c]	2	3	2	2	4	4	7
Drawings on reserves	-3	—	2	2	—	1	—

[a]Excluding the eastern states.

[b]Provisional estimates.

[c]Including depreciation and unremitted profits of foreign firms in Nigeria.

Sources: 1952-57, derived from several sources and should be regarded as illustration of long-term trends only. 1958-70, mission estimates.

estimated high of 7 percent in 1970. The absolute level of investment increased from £N10 million in 1950 to almost £N120 million twenty years later. However, total private capital inflows were insufficient to meet investment requirements during the years 1958 to 1963 and again during 1966 to 1970. Over these periods, drawings on external reserves financed a considerable share of total capital formation.

The average savings rate in Nigeria has stagnated since the early 1950s in contrast to very vigorous investment activities (Table 1-5). The aggregate data, however, obscure a very encouraging trend in private savings. The share of private savings in GNP increased steadily from an estimated 5 percent in the period 1952 to 1954 to over 10 percent in recent years, except for a drop between 1957 and 1958 which may be explained partly by the inconsistency of the two series of data. Including net factor payments abroad, domestic private savings in 1970/71 would amount to an even more impressive 17 percent of GDP. As a proportion of private income, private savings over the period increased from about 6 percent to 13-14 percent.

The government, on the other hand, has never been able to generate a sizable recurrent surplus for investment expenditure except during the early 1950s, when revenues from the rapidly expanding foreign trade sector far outstripped the growth in recurrent government expenditures. From an amount representing about 5 percent of GNP, government recurrent surplus declined over the last two decades to turn into substantial deficits in recent years.

Aggregate consumption in the economy has remained fairly steady over the last twenty years at a level of approximately 90 percent of GNP, although the ratio has apparently risen to as much as 94 percent over some periods. Within this aggregate, however, the different movements of private and public consumption ratios were clearly discernible. Public consumption rose from a low of 4 percent of GNP in the years 1952-54 to an average of 7 percent in 1966. Expenditure (defense, capital and recurrent) then rose sharply to represent 12 percent of GNP from 1966-70, then declined to 10 percent afterward.

Private consumption, which seems to have been a steady 87 percent of GNP in the 1950s, declined substantially during the last decade to about 80 percent in recent years. The national account series for 1950 to 1957 estimated an average growth of private consumption expenditure at 4 percent per annum over the period, or about 2 percent in per capita terms. From 1958/59 to 1966/67, the average growth rate of private consumption derived as a residual from the official national account estimates is about 5.8 percent in current prices, which would be equivalent to 4.3 percent in real terms, assuming that the GDP deflator is also valid for consumption expenditure. Provisional estimates for 1970/71 also indicate a real growth rate of private consumption at about 4 percent per annum since 1966/67. With a population growth rate assumed to be 2.5 percent, it would therefore appear that per capita private consumption in Nigeria has increased, on the average, at a fairly satisfactory rate of 1.5-2.0 percent per annum over the last twenty years.

International Trade

One of the most significant characteristics of Nigeria's economic development since the end of the Second World War is the rapid integration of the economy into the world market. From 1945 to the mid-1960s, the volume of Nigeria's exports increased almost threefold while imports increased eight-fold. Exports increased from 17 percent of GNP in 1950 to 20 percent in 1970 as imports increased from 12 percent. By far the largest growth in export volume came from groundnuts which increased from 180,000 tons in 1945 to over 600,000 tons in 1963, making Nigeria the world's major exporter of the product. Exports of cocoa, timber, cotton and rubber also increased rapidly over the period, leading to a diversified export economy.

In contrast to the fairly steady growth in export volume, the corresponding growth in export value was more erratic because of price fluctuations. From 1945 to 1954, export prices moved strongly in the country's favor, resulting in an increase in export values almost five times the corresponding increase in volume. The import purchasing power of Nigeria's exports rose fourfold over this period despite a significant rise in import prices. After 1954, this favorable development in terms of trade turned abruptly. On the whole prices of Nigeria's exports have declined while import prices rose continuously. Consequently, the import purchasing power of Nigeria's exports increased by only 25 percent in the decade following 1954 even though export volume increased by some 80 percent. In subsequent years the value of traditional exports largely fluctuated around a fairly stagnant level. Total exports, however, increased rapidly due to the phenomenal rise in petroleum export which amounted to £N490 million by 1971, accounting for 75 percent of total exports.

Imports also expanded at a rapid rate since 1945, increasing from less than £N20 million in 1945 to £N538 million in 1971. Changes in the composition of imports over this period are significant. Consumer imports doubled in value over the 10 years following 1950, from an average of £N45 million in the early 1950s to £N110 million at the beginning of the 1960s. Since 1960, however, extensive import substitution in items such as processed food, beverages and textiles prevented any further increase. During 1966-70 restrictive import policies even reduced the average annual value to slightly less than £N80 million. In real terms, imports of consumer goods undoubtedly declined over the period 1960 to 1970. Over the twenty-year period following 1950, consumer goods imports declined from 10 percent of total consumption expenditure to about 5 percent, or from about 60 percent of total imports to 30 percent. In 1971, however, the liberalization of imports and the postwar increase in consumer demands resulted in a 60 percent increase in consumer imports.

In line with the rapid growth of investment expenditure and industrial production, imports of intermediate and capital goods tripled over the decade following 1950, decreasing in the 1960s. Over the last twenty years, imports of machinery and equipment appear to have remained at around 40 percent of total investment expenditure outside the oil sector except during the civil

Table 1-6: BALANCE OF PAYMENTS: CURRENT ACCOUNT

(In Millions of Current £N)

	1950-52	1955-57	1961-63	1964-66	1967-69	1970-71
Exports of goods	105.9	122.6	173.8	252.0	253.4	558.4
of which:						
cocoa	26.0	25.0	33.1	36.9	52.9	69.3
groundnuts	15.0	27.0	42.0	51.9	50.3	30.9
petroleum	–	–	16.2	64.0	80.2	373.9
Imports of goods	87.5	151.0	204.4	254.8	212.8	444.6
of which:						
consumer	54.5	89.0	109.8	106.7	77.6	139.8
producer	33.0	62.0	94.6	148.1	135.2	304.7
Trade balance	18.4	-28.4	-30.6	-2.8	40.6	113.9
		— (IMPORTS)				
Net non-factor services	-1.9	6.3	-13.7	-38.5	-76.2	-80.5
Net factor payments	-3.5	1.5	-9.9	-70.3	-73.3	-215.4
				106.8	149.5	
Transfers	2.1	2.0	-2.4	1.5	11.8	11.7
Current account balance	15.0	30.9	-56.6	-110.1	-97.1	-170.3

Source: Central Bank of Nigeria.

war period when the ratio dropped to 35 percent. Intermediate goods imports apparently grew at roughly the same rate as the growth of domestic production, the larger raw material requirements of the faster growing sectors being offset by some import substitution in cement, building materials, and fuels. Intermediate and capital goods imports in 1971 were about 40 percent higher than in 1970, and accounted for 67 percent of total imports.

These changes in the trade pattern resulted in considerable fluctuations in the balance of payments accounts (Table 1-6). Sizable annual trade surpluses were generated during the early 1950s by the very favorable export conditions. As service payments were small and private foreign capital inflow amounted to about £N15 yearly, the trade surpluses were accumulated as external reserves which reached £N264 million in 1955, then equivalent to two years' imports. In 1955, however, the trade balance turned sharply into a deficit because of increasing import volume as well as deteriorating terms of trade. A trade deficit persisted annually until 1966 when import substitution and expanding petroleum export again turned the trade balance into a surplus.

The trade surpluses however, do not give the full amounts of foreign exchange remaining in Nigeria because the import substituting industries were financed to a large extent by foreign capital. Consequently, investment income accruing to non-Nigerians (i.e., factor payments abroad in the balance of payments account), increased rapidly after 1960, from a net value of £N5 million in 1960 to £N251 million by 1971. Factor payments abroad generated by the oil sector, for example, amounted to some 41 percent of the value of crude oil exports in 1971. Thus, the current account balance which first showed a deficit of £N21 million in 1955 continued to deteriorate over the 1960s, reaching a deficit of £N185 million in 1971.

Prices and Monetary Developments

Since the implicit GDP deflator is particularly susceptible to data problems, assessment of price movements in Nigeria has to be based primarily on the urban, low-income consumer price index. This index rose at an annual rate of 3.4 percent from 1960 to 1965. The food component, which has nearly half the weight in the aggregate index, showed considerable fluctuation combined with moderate increase (Chart 1-2), whereas the non-food components rose steadily at just over 3 percent per annum. During this period, the behavior of the GDP deflator was very similar to that of the urban index. After 1965, the movement of the index was dominated by fluctuation in food prices and hence diverged from the GDP deflator, which is heavily weighted with the subsistence agricultural sector. The outbreak of the civil war broke communications with the food-deficient eastern states and was preceded by population movements into these states. The consequent reduction in demand led to a drop in food prices in the rest of Nigeria during 1967 and 1968. In the following two years, as population centers in the East were recovered, food prices rose sharply. The demand for food was reinforced by the need to rebuild depleted stocks and by the requirements to replant crops in the devastated eastern states. The rate of inflation of non-food items continued at roughly 3 percent in 1968 and 1969 but accelerated to 6.1 percent in 1970.

A number of plausible explanations have been advanced for these inflationary pressures. Defense expenditure did not add to the productive capacity of the country but increased demand and may have reduced supply. Recruitment for the army drew active labor away from the agricultural sector and probably added to the demand for food due to the higher nutritional standards maintained in the army. Urban population has been estimated to grow at between 4 percent and 8 percent per year, increasing demand pressures on accommodation, transport and on the distribution of food.

"Cost-push" pressures on inflation appear to be small. Wage increases have been restricted by the government since May 1968. Some inflationary pressure may, however, have originated in the increases in indirect taxes. Import and excise duties rose from 5.1 percent of total consumption expenditure in 1967/68 to 8.3 percent in 1970/71. The delays on payments for commercial imports probably led to price increases to recover hidden finance charges, thereby adding to the increases in import prices attributable to world-wide inflation.

A major cause of the gradually accelerating price movement appears to be the easy money policy followed during this decade. The money supply, including savings deposits, increased at an annual rate of 7 percent from 1960 to 1963, keeping pace with GNP. The rate of increase rose in subsequent years, accelerating to 15 percent per annum during the period 1966-70. The ratio of

Chart 1-2: URBAN CONSUMER PRICE INDEX, 1960-1971

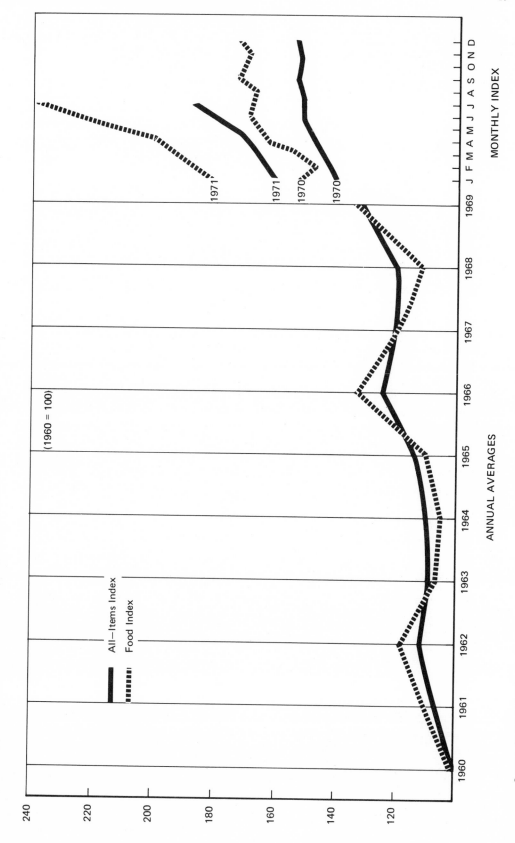

All—Items Index

Food Index

(1960 = 100)

1971

1971

1970

1970

240
220
200
180
160
140
120

1960 1961 1962 1963 1964 1965 1966 1967 1968 1969   J F M A M J J A S O N D

ANNUAL AVERAGES   MONTHLY INDEX

Source: Appendix Table

money supply to GNP rose from 11 percent in 1960 to 16.2 percent in 1970. Reflecting the development of the banking system, deposit components of the money supply expanded faster than currency. The currency-deposit ratio fell from 1.2 to 0.8 during the decade.

Before 1966, the primary source of monetary expansion was rising credit to the private sector. Corresponding to an increase of £N88.2 million in the money supply from 1960 to 1966, credit to the private and public sectors rose by £N90.8 million and £N58.1 million respectively (Table 1-7). The growth of money supply was not as rapid as the growth of credit because of the rise in time deposits and the increase in liabilities to foreigners caused by the restriction on import payments. The domestic counterpart of the latter, held by the banking system, accounted for £N86.0 million of the net change of £N132.6 million in unclassified assets during 1966-70.

Private sector credit declined in 1967 and 1968 (reflecting reduced lending by commercial banks to marketing boards), but picked up again later to register an average annual increase of 5.1 percent during 1966-70. There was a veritable explosion, however, in credit to the public sector from £N62.3 million in 1966 to £N336.5 million at the end of 1970, an average annual increase of 53 percent. From 1968, the Central Bank took the sole responsibility of financing marketing boards following the unsatisfactory operation of the commercial bill finance scheme. The last three years of the decade saw a substantial increase in credit to the marketing boards, reaching a level of £N58.7 million at the end of 1970.

Until 1966 expansion in internal public debt was evenly balanced between Treasury Bills (90 day maturity) and Development Stocks (maturity over 5 years). Subsequently, however, there has been a rapid expansion of Treasury Bills and the introduction of Treasury Certificates with maturities of one or two years from the time of issue (Chart 1-3). At the end of March 1970, Treasury Bills formed 42 percent of outstanding internal public debt, Treasury Certificates were 22

Table 1-7: EXPANSION IN MONEY AND CREDIT

			(In Millions of £N)
Net changes[a]	1960-63	1963-66	1966-70
Money supply[b]	29.3	58.9	163.9
Credit to public sector[c]	15.1	43.0	274.2
Credit to private sector[d]	45.4	53.0	83.7
Net foreign assets	-8.7	-5.1	1.3
Net unclassified assets	-12.5	-13.0	-132.6
Less time deposits	10.0	19.0	62.7
Total	29.3	58.9	163.9
Money Supply as % of GNP (average)	10.9	12.4	13.8

[a]Changes in outstanding assets and liabilities of the banking system as at end December 1970.

[b]Money Supply is defined to include savings deposits but not time deposits, the criterion being liquidity.

[c]Net of federal government deposits.

[d]Includes credit to marketing boards.

Source: Central Bank of Nigeria.

percent and Development Stocks were 32 percent.

The Central Bank has always held a substantial proportion of outstanding debt. Even more significant is the rapid growth in the holdings of commercial banks, which resulted in a sharp decline in Central Bank holdings in 1968 and 1969. The principal reason for this shift was the restrictions on payments for imports imposed in 1967/68, which resulted in a forced credit to the Nigerian economy from foreign exporters.

The payments arrears grew from approximately £N20 million at the end of 1968 to £N92 million by March 1970 and £N214 million by March 1971. Approximately half of the domestic counterpart of the payments arrears are estimated to have been deposited with the banking system. These "backlog deposits" supplied considerable additional liquidity to the commercial banks which they held in the form of Treasury Bills and Treasury Certificates. As a result, the liquidity ratio of commercial banks rose from an average of 32.6 percent in the period 1960-66 to an average of 96.2 percent during 1970. Since the required liquidity ratio has been only 25 percent, the excess liquidity has seriously hampered the implementation of monetary policy. During

Chart 1-3: INTERNAL PUBLIC DEBT, 1961-1970

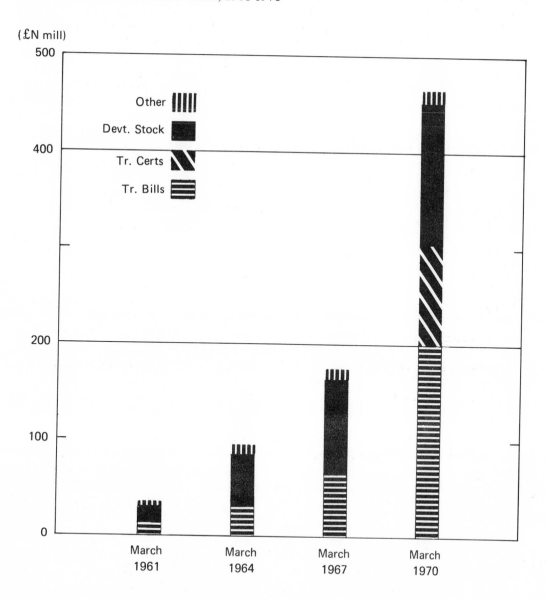

1970, commercial banks violated the official guidelines both on aggregate credit expansion and on the composition of loans and advances. The actual increase in total credit was more than twice the guideline figure, with every major sector except agriculture receiving more credit than was targeted.

Fiscal Development

Within the framework of an apparently responsive and vigorous economy described in the foregoing sections, the development effort of the public sector has been appreciably less impressive than that of the private sector. At independence, Nigeria inherited a tax structure that was not very productive and heavily dependent on indirect taxation. Combined federal and regional government revenues amounted to 11.5 percent of GDP at factor cost in 1961 and increased only to 12.3 percent in 1966/67, the last year before the civil war. Imbalance in the structure is illustrated by the fact that 71.6 percent of federal recurrent revenues came from indirect taxation in 1961, import duties alone contributing 53.8 percent. The contribution of indirect taxes continued to fluctuate around 70 percent through most of the decade, aided by an expansion of excise duties until 1966. Regional revenue, meanwhile, stagnated at about £N30 million per annum from 1962 to 1966. This meager revenue performance lasted through 1968/69, and, in the next two years, the share of non-oil revenues in GDP rose to 13.3 percent and 15.7 percent. This is less remarkable than it first appears, since increased foreign exchange earnings from oil permitted the liberalization of imports which led to large increases in customs and excise receipts.

On the expenditure side, the most striking development was the increase in expenditure on defense on both current and capital accounts; from 7.5 percent of total government expenditure (1.1 percent of GDP) in 1961, it rose to 9.4 percent in 1966 and to a peak of 41.7 percent (12 percent of GDP) in 1969/70. Even before 1966, federal current expenditure was rising at about 13 percent per annum, thereby eroding the current surplus which had amounted to 38 percent of retained revenues in 1961. Recurrent expenditure on general administration doubled from 1961 to 1966, growing only slightly thereafter. These trends took their inevitable toll on expenditure on economic and social services. This expenditure fell from 37.6 percent of recurrent federal expenditure in 1961 to 34.3 percent in 1966. By 1968/69 it had declined to 12.4 percent, also declining in absolute terms from previous levels.

In the state (regional) governments, however, recurrent expenditure on economic and social services rose from £N37.5 million (64.8 percent regional recurrent expenditure) in 1961 to £N58.4 million (67.8 percent of regional recurrent expenditure) in 1966. On the basis of available data after 1966, it appears that over 60 percent of the states' recurrent expenditures continued to be directed to economic and social services.

In 1967/68, the recurrent surplus of the combined government account which has been achieved annually since independence turned into a substantial deficit. Although the proximate cause of this transition was rising defense expenditure attributed to hostilities, recurrent expenditure of the federal and regional governments together was rising at 10.5 percent per annum even before 1967, while revenues were rising at 6 percent per annum. This financing resulted in lower capital expenditure, lower current expenditure for economic and social services and a major increase of the government's internal indebtedness. Government debts rose to 35 percent of GDP by the end of 1970, and debt service accounted for 23 percent of the government's total revenues in 1969/70.

In relation to the goal of a maximum rate of economic development, fiscal arrangements from 1960 to 1966 were not very appropriate. Current expenditure on low priority items was sometimes allowed, and the tax effort was minimal. Expenditure allocations both for capital and current expenditure could have been better designed to promote national development. Nevertheless, it is remarkable that a country with such serious resource constraints has emerged from a protracted and costly emergency without additional external borrowing. The advent of petroleum revenues has, no doubt, accelerated the fiscal recovery. But even without this, internal borrowing would still have been within manageable limits and the country would have overcome its fiscal problems in due course. This performance augurs well for the future, when fiscal management of substantially larger resources will be required.

Development Planning

Medium-term development plans have served as the main instrument for allocating public sector investments since before independence. The first plan of Nigeria was a Ten-Year Plan for Development and Welfare covering the years 1945 to 1955. By 1950, it was realized that it was not feasible to chart development over a period as long as ten years in a country that was undergoing rapid structural changes. A decision was therefore taken to break the interval into two 5-year periods and to formulate a new plan for the period 1951-56. Much of the new plan was a revision and updating of the original in the light of performance difficulties — shortages of qualified manpower and materials. On the basis of the recommendations of the 1954 World Bank mission to Nigeria and following constitutional changes in 1955, a new Economic Development Plan for the years 1955-60 was launched. The period was later extended to 1962.

Subsequently, the first National Development Plan for independent Nigeria covering the period April 1962 to March 1968 was formulated, based for the first time on an analysis of the economy and its major trends. Implementation of the Plan was interrupted during 1966 to 1970, but the federal government then prepared a Second National Plan for Reconstruction and Development covering the period April 1970 to March 1974. As its predecessors, however, the current Plan remains in essence a program of public investment activities by projects. Although sufficient safeguards exist to preserve flexibility in the Plan's project content, the intention is clearly to establish a list of selected approved projects for which resources are to be made available as a matter of development priority.

The difficulties previously encountered are fully discussed in the current Plan documents. The First Plan did not have an annual phasing, but it appears that a substantial increase over the period was envisaged, with an annual average of £N132 million projected over the period. Public investment expenditure amounted to only approximately £N64 million in the first two years, and only reached £N90 million in 1966. The main bottlenecks were evidently the lack of readiness of projects and the limited executive capacity in some sectors, although resource constraints were also operative to some extent during the Plan. In agriculture, 43 percent of the planned allocation remained unspent because of shortcomings in the design and implementation of agricultural plans. In trade and industry, only one-third of the planned allocations had been committed by the end of the Plan period, mainly because of a lack of prepared projects. The current plan document also mentions the serious management problems of railways, the Lagos Port, and of the National Shipping Line and the lack of efficiency of the Post and Telecommunications Department.

The formulation of medium-term plans, the monitoring of economic development and the decision-making process for short-term economic policy require the availability of adequate and timely information on the overall and sectoral performance of the economy and on the bottlenecks and problems which may arise from time to time. This is not provided in Nigeria, as basic statistical services are often weak or non-existent, and important quantitative data frequently become available only after considerable delay. The reasons can be found to a large extent in the absence of a strong organizational set-up with adequate staff and physical resources to discharge this function.

Economic Developments and Policies During the Civil War

The civil war which lasted from mid-1967 to January 1970 severely tested the basic strength of the economy. Unrest and uncertainty preceding the war began to disturb the normal growth of the economy in 1966, with a resultant slackening of investment activity and a fall in the rate of GDP growth. The war itself caused major losses of production and serious damage to infrastructure, notably transport and public utilities in the East and Mid-West. Elsewhere, the economy suffered from a decline in the growth investment and inadequate maintenance. The disturbances preceding the war and the war itself displaced a large number of people, many of whom were skilled workers and highly trained professionals.

Petroleum, by then a major and expanding source of foreign exchange earnings and government revenues, was the industry hardest hit. Onshore operations, which supply most of the output, came to a halt for almost fifteen months; only offshore production continued relatively undisturbed. Petroleum output in July 1967 dropped to less than 10 percent of its prewar peak of

580,000 barrels per day and remained at this low level through August 1968. Moreover, the refinery at Port Harcourt was put out of operation by military action, thereby necessitating the import of motor fuels and other petroleum products. Manufacturing in the East, then accounting for about one quarter of the country's total manufacturing output, was crippled soon after the war broke out and eventually ceased altogether. Plants and installations were seriously damaged by acts of war or fell into disrepair due to lack of maintenance. Production of food crops in the eastern states, insufficient to feed the population even in normal times, declined sharply as the war proceeded; production and export of palm produce, rubber and timber were also sharply reduced.

The war also caused a sharp decline in investment activities. Data on capital goods imports indicate that investment during the war period amounted to only two-thirds to three-quarters of the 1966 level. Net private foreign capital inflow into the non-petroleum sector decreased from £N60 million in 1965 to £N6 million in 1967. The civil disturbances and war also interrupted the rising trend in government revenues. Revenues collected by the federal government in 1967/68 and 1968/69 were roughly 10 percent lower than 1966/67 despite several revenue-raising measures. On the other hand, federal expenditures rose sharply as the result of military expenditures which increased from about £N20 million in 1966/67 to £N180 million in 1969/70. The estimated total federal budgetary cost of the war amounted to about £N300 million, equivalent to virtually all of the federal government's retained revenues.

In light of these adverse developments, the federal government's management of the economy during this period through a combination of direct and indirect controls was effective. Immediately following the outbreak of the war in 1967, the limit of Treasury Bills as a percentage of estimated federal revenues was raised from 40 to 50 percent; the export of a number of essential domestic food items was subject to licensing; a capital gains tax of 20 percent on gains accruing from disposal of assets was introduced at the beginning of the financial year. Later in the same year, a super-tax on company profits was imposed and specific import licensing introduced for a number of exporting areas and for a large number of nonessential consumer goods, including passenger vehicles. At the beginning of 1968, new currency notes were introduced in order to discourage speculation against Nigerian currency in the international money markets.

Economic policy during the remainder of the war period was directed primarily towards the protection of the country's balance of payments position which deteriorated rapidly as the result of sharply reduced petroleum and agricultural exports and rising military expenditures. In 1968, direct import controls were extended to include a wide range of essential consumer goods. Customs duties and reconstruction surcharges on most goods were also increased and excise taxes on some domestic manufactures were raised. The repatriation of profits and dividends was also prohibited during this period and government control over private financial and commercial operations was also tightened considerably.

Despite increasingly severe restrictions on external trade, it appeared that longer-term developmental requirements of the economy were not being ignored. In 1969, duties on machinery and a number of intermediate goods were substantially reduced or abolished. Throughout the war period foreign exchange reserves were maintained at roughly 3-4 months' imports equivalent and external public debt increased by less than 10 percent. Except for unremitted investment income and the accumulation of arrears on payments for commercial imports, the federal government's expenditures were financed without external borrowing; public sector deficits were met largely by borrowing from the banking system. At the same time, credit to the private sector was restricted and wages were controlled in order to contain inflationary pressures caused by the public sector's deficit financing.

The civil war also clearly demonstrated the basic strength of the Nigerian economy. Except for the war-affected areas, production of food crops continued without any significant trend. Production and export of the two major export crops, cocoa and groundnuts, also continued undisturbed by the war except for internal transport difficulties. The loss of manufacturing in the East, coupled with the severe restriction of imports, especially of textile and other consumer goods, led to sharp increases in manufacturing output in the rest of the country. Idle capacity was evidently harnessed during the war period, second and even third shifts introduced, and considerable new capacity added. After a fall of roughly 8 percent in real terms in 1967, a positive GDP growth rate was maintained during the remaining three years of the war period. By 1970/71, the first year after the war, real GDP per capita was substantially higher than in 1966/67.

Thus, Nigeria emerged from the civil war in January 1970 with a sizable but manageable internal debt; a negligible increase in external public debt; an increased level of economic activities, particularly in the manufacturing and petroleum sectors; and most importantly, with considerably increased confidence in both the underlying strength of its economy and the ability of the government to manage the large and diverse economy. These factors undoubtedly contributed to the remarkable recovery of the country from the consequences of the war and the rapid implementation of the reconstruction program which are documented elsewhere in this report. They also augur well for the future, when a substantially larger role of the public sector in the development effort than ever before will be called for.

Past Trends and Characteristics

The preceding paragraphs present some of the main features of Nigerian economic developments and policies in the past two decades. Some topics discussed were the structure and changes in the economy which offer insight into the nature of the transformation which can be expected in the future. Others were the character of the government and its policies from which some conclusions can be drawn about the likely course of public sector activities and their impact on the economy in the years ahead.

Over the past two decades, Nigeria has apparently been attractive to private investors, both domestic and foreign. Investment opportunities have existed during this period when growth of the economy averaged 5.5 percent per annum. The profitability of operating at productive capacity in a large domestic market which provided adequate investment incentives and a reasonable (sometimes even excessive) degree of protection has been clearly established in the past. This will most probably be a major element in the continued growth of private investment and savings. The large market combined with the growth stimulating impact of the oil sector make it likely that this attraction will increase further.

A gradual but marked shift from a structure in which growth originated largely in the export-oriented sectors to one which draws its impetus increasingly from production for domestic demand has been apparent in the past decade. This trend is likely to continue. The major exception will be the oil-producing sector, which will not only generate the domestic resources to permit an acceleration of economic growth, but will also provide the necessary foreign-exchange to stave off, for some time at least, the balance of payments strains usually associated with the development process. Nigeria therefore, will be able to concentrate new investment on the provision of goods and services for domestic use while still maintaining the characteristics of an export-oriented economy able to build up foreign exchange reserves.

However, the process of accelerated development may not follow an easy path. Although private investment may grow rapidly, the provision of necessary economic and social infrastructure and its proper maintenance and operation will require an equally rapid growth in public sector investment. In that respect Nigeria faces a situation where the weakness of implementing institutions at the federal and state levels is apparent and where the autonomous agencies are known more for their financial losses and inadequate management, than for their abilities to prepare and implement development programs and projects efficiently. Major efforts in institutional reform are clearly called for and, in fact, are identified in the current Plan.

Some of these problems are closely related to the lack of trained and experienced staff and management. It must therefore be assumed that the retention of, or even larger reliance on, expatriate expertise will be necessary for some time to come. In the meantime, priority should clearly be given to the training of domestic talent and capabilities in order to reduce the reliance on external technical and managerial skills over the longer run.

Without adequate effort to build institutions and to train their staff for the implementation of sound investment programs, the resources available for development may not give the returns which are essential for Nigeria to move to a higher level of development and general welfare. These resources may, for lack of development opportunities, be used for lesser priority purposes in the current government budget. Past experience points to a limited ability of the government to resist such claims on available resources. Unless there are well-established institutions which can rightfully claim a capacity to utilize substantial resources effectively, their diversion to expenditure of little or no developmental impact may be difficult to avoid.

In the chapters that follow, current economic developments and the outlook for the medium-term are discussed against this background, and an effort is made to identify the major problems and opportunities which appear to exist for those years. Some tentative projections and conclusions regarding the longer-term outlook for economic growth, the constraints and conditions governing this process, and some of the options which appear to exist for longer-term development strategy are also given. Special attention is given to the distributive aspects of growth and development, particularly to their impact on urban and rural employment and incomes. The dimensions of the latter are the subject of investigation in the following chapter.

CHAPTER 2
EMPLOYMENT AND INCOME DISTRIBUTION

Size and Shape of Employment Problems

One statement which may confidently be made about the labor force and employment situation is that the statistical data available will support no more than extremely rough judgments of the basic characteristics and the quantitative dimensions of the problems involved. The degree of uncertainty surrounding such basic data as the size, structure and rate of growth of the population, labor force and employment, is so high that any estimates are better considered as illustrative figures to aid in finding a quantitative framework for essentially qualitative propositions rather than as precisely descriptive of an existing or historical "reality".

The outlines of such a framework may be sketched in the form of a set of quasi-quantitative propositions on the size, structure and growth of the population and labor force which are supported by a variety of sorts of "evidence" ranging from statistical sources of varying scope and unreliability to quantitative judgments of informed observers.[1]

(a) The rate of growth of the population has accelerated to about 2.5 percent a year and is likely to increase further with declining mortality.

(b) Because of high fertility rates, the population is "young" with a "dependency ratio" of nearly 1:1.

(c) The rate of growth in the labor force is of the same order of magnitude as the rate of population increase — perhaps slightly less — but is likely to increase.

(d) The absolute annual increase in the labor force is in the neighborhood of half a million workers with the annual number of new entrants to the labor force some 10 percent to 25 percent higher.

(e) The overall labor force participation rate is roughly 40 percent and may be expected to decline slightly over the next 15 years.

(f) With about four-fifths of the population living in rural areas, a similar percentage of the new entrants to the labor force will be coming from rural backgrounds.

(g) The working age population is highly mobile, especially over short-to-medium-range distances; gross migration rates from rural areas approach 75 per thousand and residential turnover in urbanized areas is extremely high.

(h) There are wide disparities in density of population among regions and states with some rural areas extremely densely populated.

(i) The long-term effects of internal unrest on movements of population are difficult to determine; it appears that the past pattern of movement from relatively densely populated areas in the east to the more sparsely populated regions has been disrupted.

(j) Ethnic and language factors may have become more important in determining internal migration so that movements will more closely follow economic opportunities within ethnically defined regions.

(k) Growth of the principal urban centers is most probably in the range of 4 percent to 8 percent a year with most expansion in the federal and state capitals.

(l) There is little data on unemployment, but what evidence there is tends to confirm the usual expectation that open unemployment is primarily an urban phenomenon and is heavily concentrated in the younger age groups and among school leavers.

Nigeria is facing the now familiar employment syndrome of having to absorb rapidly increasing numbers of a youthful and primarily rural work force into productive and remunerative activities. The potential income opportunities of the urban economy and the small but vigorously growing industrial sector inevitably attract increasing numbers from rural into urban areas. The central issue is the impact of development on the relative income opportunities in the "rural" and "urban" sectors and in the "traditional" and "modern" activities within those sectors.

---

1. To a considerable extent these propositions also roughly summarize some of the common characteristics of the estimates and projections produced by Nigerian and other sources. See Nigerian, UN and ILO Populations and Labor Force estimates. (Statistical Annex Table 1-5.)

Employment Structure, Income Differentials
and the Problem of Rural-Urban Balance

The Labor Force Sample Survey of 1966/67 showed about 95 percent of gainfully occupied persons in Nigeria as own-account or unpaid family workers and only some 5 percent as employees. Of the former, three-quarters were engaged in agriculture. Even in urban areas, only one-fifth of non-agricultural workers were reported as having the status of employees, and the other 80 percent were apparently heavily concentrated in trade and service activities. It is difficult to establish the rate at which changes in these patterns are being imposed by the process of development. There is little doubt, however, about a well-established trend in the movement of population from rural to urban areas and the associated shift in employment from agricultural to non-agricultural activities.

On the basis of some crude assumptions regarding the size of these movements, a rough idea can be found of the magnitude of the changes implied by a continuation of these trends. If net migration out of rural areas is as high as half the estimated natural rate of increase of 2.5 percent, the urban population will continue to grow at over 6 percent a year for the next 10 to 15 years. In absolute terms, this would involve a shift of roughly 600,000 to 700,000 persons annually from rural to urban areas, implying an increase in the urban labor force of the order of 250,000 to 300,000 per year. These are probably upper limits to the rate of increase in urban labor supply, implying the absorption in the urban economy of about half the total annual increment in the labor force. Nevertheless, with total wage employment in the urban sector currently at only about one million workers, it is clear that by far the greatest proportion of the increment to the urban work force will be forced to seek employment in occupations where permanent status as wage or salaried employees is the exception rather than the rule.

For most of the Nigerian work force, employment is less a matter of finding a "job" in the sense of achieving an enduring status as an employee than of piecing together a set of income generating activities which together are (hopefully) sufficient to provide a "living." This is well recognized in the agricultural or "subsistence" sector where the problem of employment is usually explicitly conceived not as that of creating "jobs" but of providing the means whereby rural householders can employ labor effectively to achieve more adequate and increasing levels of income. The achievement of employee status — an enduring formal employment relationship — is for most workers unattainable.

A distinctive feature of the continual search for informal earning opportunities, which characterizes Nigerian labor markets, is the complex set of relationships between the urban and rural sectors and between wage and non-wage activities, both by way of movements of people as well as through income transfers. While it is not possible to quantify the structural links between the rural and urban economies, there is considerable evidence that they are strong and pervasive in their effects on the movement of workers and the redistribution of income through transfers in cash and in kind.[2] The existence of such links undoubtedly increases the sensitivity of labor market responses within the economy by providing a network for the transfer of information on relative income opportunities and mechanisms for financing the movement and search activities necessary for their exploitation.

The central employment issue in Nigeria's development can be identified in aggregative terms with the problem of "urban drift" — of coping with the movement of labor from the rural to urban areas. This movement is generated and sustained by a profoundly purposeful evaluation of relative economic opportunities in the two sectors.

Despite lack of data on the structure of incomes in Nigeria, there is considerable evidence that income differentials between rural and urban occupations are substantial. According to surveys made for the Adebo Commission, *minimum* pay for urban workers ranges from 1.5 to 2.5 times

---

2. An illustration is provided by the experience in the East Central State with an attempt to improve state finances by the imposition of a 25 percent forced saving scheme on state employees. According to state officials, the scheme was abandoned after one year largely because the impact was felt primarily in the rural areas in the form of reduced transfers by state employees to village households.

average farmer income. Annual earnings of paid agricultural workers have been estimated for 1967 at less than 45 percent of average earnings for workers in wage and salary employment, a decline from about 58 percent in 1960.[3] With differentials of this magnitude, the rural household is unlikely to be able to find a better investment than supporting one of its younger members in an effort to become established in the urban economy even if that effort involves an extended period of employment search or unemployment.

Moreover, differences in the *distribution* of rural and urban incomes provide an additional rationale to motivate the search by younger workers for employment in the urban economy. Since urban income opportunities are likely to be distributed skewed toward higher incomes, the probability of achieving a *high* income will be greater in the urban sector. To the extent that

Table 2-1: EMPLOYMENT STATUS IN RURAL AND URBAN AREAS, BY INDUSTRY

	Urban	Rural (Percent)
Agriculture	25.7	80.0
Employers and own account workers	20.3	46.4
Employees	0.6	0.8
Unpaid apprentices and household workers	4.8	32.9
Non-Agriculture	74.3	20.0
Employers and own account workers	47.9	17.1
Employees	21.0	1.5
Unpaid apprentices and household workers	5.4	1.4
of which:		
Manufacturing	(17.1)	(8.5)
Construction	(2.1)	(0.3)
Commerce	(33.0)	(0.2)
Transport and communication	(3.7)	(9.3)
Services	(17.6)	(1.4)
Other	(0.6)	(0.1)
Total	100.0	100.0

Source: 1966/67 Labor Force Sample Survey.

3. S.A. Adebo, "Prices, Wages and Costs," *Conference on National Reconstruction and Development in Nigeria, 1969.*

aspirations are focused on achieving "success," i.e., reaching higher levels of income rather than simply maximizing expected income, seeking work in the towns is a strategy maximizing the probability of *success.*[4]

When one turns to consideration of the general pattern of demand for labor, it is starkly revealed by considering likely future developments in the economy that the bulk of the anticipated increases in national income will arise in non-agricultural sectors which account for a relatively small proportion of direct employment and for which the employment elasticity of increases in output is generally believed to be low. The petroleum sector in Nigeria represents, of course, an extreme case of the more general phenomenon.

From the mission projections, it would appear that over 50 percent of the increment in gross domestic product over the next 15 years will arise in non-agricultural sectors (excluding trade and services) which provide employment for less than 20 percent of the work force. Since direct expansion of employment opportunities within the sectors contributing disproportionately to the growth of output will be too limited to serve as a major vehicle to spread the benefits of development broadly throughout the population, the crucial determinants of the employment and distributional impact of development will be the indirect effects transmitted to other sectors.

We may therefore conclude that: a) first and perhaps foremost, the large net movements of workers out of rural and agricultural activities must be expected to continue, with the result that the employment problem will continue to have its deepest roots in the rural sector but its most visible manifestation in the urbanized areas; b) the rate at which these structural shifts in employment take place will depend to a large extent on the impact of development and economic policy on the pattern of relative income opportunities and demand for labor in both the rural and urban sectors; c) effective policies to deal with the structural shifts in labor force and employment must take account not only of the interaction between the agricultural and non-agricultural sectors and the basic differential in rural and urban incomes, but also of the intra-sectoral structure of wages and incomes, particularly in urban and non-agricultural occupations; and d) since new labor force entrants and younger workers are bound to be disproportionately affected, education and training must have a central place in employment policy formulation.

Table 2-2: EMPLOYMENT STATUS IN AGRICULTURE AND
         NON-AGRICULTURE, 1970

			(Percent)
	Agriculture	Non-Agriculture	Total
Wage employment	0.7	5.1	5.8
of which:			
Large- and medium-scale	(0.3)	(2.9)	(3.2)
Small-scale	(0.4)	(2.2)	(2.6)
Own account and unpaid household workers and apprentices	69.1	25.1	94.2
Total	69.8	30.2	100.0

Source: Second National Development Plan 1970-1974, p.327, Table 4.

4. Cf. Stephen Michelson, "Rational Income Decisions of Negroes and Everybody Else," *Industrial and Labor Relations Review,* October 1969.

Agricultural Development, Rural Incomes and Employment

One hardly need emphasize that Nigeria's future with respect to increasing income disparities will depend primarily on the course of agricultural development. The links between rural and urban labor markets exemplified by the flow of labor into the towns in search of employment in response to prevailing income differentials are only one aspect of the basic problem of insuring that the mass of the population has a proper share in the benefits of economic growth. Under the most optimistic assumptions on expansion in non-agricultural sectors over the next decade or two, the economic well-being of the great bulk of the population as well as that of the major part of new entrants to the work force will remain dependent upon the growth of incomes and employment opportunities in agriculture. The necessity for retaining most of the labor force in the rural areas and the importance of agricultural prosperity point to Nigeria's urgent need for improving rural living through an increase in income levels resulting from increased agricultural and agriculturally related output.

With less than 40 percent of the estimated total area reasonably suited for agriculture currently being farmed, it would appear that the potential absorption of labor into agriculture is not limited by a shortage of land. This is somewhat deceptive in that much of the unused land lies in the large middle belt of the country, where transport problems and the tsetse fly present major obstacles to the development of the type of mixed farming for which it is most suited. In the tree crop belts of the south as well as in parts of the northern region, there is evidence that population densities have reached the point where, under prevailing agricultural techniques (particularly shifting cultivation and nomadic grazing), levels of fertility and productivity are already adversely affected. Consequently, the opening of new areas for cultivation as a means by which the growing population may secure a livelihood does not offer an easy avenue for generation of rural employment. If a *rural transformation* is to take place, it necessarily will involve not only the absolute expansion of agricultural activities but the whole range of changes necessary to raise the level of agricultural productivity and incomes.

Price policies alone, although a central and essential element in agricultural development, cannot be expected to yield either a substantial reduction in urban-rural income differentials or major improvements in intra-sectoral income disparities. To serve the latter objectives, supplementary methods which have a broad and immediate positive impact on the income position of the rural population must be sought. In general, distributional and employment considerations would seem to favor devoting substantially increased resources to improving rural infrastructure — roads, transport, storage and marketing facilities, rural public services, etc. — and to providing inputs necessary to support higher levels of technology on rural smallholdings — improved seeds, fertilizer, power implements, training and extension services. The strategy underlying emphasis on such components of a rural development program would be to achieve significant, and relatively quick increases in the incomes of agricultural smallholders and, at the same time, generate increasing non-agricultural employment opportunities in rural villages and towns.

Urban Labor Markets, Wage Structure and Open Unemployment

It has now been almost accepted as *conventional wisdom* that the unemployment problem in developing countries in its most visible form — open unemployment in urban centers — is associated with labor market imperfections which maintain urban wage differentials at inappropriately high levels and even result in their widening, despite growing unemployment. To what extent such an analysis is applicable to Nigeria is difficult to establish without more knowledge and understanding than is now available. Additional information is needed on the structure and operations of labor markets, the patterns and trends in relative earnings and wage rates, and the mechanisms of wage determination within the Nigerian institutional setting.

For purposes of analysis at least three reasonably distinct *markets* or employment categories in the urban areas may be distinguished — civil service and public sector employees, workers in the larger-scale industrial establishments or other *modern* enterprises, and the *residual* market of the self-employed, casual, or family workers in small workshops, and various trade and service activities. Available information on relative earnings (relating almost entirely to wage and salary employment in larger enterprises and the public service) indicates that inter-sectoral and occupational differentials are indeed high and perhaps increasing.[5] To appraise the significance of this requires an explanation of the reasons underlying such earnings patterns, and the extent to which they represent deviations from more economically justifiable wage structures. With the government as the major employer of hourly and salaried labor, it is apparent that observed earnings of urban employees will depend in large measure on prevailing government pay scales. Government decisions on employment levels are not as closely linked with wage scales as is presumed to be the case in private profit-making enterprises. The opportunity costs to the economy of inappropriate wage and salary rates may take different forms depending on the corresponding decisions on government staffing and the level of public activities.

With regard to the latter, given budgetary limitations, higher costs of public services may lead to adverse effects on the level and composition of public development expenditure. Excessively high government payrolls not only will tend to reduce the rate of public saving and investment accomplished over government budgets, but also provide the vehicle for supporting higher rates of private urban consumption by public employees, which may be particularly serious in the Nigerian context because of the higher import component of urban consumer demand. The effects on the composition of public expenditure may also present serious problems, especially when account is taken of possible *negative feedbacks* in the interactions between government wage decisions and public development expenditure policies.

When it comes to misallocations in the use of labor in the public sector (for any given level or pattern of government activities), attempts to economize on high cost employees may lead to *understaffing* in critical occupational positions. If such *understaffing* does not occur, there is still the possibility of efficiency losses because individuals will be attracted into government positions by high salary scales even though their productive talents could be better used in other professions or occupations. If neither situation applies — i.e., despite excessive pay rates there is overstaffing, or at least no understaffing and alternative productive contributions by the workers outside the government are less than inside (possibly even zero) — public employment takes on more the character of a vehicle for accomplishing transfer payments to those fortunate enough to obtain a government job.

It is therefore difficult to establish whether or to what extent government pay scales are excessively high in relation to supply and demand for different categories of employees. Certainly the wide differentials between high and low level occupations in government service observed in Nigeria cannot provide an a priori case that upper level categories are too highly paid. The persistent and extreme shortages of highly qualified personnel in both public and private employment would be consistent with a steep gradient in the occupational earnings scale. Moreover, available information suggests that government wage scales are not widely out of line with those prevailing in the modern private sector, except perhaps at the lowest skill levels.

None of these concerns about the effect of the wage structure in public employment equals in importance the possible influence of government decisions on wage and salary determination in the modern private sector, mainly through potentially effective governmental pressures, particularly on the larger or foreign-owned enterprises, to follow the government's lead in setting wage and salary rates.

It may perhaps be pointed out, however, that evidence is lacking either to establish that this problem is a serious one or, more importantly, if it is, that its principal roots lie merely in the policy actions of government, unions and modern enterprises. By and large, the evidence for the latter propositions boils down to the absence of a persuasive economic explanation for the fact that wage and salary levels in government and modern enterprises appear to be higher than those in the "residual" urban labor market, despite an excess of workers desiring jobs in those sectors (at least at the lower skill levels). Without a reliable basis — analytical or empirical — for the ascription of casual importance to *institutionally* determined wage decisions or exogenous policy variables, there would seem to be little support for attempting to impose a greater degree of governmental control over the wage structure in order to obviate the adverse employment effects of the wage differential in the modern and *residual* labor markets.

5. Cf. S.A. Aluko "Prices, Wages and Costs," *Conference on National Reconstruction and Development in Nigeria,* Ibadan, 1969; O. Teriba and O.A. Phillips, "Income Distribution and National Integration," *Nigerian Journal of Economic and Social Studies,* March 1971.

Table 2-3: SOME INDICATORS OF PUBLIC/PRIVATE WAGE AND SALARY DIFFERENTIALS

(£N)

	Government Sector	Quasi-Government Sector	Private Sector
Entry point for daily paid and unskilled labor	90	90	50.8- 174
Initial salary of graduate entrants (non-professional)	648- 720	850-1,200	850- 1,500
Initial salary of professional entrants	840- 950	950-1,200	1,200- 1,600
Chief executives, i.e., permanent secretaries, directors of companies and general managers of public corporations	3,000-3,250	3,000-4,500	5,000-12,000

Source: O. Teriba and O.A. Phillips, "Income Distribution and National Integration," p. 102.

Moreover, the higher wage levels in modern, large-scale establishments are usually believed to affect adversely employment expansion by encouraging excessively capital-intensive production processes. Not only is there the question of by how much employment opportunities would increase in those establishments with the elimination of any wage differential, but also account must be taken of the adverse effects on employment in the smaller, less modern establishments when these were confronted with the loss of the advantages they presumably enjoy from relatively lower wage levels. The differential in wages between the larger capital-intensive and smaller scale, more labor-intensive enterprises, is, however, probably of considerably less importance to the expansion of employment than access to and relative costs of non-labor inputs such as capital, managerial resources, technological expertise, etc. The relative advantages that the modern sector enjoys in these respects probably dwarfs in importance any relative wage differential in reducing the employment elasticity of output increases.

If this is the case, the presumptively detrimental effects on employment of higher wage levels in the modern sector are a less appropriate focus for government employment policy than the relative disadvantages faced by the smaller scale, more labor-intensive enterprises in obtaining capital, in benefiting from investment incentives, in introducing improved technology and in employing more efficient managerial and marketing techniques.

Money Wages, Urban Incomes and Inflation

Continuing and possibly accelerating inflation poses the most immediate threat to the employment and distributional objectives of Nigeria's development. The substantial increases in prices in the past several years have their origins in the disruptions and financial instability associated with the country's internal unrest (see Chapter 4). The inflationary problems, nevertheless, cannot be expected to recede as a natural consequence of economic recovery and reconstruction. Unless monetary and fiscal management succeeds in re-establishing a reasonable degree of internal financial stability, there are reasons to believe that the wage-price mechanism in the urban sector will aggravate the disparities in income and employment opportunities.

The lack of reliable and comprehensive data on current wage and price movements make it difficult to judge the full dimensions of the problem, but the broad outlines are clear. Excessive monetary demand appears to have its greatest impact on food prices because of the difficulties of obtaining rapid increases in urban food supplies. Although the lower income self-employed and casual urban workers may feel the increases in the cost of living most severely, the workers in wage-employment may be better placed to protect their real income position through money wage increases. In particular, the government, as the principal employer of wage and salary employees, is almost certain to place great weight on the cost of living in its decisions on wage increases. This is partly as a matter of general policy, but also because of sensitivity to organized pressure by trade unions, which in Nigeria have their principal strength among public employees. With government payrolls accounting for an estimated 50 percent of public recurrent expenditure, the direct impact on public budgets of government wage increases is large and immediate, and poses the problem of financing the increased level of expenditure in a way that does not simply add to the inflationary pressure. The federal structure of government and the role of petroleum in the structure of government revenues contribute further complications. This occurs since government wage decisions have, by far, their greatest budgetary impact on state, local and other statutory authorities, while the bulk of the anticipated increases in oil revenues will accrue to the federal government.

While the expected increases in oil revenues are sufficient to cover the additional federal employment costs stemming from recent wage and salary awards in the public service and to accomplish the necessary transfer to other governmental bodies without incurring a deficit on the current account of the federal budget, this does not obviate the need for concern about the inflationary impact. If the resulting increases in urban consumer demand lead to a further spiraling of urban food prices, the foundations are laid for continuing rounds of wage increases. Measures to moderate the rise in urban prices through liberalization of imported consumer goods (such as have already taken place) though an important and desirable element of stabilization policy, do not offer a long-run solution. The fundamental policy issue is the extent to which the fiscal and foreign exchange resources provided by the increases in oil revenues are to be used to finance higher levels of investment and development rather than to support higher consumption for those sectors of the urban population which are best placed to maintain and improve their real income position. The ramifications of this basic issue for general economic policy are pursued in other parts of this report.

The Adebo Commission report itself laid great emphasis on the importance of anti-inflationary measures if the wage increases it recommended were not simply to aggravate the situation. To quote:

> "No previous Nigerian commission on wages and salaries was so preoccupied as we have been with the incidence of the cost of living... Our appointment synchronized more or less with the end of a civil war that had dammed up purchasing power for some two and a half years, and upset production, marketing and distribution patterns. The resulting inflationary situation was of extraordinary magnitude, but it was to a significant extent curable. It was clear to us that, unless certain remedial steps were taken and actively pursued, a pay award would have little or no meaning and could indeed make matters worse."[6]

Moreover, in arriving at its recommendations, the Commission gave explicit attention to the position of other groups in the economy — particularly rural workers and the self-employed — and to the relation of government pay scales to wage rates in the private sector. In general, the report gives every indication that these considerations weighed heavily in its decision to award increases falling considerably short of the almost 50 percent measured increase in the cost of living since 1964, the date of the last previous general review of wages and salaries.

From the trade union side, the threat to wage stability appears minimal since the unions do not seem to have either the organizational strength or the financial resources to enforce wage demands independently of government wage awards, at least when prices are reasonably stable.

The prospects for bringing inflation under control and avoiding the misuse of resources and the distributional inequities associated with a wage-price spiral are primarily dependent upon the government's capacity for monetary and fiscal management. The level and structure of demand

6. Second and Final Report of the Wages and Salaries Review Commission, 1970-71, p. 9.

must be in accord with the resource availabilities and patterns needed to achieve its investment and development objectives.

Employment Policy and Planning

The magnitude and structure of Nigeria's employment problems are such that they will not yield easily to short-run or narrowly conceived employment programs. Certainly over the current Plan period and beyond, improvements in income and employment position for most workers and, more particularly, for most of the new entrants to the work force, will continue to depend largely on developments in the agricultural, small industry and service sectors for which detailed planning and administrative implementation presents the most difficult problems. For this reason, if for no other, the basic strategy followed in the allocation of development resources and the corresponding structure of incentives generated by government development policies will continue to be of decisive importance to the achievement of employment and distribution objectives. The obvious implication — that employment and distribution cannot be treated independently of general development policies — does not, of course, mean that specific employment-oriented programs are of little importance or significance, but simply that their role can be assessed only in the larger developmental context.

There is some question whether the present organization of planning and policy-making provides an effective mechanism through which such appraisals can take place. The National Manpower Board, which apparently was established to be a major vehicle for analyzing the manpower implications of development plans and introducing employment considerations into the economic policy formulation process, has not achieved its potential in this regard. For it to do so would require considerable strengthening of the Board's secretariat (the Manpower Division of the Ministry of Economic Development), and probably a substantial reorientation of the secretariat's work. In past years much of this work has been data collection, requirement surveys etc., which under normal circumstances are perhaps the proper responsibility of other ministries and the Federal Office of Statistics. Lack of statistical data and information make it understandable that the Manpower Board has felt constrained to remedy some of the deficiencies through its own effort. However, it would seem that its more proper function is to make sure that the various agencies of government are developing the interest and capacity to provide basic data on employment and manpower aspects in their own areas of activity, for their own purposes as well as for the Manpower Board. The professional and analytic resources of the board secretariat could then be devoted in greater measure to the analysis of the substantial issues of how employment and income distribution objectives must be taken into account in basic decisions on investment allocation, industrialization, agricultural development, education and training, wage, price and fiscal policy, etc., which determine the course of Nigeria's development.

CHAPTER 3
INVESTMENT PROGRAMS AND POLICIES

Public Investment

The composition of the public investment program is described in the Second National Development Plan and in the twelve State Government Plans[1] which are summarized in Statistical Annex Table 30. The National Plan includes allocations for the investment programs of each state.

The public investment programs are implemented through the federal and state governments' capital estimates, and through the capital budgets for the federal corporations. No federal capital estimates were published for 1970/71, and capital funds were only released during this period in respect of continuing projects. The reason for this was not only that the Plan had not been approved, but also that the budgetary and foreign exchange position demanded continued stringency. However, the state governments and statutory corporations were operating with capital budgets during 1970/71, albeit for rather limited amounts.

In April 1971, the federal government approved capital estimates for 1970/71 and 1971/72. Contrary to the usual practice whereby unspent capital allocations lapse at the end of the fiscal year, this two-year capital budget allowed for funds unspent in 1970/71 to be carried forward to 1971/72. So far as the federal government departments are concerned, the capital estimates closely reflect the Plan allocations for 1970/71 and 1971/72. The effect of the two-year capital budget, taken together with the limited investment carried out in 1970/71, was that nearly all federal departments had capital funds available in excess of what they could reasonably have been expected to spend efficiently in 1971/72.

Control over the content of the investment programs is maintained, since projects not included in the Plan cannot be carried out without approval of the Federal Executive Council. This is the case both with respect to federal government departments and the statutory corporations. Furthermore, revisions to the State Plans also have to be approved by the Supreme Military Council, on the recommendation of the Federal Commissioner for Economic Development. The capital budgets of the Statutory Corporations are not published and are not readily available, but are thought to correspond to the Plan. The capital budgets of the state governments are published, but with some delay. With some exceptions, these capital estimates correspond to the Plan allocations, and in those cases where discrepancies have emerged, they are in the process of being reconciled through the Federal Ministry of Economic Development.

In accordance with the Plan, the government has prepared a progress report on plan implementation.[2] The report is a review of economic development during 1970/71 and of the implementation of the Plan in respect of policies, institutions and the execution of the public investment programs. The report also includes some preliminary data for public investment programs during the first six months of 1971/72 (that is, up to September 1971), as well as for 1970/71.

The Second Plan provides for a number of new institutions in the public sector and for improved administrative arrangements for planning and implementing public sector programs. There has been significant progress in this respect. A Central Planning Office has been set up within the Federal Ministry of Economic Development and Reconstruction which is meant to replace the Economic Planning Unit, and the new office is in the process of being staffed. The joint Planning Board has also been set up, comprising officials of the federal and state governments, the Central Bank and the Nigerian Institute for Social and Economic Research (NISER). Planning sections in several federal executive ministries have started to function (Transport, Education, Communications) and initial steps have been taken to establish the National Economic Advisory Council which will be composed of senior officials of the economic ministries, the universities and the private sector.

Table 3-1 summarizes the implementation of the Plan during 1970/71 and 1971/72, and provides a comparison with the Plan targets. Against total planned public investment in 1970/71 (excluding defense) of £N175 million actual expenditure was about £N100 million. In 1971/72,

---

1. Cf. Summary of the Plan in Ch. 3 of Economic Report AW22a, January 21, 1971.

2. Second National Development Plan, First Progress Report, 1972.

Table 3-1: PLAN IMPLEMENTATION

(In Millions of £N)

	1970/71[a]	Apr-Sept 1971[a]	Apr-Mar 1971/72	1972/73	1973/74	1970/71- 1973/74
Plan targets			(at current prices)			
Nominal total public investment	222		265	253	208	948
of which:						
Federal government	79		105	85	66	335
Federal corporations	39		34	39	31	143
State governments	104		126	129	111	470
Less underspending and transfers	47		67	64	44	222
Total public investment	175		198	189	164	726
			(at constant 1970/71 prices)			
Total public investment[b]	175		195	184	158	712
Expected implementation – low range	(actual)	(provisional)	Estimated			
Total public investment	100	71	150	195	210	655
of which:						
Federal government	34	18	40	65	70	209
Federal corporations	12[c]	6[c]	20	30	35	97
State governments	54	47	90	100	105	349
Expected implementation – high range						
Total public investment	100	71	160	215	237	712
of which:						
Federal government	34	18	40	70	77	221
Federal corporations	12[c]	6[c]	20	35	45	112
State governments	54	47	100	110	115	379

[a]Implementation data for 1970/71 and the first six months of 1971/72 are from the draft progress report and may not be complete.

[b]Plan targets deflated by the Plan's projected GDP deflator.

[c]Excludes some statutory corporations for which data are not available.

Source: Plan, pp. 58, 92, 269-272, draft progress report and mission estimates.

provisional data for the first six months indicate capital expenditure of £N71 million, which could reach about £N160 million for the year as a whole. The progress report does not estimate likely investment for the remaining two years of the Plan. The mission has, however, estimated the rate of investment which could materialize during 1972/73-1973/74 given continued improvement of executive capacity, and on the basis of likely investment programs in some of the main sectors. Table 3-1 also illustrates the rate of investment ("high range") which would be required if the total investment included in the Plan were to be realized, in financial terms, during the 1970-74 Plan period.

The most difficult aspect to evaluate is the effect on Plan implementation of changes in the cost of investment. It has been clear for some time that the Plan allocations for a number of projects are insufficient to complete them. In other cases, financial allocations have been made for rather ill-defined expenditure programs, and it is not possible to determine in physical terms what the investment target was to which the allocation was initially related. Even when the scope of projects is defined, cost overruns have not been due purely to inflation; specifications have been increased in some cases, and in others preparation of the projects has revealed that the initial allocations were unrealistic. It is therefore not possible to evaluate Plan implementation in physical terms, or to deflate Plan investments to the national prices used in the preparation of the Plan, and thereby to obtain some estimate of public investment in *real* terms.

The progress report on Plan implementation considers implementation performance primarily in terms of the financial targets, with only limited attention being paid to physical execution. This is understandable, but provides only a partial picture of what is actually happening. A full assessment would require either a thorough recosting of the Plan investment programs, or detailed reporting of physical indices of execution (miles of road, houses connected with water or electricity, schools constructed, jobs created, etc.).

A case in point is the road program. The initial allocation for the federal road rehabilitation program was £N33 million, of which some £N7 million was spent during the first eighteen months of the Plan. Allowing for the fact that this only represents one construction season,[3] this performance could be regarded as quite successful were it not for the fact that, on the basis of current construction prices, the rehabilitation program has now been revalued to £N64 million. One state has revalued its road construction program, indicating a 50 percent inflation in the price of the planned projects;[4] while another has more than doubled the price of its road program.[5] Otherwise the states have not undertaken a revision of the planned allocations for roads, or for other sectors.

This revaluation has serious implications for the financial planning of the remaining two years of the Plan. While some states may not spend their planned allocations, although their actual programs cost twice the estimate, it is quite possible that a number of other states may find that their investment cost will exceed Plan allocations by 1974, even though their programs will not have been fully implemented. Unless such situations are revealed and approved at an early stage it is possible that several states may experience financial difficulties in the course of the next two years. It is important that all revisions in the cost of planned investments be brought to the attention of the federal government in a systematic and timely way so that the necessary action can be taken to make additional funds available, if they are required. This problem is only a specific example of the general problem of federal allocations to state governments discussed in Chapter 4.

The performance of the various state governments in the implementation of their public investment programs varies widely from state to state. In those states where there was a continuing development program predating the current Plan the level of investment was high compared with Plan targets while others have implemented only a fraction of their targets during the first eighteen months of the Plan. There are many reasons for this situation. In some states, particularly the new states with relatively weak administrations, executive capacity is an absolute constraint. In others, the financial constraint referred to is already being felt. There is also the fact that compared with

3. The rainy season ends about September when mobilization on new projects usually begins.

4. Refers to Western State. Plan allocation is £N8.4 million revised to £N12.8 million. Implementation is reported at £N6.7 million in 1970/71, but the projects reports only account for £N1.3 million.

5. Lagos State. Inflation entirely due to contract price of Lagos-Badagri road. This is now expected to be carried over, in part, to the next plan.

their executive capacity, some state plans are more ambitious than others. A detailed state-by-state review of Plan implementation is contained in the government's progress report.

Much of the Federal Statutory Corporations' investment in 1970/71 was accounted for by expenditure on telecommunications. Performance in other areas was limited in that year. In the longer term the level of investment in the Corporations must improve if serious bottlenecks are to be avoided.

Table 3-2 indicates the main components of nondefense public investment by sector in 1970/71 and the projected composition of this investment through the end of the current Plan period.

Table 3-2: PUBLIC INVESTMENT: ACTUAL AND PROJECTED SECTORAL ALLOCATION[a]

					(£N Million at Constant 1970/71 Prices)
Sector	1970/71[b]	1971/72	1973/74	1974/75	1970/71-1973/74
	actual		projected		
Total	100	160	200	225	685
Fuel and power	6	10	10	15	41
Transport	37	55	70	65	227
Communications	9	10	10	10	39
Water supply	5	10	10	12	37
Health	3	5	10	10	28
Education	10	20	25	30	85
Agriculture[c]	10	15	20	20	65
Industry	5	10	10	15	40
General administration	5	15	20	30	70
Other	10	10	15	18	53

[a]The estimates of total public investment shown here fall approximately mid-way within the range presented in Table 3-1.

[b]Data for 1970/71 are from the draft progress report and may not be complete.

[c]Includes livestock, forestry and fishing.

Source: Draft progress report and mission estimates.

Apart from the road program, the main components of the growth of federal investment are the agriculture and industry programs. These are also the most problematical. For agriculture, the main problem is project preparation, which is not going ahead as rapidly as would be required if the Plan were to be implemented, especially where major projects with direct federal participation are concerned. In the industry sector, implementation of a number of projects depends on foreign technical associates who have not yet been forthcoming in all cases.

In the longer term, the government could clearly finance a much higher level of public investment than that envisaged in the present Plan. The following numerical exercise illustrates the magnitudes that the mission has in mind. In 1970/71, total fixed investment in the non-petroleum sectors was about 14 percent of GNP, equivalent to about £N340 million. Public (non-defense) investment accounted for about 30 percent of this, that is to say no more than 4½ percent of GNP. By the end of the Plan period, following prewar trends in the rate of investment, the rate of non-petroleum investment can be expected to rise to about 17 percent of GNP of which the public sector would account for about 40 percent. By 1978/79, non-petroleum investment may well have risen to about 19 percent of GNP, and it is not unreasonable to expect that public investment would continue to account for 40 percent of that amount. With GNP of £N4,800 million (in

1970/71 prices) projected for 1978/79, this would mean public investment of some £N350 million to £N400 million in that year. In other words, the average rate of growth of public investment between 1970/71 and 1978/79 could be about 18 percent per year.

Alternative development strategies for the economy and the present status of preparation of investment programs in the various sectors are discussed later in this report. However, the mission has found it useful to prepare, as a frame of reference, an estimate of the composition of the public investment program assuming total investment approximately as described above, and taking account of the existing work in the various sectors. The result of this exercise is shown in Table 3-3.

Table 3-3: TENTATIVE PUBLIC INVESTMENT PROGRAM 1974/75-1978/79

					(£N Million at 1970/71 Prices)
	1974/75	1975/76	1976/77	1977/78	1978/79
Total	250	280	310	350	380
Economic (56%-60%)	140	158	180	206	230
Social (29%-25%)	72	81	87	91	95
Administration (15%)	38	41	47	52	55

Source: Mission's estimates.

Allocations for most classes of overhead investments are based on present expectations of requirements. Investments in the productive sectors are only a minor part of total investment in these areas and depend to a large degree on the extent of public participation in, for example, the manufacturing industry or large-scale agricultural projects. They also depend on the speed at which the corresponding projects are carried out, particularly the large-scale industrial projects.

There will be increasing scope for capital transfer from the public to the private sector. Industrial and agricultural credit facilities and eventually home mortgages and the acquisition of equity in private enterprises may be increasingly financed through transfers from the government budget. Thus, even if direct public investment in productive activities does not increase as rapidly as suggested, the federal and state governments may well finance intermediary institutions investing in those sectors. The establishment of the federal government's Industrial and Commercial Credit Bank announced in the 1972/73 Budget appears to be a first step in this direction.

Investment allocations for social services and government administration are particularly tentative. Much work is required before health and education programs can be determined so far ahead, and the requirements for administrative buildings are not known. The allocations are based on approximately maintaining current proportions of investment in these sectors.

In terms of present executive capacity the program outlined in Table 3-3 is indeed ambitious. The mission considers that, in the absence of the financial constraints that have been encountered in the past, more can be achieved. There is time to improve executive capacity in the different sectors and to establish new institutions, both for the preparation and implementation of projects in the public sector, and for channeling funds to the private sector.

Pre-investment

A recurring theme is the need for long-range planning to insure that necessary pre-investment work is carried out for timely execution of development plans. This is a question of insuring that necessary staff is available with the appropriate training and of allowing enough time for work to be completed. Much of the shortfall in public investment during the first two years of the Plan has not been due to any failure of executive capacity as such, but to over-optimism as to the lead time required to prepare the planned investments. Whereas much of the pre-investment work required for the current Plan is now in hand, the longer-term demand for these services corresponding to the higher level of investment envisaged may well be in excess of available capacity.

Pre-investment activities are carried out by the planning and development staff in many federal and state government ministries and in public corporations. These, in turn, contract out a variety of tasks to a wide range of consulting firms, or employ foreign professional staff to assist in this work. Presently, outside the planning functions of government ministries, most of the pre-investment capacity is still based on expatriate skills. While some ministries of works employ Nigerian engineers able to undertake design work, the available technical personnel employed by the government are usually used for supervision of on-going work, and in the case of externally financed projects this function is still being contracted to outside firms.

While consultancy firms and other sources of technical assistance are supplying trained and, at times, highly experienced staff, these firms sometimes suffer from lack of continuity and, consequently, from a limited knowledge of Nigeria. While a few firms have built up a sustained volume of business, especially in road transport, and can build on their past knowledge, the prospective growth in public investment, and in investment generally, means that this accumulated experience will be increasingly spread.

In the past, external agencies have been associated with many of the large projects included in the development plans, employing foreign consultants to prepare and supervise projects. In the future, the government can be expected to finance an increasing share of its investment directly from its own resources and to direct its attention toward the employment of Nigerians for this purpose. There are several way of approaching this changed situation.

Nigerian consultancies. Some all-Nigerian consultancies exist and these can be expected to expand. Nevertheless, the effect on overall capacity will be limited for some time to come, even with strong government encouragement. These firms are apparently still quite small and are not equipped to undertake large projects.[6] They seem to be concentrated in professions related to the building industry (architects, quantity surveyors, etc.), while few are working on civil engineering and hardly any on industrial projects or in economic consultancy.

Partnerships. One way Nigerian professionals can obtain appropriate experience with a firm large enough to work on a wide range of projects, or on larger projects, is through partnerships. The federal government increasingly requires that foreign consultancies entering the country associate themselves with a Nigerian firm. The principal drawback to this policy is the paucity of Nigerian firms able to sustain the local side of the partnership. The danger is that, pressed too far, the policy may lead to a number of very unequal partnerships, and at worst, the deliberate creation of sleeping partners whose only role would be to fulfill official requirements.

Government employment. The federal and state governments already employ engineers, economists and other professionals and would employ more were they available, especially in the newly created states. Usually long-range planning work is done within government ministries, and available trained personnel concentrated in this area. Even so, some states have used technical assistance for development planning, and some consultants are employed on planning at the federal level, notably in the transportation sector.

On the other hand, sector surveys, feasibility studies, design work and eventually project supervision, could be contracted to outside firms, and in the majority of cases probably should be. An attempt to do otherwise might prove unsuccessful. It would be inconsistent with the development of Nigerian firms, and in any case there is so much demand in the private sector that government departments find it difficult to deter experienced professionals from joining private consultancies.

In the area of project supervision, the government cannot entirely delegate its responsibilities to private firms, because the ministries are, and should be, accountable. While some state ministries still need outside support for this work, given the overall requirements for experienced profes-

---

6. Recently, the design of about forty new culverts on the Shagamu-Benin Road was divided among about ten Nigerian firms.

sional services, it would not be unreasonable to expect that this function would be progressively taken over by engineers employed by government departments, particularly as project supervision provides a training ground for engineers.

Nigerianization. Foreign consulting firms can be expected to continue to provide the bulk of the pre-investment capacity in Nigeria, and in the context of a rapid growth in investment, public and private, expand their activities. It is necessary to reconcile this expansion with the objective of employing and training an increasing proportion of Nigerians. The Quota Board might consider linking increased employment of foreign technicians with a corresponding quota of Nigerians. Because most pre-investment contracts are financed by external agencies, these requirements could be reflected in the policies of these companies.

Technical assistance. It is also possible to recruit individuals or groups directly through official technical assistance channels. This approach is relatively inexpensive compared with consultancy fees and is conveniently suitable for the recruitment of operating personnel in educational and health services, but it has proved difficult to build up the stable and balanced teams required for major pre-investment work on this basis. In practice, this approach is most widely used by those state governments which have fewest Nigerian graduates to staff technical ministries, and while some are involved in pre-investment work, it does not offer an effective solution to the overall demand for professional services of this kind.

The Universities. The expansion in higher education and the prestige attached to the universities has resulted in a large proportion of highly trained Nigerian professionals working on university faculties. Not unnaturally, the government has looked to the universities for assistance in preparing development plans, and providing economic advice in various sectors. This tendency will doubtless be developed and should be encouraged. However, for this to be successfully developed, it will be necessary to plan carefully. While the development of Nigerian universities is striking, their resources are limited. Practical research related to government development plans should not be to the detriment of university teaching, and the work should not be undertaken on too broad a front. Notwithstanding the substantial scope for increased activity in this direction, external agencies may also have a role insofar as they are able to associate research contracts to Nigerian research institutes with additional trained staff from abroad.

Private Investment

A realistic assessment of the policies and problems of private industry is made in the Second Development Plan, followed by a number of specific policy recommendations. The relatively low value-added content of industrial output, the discrimination against the production of intermediate and capital goods, the disincentives for producing processed export goods and the relatively minor, and rather unsuccessful role of the public sector's own investments are analyzed in some detail.

The Plan stresses the need to increase the value-added content of domestic output, while simultaneously reducing that portion transferred abroad, and specifies certain means to accomplish this. First, there is a list of priority industries which includes, among others, industries processing agricultural products, petrochemicals, integrated textiles, iron and steel, vehicle assembly, new exporting and further import substitution industries. Revisions of the industrial incentives system are envisaged in order to direct private investment in line with the Plan's priorities. These measures, therefore, will be discriminatory, but are not further specified. Within this setting, special assistance is to be given to Nigerian enterprise, both in the form of financing and training. The public sector's direct investments in manufacturing are planned at about 20 percent of those expected to be made by the private sector.

The Second Plan projected private investment in manufacturing at £N379 million, rising from £N75 million in the first year, 1970/71, to £N117 million in 1973/74. The average rate of increase was expected to be 16.5 percent per year. Provisional figures for 1970/71 indicate that private investment in manufacturing amounted to an estimated £N90 million, substantially exceeding Plan targets. There is little doubt that private investment in manufacturing will remain above Plan targets, judging from the number of new ventures now being started in reaction to the strong upward move of domestic demand. As most of these new industries are financed from abroad and are of the same character as existing industries, there is a strong impression that this development is not in accordance either with the government's preference for joint ventures with foreign capital, or with its objective to maximize value-added as a proportion of gross output. Moreover, in view of the long gestation periods of many high value-added industries, it would be unreasonable to expect very rapid change in the structure of manufacturing output and value-added.

The Plan target for private investment in activities other than manufacturing and mining is £169.8 million, 72 percent of which is in the non-corporate sector (primarily peasant agriculture and housing). The Plan estimates presented for these sectors may in themselves be realistic and represent the capacity to save in the non-corporate sector rather than in their investment needs. Here, however, the Nigerianization issue is particularly important as existing foreign investments are large, especially in trade and construction, probably amounting to several times the total involved in the manufacturing sector. The investment funds that would be required to finance the prescribed participations far exceed the available savings in the non-corporate sector.

Moreover, there is a danger that the policy to reduce the share of value-added which flows abroad may be pushed too hard. A recently issued decree provides that a number of manufacturing and commercial activities are to be reserved entirely for Nigerian enterprise after 1974. In the manufacturing sectors these embrace an estimated 8 percent of value-added in large-scale establishments. A second group of manufacturing establishments, covering about 40 percent of value-added, is listed for the purpose of increasing indigenous participation to 40 percent equity. Small ventures in this category may be completely barred to foreign investment.

Nigerianization is also pursued in the form of training indigenous staff and management to operate firms which still use substantial numbers of expatriates. A financially well-endowed industrial training scheme has just been launched. For some time, expatriate quotas have been tightened and may now be harming efficient operations in a number of cases. Admittedly, the task of balancing desires for speedy Nigerianization of staff and management in foreign-owned operations with the need to maintain and improve industrial efficiency is a delicate one. The government does, however, realize that for years to come a degree of dependence on expatriates will be unavoidable, and that a balance must be struck between the objectives of growth and domestic ownership.

Private investment including that in the oil producing sector will almost certainly exceed Plan targets by a substantial margin. Outside the oil sector, an investment level and growth rate beyond the Plan's forecasts are also possible, provided that the government implements an appropriate incentives policy and follows a carefully charted course on the issue of indigenization, accompanied by clear and unequivocal statements of intent in the matter. Public investment is continuing to fall short of Plan targets but could exceed Plan levels in the later years if delayed projects are actively implemented and new ones initiated in the near future.

From this, it appears realistic to conclude that the investment rate (including oil) during the balance of the Plan period may remain at the high level of about 20 percent of GNP at market prices estimated for 1971/72. Excluding the oil sector, the rate may possibly rise from 16 percent in 1971/72 to 17 percent in 1973/74 as compared to about 13 in 1960-66.

CHAPTER 4
FISCAL AND MONETARY TRENDS AND PROSPECTS

The fiscal year 1971/72 (April-March) saw a reversal of the deterioration of the government's accounts which began in the early sixties and accelerated during 1966-70. The very substantial deficits which had become a common characteristic of government finance at almost all levels and the consequent need to rely heavily on Central Bank finance have now been replaced by a sizable surplus in the federal government's account which more than compensates for expected overall deficits at the state level. Thus, for the first time in Nigeria's history since independence, the government's overall accounts are in surplus, and short-term indebtedness can be reduced.

This rather dramatic transition has not come about as a result of reduced expenditure — which might be expected at least in the defense area — although the share of government expenditure in GDP has declined somewhat from the extremely high level of 29 percent in 1969/70. The major determinant of the favorable turn has been the large increase of revenues originating in the oil-producing sector because of rapid production and export growth as well as a consequence of the recently negotiated increase in the posted (tax reference) price. The order of magnitude can be indicated by reference to the revenues accruing from the oil sector in 1966, when they amounted to £N13.3 million or 7 percent of all current revenues (federal and state together). The estimate for 1971/72 is £N320 million or nearly 50 percent of total revenue. The outlook for the financing of the public sector in the next years is dominated by this single factor, as further major increases in oil revenues are expected.

Implementation of the 1970/71 and 1971/72 Budgets

Federal government revenues in 1970/71 were about threefold greater than in 1969/70, having risen from £N218 million to an estimated £N646 million. Of this increase, oil revenues (rents, royalties, and profit taxes) contributed about two-thirds and the remainder came almost entirely from import and excise duties. The liberalization of imports and adjustments of some duty rates were the main causes of this rapid increase in indirect taxes (Table 4-1).

Larger federal revenues imply larger transfers to the states on the basis of the existing revenue sharing arrangements. In addition, the states, judging by their budgets for 1971/72, expected to increase significantly their own revenues. However, as substantial rate reductions were introduced in the personal income tax (a state subject) and no steps were taken to introduce a general sales tax, the budget estimates for the states' own revenues appear to have been rather optimistic. Actual receipts may, in fact, have been less than £N50 million in FY 1971/72. The degree to which the states rely on transfers from the federal government is thus increasing rapidly. Before 1966, their own current revenues amounted to about 35-40 percent of their total current receipts, but in 1971/72 this may have declined to a little over 20 percent.

An important feature of the development of government revenues is the fact that the favorable fiscal situation and prospects have come about without more than minor changes in the tax structure. The existing tax structure is not particularly balanced, nor is it adequately geared to Nigeria's development objectives. Revenues from the oil sector will conceal part of this problem in the coming years so far as the federal government's financial position is concerned. This may, in turn, lead to the neglect of tax reforms which would be desirable for purposes of protecting domestic production, changes in the distribution of income and price stability.

Current Expenditure

In 1966/67, federal recurrent expenditures were still slightly less than federal revenues after allowing for statutory transfers to the regions. Between 1966/67 and 1971/72, federal recurrent expenditure tripled. The surplus on current account last year followed a series of large annual deficits (Table 4-2). The state governments maintained a current surplus in 1969/70 equivalent to about 15 percent of current expenditure. Although complete information on expenditures of the state governments in 1970/71 and 1971/72 is not yet available, it appears that rapidly rising current expenditures have at least kept pace with the increase in state government revenues arising from higher transfers from the federal government.

Table 4-1: FEDERAL AND STATE GOVERNMENT REVENUES AND TRANSFERS, 1969/70-1971-72

	1969/70 Actual	1970/71 Actual	1971/72 Budget	1971/72 Mission estimate
				(In Millions of £N)
Federal Government Current Revenues	217.9	377.8	475.8	646
Import Duties	80.1	115.5	96.8	155
Excise Duties	39.2	65.9	82.2	82
Oil Revenues	34.0	102.8	225.5	320
Other (tax and non-tax)	64.6	93.6	71.3	89
Less revenues transferred to states	89.7	143.4	126.0	176
Federal Government Retained Revenues (1-2)	128.2	234.4	349.8	470
State Government Current Revenues	36.1	45.0[a]	66.0	50
State Government Current Receipts (2+4)	125.8	188.4	192.0	224
Total (Federal, State) Current Revenues as % of GDP (at factor cost)	13.9	17.8	—	24

[a]Provisional estimate.

Defense and security expenditures at over 60 percent of federal current expenditures were the dominant item in 1969/70 and 1970/71. Although increasing in absolute amount in the past fiscal year, their share declined slightly, as other expenditures, notably for economic and social services, rose. The federal government's outlays for maintenance and operation of the country's economic and social infrastructure averaged about £N21 million per year from 1961-66. Table 4-2 (line 1.b) shows that in 1970/71 these outlays were still at the same level. The rise to an estimated £N30 million in 1971/72 is the first major increase in the country's history, notwithstanding the significant additions which have been made to Nigeria's economic and social infrastructure since independence. There is no comprehensive information available to judge whether expenditures for maintenance and operation at the 1971/72 level were adequate. However, a crude comparison with the value of total federal investments in economic and social infrastructure since independence would suggest that further increases will be needed in the coming years.[1]

Public debt charges, the other major federal expenditure item on current account, largely represent the burden imposed by internal borrowing to finance budget deficits during 1966-70. The rapid increase of current revenue has reduced this burden considerably since 1969/70 when debt servicing claimed almost 27 percent of federal current receipts and 45 percent of retained revenues. In 1971/72, these rates dropped to 8 percent and 11 percent, respectively.

The bulk of total public spending for economic and social services in Nigeria is borne by the states in accordance with the existing distribution of sectoral responsibilities between the federal and state governments. A large part of state current expenditure falls in this category, and the

1. Capital expenditures for economic and social services between 1961 and 1966 amounted to £N145 million; assuming recurrent costs conservatively at 15 percent, and adding this to average current expenditures in the base period would give a "need" of £N40 million.

growth of these outlays in recent years is more in line with past levels of capital expenditure for economic and social infrastructure than is the case with regard to the federal government. State expenditure since 1967 also shows a rapid increase under the general administration heading, reflecting the creation of the twelve states and eight new government administrations in that year.

Prior to 1966, the federal and regional governments generated surpluses on current account which averaged about 2 percent of GDP. During 1966 to 1970, this turned into an annual average deficit of more than 2 percent of GDP. The estimated surplus of £N169 million last year amounted to roughly 7 percent of GDP and, for the first time, provided a comfortable basis for financing capital expenditure.

Capital Expenditure

The composition and implementation of the combined 1970/71-1971/72 capital budget was discussed in some detail in Chapter 3. As shown in Table 4-3, the estimated surplus on current account in 1971/72 was more than sufficient to finance all government capital expenditure. As the flow of external resources was also relatively large because of expanded program lending, the overall budget of the federal and state governments was probably in surplus for the first time since independence.

Table 4-2: FEDERAL AND STATE CURRENT EXPENDITURES 1961/70-1971/72

				(In Millions of £N)
	1969/70	1970/71	1971/72	
	Actual	Actual	Budget	Mission estimate
Federal Government Current Expenditures	296.1	271.4	242.1	315
Defense, security[b]	192.1	172.8	130.3	195
Economic and social services	18.3	21.9	28.8	30
Debt service	58.1	45.9	38.7	50
Other expenditures	27.6	30.8	44.3	40
State Government Expenditures	111.6	170.0[a]	183.2	210
Economic and social services	69.1	110.0	na	na
Other expenditures	42.5	60.0	na	na
Current Surplus (+) or Deficit (−)	-153.6	-18.6	+115.3	+169
Federal government	-169.1	-37.0	+106.5	+155
State governments	+15.5	+18.4	+8.8	+14

[a]Provisional estimate.

[b]Includes capital expenditures.

The presentation of Table 4-3 obscures the considerable differences between the financial position of the federal government and that of the state governments. In 1971/72 the overall surplus in the federal accounts is estimated at about £N100 million whereas the combined accounts of the states may show an overall deficit of about £N85 million.

Not enough is known about the recent and current fiscal position of the states to venture estimates on budget implementation by each individual state. It is known that in 1969/70 the actual accounts of the states varied widely; for later years only budget data and limited expenditure and revenue data collected by the Central Bank are available.

Table 4-3: FEDERAL AND STATE CAPITAL EXPENDITURE FINANCING, 1969/70-1971/72

	1969/70 Actual	1970/71 Actual	1971/72 Budget	(In Millions of £N) 1971/72 Mission estimate
Total Capital Expenditures	64.2	90.7	241.3	151
Federal government[a]	22.5	36.8	119.4	51
State governments[b]	41.7	53.9	121.9	100
Finance from				
Current account surplus[c]	-153.6	-18.6	115.3	169
External borrowing (including grants)	2.0	0.2	69.5	
Loans to states from marketing boards	8.7	8.8	6.0	
Other internal borrowing[d]	207.1	100.3	50.5	

[a]Excluding defense capital expenditure and capital transfers to the states; including loans and grants to federal statutory corporations.

[b]Including expenditure financed by federal capital transfers.

[c]Federal and state governments.

[d]Residual item.

Inflationary Pressures

An intensification of the inflationary pressures discussed in Chapter 1 caused the urban consumer price index to increase by 13.8 percent from 1969 to 1970 and by 15.2 percent for the first ten months of 1971 as compared with 1970 figures. The increase in 1971 was due almost entirely to a 27 percent increase in the price of food. While no information is available on the pace of inflation in rural areas, there is some evidence that the increase in food prices has not been confined to the major cities. This suggests that the rapid expansion in the supply of money and credit may have contributed to the severe inflationary pressures over the last two years.

Money supply (including savings deposits) held outside the government sector rose from £N263 million in December 1969 to £N400 million in December 1971, an increase of 52 percent in two years. Since the commercial banking system is predominantly urban, most of this new purchasing power was injected into the cities. Outstanding internal public debt expanded further by 12.6 percent from December 1970 to October 1971. The percentage held by the banking system fell from 65.3 percent to 51.4 percent, but there was no change in the liquidity structure of the debt. At the end of October 1971, more than two-thirds of the outstanding government debt held *outside* the federal government and the Central Bank had a maturity of less than one year (Table 4-4).

Strong inflationary pressures will persist in the foreseeable future. The Adebo Salary Award and the anticipated extension of similar wage increases to other government personnel and employees in the private sector will introduce new cost pressures. As outlined in Chapter 2, population and per capita income will continue to grow faster in urban than in rural areas, placing a heavy strain on the inadequate transport and storage facilities for food and accelerating urban inflation. Since more than half the federal government revenues will be derived from essentially enclave type petroleum operations, not only the size but the composition of government expenditure becomes vitally important in assessing the inflationary impact of fiscal policies.

Table 4-4: MATURITY OF GOVERNMENT DEBT[a] (October 1971)

			(In Millions of £N)
	Less than 1 year	1 year and above	Total
Total	388	175	563
Currency	181	—	181
Treasury Bills	153	—	153
Treasury Certificates	51	52	103
Development stock	3	123	126
Percent	68.9	31.1	100.0

[a]Debt, defined to include currency held outside the federal government and Central Bank.

Source: Data provided by Central Bank of Nigeria.

In summary, past increases in money supply, the high liquidity of the banking system, the short maturity structure of the public debt, the flood of pent-up wage increases, distribution bottlenecks, continuing demand pressures and a rising level of government activity, all set the stage for persistent inflation. This context is particularly relevant for the following discussion of fiscal and monetary prospects.

Fiscal Prospects and Policies

The Government of Nigeria is in the favorable position of having firm and rising flows of revenues. Thus, the mobilization of resources at the federal level has, for the time being, ceased to be a problem. The government's current fiscal concerns relate to the employment of resources in a non-inflationary way, their allocation over a variety of alternative uses and the efficiency with which such alternatives can be implemented. Developing and sustaining momentum in the implementation of the Second Development Plan now require the utmost diligence of the government at all levels. Therefore, it is understandable that preparation for the next five-year period has only just begun except in those cases where the preparation of sector plans required a longer perspective than is covered by the current Plan.

The transformation of the public sector's financial position and the wider range of alternatives which are now feasible require that increased activity be generated as soon as possible. The rapidly changing financial position should be accompanied by early consideration of alternative policy options, as their choice will determine the institutional and organizational arrangements which must be made in advance of project implementation. This applies most critically to the agricultural sector where present institutions have several weaknesses. If the government were, for example, to decide that it is desirable to triple or quadruple presently low expenditure on agricultural development from the beginning of the Third Development Plan, there would probably be no financial constraint on doing this. However, unless specific organizational arrangements are made now and proper channels for coordination and communication, horizontally as well as vertically, are established, such an increase in expenditure could easily lead to a wasteful use of resources.

The urgency to begin longer-range planning is heightened by several other considerations: there is an apparent weakness of present agencies and institutions in charge of development program implementation — if their responsibilities are to expand, their strength must keep pace — the distribution of responsibilities among the federal and state governments means that executing agencies must be built and strengthened in all the states as well as at the center and that appropriate coordination machinery must be developed; lack of foresight and hasty consideration of only a limited number of alternatives may result in allocations of resources which are less than optimal. The needs of Nigeria's population are so pressing, and, even with efficient use of oil resources, will be so persistent that the search for priorities in spending and institution-building cannot be delayed.

In what follows, the mission has attempted projections of the public sector's revenues and expenditures through the remaining years of the current Plan. For these years, a reasonably firm basis can be claimed, drawing not only from the Plan document itself, but also from the available information on actual developments during the first eighteen months of the Plan. Chapter 8 analyzes the more distant future for which the estimates are by their nature more tentative, and can be described as conditional projections. Assumptions are made, and specified, for some of the main variables and at that stage alternative assumptions are made in order to derive an impression of the orders of magnitude for the effects of alternative courses of action.

Table 4-5: PROJECTIONS OF GOVERNMENT REVENUES, 1971/72-1973/74

	1971/72 estimated	1972/73[a] projected	1973/74[a] projected	Average annual rate of growth (%) 1971/72-1973/74
				(In Millions of Current £N)
Federal government revenues	646	745	880	16.7
Oil revenues	320	400	500	25.0
Import duties	155	160	170	4.7
Excise duties	82	85	100	10.4
Other current revenues	89	100	110	11.2
State revenues	50	60	65	16.4
Total government revenues	696	805	945	16.7
Federal government retained revenues	470	550	660	18.5
Transfers to states	176	195	220	11.8
Total states' current receipts	226	255	285	12.7

[a]Changes in import and excise duty rates announced in the 1972/73 Budget have been taken into account in these projections.

Allocation of Revenues

The projections (Table 4-5) clearly demonstrate the buoyancy of revenues that can reasonably be expected; during the three years of the current Plan period, the average elasticity of government revenues to GDP is of the order of 1.65. However, the projection also indicates that the present revenue distribution system will yield a rate of growth of transfers to the states which is below the rate at which federal government revenues rise. As a consequence, the share of the states in total revenues declines from 45 percent in 1970/71 to 30 percent by the end of the current Plan.

The present allocation of revenues to the states therefore appears to be inadequate in relation to the role which state governments are expected to play in implementing development projects and programs, and in the operation and maintenance of existing and planned economic and social infrastructure facilities. Under present arrangements, there is no guarantee that the states (individually or collectively) will be provided the resources which they need to meet the objectives of national and regional growth or distribution of incomes and public services. Moreover, the present system provides no positive incentives to the states to increase their own resources. In the past, since transfers from the federal government have often been inadequate against expenditure obligations, the states have frequently placed heavy reliance on resources from the marketing boards. This has indirectly put an inequitable burden of state financing on the producers of export crops. In order to create more scope for a rational agricultural price policy, it appears necessary to free state governments from the reliance on marketing boards for revenue. This could be achieved by raising resources from other sources, including the non-agricultural tax base of the states themselves, or through additional transfers from the federal government in the form of matching grants in some specified proportion to the amounts of additional resources which the states themselves generate.

The existing distribution system also has the weakness of not being geared to the specific current and capital requirements of the states. This is a major defect when seen in the light of the wide disparities between the states in terms of the provision of economic and social services. From a development point of view, it is important that allocations of revenue to the states are adequate to insure full use of existing infrastructure capacity while providing adequate funds for its operation and maintenance, provide for the creation of new facilities where these are most needed, and create incentives for the states to generate additional revenues of their own without jeopardizing an improved agricultural price policy.

Government Expenditure

In projecting government expenditure it is difficult to make separate projections for the different levels of government. Much will depend on the distribution of their respective responsibilities. The claims on revenues for current expenditure are particularly difficult to project, as some elements depend heavily on political and social considerations. The main initial assumptions are as follows: the additional public sector costs associated with the Adebo and subsequent salary awards are all to be met, directly or indirectly, from the federal budget; the annual increase of personnel expenditures (including armed forces) could well be some £N40 million, if not more. The estimates are reflected in each of the usual categories of public expenditure. As a consequence, defense expenditure in 1972/73 will rise by the amount of the assumed salary increase; the same level, in real terms, is assumed for 1973/74 and this results in a gradual decline of their share, including defense capital expenditure, in GDP from the present high level of 6.7 percent to less than 6 percent by the end of the current Plan period.

Expenditure for debt servicing has been assumed constant at £N55 million per annum. This would imply substantial but decreasing roll-overs of short-term debt and only modest reductions of the outstanding amounts in earlier years. Debt retirement will, however, increase over time. All other federal expenditure is assumed to increase by about 15 percent per year after allowing for the current salary increases; expenditure by the state — largely for economic and social services — increases at the same rate (Table 4-6).

Rapidly increasing surpluses on current account are found when projecting on this basis, from an impressive 5.7 percent of GNP in 1971/72 to 7.5 percent in 1973/74. As was observed with respect to revenues, here the difference between the financial prospects of the federal and state governments comes even more sharply into focus, with virtual balances projected for the states' current accounts whereas the federal government's surplus almost doubles between 1971/72 and 1973/74.

No separate projections are made for capital expenditure by federal and state governments. Instead, a functional projection of government investment by sectors of the economy has been attempted, taking into account both estimated requirements and the public sector's capacity to implement investment programs and projects. This implies that suitable revenue-sharing arrangements will be implemented to match available resources to the needs of individual states. On this basis, government public investment could reach (as described in Chapter 3), a level of roughly £N185 million by the end of the current Plan period. This figure is based largely on projects presently being implemented or fully prepared and ready for execution in the next few years.

Table 4-6: CURRENT EXPENDITURES AND SURPLUSES, 1971/72-1973/74

(In Millions of Current £N)

	1971/72	1972/73	1973/74	Average annual rate of growth (%) 71/72-73/74
Federal Government				
Retained Revenues	470	550	660	18.5
Federal current expenditures	315	355	375	9.1
Federal current surplus	155	195	285	35.0
State Governments' Total				
Current Receipts	226	255	285	12.8
States' current expenditures	210	250	290	17.5
States' current surplus	16	+5	-5	—
Total Current Surplus as % of GDP	5.7	6.0	7.5	

aIncluding defense capital expenditures.

Substantial spending on these projects will spill over into the next Plan period.

As shown in Table 4-7 current budget surpluses are projected to exceed the amounts which can reasonably be expected to be invested by the federal and state governments, and overall budget surpluses of 2-3 percent of GNP can be anticipated on this basis by the end of the current Plan period. These projections do not allow for capital transfers to federal statutory corporations which amounted to some £N5 million in 1970/71; nor do they take into account actual or anticipated official capital receipts from abroad which are likely to be substantial. In considering the alternatives for the use, or non-use, of these resources, the mission has deliberately chosen to address this issue in the context of the next Plan period (which is the subject of Chapter 8), and to leave open the question of disposition of budget surpluses in 1972/73 and 1973/74. It should be noted, however, that these additional sources accrue to the government in the form of foreign exchange and may initially be used for strengthening reserves which at present cover only some two months' imports. Also, developments in the remaining two years of the current Plan period depend a great deal on the degree to which the government is able to control inflation. As stated earlier in this chapter, there is considerable uncertainty about the origins of the current inflation and about the effectiveness of the monetary measures presently at the government's disposal. In this context, the implementation of the Adebo Award for substantial wage and salary increases may add in a major way to inflationary pressures, particularly in the urban areas. These developments will have a substantial impact on the actual outcome of governmental accounts over the next two years.

Anti-Inflationary Policy

Recognizing the adverse impact of inflation on the development strategy of the country, the government has attempted to combat inflation using a variety of measures:

Price Control Board: A Price Control Board, established in May 1970, is empowered to impose controls on a wide range of essential commodities including textiles, drinks, building materials, tinned meat and fish, pharmaceuticals, salt, flour and motor vehicle and bicycle parts. Conspicuous omissions are staple food items and the board has not attempted to control prices of all the items mentioned above. So far, the board has concentrated its efforts on items which have clearly identifiable wholesale and retail channels, making supervision less difficult. Some success

Table 4-7: FINANCING OF GOVERNMENT CAPITAL FORMATION 1971/72-
1973/74

	(Millions of Current £N)		
	1971/72	1972/73	1973/74
Total government capital formation[a]	145	180	185
Current surplus, federal and state governments	169	200	280
Overall budgetary surplus[b]	24	20	95
Overall budgetary surplus as % of GNP	0.8	0.6	2.5

[a]Excluding defense capital expenditure.

[b]Excluding receipt from external borrowing and loans and grants to statutory corporations.

has been achieved in controlling the prices of soft drinks, sugar and milk; but little or no success
has been achieved for other commodities, despite strenuous efforts to control beer and textiles.

Import Liberalization: In April 1971, the government liberalized the import of consumer and
other goods as a deliberate and explicitly anti-inflationary move. The almost 60 percent increase in
consumer goods imports which resulted during the following year was undoubtedly a major
dampening factor on the upward movement in the prices of most manufactured goods. However,
the liberalization measures did not extend to major food items such as rice, wheat, stockfish, fresh
meat and vegetables. The problem of inadequate supply of major food items remained during 1971
and the increase in the food component of the urban consumer price index actually accelerated
during 1971 as compared to 1970.

National Supply Company: Another method being tried to restrain inflation is for the government to enter the distribution business directly. A National Supply Company has been established
to arrange bulk purchases of selected commodities for subsequent sale to the public. Assistance in
price control is only one of the objectives of this company. Other objectives are to arrange
bilateral trade, especially with the socialist countries, to phase out the crown agents, to encourage
local procurement and to establish training facilities for business and commercial management.
The initial trading capital provided by the federal government is £N1.5 million.

The first task of the National Supply Company will be to distribute 50,000 tons of flour and
150,000 tons of cement currently being imported. The major hurdle it will face, however, is the
absence of its own retailing facilities. The distribution will be handled by state trading companies
to be set up in each state. So far only six states — Western, Mid-Western, East Central, Kwara,
Kano and North Central — have set up these companies. They will not have direct contact with the
consumer, but rely on normal trade channels. Therefore, the only means of enforcing price control
will be through retail price maintenance agreements and a system of registered wholesalers. There
are no indications as yet that this new company has had any impact on price movement.

Credit Guidelines: Credit guidelines, issued by the Central Bank early in 1971, specified a
growth of 8.4 percent in total advances by commercial banks over the corresponding month of
1970. The actual expansion of credit was much higher; the deviation from the guideline being 66
percent at the end of April (when the guidelines were introduced) and 32 percent at the end of
December. The actual credit outstanding at the end of the year compared with the guideline target
is shown in Table 4-8 which also indicates that the sectoral composition of bank credit deviated
considerably from the guidelines. Advances to agriculture fell short of the guideline objectives,
while there were large positive deviations in all other areas.

Another feature of the guidelines issued to commercial banks was that a minimum of 35 percent of outstanding loans should be made to Nigerian borrowers. Only a few banks consistently
satisfied this requirement, although, by and large, it was not breached by wide margins. The
minimum percentage was recently increased to 40 percent.

Table 4-8: ACTUAL CREDIT OUTSTANDING AND CORRESPONDING GUIDELINE AMOUNT, DECEMBER 1971

(In Millions of £N)

	Guideline	Actual	Excess of Actual above Guideline (%)
Total	190.5	251.0	32
Agriculture, forestry and fishing	5.3	4.6	-13
Manufacture, mining and construction	66.5	84.4	27
General commerce	88.0	110.6	26
Services	11.0	17.7	61
Others	16.0	33.7	111

Whether credit expansion was actually less than it would have been in the absence of guidelines is difficult to assess. It is clear, however, that the guidelines were not closely observed, despite warnings by the Central Bank. The principal reason for this is the excessive liquidity of the commercial banking system. Whereas the required liquidity ratio has been 25 percent, the actual liquidity ratio was over 90 percent during the first quarter of 1971 and was still 62 percent at the end of August despite the imposition by the Central Bank of special reserve requirements against "backlog deposits." In this situation, raising the rediscount rate is unlikely to have more than a symbolic effect, since higher interest rates can be passed on to the borrower in an inflationary environment. Credit guidelines could not be regarded as a credible anti-inflationary device unless the Central Bank was willing to take concrete punitive measures against banks which violate guidelines or regain control of the monetary system by mopping up excess liquidity. The use of guidelines with respect to total credit outstanding was abolished early in 1972, while guidelines on the sectoral composition of commercial bank credits remain in effect.

Stricter monetary discipline has become vital to the control of inflation. As noted earlier in this chapter, inflationary pressures are likely to persist in the foreseeable future. There are a variety of measures, currently within the power of the federal government and the Central Bank, which would contribute toward mopping up excess liquidity. One option is to raise the required liquidity ratio substantially. Another is to step up the sales of long-term debt outside the banking system, using the proceeds to retire outstanding Treasury Bills and Treasury Certificates. A third option is to remove Treasury Certificates from the list of assets included in calculating the liquidity ratio of commercial banks. A fourth option would be to go over to a cash reserve system, at the same time increasing the discount rate to discourage rediscounting of Treasury Bills. A fifth option would be to call for special deposits against the commercial credit generated by the 90/180-day import credit system. No doubt there are other ways to reduce excess liquidity. An appropriate choice of measures would not only meet the immediate anti-inflationary objective but would also make the banking system more responsive to the development needs of the country.

CHAPTER 5
THE BALANCE OF PAYMENTS AND AID REQUIREMENTS

Since independence, Nigeria has had to tailor its imports of goods and non-factor services to the limited foreign exchange resources obtainable from exports and foreign, primarily private, capital. Nigeria possessed foreign exchange reserves of approximately £N200 million in 1960. These were drawn down to less than £N100 million by the end of 1963 and were held at that level until 1967. From 1964 onward, higher import tariffs, quantitative trade restrictions and restrictive credit policies were introduced from time to time to stem the outflow of foreign exchange. In 1967 and 1968, following the devaluation of sterling, specific import licensing was extended to cover areas of origin as well as particular types of commodities. Additional tariff increases and import prohibitions further tightened control over imports, and the allocation of foreign exchange for imports and other current payments became subject to an elaborate rationing system which involved increasing delays.

Between 1960 and 1965, private capital inflows net of investment income payments were strongly positive, and, after the initial post-independence draw-down of reserves, were by far the largest source of external finance to meet the country's growing current account deficits. Since 1966 investment income payments have exceeded inflows of new private capital. In 1967, the outbreak of hostilities curtailed petroleum production and also led to a sharp drop in private capital inflows in both the oil and non-oil sectors (from £N87 million in 1966 to £N44 million the following year) and this also coincided with a significant fall in traditional exports. In that year Nigeria suffered an overall balance of payments deficit of £N43 million and reserves dropped to £N51 million — the level at which they were to remain throughout 1966-70. Prior official capital inflows were less than half the net amounts received from private sources, although there was a significant increase over time. Here also civil unrest disrupted the course of events, and for five years after 1965 net official capital receipts were only a minor item in the balance of payments.

By the mid-sixties the Nigerian balance of payments was on the threshold of a structural transformation resulting from the initiation of crude oil production on a substantial scale. Hostilities delayed — and, in fact, briefly reversed — this development, but by 1969 oil exports were again rising, and in the following year yielded earnings of nearly £N260 million as compared with receipts of £N184 million from all other exports combined. The rapid growth of oil exports since 1970 and the anticipation of further substantial increases in petroleum receipts through the middle of this decade have enabled the government to abolish many of the import controls and exchange restrictions imposed in recent years and to liquidate the backlog of short-term commercial liabilities incurred between 1967 and 1971. It now appears that commercial policy may henceforth be tailored primarily to meet the social and economic needs of the economy rather than to meet balance of payments or revenue considerations.

The following section provides a brief historical review of the various elements in Nigeria's balance of payments and projects the probable development of the country's external accounts through 1973/74, the last year of the current Plan period. It should be emphasized at the outset that these projections are particularly sensitive to price developments in the economy. The following balance of payments projections presuppose a substantial diminution in the rate of domestic inflation over the next few years. Were this not to occur, expenditures abroad would almost certainly be well above the rates suggested here and the country's balance of payments position would be considerably weaker.

Chapter 8 discusses Nigeria's probable aid requirements and concludes that, despite the favorable short-term outlook for the balance of payments, foreign assistance may have a very important role to play in the country's future growth and development. The case for foreign aid rests mainly on the contribution that donor countries can make toward providing the skills, organization and institutions that Nigeria requires.

Balance of Payments

Petroleum Impact

A full description and analysis of the petroleum sector's recent and prospective impact upon the Nigerian economy is contained in Chapter 6. Table 5-1 summarizes the major developments in the oil sector as these have affected Nigeria's balance of payments since 1968; Table 5-8 identifies the major petroleum sector components in the balance of payments projections through 1973/74 and contains a summary item indicating the total net impact of this sector.

Table 5-1: IMPACT OF THE OIL SECTOR ON THE BALANCE OF PAYMENTS, 1968-71

(In Millions of £N)

	1968	1969	1970	1971[a]
Production (million barrels)	52.0	197.0	396.0	558.0
Gross export value	37.8	130.8	254.7	489.1
Imports of goods and services[b]	-38.5	-134.7	-199.8	-279.6
Current account balance	-0.7	-3.9	54.9	209.5
Net capital inflow	28.7	57.2	77.0	83.3
Net petroleum impact	28.8	53.3	131.9	292.8

[a]Provisional.

[b]Includes investment income.

Source: Central Bank of Nigeria and mission estimates.

In 1966, oil exports, which began in 1958, amounted to £N92 million or one-third of total exports and petroleum sector factor payments, which had been negligible two years earlier, were £N57 million, substantially exceeding foreign investment income originating elsewhere in the economy. By 1969 petroleum production was well above the 1966 level. Between 1969 and 1970 output doubled to over 50 million tons valued at £N265 million and yielding net foreign exchange receipts of £N130 million. Petroleum exports in 1971 amounted to £N489 million, with net receipts of £N293 million.

While the recent rate of growth of oil production is not likely to be maintained, total output should continue to rise at least through the 1970s to reach a level of 3 million barrels per day. On this basis and assuming a continued increase in the export (realized) price according to current trends, the value of Nigeria's oil exports may be of the order of £N1.5 billion by the end of the decade, of which roughly two-thirds will accrue to the government and represent a positive item in the net balance of payments.

Trade

Non-petroleum Exports. Nigeria's non-oil exports grew from £N160 million in 1960 to a peak of £N195 million in 1965 and since then have fluctuated generally within the range of £N170 million to £N190 million. The 22 percent growth of exports during the first half of the sixties was largely concentrated in the period 1963-65. As can be seen from Table 5-2 and Chart 5-1, the export boom in the years 1963-70 resulted primarily from the coincident occurrence of good harvests and good prices for Nigeria's principal agricultural exports: cocoa, groundnuts and palm produce. Indeed, in 1965, groundnuts, palm produce and cotton brought prices that were close to or better than those to be seen during any of the preceding or following five years.

From the late fifties until the mid-sixties only cocoa showed fairly consistent steady growth in export volume, reaching a peak of 255,000 tons in 1965. Groundnut produce exports expanded from 1961 to 1963 and since then have fluctuated rather widely. In 1968 they hit an all-time high of over 900,000 tons and then plunged to a 10-year low in 1970, falling yet further in 1971. Even before then, exports of palm produce, grown principally in a belt from the West to the Southeast, were declining. Palm kernel exports fell precipitously and, despite some recovery, remain well below their former levels.

It is, in part, against this background that the projections for Nigeria's traditional exports through the mid-seventies must be viewed. Table 5-3 sets forth the quantity and price projections that have been used in deriving estimates of export earnings from the major agricultural export commodities. These projections are drawn from the report of the Bank's agricultural sector mission which visited Nigeria in mid-1971. That report provides a full discussion of the assumptions underlying these projections and of the obstacles that are likely to inhibit a more rapid expansion of traditional exports over the medium term. It should be noted that no allowance has been made for the possible appearance of any new agricultural export commodity, e.g., cassava products.

The projected volume of tin exports is based on the assumption that Nigeria will be able to take full advantage of its quota under the International Tin Agreement. In fact, the Nigerian tin industry is presently facing financial difficulties due to high export taxes and rising production costs. If these are not alleviated, tin production may not grow as fast as projected. Exports of hides and skins and timber and plywood have been conservatively projected to rise annually by 3 percent and 5 percent respectively in real terms during the 1970-75 period. In both cases, export growth is expected to be limited by the rise in domestic consumption of these products. Moreover, forestry exports are also likely to be affected by rising production costs, reflecting the increasing difficulty of extracting export timber. Although some marginal exports of low quality cotton may continue indefinitely, by 1975 Nigeria will probably be a net importer of cotton. The volume of all other exports, which amounted to only £N15 million in 1970, is projected to rise by 4 percent (5 percent in value terms) per annum for the next five years.

Chart 5-1: NIGERIA: NON-PETROLEUM EXPORTS, INDEX OF VOLUME AND PRICE, 1963-70

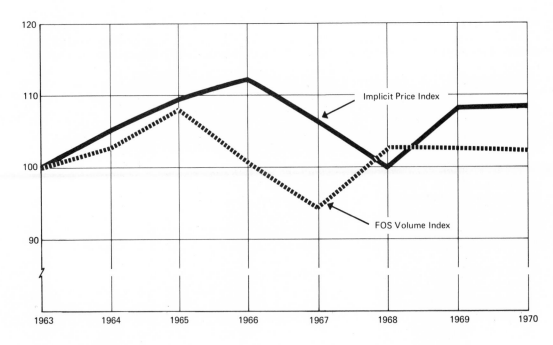

Table 5-2: NON-PETROLEUM EXPORTS, INDEX OF VOLUME AND PRICE 1963-1970

SITC Sections	Principal Commodities		1963	1964	1965	1966	1967	1968	1969	1970
0 & 1	Cocoa	Value (£N mil.)	37.0	47.2	49.8	37.7	62.6	65.7	69.8	83.9
		Volume index (1963=100)	100.0	99.8	142.0	118.9	149.1	137.5	123.1	128.0
		Implicit price index (1963=100)	100.0	128.0	95.0	86.0	113.0	129.0	153.0	177.0
2	Groundnuts, palm kernels, cotton and cottonseed, hides and skins, rubber, wood	Value (£N mil.)	96.8	93.2	100.2	100.4	70.2	71.1	73.1	61.4
		Volume index (1963=100)	100.0	98.6	92.9	91.5	73.3	84.8	67.5	73.6
		Implicit price index (1963=100)	100.0	98.0	111.0	113.0	99.0	87.0	112.0	86.0
4	Vegetable oils (groundnut, palm and palm kernel)	Value (£N mil.)	16.1	19.4	24.3	24.5	12.4	12.9	15.3	16.5
		Volume index (1963=100)	100.0	183.4	125.1	137.2	32.4	78.2	75.8	67.4
		Implicit price index (1963=100)	100.0	66.0	121.0	111.0	238.0	102.0	125.0	152.0
0-2, 4-9	All exports except crude oil	Value (£N mil.)	164.6	178.3	195.1	185.5	164.7	169.0	183.6	183.5
		Value index	100.0	102.9	108.0	100.3	94.0	102.9	102.8	102.7
		Volume index	100.0	105.3	109.7	112.4	106.4	99.8	108.5	108.6
		Implicit price index	100.0	108.3	118.5	112.7	100.1	102.7	111.5	111.5

Sources: Value figures, *Review of External Trade*. Volume indices, Federal Office of Statistics.

Table 5-3: ACTUAL AND PROJECTED EXPORTS OF NON-PETROLEUM
PRODUCTS 1970-75

(Values in £N Millions)[a]

	1970	1971	1972	1973	1974	1975
	Actual	Provisional	—	Projected	—	
Cocoa						
Tons ('000)	211.0	283.0	230.0	240.0	250.0	265.0
Value (1970 prices), f.o.b.	74.3	99.6	78.0	81.7	84.7	89.9
Price index (1970=100)	100.0	77.0	87.0	82.0	76.0	72.0
Value (current prices)	74.3	77.0	67.9	67.0	64.4	64.7
Groundnut products						
Tons ('000)	535.0	256.0	593.0	620.0	660.0	700.0
Value (1970 prices), f.o.b.	38.9	18.6	43.2	45.1	48.2	51.0
Price index (1970=100)	100.0	121.0	93.0	90.0	87.0	83.0
Value (current prices)	38.9	22.6	40.2	40.6	42.0	42.3
Palm kernel products						
Tons ('000)	247.0	303.0	317.0	340.0	365.0	400.0
Value (1970 prices), f.o.b.	16.1	21.1	20.6	22.2	23.8	26.1
Price index (1970=100)	100.0	90.0	92.0	88.0	84.0	80.0
Value (current prices)	16.1	18.0	19.0	19.5	20.0	20.9
Rubber						
Tons ('000)	60.7	48.0	62.0	64.0	66.0	69.0
Value (1970 prices), f.o.b.	8.7	6.9	9.3	9.7	9.9	10.4
Price index (1970=100)	100.0	86.0	91.0	87.0	83.0	79.0
Value (current prices)	8.7	5.9	8.5	8.4	8.3	8.2
Raw cotton						
Tons ('000)	27.8	25.1	15.0	10.0	5.0	3.0
Value (1970 prices), f.o.b.	6.6	6.0	3.8	2.6	1.3	0.8
Price index (1970=100)	100.0	103.0	98.0	97.0	96.0	95.0
Value (current prices)	6.6	6.2	3.8	2.5	1.2	0.8
Tin metal						
Tons ('000)	10.7	8.1	12.2	12.9	13.5	14.2
Value (1970 prices), f.o.b.	16.9	12.8	18.9	20.1	20.9	22.1
Price index (1970=100)	100.0	95.0	98.0	97.0	96.0	95.0
Value (current prices)	16.9	12.1	18.5	19.5	20.1	21.0
Hides and skins						
Value (1970 prices)	2.8	2.3	3.2	3.3	3.4	3.5
Value (current prices)	2.8	2.4	3.3	3.4	3.5	3.6
Timber and plywood						
Value (1970 prices)	4.0	4.1	4.4	4.6	4.9	5.1
Value (current prices)	4.0	3.6	4.5	4.8	5.1	5.5
Total, major exports						
Value (1970 prices)	168.2	171.4	181.4	189.3	197.1	208.9
Value (current prices)	168.2	147.8	165.7	165.7	164.6	167.0
Misc. exports (current prices)	15.4	18.6	17.0	17.9	18.7	19.7
Total non-petroleum exports (current prices)	183.5	166.4	182.7	183.6	183.3	186.7

[a]Current prices refer to current dollar prices.

Source: Nigeria Trade Summary and IBRD estimates.

The only new products which now seem likely to appear on the export list by 1975 are Liquefied Petroleum Gas (LPG) and perhaps ethylene. By the middle of the decade, an LPG facility should be in production with an annual export capacity of approximately 300,000 tons. At the same time, an ethylene plant based upon either methane from the LPG operation or upon natural gas could be generating exports of 100,000 tons per year. Each of these products could yield foreign exchange receipts of approximately £N2 million per year. (The prospects for exports of liquefied natural gas are discussed in Chapter 6.)

The estimates of the volume and value of Nigeria's traditional exports through the seventies were made prior to the 1971 international currency realignment. However, it would appear that the effects, if any, of exchange rate adjustments on Nigeria's non-oil export earnings will be slight.

Imports. At the end of hostilities the Nigerian Government relaxed import restrictions while maintaining licensing controls over most items. In April 1971, there was a more complete liberalization of imports and most specific-license requirements were dropped. Duties on a few consumer goods were raised slightly, replacing a cumbersome two-tier system which had involved an upper rate of 15 percent. The effects of these liberalization measures are evident in the growth of imports during the past two years, as imports rose by 52 percent in 1970 and by a further 42 percent in 1971.

Chemicals, manufactured goods and machinery and transport equipment have been the fastest growing import categories and now account for 80 percent of total imports as compared to 70 percent in 1969. Within the manufactured goods group, cement and other building materials, paper and textile products and tubes and pipes (presumably destined for the petroleum industry) account for the bulk of imports and the most rapid growth. Commercial road vehicles and textile machinery have been major import items within SITC Section 7 (Table 5-4).

Table 5-4: IMPORTS BY SITC SECTIONS

(In Millions of £N)

SITC Section	1969	1970	1971[a]	Percentage increase 1969-70	Percentage increase 1970-71
0 Food and live animals	20.9	28.9	44.1	38	53
1 Beverages and tobacco	0.8	2.0	2.2	150	10
2 Crude materials inedible except fuels	5.7	8.3	10.2	46	23
3 Mineral fuels, lubricants and related materials	15.6	11.0	4.5	-30	-60
4 Animal and vegetable oils and fats	0.2	0.4	0.4	100	–
5 Chemicals	30.4	44.2	61.0	45	38
6 Manufactured goods classified chiefly by material	72.0	113.0	159.7	57	41
7 Machinery and transport equipment	73.2	141.3	214.4	93	52
8 Miscellaneous manufactured articles	13.4	19.8	34.3	48	73
9 Commodities and transactions not classified according to kind	16.4	9.3	7.4	-43	-20
Total	248.7	378.2	538.2	52	42

[a]Provisional.

Source: Review of External Trade.

The value of imports of both raw materials and capital goods in 1970 was twice the 1964 level. Nearly half the 130 percent growth of imports over the past two years is attributable to capital goods whose share of total imports rose from 37 percent in 1969 to 43 percent in 1971. Intermediate goods, other than fuel, have risen roughly in line with total imports, accounting for 23 percent of the total growth. Imports of fuel fell sharply after mid-1970, following the reopening of the petroleum refinery near Port Harcourt (Table 5-5).

The share of consumer goods in total imports remained close to 30 percent over the past two years, and in real terms the value of such imports in 1971 was more than twice the 1969 level. It is noteworthy that the value of consumer goods imports in 1970, despite having risen sharply from the 1966-70 level, was still below that of 1964. An overall decline in consumer goods imports actually began before the civil war and has not been without some significant shifts in the composition of such imports during the second half of the sixties. In particular, there has been marked import substitution in textiles. The value of textile imports in 1970 was only about 60 percent of its prewar level. By contrast, imports of food, which had been declining from 1960 to 1964, began to rise shortly before 1966 and in 1970 were above their 1966 level, despite having been sharply depressed between these years. Some of the increase in food imports in 1970 undoubtedly reflected postwar relief shipments, but the rising trend continued into 1971 and the country had record food imports that year (Statistical Annex Table 16).

Table 5-5: IMPORTS BY ECONOMIC USE

	1964	1968	1969	1970	1971[a]	1964	1968	1969	1970	1971[a]
			£N Million					Percentage Distribution		
Consumer goods	109.5	65.5	73.8	108.9	174.7	43	35	32	30	33
Intermediate goods	63.9	56.3	72.6	104.4	128.3	25	30	31	28	24
of which, fuel	19.5	14.6	15.6	11.0	4.5	8	8	7	3	1
Capital goods	80.1	66.6	85.9	115.6	228.8	32	35	37	42	43
Total	253.5	188.4	232.3	368.9	532.0	100	100	100	100	100

[a]Provisional.

Source: Federal Office of Statistics.

To some extent, Nigeria's recent trade data are probably distorted by: inventory accumulation; the inclusion, without explicit identification of, military imports; and implicit interest charges added to import prices to cover payment delays. In the absence of any data on these several factors, however, it is not possible to estimate their quantitative significance.

The import projections detailed in Table 5-6 were derived basically from the model described in Chapter 8 and Chapter 9 and follow from the "high public-sector expenditure" option there described. For the balance of the current Plan period total non-petroleum imports measured in constant prices are likely to grow moderately, compared with the rates of growth recorded during 1970 and 1971. That is, after more than doubling during the first two years following the period of unrest, imports are expected to return temporarily to a growth path reminiscent of that prevailing during the first half of the sixties. A number of factors account for the projected abrupt slackening in the medium-term rate of import growth: the backlog of consumption and inventory demand for imports which built up during 1966-70 has presumably now been satisfied; most quantitative import restrictions were abolished by early 1971 and, barring an unexpected general reduction of tariffs, there would not appear to be much further scope for import liberalization;

and investment, after being depressed for a number of years, is now back at a high level and unlikely to rise much further as a share of GNP. Consequently, as the rate of growth of investment subsides, there should be a corresponding slowdown in the growth of capital goods imports. Also, with the recovery of private investment in manufacturing and the freeing of capital and intermediate goods imports, the rate of import substitution is expected to rise. Domestic production of textiles and other non-food consumer goods is anticipated to outpace the growth of domestic demand during the next few years.

Table 5-6: IMPORT PROJECTIONS

(£N Million at Constant and Current Prices)

	1970/71 Actual	1971/72 Estimated	1973/74 Projected	Annual Average Growth Rates (%) 1970/71- 1973/74
Constant (1970) prices				
Consumer goods				
Food	34	40	55	17.4
Textiles	21	20	20	-1.5
Other	65	80	85	10.2
Total	120	140	160	10.1
Intermediate goods	112	145	160	12.6
Capital goods and transport equipment	152	210	245	17.2
Total non-oil imports	384	495	565	13.7
Current prices				
Import price index	100	103	105	1.6
Total non-oil imports	384	510	595	15.7
Oil sector imports	28	40	45	17.1
Total imports of goods	412[a]	550	640	15.8
Imports of NFS (net)	112	105	110	0.6
Non-oil sectors	31	25	35	2.1
Oil sector	81	80	75	-3.8

[a]1970/71 import figures based on customs data. Total differs slightly from that shown in the balance of payments.

For the period 1970/71-1973/74 the real rate of growth of non-petroleum imports is projected to decline from almost 30 percent in 1971/72 to 12 percent 1972/73 and to 4 percent in 1973/74, yielding an annual average rate of growth of 14 percent over the period as a whole. Imports of capital goods are expected to show the largest absolute (£N100 million) and percentage (17 percent per year) gain, while intermediate goods imports are expected to rise nearly 13 percent per annum.

Other Current Account Items

Non-factor Services. From 1960 to 1966 Nigeria's net import of non-factor services, excluding those for the petroleum sector, averaged about £N14 million per year and showed only a modest upward trend. Net service payments jumped abruptly to nearly £N40 million in 1967 and were £N45 million in 1969, reflecting the very sharp increase in unspecified government payments abroad, but then declined slightly to £N37.5 million in 1970. During the five years 1966-70 exports of non-factor services averaged £N25 million per year and fluctuated only slightly. These movements of non-factor services, excluding the petroleum sector, from 1966-1970/71, are summarized in the following table, together with the mission's estimates for 1971/72 (in £N million):

	1966	1967	1968	1969	1970	1970/71	1971/72
Payments	52.8	60.8	61.4	74.1	60.8	56.0	51.0
Receipts	24.8	21.6	24.9	29.2	23.3	25.0	26.0
Net	28.0	39.2	36.5	44.9	37.5	31.0	25.0

It does not seem likely that non-factor service payments, having dropped back to the amount reached in 1966, will decline further. On the contrary, most service items can be expected to rise, particularly as exchange restrictions affecting trade and foreign travel are relaxed. Therefore, in projecting non-petroleum non-factor service payments it is assumed that, in real terms, this item will grow at the same rate as total GNP and be subject to the same price inflation as other imports. Projected non-factor service receipts are based on the recent average level of £N25 million per annum, inflated by the rate of growth of non-petroleum GDP.

Factor Payments. The projections of net factor payments outside the petroleum sector consist basically of three components: profits from direct investments; interest on external public debt; and interest earned on reserve assets. The base year (1970) value of foreign, privately owned, non-petroleum productive assets is estimated at £N300 million. To compute returns in the private sector this stock has been depreciated at a rate of 10 percent per year and augmented by the projected annual inflow of private direct investment. The annual return on investment, thus adjusted, has been assumed to be 15 percent. Projections of interest payments on official capital with respect to loans outstanding as of June 30, 1971, are based on knowledge of the terms of individual loans. In projecting interest payments on future loans it has been assumed that two-thirds of all new commitments would be on conventional terms and one-third on concessionary (DAC) terms. To compute the government's interest income on its reserve holdings a rate of return of 5 percent was applied to that portion of projected gross reserves not accounted for by gold, Special Drawing Rights (SDRs) and the country's international monetary position.

By conventional standards Nigeria enjoys a very low debt service ratio (about 3 percent of exports in 1971/72). However, in Nigeria, as in any country where there is a large, foreign-controlled extractive industry, factor payments abroad are a very significant item in the balance of payments and are directly and functionally related to those exports which dominate the receipts side of the current account. Therefore, a better measure of the contractual foreign obligations is the ratio of debt service plus factor payments to exports, rather than simply the debt service ratio itself. Factor payments plus debt service are expected to consume nearly one-third of Nigeria's export receipts throughout the seventies. Similarly, the ratio of debt service plus net factor payments to gross domestic savings, after falling sharply in 1971/72 largely in response to the terms of petroleum agreements negotiated early last year, is projected to remain at just over 30 percent for the balance of the Plan. The ratio of debt service plus net factor payments to exports and to gross domestic savings is shown below.

	1970/71	1973/74
To exports	33%	33%
To gross domestic savings	47%	34%

Transfers. Prior to 1966, Nigeria enjoyed a small but rising amount of net official transfers which were, until 1965, more than offset by private remittances abroad. During the hostilities private transfers became a positive item in the balance of payments, while official transfer receipts rose substantially. In 1970, total transfer receipts amounted to £N22.5 million, of which nearly £N16 million was in the public sector. This inflow reflected, in part at least, relief shipments and grant rehabilitation assistance extended to Nigeria following the cessation of hostilities. This flow of resources began to taper off after mid-1970. During the first quarter of 1971/72 total transfer receipts amounted to an estimated £N2.4 million and this rate has been projected for the full year. Thereafter, such receipts are expected to decline somewhat further before leveling off at £N5 million in 1973/74. This presupposes that official grants will revert to the average level of 1962/65 (also the level assumed in the Plan) and that private transfer receipts will, over the longer term, be a negligible item.

Short-Term Liabilities

The Backlog. During 1966-70, the Nigerian Government rationed foreign exchange for most imports and other current payments. Early in 1968 exchange control procedures were introduced whereby importers, through the commercial banks, were required to apply to the Central Bank for foreign exchange in one of four categories, depending upon the priority classification of the payment to be made. Since foreign exchange earnings fell short of the nation's needs during the period of unrest and external reserves had already fallen below £N50 million, there developed a backlog or "pipeline" of applications for foreign exchange at the Central Bank.

In early 1970, the backlog of exchange applications at the Central Bank amounted to approximately £N50 million. The wartime system of rationing foreign exchange and allocating it among different classes of imports, service payments and other current obligations was maintained throughout 1970/71. As imports increased substantially that year, with considerably smaller growth in export earnings,[1] the backlog grew and payment delays became longer. At the end of 1970 payment delays for high-priority Category B imports were approximately four months and for imports in Category D the payments lag was over five months.[2]

The backlog continued to grow steadily during the first three months of 1971. By March 31, Nigeria's short-term commercial liabilities reached approximately £N220 million. On that date, the backlog was "frozen" and a new payments system was introduced. As foreign exchange earnings from the oil sector rose during 1971/72, repayments were made in successive stages during the year and the entire backlog was liquidated by February 1972.

The New System (1971). The decision of the government to freeze the old backlog and to introduce a new import payments system in April 1971, marked a turning point in the country's foreign exchange administration. Uncertainty on when foreign exchange might be released in payment for a particular import, rather than simply delays as such, had become a principal objection to the exchange control practiced during the years 1966-70 and 1971. Moreover, since the govern-

1. The payment of petroleum royalties and taxes lagged substantially behind oil shipments.
2. With respect to Category A items, embracing various types of personal remittances, insurance and freight payments covering Nigerian exports and the importation of educational materials and chemicals for agricultural purposes, foreign exchange was released immediately upon application to the Central Bank.

ment did not allow the payment of explicit interest charges covering the period of payment delay attributable to the foreign exchange control procedures, exporters presumably inflated their invoices arbitrarily to recover the extra financial costs associated with the Nigerian trade. Thus, the system was both cumbersome and expensive.

On April 1, 1971, a new import payments system was introduced simultaneously with the freezing of the old backlog, the abolition of most specific import license requirements and the general liberalization of imports formerly subject to quantitative restrictions. The new procedures provided for the regular release of foreign exchange for imports 90 or 180 days after the arrival of the merchandise. This system was further liberalized at the beginning of the current fiscal year. Originally, somewhat less than one-half of all commercial imports fell into the 90-day category which embraced such major items as essential raw materials, salt, sugar, cement, agricultural chemicals and plant and machinery valued at less than £N25,000. Most other imports – representing about one-third of the total – fell into the 180-day category. Recently, flour, buses, vehicle components for local assembly and other spare parts have been added to the 90-day category and the payment limit on plant and machinery has been raised to £N50,000. Special arrangements are in force with respect to imports of plant and machinery valued at more than this amount. For these imports 15 percent is payable against documents or upon the signing of a contract; 15 percent at the time of delivery, and the balance, depending on the value of the equipment, over a period of up to four years.[3] The Exchange Control Orders which specified these payment terms made no explicit mention of the interest charges which would be permitted in connection with these mandatory supplier credits. However, the Orders have indicated that the Central Bank would be required to approve the supplier-credit terms arranged by the importer, and this provision presumably provides authority for the Central Bank to reject arrangements which, in its view, contain excessive interest charges.

A significant volume of imports is not covered by the mandatory 90-day or 180-day trade credits. Some of these imports are for the public sector or financed by public and private capital inflows and hence not subject to foreign exchange restrictions. Others are covered by the deferred payment provisions applicable to plant and machinery; and some are financed by other suppliers' credits or *free* foreign exchange, i.e., exchange held or obtained by Nigerian nationals without recourse to the Central Bank.

From all accounts, the 90/180-day credit system is working satisfactorily. The system has not necessarily reduced the delays in releasing foreign exchange to importers – except as compared to the situation prevailing immediately before the old backlog was frozen – but it has established predictability and regularity in foreign exchange administration.

The current system of compulsory trade credits also implies the accumulation of short-term liabilities. It is estimated that the effect of the new payments system was to create trade credits on Nigeria's behalf of approximately £N150 million by the end of fiscal year 1971/72. That is, the 90/180-day system, together with deferred payments for machinery imports, resulted in gross short-term private capital inflow equivalent to the value of approximately three months' imports. This, of course, partly offset the impact of the liquidation of the old backlog, so that the net effect was a reduction of approximately £N70 million in Nigeria's short-term indebtedness.

Private Long-Term Investment

The analysis of private foreign investment, particularly for recent years, is hampered by the lack of a consistent set of statistics and the fact that exchange controls have restricted the repatriation of profits and dividends since 1966. Balance of payment data indicate that net private investment inflows in the non-petroleum sectors reached a peak of just under £N50 million in 1964, having doubled since 1960, the year of independence. In 1967, net private non-oil investment virtually disappeared, but in 1968 and 1969 receipts from this source averaged almost £N30 million and in 1970 were back to over £N40 million. Throughout the past decade direct investment has been the major element in private capital inflows, although cumulatively other long-term private investment contributed £N90 million to the country's foreign exchange earnings. By 1969,

3. During 1971/72 only 5 percent was payable against documents. Payment periods ran as long as 7 years.

however, inflows of private capital, other than direct investment, had ceased to be a significant item in the balance of payments.

Statistical Annex Table 19, based on data collected by the Central Bank of Nigeria in response to its annual investment surveys, presents a breakdown of foreign investment into Nigeria from 1961/69 by sector and by source of funds. Unremitted profits have been the principal source of new foreign investment funds since the mid-sixties. During the past decade, the petroleum sector has accounted for more than half of all new foreign private investment. Of the remainder, roughly 50 percent has gone into manufacturing and processing and about 30 percent into trading and business services. There has been very little foreign investment in agriculture, transportation or the construction industry.

In projecting private, non-oil foreign investment inflows it has been assumed that direct investment in real terms will be maintained at the 1970/71 level of just under £N50 million. Other private foreign investment is a negative item through 1974/75 (after which it is not included in the projections) reflecting simply the amortization of the loan capital provided during the sixties.

The projections of foreign private capital outside the oil sector are subject to particularly wide margins of error, since much will depend upon the rate of enforced Nigerianization of privately-owned foreign businesses and the government's policy with respect to the repatriation of foreigners' receipts from the sale of businesses which are Nigerianized. The projected net inflow of private capital outside the oil sector during 1970/71-1973/74 is £N135 million or about the same as that contemplated by the Plan. The detailed basis for projecting oil investment is discussed in Chapter 6.

Official Capital

Nigeria did not succeed in mobilizing a substantial inflow of official capital until the mid-sixties. In 1964 and 1965 net official capital receipts averaged £N15 million per year, whereas during the first four years of the decade they had averaged less than £N5 million annually. As noted earlier, the disturbances of 1966-70 interrupted the flow of foreign aid to Nigeria. Some major aid-financed projects, notably the Kainji Dam, were carried to completion during this period, but, in general, hostilities interfered with project implementation and virtually halted new project preparation.

Commitments. During 1966-70, only a few long-term aid commitments (including three Bank loans) were negotiated. These, together with commitments inherited from the prewar period, provided an aid pipeline of £N78 million at the end of 1969/70. Aid negotiations during the past two years led to commitments in the first 18 months of the Plan period, i.e., through September 30, 1971, of approximately £N73 million. Of this amount, substantially more than half was in the form of program or commodity assistance.

It has been assumed for the projections through 1973/74 that total project aid inflows might reasonably average about £N35 million for each of the first three years of the present Plan period and then rise gradually to £N50 million by mid-decade. This is not to suggest, however, that Nigeria may not in fact obtain a much larger bilateral and multilateral commitment and disbursement level in the course of the next Plan period. Nigeria's medium- and long-term aid requirements and proposals for a foreign assistance strategy are discussed at greater length in Chapter 8.

Disbursements. Gross disbursements of long-term official capital amounted to an estimated £N12 million in 1970/71.[4] During 1971, disbursements are estimated to have been above £N50 million, reflecting in large part the impact of the program assistance negotiated from several donors between the end of 1970 and the middle of 1971. At the same time, however, disbursements against project loans were also up substantially as work resumed on projects interrupted by unrest and as new projects were launched within the context of the Second Development Plan.

On the basis of the foregoing estimates and assumptions, net official capital inflows to Nigeria are estimated to have risen from an annual average of £N5 million in 1969/70-1970/71 to approximately £N50 million in 1971/72 when program aid receipts accounted for about 60 percent of the

---

4. There are serious discrepancies in the available data, and it is impossible fully to reconcile information provided by the Central Bank in the context of the balance of payments and that emanating from the Ministry of Finance through which all foreign assistance receipts are nominally channeled.

Table 5-7: PROJECTED COMMITMENTS AND DISBURSEMENTS OF OFFICIAL
CAPITAL, 1969/70-1973/74

(In Millions of £N)

	1969/70	1970/71	1971/72	1972/73	1973/74
Commitments					
Prior to 9/30/71 (actual)	14.5	18.4	54.9	–	–
After 10/1/71 (projected)	–	–	25.0	35.0	40.0
Disbursements					
Project loans	– }	12.0	25.9	32.9	25.0
Program loans	– }		32.1	9.1	–
Total	–	12.0	58.0	42.0	25.0
Amortization	–	6.6	6.7	7.1	7.5
Net official capital	4.6	5.4	51.3	34.9	17.5
Outstanding and undisbursed, year-end	78.1	84.5	106.0	99.0	114.0

Source: Central Bank of Nigeria and mission estimates.

total. Net official capital movements are likely to drop off to about £N17 million in 1973/74 before resuming a gradual upward growth.

Summary of the Balance of Payments Prospects

In 1970/71 Nigeria's holdings of gross reserves increased, but were counterbalanced by the accumulation of short-term commercial liabilities. By the end of that year reserves had risen to approximately £N105 million – almost double their level at the end of 1970 – but the backlog of import payments stood at approximately £N220 million or more than twice the level of a year earlier. Then followed a substantial improvement in the net international liquidity position. Although gross reserves (excluding an SDR allocation) rose by less than £N10 million, net short-term liabilities (excluding those related to oil company accounts) were reduced by approximately £N70 million, reflecting the elimination of the former backlog of commercial arrears and the partly offsetting accumulation of new trade credits under the 90/180-day credit system. The improvement in the balance of payments last year was wholly attributable to the petroleum sector whose net positive impact rose by £N200 million to £N365 million, thus countering a further deterioration of more than £N100 million recorded by the rest of the economy.

As a consequence of the rapid rise in oil exports, Nigeria's resource balance (net exports of goods and non-factor services) in 1971/72 is estimated to show a surplus of approximately £N65 million, an improvement of £N115 million over 1970/71. Assuming that the rate of import growth declines substantially over the next two years as projected, this surplus could increase further to some £N250 million by the end of the current Plan period (1973/74). However, because of the corresponding increases in investment income paid abroad – mainly from the oil sector – the current account deficit is likely to persist although declining in magnitude from the estimated £N120 million in 1971/72. The inflows of private and official capital are expected to exceed these deficits and an overall balance of payments surplus is likely to result. This should enable the

Table 5-8: ACTUAL AND PROJECTED BALANCE OF PAYMENTS 1970/71-1973/74

(In Millions of £N)

	1970/71 Actual	1971/72 Provisional	1973/74 Projected	Average Annual Growth Rates (%) 1970/71-1973/74
Current Account				
Merchandise exports				
Oil	293	540	800	40.0
Other[a]	188	180	195	1.2
Merchandise imports	-419	-550	-640	15.2
Imports of non-factor services (net)	-112	-105	-110	—
Resource Balance	-50	65	245	—
Factor income payments				
Oil sector[b]	-97	-140	-250	37.0
Other	-56	-54	-65	5.1
Transfers	20	10	5	—
Current Account Balance	-183	-119	-65	—
Capital Account				
Long-term capital (net)	115	125	120	—
Private, oil sector	28	35	35	—
Private, other	5	50	15	—
Public	-37	-40	5	—
Private short-term (net)[c]				
Oil sector	122	-70	-50	—
Accumulation/liquidation of commercial arrears	233	100	125	—
Capital Account Balance	41[d]	-19	60	—
Overall balance	5	5	5	—
Special Drawing Rights allocations	-46	+14	-65	—
Net changes in reserves (incl. SDRs) and official and other private short-term capital movements (increase, -)	165	365	552	49.0
Memorandum Items	-251	-364	-457	22.1
Net impact of the oil sector				
Net impact of the non-oil sector[e]				
Ratio of debt service and factor payments to exports (%)	34	29	33	—

[a]Export figures are slightly higher than those shown in Table 5-3 because of a balance of payments adjustment factor.

[b]Because of lags in the payment of petroleum taxes, factor payments as reflected in the national accounts differ from those shown here by the amount of oil sector short-term capital movements.

[c]Refers only to oil sector and non-oil movements associated with commercial arrears.

[d]Includes errors and omissions of -£N9.

[e]Excludes short-term and official capital.

government to liquidate the remaining short-term liabilities and perhaps to increase the level of external reserves over the remaining two years of the current Plan period. Actual and projected development of the balance of payments is shown in Table 5-8.

The principal argument for maintaining and increasing current levels of international and bilateral capital aid to the country is, however, not based primarily in the short- or medium-term balance of payments situation. Rather, Nigeria's case for foreign assistance rests mainly upon the need for institution building, planning and the general strengthening of administrative machinery, if growth is to be maintained. For the time being, many of the skills necessary for development can only be acquired in adequate volume from abroad. Some of these are perhaps most economically and efficiently found and applied in association with those types of capital projects typically financed under foreign assistance programs.

Nigeria currently enjoys a low-debt service ratio (about 3 percent of exports in 1971/72) and clearly could absorb a very substantial volume of additional borrowing on conventional terms without meeting debt servicing problems.

On the basis of its low per capita income, Nigeria would be eligible for soft-term lending. The more public investment Nigeria can finance with concessional aid over the next few years, the more net resources (after debt service) the country will have available to support a greatly expanded investment program in the future when the need for resource transfers may again become large and when the contribution of petroleum revenues and external assistance will be much smaller in terms of the country's requirements and absorptive capacity.

The fact that Nigeria temporarily may appear to have surplus resources, in the aggregate, emphasizes the issues of resource allocation and effective use. The capacity to prepare programs and projects in priority sectors and to build institutions capable of their implementation will require very substantial efforts. By selecting projects for financing in priority sectors and areas, and by helping in the process of institutional improvement, aid can assist the government in its own efforts to allocate resources in accordance with national priorities.

The expertise that should be associated with foreign assistance is currently in short supply. Aid programs can augment managerial and technical capacity where it is most needed, and, where foreign and domestic resources are being used in combination, can help to insure that both are used effectively.

Nigeria's absorptive capacity — and hence its effective need for capital — could rise more rapidly than the supply of assistance funds, given a reasonable effort to expand and strengthen executive capacity, including project preparation and implementation within the federal and state governments, the statutory corporations and the private sector. With rapidly expanding investment activity, official capital inflows as a proportion of investment requirements could well decline. While the availability of financial aid is not now a significant restraint on the overall level of investment, it could well become so before the end of the decade.

The currently favorable economic conditions and prospects give the government and donors alike an opportunity to formulate an aid and development strategy based on long-term assessments of the country's opportunities, priorities and potential. The Bank, through its recent sector studies, has already made a start in this regard, but much remains to be done. In particular, consideration of the medium-term aid requirements should not be so much in terms of the additional financial resources that can be mobilized from abroad, as in terms of what real contribution external assistance can make toward preparing the way for future self-sustained growth based primarily upon the country's own resources.

CHAPTER 6
PETROLEUM

Petroleum is by far the most dynamic sector in Nigeria today. Production of crude oil has increased rapidly since the first commercial discovery in 1956 and has now reached a level of 1.7 million barrels per day. Exports of crude oil will represent about 75 percent of total export earnings this year. By the end of this decade, value added in petroleum mining is likely to represent some 20 percent of GDP.

Production and Disposal of Crude Oil

The petroleum industry has always been dominated by Shell/BP Development Company of Nigeria, Ltd., a joint venture of Royal Dutch Shell and British Petroleum, which began exploration in Nigeria in 1938 and made Nigeria's first commercial discovery at the tertiary area of the Niger Delta in 1956. Extensive exploration followed and, in subsequent years, the Nigerian Government granted exploration rights to fifteen other groups. Six groups are now producing under 30-year mining leases for onshore areas and 40-years for offshore areas. Shell/BP's concessions account for 60 percent (17,000 sq. miles) of the total area under these mining leases, with Gulf (5,000 sq. miles), Agip/Phillips/NNOC (2,000 sq. miles), Safrap/NNOC, Mobil, and Chevron/Texaco (1,000 sq. miles each) sharing the rest.

The success ratio of drilling has been very high, on the average 43 percent of all exploration wells resulted in new fields, and 84 percent of appraisal and developmental drillings were successful. About 200 oil fields have been discovered to date with proven recoverable reserves of about 12 billion barrels. This represents about 1.8 percent of total world reserves, or about 20 percent of total reserves in Africa. At the current rate, proven reserves represent about 20 years of production, and potential reserves in existing concessions are believed to be much larger.

Production of crude oil, increasing rapidly after the first commercial discovery in 1956, reached almost 600,000 bls/day in mid-1967 when internal trouble caused all onshore areas to cease operation (Statistical Annex Table 44). Recovery since 1970 has been remarkable and production could reach 2 million bls/day. About 77 percent of current production is onshore, almost entirely by Shell/BP, although production costs including depreciation are somewhat higher.

Nigerian crude oil varies between light crude of 45° API gravity and heavy crude of 21° API, with a weighted average of about 32°. Sulphur content, averaging 0.2 percent, is very low.

More than 95 percent of total crude oil produced is exported. In 1970, 72 percent of total exports went to Western Europe, 16 percent to North America and 12 percent to South America. During the first half of 1971, the United States replaced the United Kingdom as the largest single market, receiving 20 percent of total exports. Loading facilities presently under construction will be able to handle more than 2.5 million bls/day, sufficient to cope with expected export over the next 3 years, and accommodate tankers of all sizes.

Nigeria's only refinery was established in 1965 at Alese Eleme near Port Harcourt. It is operated by the Nigerian Petroleum Refinery Company, a joint venture of the Nigerian Government (55 percent), Shell (22.5 percent) and British Petroleum (2.25 percent). Its present capacity of 60,000 bls/day is adequate to meet local demands, but its output of motor spirit, kerosene and aviation turbine fuel is expected to be short of the rapidly increasing demands by 1973. A second refinery to process 50,000 bls/day is included in the Plan but construction has been delayed, primarily because of the complex economic and political factors involved in site selection.

Natural Gas

All natural gas currently produced in Nigeria is a by-product of crude oil production, and reserves of natural gas roughly followed the growth of proven recoverable reserves of crude oil. The average ratio of associated gas produced with crude oil is about 750 cu ft. of gas per barrel of crude. Total reserves of natural gas are presently estimated at about 50×10^6 MM cu ft.

In 1970, about 98 percent of the estimated 280×10^3 MM cu ft. of gas produced in association with crude oil was flared. Only 4×10^3 MM cu ft. was consumed usefully, about half by the petroleum mining industry itself; of the remaining 2.3×10^3 MM cu ft., 70 percent was sold to gas-fired power stations situated near the oil fields and 30 percent to manufacturing industries in the eastern states.

National Oil Corporation

In accordance with its intentions expressed in the Plan, the government established the Nigerian National Oil Corporation (NNOC) in May 1971 to engage in all phases of the industry from exploration to refining and marketing. The corporation is run by a board of directors representing both the government and the private sector and is headed by the permanent secretary of the Ministry of Mines and Power. It functions as an independent corporation subject to all financial obligations applicable to petroleum companies but is initially financed by federal loans and grants.

NNOC's activities are presently limited to participation in new and existing exploration companies. Upon incorporation, NNOC was assigned a 35 percent equity share in the French company Safrap operation in Nigeria, part of the government's settlement with the company. Current output of Safrap is about 40,000 bls/day but NNOC's interest will rise to a maximum of 50 percent when output exceeds 400,000 bls/day. In 1971, NNOC also took the government's option of 33-1/3 percent equity position in Agip/Phillips' operation. Agip/Phillips' present production is also about 40,000 bls/day which, together with Safrap's production, accounts for about 5 percent of total Nigerian output. NNOC's shares in both these companies will be paid for through revenues accruing from future production.

NNOC also has a 51 percent option on any commercial discoveries made in the concessions awarded to Occidental, Japan Petroleum, Deminex/Niger, Monsanto/Niger and the Nigerian firm of Henry Stephens & Sons during 1971. In addition, NNOC now has exclusive exploration rights in all areas except those for which concessions have already been awarded. The government plans to have NNOC engaged in actual exploration and production, possibly with international oil companies or other groups as contractors or minority partners.

Government Revenues

At present, petroleum remains a typical enclave industry whose contribution to the economy is limited largely to its contribution to government revenues and foreign exchange earnings. The government receives revenues directly from petroleum exploration and producing companies in the form of oil and natural gas royalties, profit taxes, rentals for oil exploration and mining leases, premia paid for the acquisition of concessions; and miscellaneous fees such as oil pipeline fees. In line with the rapid development of exploration and production, government revenues from the petroleum sector rose from less than £N1 million in FY 1959/60 to £N320 million in FY 1971/72, or from less than one percent of total federal government revenues to about 50 percent. Over this period, royalties and profit taxes replaced rentals and premia as the major sources of government revenues and now account for over 90 percent of total government revenues from petroleum (Statistical Annex Table 47).

In May 1971, the royalty and profit taxes accruing to the government per barrel of crude oil produced were increased substantially as the result of revised agreements between the Nigerian Government and the petroleum companies, which are effective retroactively from March 20, 1971 to December 31, 1975. The major feature of these agreements related to the posted price of crude oil, the tax reference price used since 1967 for computing petroleum royalties and profit taxes. The agreements immediately increased the base posting of Nigerian crudes by U.S.$0.36 per barrel and eliminated a number of deductions previously permissible. In addition, the agreements included premia for Nigerian crude's low sulphur content and geographical advantages as well as escalation provisions, thus resulting in a U.S.$1.03 increase in the tax reference price. The structure of the tax-reference price from January 1970 to March 1971, and from then until December 31, 1975 according to the stipulations of the 1971 agreements are given in Table 6-1.

Accompanying the increase in the tax reference price, the tax rate on the petroleum companies' profits was increased from 50 percent to 55 percent and a number of modifications to the computation of profit taxes and royalty assessments were agreed. The net effect of these changes

Table 6-1: PETROLEUM PRICE STRUCTURE

(U.S. $ per Barrel of 34° API Crude)[a]

	Jan-Aug 1970	Sept 1970-Mar 1971	Mar 20-Dec 31, 1971	1972	1973	1974	1975
Base posting	2.170	2.420	2.780	2.780	2.780	2.780	2.780
Less:							
Harbor dues	-.060	-.060	—	—	—	—	—
Gravity allowance	-.019	-.019	—	—	—	—	—
Percentage allowance[b]	-.137	-.153	—	—	—	—	—
Marketing allowance[b]	-.005	-.005	—	—	—	—	—
Plus:							
Low sulphur premium	—	—	.100	.120	.140	.160	.180
Suez premium[c]	—	—	.120	.120	.120	.120	.120
Freight premium[d]	—	—	.090	.090	.090	.090	.090
Annual 2.5% escalation	—	—	.072	.072	.148	.227	.310
Annual 5¢ escalation	—	—	.050	.050	.100	.150	.200
Tax-reference price	1.949	2.183	3.212	3.232	3.378	3.527	3.680

[a]At May 1971 exchange rate.

[b]These allowances were retroactively eliminated by the 1971 Agreements.

[c]In effect only when Suez Canal is closed.

[d]Subject to variations according to movement of world scale freight rates. Premium in April 1972 was $0.015.

Source: Unpublished agreements between the Nigerian Government and petroleum-producing companies.

on government revenues per barrel of crude oil produced in established onshore and offshore fields is summarized in Table 6-2. The 1971 agreements also provided for an acceleration in the payments of royalties and profit taxes, effectively reducing the lag in payments from the six to nine months under the old schedule to about three months by 1973.

These developments, together with a 30 percent increase in the level of production, resulted in an increase of total government oil revenues from £N98 million in FY 1970/71 to about £N320 million in FY 1971/72. Royalties generated in 1971/72 are expected to be roughly double the 1970/71 total of about £N35 million, while profit taxes are expected to increase from approximately £N100 million to £N263 million. While total government revenues, including rentals and indirect taxes, accruing from production over 1971/72 should amount to about £N360 million, delayed payments of royalties and profit taxes will probably reduce actual receipts by some £N40 million.

Table 6-2: ESTIMATED REVENUE TO GOVERNMENT PER BARREL OF 34° API CRUDE

(U.S. $)[a]

	Jan-Aug 1970	Sept 1970- Mar 1971	Mar 20- Dec 31, 1971	1972	1973	1974	1975
Tax-reference price	1.949	2.183	3.212	3.232	3.378	3.527	3.680
Profit tax assessment							
Onshore	.630	.730	1.300	1.320	1.400	1.470	1.550
Offshore	.660	.770	1.350	1.360	1.440	1.520	1.600
Royalty assessment							
Onshore	.230	.260	.400	.400	.420	.440	.460
Offshore	.180	.210	.320	.320	.340	.350	.370
Total government's revenues[b]							
Onshore	.860	.990	1.700	1.710	1.820	1.910	2.010
Offshore	.840	.980	1.670	1.680	1.780	1.870	1.970

[a]At May 1971 exchange rate.

[b]Including rentals and custom duties which are offsets against assessed royalty and profit tax.

Source: Mission estimate.

Petroleum's Contribution to Foreign Exchange Earnings and National Income

In addition to the companies' payments to the government, the sector contributes to foreign exchange earnings through the companies' purchase of goods and services not financed by local proceeds. Net local payments for goods and services by the petroleum sector increased from about £N9 million in 1963 to £N42 million in 1971. Thus net foreign exchange earnings of the sector increased from £N14 million to £N293 million over the period, or from 7 percent of total imports of goods and non-factor services to about 47 percent (Table 6-3).

Table 6-3: CONTRIBUTIONS OF PETROLEUM SECTOR TO THE NIGERIAN ECONOMY

(In Millions of £N)

	1964	1966	1968	1970	1971[a]
Gross proceeds	33	101	38	265	508
Value-added (factor costs)	15	76	17	208	450
Wages and salaries	2	3	2	4	6
Government income	11	16	15	81	248
Investment income	1	57	—	123	196
Value-added as % of total GDP	(1%)	(5%)	(1%)	(9%)	(17%)
Net foreign exchange earnings	25	43	29	132	293
As % of Total imports of goods, NFS	(9%)	(14%)	(11%)	(28%)	(47%)

[a]Provisional.

Source: Central Bank of Nigeria and mission estimates.

Value-added of the petroleum sector increased tenfold in the three years 1964-1966, reaching a level of £N76 million in 1966. It then dropped sharply in 1967 and 1968, but recovered to £N208 million in 1970. Value-added as a ratio of gross proceeds of the sector increased from 34 percent in 1963 to 89 percent in 1971 because of a sharp decline in production costs per barrel as the level of output rises.

The petroleum sector's contribution to GNP is considerably smaller than its contribution to GDP because investment income abroad represents a very large proportion of total income generated. In 1970, investment income abroad accounted for almost 60 percent of total value-added, with the sector's contribution to GNP only £N85 million or about 4 percent of total GNP. However, the 1971 agreements increased Nigeria's share in total value-added considerably and the share of investment income abroad in total value-added declined to 43 percent in 1971 and will decline further to about 30 percent in the next few years. Petroleum's contribution to GNP in 1971 is estimated to amount to £N254 million, representing about 11 percent of GNP.

Future Prospects

In physical terms, the longer term prospects for a continued rise in the crude oil production of Nigeria are very favorable. Intensive exploration activities have so far been limited to the tertiary area of the Niger delta, with highly encouraging success ratios. While exploration in onshore cretaceous areas was impeded by internal unrest, discoveries have been made, and the prospects for oil formation in commercial quantities are good. The offshore areas which the government has reserved for the National Oil Corporation also have considerable potential.

Nigeria's position in the international petroleum picture was particularly attractive in recent years for several reasons. One is its proximity to its primary markets in Western Europe and to its secondary markets in North and South America. Since the closing of the Suez Canal, Nigerian crude oil benefited from a substantial freight cost advantage as compared with petroleum produced in the eastern side of the Suez. Secondly, the low-sulphur content of Nigerian crudes represents a major qualitative advantage for Nigeria over all major producers except Libya and Indonesia whose oil is also low in sulphur. Before the May 1971 agreements, the landed cost of Nigerian crude in the major markets was considerably less than that of its competitors even discounting the differences in quality. (Statistical Annex Table 45 gives a comparative analysis of relative costs of major suppliers' crude oils landed at Rotterdam and New York in January 1971. These cost differentials undoubtedly account, at least in part, for the recent intensive exploration efforts in Nigeria.)

The May 1971 agreements altered the situation considerably. The increase in the tax liabilities of the petroleum companies operating in Nigeria was significantly higher than parallel increases negotiated in other oil producing countries. As compared to the U.S.$0.70 increase in the tax-paid cost of Nigerian crudes, the Teheran Agreement increased the tax-paid cost of Middle Eastern crudes by only $0.30 to 0.34, while the Tripoli Agreement increased the tax-paid cost of Libyan crude by $0.62. This relatively higher increase in tax costs resulted in a landed cost of Nigerian crudes at Rotterdam in July 1971 roughly comparable to Libyan crudes, but about $0.17 higher than the high sulphur content Middle Eastern crudes. In the American market, the price of Nigerian crudes is still relatively attractive as compared with Libyan and Iranian crudes, but reached $0.50 higher than Venezuelan crudes in 1972.

It therefore appears that the relative position of Nigerian crudes in the major markets over the medium term will be primarily a function of freight rates and the price differentials given to low sulphur content crudes in the major markets. The outlook seems to indicate a continued decline in freight rates which would make Nigerian crude less competitive with Middle Eastern crudes. However, low sulphur fuel will probably command an increasingly higher price relative to high-sulphur fuel, particularly if European countries introduce sulphur restrictions. Nigeria should also benefit somewhat from the apparent conservation policy presently pursued by Libya, the major producer of low-sulphur crude.

In view of these conflicting trends, output projections of Nigerian crude oil can only be highly speculative. However, considering that export facilities for a total capacity of about 2.5 million bls/day have already been completed, or are in the process of completion, daily output in Nigeria will most likely reach that level by 1974. On the other hand the rate of growth should decelerate over this period and after a level of 3 million bls/day is reached (probably in the late 1970s) production is likely to increase only in line with the expected rise in international demand for petroleum.

Estimated contributions of the petroleum sector to the economy on the basis of these projections from 1971/72 to 1975/76 are presented in Table 6-4. Projected realized price (actual price received by the petroleum companies) of exports is based on the assumption that companies' take per barrel will remain constant over the period, i.e., that the tax increases included in the five-year agreements will be passed on completely to the consumer. A continued but slower decline in production costs per barrel is also assumed.

Table 6-4 also gives the projected local cash transactions as derived from the overall balance of payments accounts of the sector based on assumed investment expenditures of £N125 and £N135 million respectively in 1971/72 and 1972/73, then gradually declining, in line with the decelerated growth of output, to about £N100 million by 1975/76. The net balance of projected local cash transactions would represent net foreign exchange earnings of the sector if investment continues to be financed entirely by the international companies. However, net foreign exchange earnings would be reduced by the extent to which the National Oil Corporation's participation is achieved during this period, although in the longer run, participation would increase the net foreign exchange earnings of the sector by increasing the Nigerian share in factor income generated.

Long-term prospects for export of liquefied natural gas are also very favorable, particularly to the East coast of the United States. The potential demand for liquefied natural gas (LNG) is very large, mainly due to the shortage in world energy supply caused by delays in the development of commercial nuclear energy. The Nigerian oil-field gas has the further advantage of being sulphur-free and unassociated gas fields are close to the coast.

Several LNG projects are under consideration. The present government project to export liquefied petroleum gas is likely to be expanded at a later date to include export of LNG. A proposed LNG project in a relatively advanced stage of preparation is likely to involve an intake capacity of 800 million cu ft/day. Annual export revenues from a project of this scale would be of the order of U.S.$200-300 million. Investment in infrastructure, liquefaction plants and tankers would probably exceed U.S.$1,000 million. Several other projects are also believed to be under consideration by the government.

All these LNG projects are at an early stage and exports within the next five years are very unlikely. A major uncertainty that remains relates to the American Government's natural gas import and pricing policy. Furthermore, the Nigerian Government appears to be interested in a majority share participation in all LNG ventures. As investment costs are very large, export proceeds accruing to Nigeria for several years after completion of the project would be required to finance the government's (or NNOC's) equity participation. Therefore it is unlikely that the economy would receive net income from the exports of LNG until at least the 1980s.

Policy Issues

There are two central issues with respect to government policies toward the petroleum sector: the division of net income per unit output between the government and the producing companies, and the time-phasing of the expected total flow of *national* income from the sector. The former is unlikely to be an urgent issue over the next year or so since the government's take per barrel of crude oil produced is now governed by the May 1971 agreements with the producing companies. Furthermore, Nigeria joined the Organization for Petroleum Exporting Countries (OPEC) in June 1971, thereby committing itself more to a unified position with other exporting countries. There is certainly little economic incentive for Nigeria to pursue an independent policy with respect to taxation. As discussed earlier, the tax-paid cost of Nigerian crudes is now more or less in line with that of competitive suppliers and any unilateral increases in the share of net income accruing to Nigeria in the foreseeable future therefore are likely to occur only as the result of parallel increases in other producing countries.

The second issue is more complex. The government of a petroleum producing country can increase future income accruing to the economy at the expense of current income either by limiting the rate of extraction, or by acquiring equity shares in the producing companies. Therefore it has a certain degree of freedom concerning the time-phasing of national income flows from given reserves of oil.

Limiting output for purposes of "conservation of wasting assets" is not yet a real issue in Nigeria. As the petroleum industry is still at a relatively early stage of exploration, the extent of total reserves is still unknown. It seems unlikely that a policy of conserving an asset whose magnitude is still unknown would be pursued in a country with Nigeria's overall needs. Conservation policy in Nigeria in the near future is likely to be limited to a careful scrutiny of output from

Table 6-4: PROJECTED PETROLEUM SECTOR ACCOUNTS

(In Millions of Current £N)

	1971/72	1972/73	1973/74	1974/75	1975/76
Average daily production (mil. bls.)	1.60	1.90	2.25	2.49	2.70
Realized price (U.S. $/bl.)[a]	2.65	2.68	2.79	2.89	3.00
Contribution to Gross Domestic Product					
Gross proceeds	560	670	825	945	1,055
Exports	540	648	800	920	1,030
Local sales	20	22	25	25	25
Intermediate inputs and harbor dues	63	72	79	86	91
Value-added	497	598	746	859	964
Wages and salaries	7	8	9	10	11
Government income[b]	350	410	485	580	655
Investment income[c]	140	180	252	269	298
Balance of payments					
Exports f.o.b.	540	648	800	920	1,030
Imports c.i.f.	-40	-45	-46	-45	-44
Trade balance	500	603	754	875	986
Non-factor service payments	-80	-85	-75	-72	-68
Investment income[c]	-140	-180	-252	-269	-298
Current balance	280	338	427	534	620
Direct investment	125	135	120	110	100
Short-term capital[d]	-40	-20	+5	-10	-15
Overall balance	365	453	552	634	705
Local cash transactions					
Government income generated	350	410	485	580	655
less payment lags[d]	-40	-20	+5	-10	-15
Government income received	310	390	490	570	640
Custom duties and other government revenues	10	10	10	10	10
Other local payments	65	75	77	79	80
less local proceeds	20	22	25	25	25
Net balance	365	453	552	634	705

[a]At May 1971 exchange rate.

[b]Profit taxes, royalties and rentals.

[c]Residual item representing proceeds not remitted to Nigeria.

[d]Resulting from time lags in payments of royalties and profit taxes. Inflow in 1973/74 (negative lags) due to acceleration of payment provided for in current agreements.

Source: Mission estimates.

established fields to insure that an abnormally rapid rate of extraction is not pursued to the extent that total recovery from the fields is diminished substantially.

Participation is a far more urgent issue. Participation in the equity and control of petroleum companies is now the explicit policy of the major oil exporting countries, including Nigeria. As the returns to investment in the producing companies are likely to be high, participation appears to be a financially attractive option for the investment of current resources which might otherwise be used for less productive purposes. An increased role for Nigerians in the country's major industry would also seem to be politically and socially desirable.

Obviously, a crucial parameter in the policy decisions concerning participation is the relative profitability of the economy's investment in petroleum as opposed to alternative investment opportunities. The probable cost of participation, however, is difficult to estimate. OPEC favors the *net book value* method for the valuation of the concessions and corresponding payments to the oil companies. The companies, on the other hand, would probably negotiate for valuation closer to the discounted stream of future net earnings accruing to the present concession holders. The cost of participation therefore largely depends on the results of negotiation within a very wide range. Furthermore, the exact nature of participation still needs to be defined in Nigeria as well as in other OPEC countries. Consequently, it is impossible now to speculate as to the likely return of participation to the economy.

Unlike most major oil producing countries, Nigeria's available resources from petroleum are not large compared with the needs of the population. Government revenues from petroleum are unlikely to approach the order of magnitude in, say, Iran or Venezuela on a per capita basis.

			(U.S. $)
Oil Revenue per Capita	Nigeria	Iran	Venezuela
1970 (actual)	4	37	125
1975 (projected)	25	80	190

Government policies toward the petroleum sector may therefore need to be pursued quite independently from countries whose oil revenues and income per capita are far larger than Nigeria.

CHAPTER 7

AGRICULTURE, MANUFACTURING, EDUCATION AND INFRASTRUCTURE

This chapter reviews and summarizes recent developments and future prospects in agriculture, manufacturing and infrastructure (education, transport and public utilities). Agriculture and transport were the subjects of separate sector missions by the IBRD; and education by a Unesco Project Identification Mission during the first half of 1971.

Agriculture

Despite the growing importance of other sectors, oil and manufacturing in particular, agriculture, including forestry and fishing, which accounted for about 50 percent of GDP at current factor cost in 1970/71, will remain a key factor in Nigeria's economic development as the largest employer of labor (about 72 percent of the labor force in 1970/71), the principal source of food and raw materials for the increasing population and a significant, albeit relatively declining, earner of foreign exchange. The acceleration of agricultural growth, therefore, and the provision of additional employment opportunities in the sector, are crucial to the country's future progress.

There are considerable opportunities for growth in the sector, based primarily on the existence of expanding markets, foreign and particularly domestic, for Nigeria's agricultural output; the abundance of land and human resources whose diverse productive capacities are presently underutilized; and the availability of improved technology, the exploitation of which could increase productivity substantially. The constraints, on the other hand, are several: low producer incentives; transport and distribution bottlenecks; inadequate machinery for planning, coordinating and implementing a coherent national policy for rural and agricultural development; insufficient qualified manpower; and shortages of improved seeds, fertilizers, chemicals, credit and other farm inputs.

Market Prospects

Nigeria is the world's largest exporter of groundnuts and, until recently, of oil palm products. It is the second largest exporter of cocoa. Rubber and cotton, though only a small part of world trade, have also been important sources of foreign exchange. In 1970, these five products accounted for 30 percent of total exports and 70 percent of non-oil exports. World demand for agricultural exports is projected to continue rising by 2-3 percent annually over the next ten to fifteen years. However, expected price declines, caused by even greater increases in world supply, will require Nigeria to expand its exports substantially if total earnings from these products are not also to decline. Moreover, given lower unit prices, the returns to producers and incentives to increased output will, unless productivity is improved and the margin between export and producer prices is narrowed, continue to fall. Domestic consumption will account for the largest increases in demand for most products. Demand for sugar, animal products, fish and paper products in particular is expected to rise in response to population growth, urbanization and rising incomes. Export demand for cocoa and rubber is also expected to double by 1985. The large increase in domestic demand for palm oil and cotton may absorb most, if not all production before 1985 and the growth of the textile industry threatens to outstrip local production. Prospects for satisfying domestic demand for beef and dairy products internally during the next ten years are poor and, in the absence of increased imports of these goods, prices will continue to rise.

Natural Resources

Most of the agricultural production is concentrated in relatively few areas — mainly in the tree crop belts in the South and the groundnut and cotton belts in the North. However, the Food and Agriculture Organization estimates that the total area cropped is probably little more than one-third of the land judged suitable for agriculture and less than a quarter of that judged potentially suitable. Moreover, the agricultural resources available are not utilized intensively. Traditional shifting cultivation is widespread with the result that much of the land at any one time is in bush fallow. The technologies used are generally very unsophisticated. There is little use of manure, chemical fertilizers and pesticides, and on-farm capital investment in fences, irrigation, wells, roads or buildings is small. Despite the importance of export crops, little medium- and long-term capital is employed. There is relatively little specialization in production which, even in specialized cash crop areas, is often directed first to satisfying family food needs. Since the effective demand for farm labor is limited, there is a surplus supply in some areas of family and employable labor except at seasonal peak periods.

Available Technology

Improved planting materials and cultivation practices already developed for several crops, if adopted, could significantly raise present yields. Tree crops, groundnuts and cotton offer the best prospects for immediate application. Improvement in processing would increase rubber and oil palm production. Improved technology would increase yields of sorghum, rice, maize, yams and cassava, although the outlook for immediate general application is more limited. However, given work already done or under way in Nigerian institutions and the possibilities opened up by the new International Institute of Tropical Agriculture, suitable high-yielding varieties of sorghum, maize and rice should be available for multiplication by the mid-1970s. If facilities for seed multiplication and distribution to farmers are in place and an adequate system for providing farm inputs is ready, a major breakthrough in cereal production could occur by the early 1980s.

The recently created Agricultural Research Council will, it is expected, remedy the absence of overall direction and coordination of agricultural research. So far, most of the research has concentrated on technical optima for individual crops — mainly export crops — rather than on the entire farming system and on integrating improvements within the system.

Development Constraints and Needs

Land. The total land area of Nigeria is 228 million acres of which 84 million acres are judged to be of medium and high productivity and reasonably suitable for agriculture. This figure does not include areas that might be suitable for range farming. Applying modern technology and making needed improvements, this area could potentially be increased to about 179 million acres.

The degree of utilization of these land resources is still very low. The area presently cropped represents only 25-35 percent of the suitable 84 million acres and only 11-16 percent of the land potentially suitable for agriculture. With traditional shifting cultivation practiced widely, much of the land farmed at any time is in bush fallow. There are also large areas which are not farmed at all.

Although in aggregate land is relatively abundant, population pressures have become serious in the tree crop belts in the South and in the groundnut and cotton belts in the North. Fallow periods under shifting cultivation have become too short to restore fertility in some areas. The original cropping cycle of 10-15 years in large segments of the tree crop belt has already been reduced to 5 years. In the North, extension of cultivation has reduced the grazing area for nomadic herds, resulting in over-grazing and erosion.

An area which is still under-populated and under-farmed is the vast middle belt covering approximately 75 million acres. Very little has been done to date toward developing this area, which could become the mixed farming area *par excellence* of Nigeria. The major obstacle is the prevalence of the tsetse fly, but its elimination can be economic in the middle belt provided the area is brought into continuous and intensive use.

Techniques. Production is carried out almost entirely by small farmers with holdings of 3 to 7 acres growing a variety of crops, usually including their subsistence needs of food crops. In 1963, about 40 percent of farmers in the northern states and over 60 percent in the southern states held less than 2.5 acres. 90 percent of the output of oil palm comes from small semi-wild groves.

The implements used in farming are hoes, cutlasses and other primitive hand tools. Use of ox-drawn implements is limited by climatic conditions such as the tsetse fly and the shortage of fodder. Use of power equipment and machinery is almost nil.

Input. The use of improved inputs is extremely limited. Use of chemical fertilizers of all types reached a peak of 65,000 tons in 1967 for a harvested acreage of about 29 million acres. This represents an average of only 5 lbs. per acre. There is no local production of fertilizer, and very little private sector participation in distribution. Fertilizer is imported in bulk and distributed through the extension services and local agents. However, adequate supplies frequently are not available when farmers need them.

The supply of suitable planting materials is seriously deficient for tree crops. Seed production is inadequate even for present needs of cocoa planting and for any large expansion of rubber and oil palm. The distribution facilities for cottonseed and groundnuts will have to be expanded drastically to cope with the rising demand for improved planting materials. Supplies of improved materials for food and feed crops scarcely extend beyond those used for research and experimentation.

Insecticides and other farm chemicals are particularly important for cocoa, oil palm, rubber and cotton, and projected increases in output will require a vastly improved supply network. Further study is also required to assess technical and economic feasibility and possible harmful effects on the environment.

Irrigation. Annual rainfall ranges from 20 inches in the North to about 160 inches in the South Eastern region of Nigeria. About 30 percent of the country receives less than 40 inches per annum. Only 36,000 acres are now irrigated, mostly in the North Western, North Eastern and Kwara States and more irrigation is probably necessary to achieve projected expansion in the output of wheat, sugarcane and rice. The Second Development Plan seeks to increase the irrigated area to 160,000 acres by 1974 and 610,000 acres by 1980.

The major problem in expanding irrigation is the absence of basic data to plan projects. Hydrologic data are meager or non-existent; topographic and soil and land surveys are yet to be accomplished; cropping programs need to be established and crop soil acceptances and crop husbandry procedures need to be investigated. These will require considerable time, making it very unlikely that Plan targets, even if found to be justified, will be met. On a very optimstic estimate, no more than 500,000 acres could be brought under irrigation by 1985, contributing an increase in agricultural output of only 3 percent. The same result can be achieved with much less investment by extending the area cropped under rain fed cultivation — currently only 30 million acres out of a possible 80 million acres of arable land.

Tenure. Land tenure systems vary among ethnic groups but a common feature is the absence of individual ownership. In the coastal states, land is regarded as the joint property of the community and the right to cultivate is given to individuals by the traditional head of the community. In the fallow period, land reverts back to the community, although trees are regarded as the property of the man who plants them. Such a system discourages individual investment in conservation, and improvement of land makes it difficult for a farmer to obtain loans using his land for security. In the northern states, land is owned by the state and tenure is on the basis of customary usufruct, a system that leads to friction between herders and farmers.

In many parts of the country the system is already in transition. While there is no need for a major program of land reform, there is need for changes in local legislation that will help the transition to individual tenure and for policies to promote improvement of commercial grazing areas.

Marketing. State marketing boards constitute the exclusive ultimate purchasers of cocoa, groundnuts, cotton, palm produce and a number of minor commercial crops. The major commodities not controlled by marketing boards are rubber and food crops.

Although the original objective in establishing the marketing boards was to stabilize prices earned by farmers and to improve the marketing organization, they have been used during the sixties as a convenient instrument for taxing agriculture. The emphasis on raising revenues has resulted in producer prices being set at roughly half the unit value of exports. Consequently, the return to the farmer engaged in production of export crops is low. At current producers' prices, the gross return per man-day of labor is less than 4 shillings in groundnut and cotton production; the return on the investment required to establish a nucleus plantation of oil palm is only about 5 percent.

In recent years producer prices have risen substantially: cocoa by 57 percent from £N96 per ton in 1968/69 to £N151 in 1970/71; groundnuts by 36 percent from £N43 to £N55 per ton in 1968/69. The producer prices of palm products have risen slightly in 1970/71, from £N41 to £N44 per ton for palm oil and from £N29 to £N30 per ton for palm kernel. Maintenance of these producer prices will necessarily involve a reduction in revenues generated by marketing boards since world prices of cocoa, groundnuts and cottonseed are all expected to drop slightly over the next 5 years.

The marketing board system has also been criticized for inefficiencies in operation. The major items of expense are the buying allowances to the licensed buying agents, transport costs and general and administrative expenses. These amount to about £N20.5 per ton for groundnuts, £N18.6 per ton for cocoa and £N11.7 per ton for palm kernels. It has been estimated that determined efforts to improve efficiency might reduce expenses by 20 percent.

The system of licensed buying agents has also come in for criticism. There is some evidence that the allowances paid to them are excessive and, further, the marketing boards have no effective control over the prices paid to the farmer by the licensed buying agents. There is considerable scope for licensed buying agents to short-change producers on weight and grade of produce purchased.

The marketing of products not controlled by the marketing boards is handled by a traditional, fragmented system. Various studies on the marketing of foodstuffs have concluded that, given the existing infrastructure, traders were reasonably efficient and achieved a considerable degree of inter-market coordination. The infrastructure, however, is inadequate. Poor transport links tend to cause seasonal price variations in small isolated markets. Storage costs are as high as 2.5-3 percent of the value of produce stored per month. Lack of adequate wholesale market facilities inhibits the inflow of perishable foodstuffs into the cities, widening the spread of prices between urban and rural centers. The high cost of distribution of foodstuffs has probably contributed to the increase in urban food prices.

Transport. Transport is the principal component of marketing costs. It accounts for 30-40 percent of total marketing costs for cotton, 35-55 percent for groundnuts and about 20 percent for cocoa. The transport network and the main arterial roads are in poor condition because of vehicle overloading and inadequate maintenance. These roads are vital in moving export crops to the ports. The railways have been unable to service traffic demand adequately, resulting in increased transport costs. For example, from 1967 to 1970 the number of cattle moved by rail halved both in absolute numbers and as a percentage of total cattle moved. The alternative modes of transport, road and hoof, involve higher direct costs and higher mortality rates.

Since there is little animal transport, a farm family's marketed output is limited largely to the amount of goods which can be moved by human power unless there is an adequate network of feeder roads. Greater attention will have to be given to the development of feeder roads to facilitate the distribution of farm inputs, and economically evacuate produce.

Credit. Lack of agricultural credit is increasingly singled out as a major handicap. Institutional credit has been available to farmers for the past two or three decades but has not been successful. The only institutions now in operation in the Western and Mid-Western States do not have active credit programs and are concerned only with collecting old debts. Commercial banks have extended credit to some large-scale plantations but not to small farmers. Agricultural cooperatives reach less than 5 percent of the farming population. They have limited financial programs, most of which go to marketing and they provide negligible credit for production purposes.

Improved income for farmers and the modernization of agriculture will bring forth a rising demand for credit. On the basis of present plans for the replanting of cocoa, rubber, and palm oil alone, annual credit needs are estimated at about £N11 million by 1980. Credit needs for production of cotton and groundnuts could exceed £N5 million by 1980.

The absence of a federal institution is being remedied by the establishment of a National Agricultural Credit Bank. The bank will lend money for credit projects which would be administered by the states or state institutions. The Second Development Plan has earmarked £N6 million for the Bank over the next five years. Since farmers now incur interest charges somewhere between 24 percent and 50 percent, the Credit Bank should be able to charge interest rates high enough to cover expenses.

Research. Research has been conducted in a number of semi-autonomous institutions situated in the various ecological regions in the country. Export crops have received the main emphasis while food and feed crops have been comparatively neglected. The best prospects of immediate application are for tree crops, groundnuts and cotton, where experimental yields have been two to three times higher than present yields. By the mid-70s suitably high-yielding varieties of sorghum, maize and rice should be available for multiplication. There are possibilities for increasing yields of yams and cassava but further work needs to be done to develop disease-resistant varieties and improve farming practices.

Much of the problem in research has been the absence of overall direction. The Agricultural Research Council has recently been set up to remedy this. Another drawback has been that research has sought technical optima for individual crops instead of focusing on the total farming system and on integrating improvements within that system.

There is inadequate agro-economic data on basic economic limitations, such as the shortage of labor at key periods in the cropping year, to provide complete guidance for re-orientation of technical research programs. There is urgent need for more studies of the type now being carried out by the Rural Economic Research Unit at the Institute of Agricultural Research.

Manpower and Coordination. Inadequate overall planning and coordination at the federal level is an impediment to agricultural development. Until recently, the principal responsibility of the Federal Ministry of Agriculture and Natural Resources was limited to research. The links between the federal and state Ministries of Agriculture are weak, making it difficult to monitor the implementation of projects in the Development Plan. The present system also tends to discourage regional specialization based on comparative advantage.

Moves to strengthen the state ministries have come up against the shortage of suitably qualified personnel, necessitating consideration of large-scale outside assistance.

Perhaps the most serious restraint on agricultural development is the shortage of qualified personnel for planning and project preparation at the state level. With few exceptions, state staffs have no more than one year's experience in planning or project work. Present training facilities are inadequate. In the long run, an increased supply of manpower should be forthcoming from the educational system. What is urgently needed is the establishment of *ad hoc,* in-service training centers to solve the short-term problem.

One of the most important constraints to the realization of the agricultural potential is the low price incentive to producers to increase output which, in tree crops, operates at two levels: on the extent of new planting or replanting, whose effects are not felt for several years, and on the level of annual output. The original objective of the marketing boards, which are the exclusive ultimate purchasers of cocoa, groundnuts, cotton, palm produce and several minor commercial crops, was to stabilize prices paid to farmers and to improve the marketing organization. However, during the 1960s they were used as a convenient instrument for taxing agriculture. Their emphasis on raising revenues, which until recently were an important source of capital for the state (and previously regional) governments, has resulted in producer prices set at roughly half the unit value of exports. Consequently, the returns to farmers engaged in export production are low. Although producer prices have increased substantially in recent years, their maintenance at current levels, in view of generally declining world prices for agricultural products, will necessarily result in reduced revenues generated by the marketing boards. Two critical policy issues therefore arise: to what degree can other sources provide the state governments with revenue hitherto drawn from agriculture through marketing board surpluses, and what reorganization in the marketing system is needed to reduce its high costs and enable it more accurately to relay market opportunities to producers. Major reductions in revenue from export crops, increased private participation in competitive marketing arrangements and a review of marketing board policy and staffing are possibilities for consideration.

Given the difficulty of planning and coordinating agricultural investment by twelve states, the Bank's study looks to a strengthening of both the authority and administrative capacity of the Federal Ministry of Agriculture and Natural Resources, increasing the executive and planning capacities of state governments, improving federal-state links in agriculture and developing sufficient numbers of qualified personnel to staff agricultural organizations and programs. The study made detailed recommendations designed to insure that improved techniques and inputs — fertilizers, credit, research and extension services — are taken up by the agricultural sector. The study also outlined a strategy and program for development whose long-term objective would be to transform agriculture from its present low technology, semi-subsistence character to a more modern, market-oriented one, based on greater regional specialization.

If immediate steps are taken to improve producer price incentives, the supply of farm inputs and transportation, and to restore production in the East, agricultural output could achieve an average annual growth rate of 3 percent through 1975, provided weather is favorable and food output responds to the pressures of demand. This would still be less than 3.3 percent average annual increase recorded from 1958/59 through 1966/67. In the longer term, provided that appropriate measures are taken to overcome the constraints noted above, the annual rate of growth could reach 5 percent by 1980.

Manufacturing

Since independence, manufacturing has grown very fast: the increase in value-added in all manufacturing averaged over 11 percent annually and, in large-scale manufacturing alone over 15 percent annually. Development began from a small base, however, and manufacturing's contribution to GDP is still well below 10 percent. In recent years the rate of growth, at least in large-scale manufacturing, has been about 20 percent annually. The surplus capacity of earlier years has disappeared in many industries and recent increases in output have not kept pace with the rapid growth of consumer demand. Vigorous investment activity and lively foreign interest in new ventures have resulted.

Structure, Location and Size

The largest manufacturing group – with 10 or more employed – is the food, drink and tobacco industry, which over the years has maintained its roughly 30 percent share of total large-scale manufacturing value-added; textiles have expanded and now account for about 16 percent. Other relatively fast growing industries, though smaller than textiles, were clothing and footwear, paper products and metal goods. The industrial structure therefore remains little diversified. The available statistics also indicate that industries with relatively low value-added per unit of output have grown faster than high value-added industries. On average, value-added amounted to only 26 percent of gross output in 1967, the last year for which complete data are available. Backward and forward integration are not significant.

Although the Lagos area contains the largest concentration of industries, its share in value-added has declined in recent years; mainly because of substantial industrial growth in the North, in the Kaduna-Kano-Zaria triangle. Industrial activity outside these two growth poles is small at present.

There is no comprehensive census of large- and small-scale industrial establishments. Cottage industry may embrace some 900,000 households (1964). Small-scale establishments exist in large numbers in most urban areas, although their density tends to be higher in the cities and administrative centers where there is considerable wage employment, compared with the traditional towns of the North and the West. Total employment in urban small-scale industry may exceed 100,000, compared with 77,000 (1967) in large-scale manufacturing.

On the basis of a 1960 survey of eastern Nigeria, small-scale manufacturing establishments may total about 35,000 to 40,000, of which about 40 percent are one-man operations. However, a comparison of these data with the 1967 Industrial Survey indicates considerable underestimation of the number of enterprises with 10-19 employees. Of the largest enterprises (500 workers or more), there were 29 establishments in 1967 (less than 6 percent of the [underestimated] total number of large-scale establishments in the survey), producing 46 percent of total value-added. Although publicly owned enterprises accounted for only 0.7 percent of large-scale value-added in 1967, they accounted for 18 percent of total paid-up capital and almost 6 percent of total employment, indicating the limited success of the public sector manufacturing ventures. Few of these projects are profitable, largely because of mismanagement. Foreign investment accounts for 70 percent of total paid-up capital (1967) and is particularly important in beverages and tobacco, textiles, chemicals, cement and metal goods. British companies accounted for 64 percent of total foreign investment in 1964, followed by American, Lebanese and Dutch investments.

Import Substitution and Export Processing

A 1969 survey revealed that industrialization had hitherto been primarily induced by the protective policies of the government, rather than tax incentives or the availability of cheap labor and raw materials. Private import substituting ventures have been considerably more efficient than those undertaken in the public sector. Imports accounted for about two-thirds of total domestic demand for manufactured products in 1963, less than half in 1968 however, and about 35-40 percent by 1970. Most important substitution occurred in textiles, beverages and tobacco and in metal goods. As these figures indicate, there is still room for further import substitution, particularly in textiles.

Export processing industries have grown relatively slowly. Their share in large-scale value-added declined from 50 percent to 25 percent between 1958 and 1967. Their growth is often limited by the growth of agricultural supplies; incentives and protection have clearly been inferior to those given to import-substituting industries. However, there is substantial potential for growth in export processing, subject to the adoption of appropriate incentive policies and the identification of new markets.

Competitiveness and Profitability

A previous IBRD study calculated the level of effective protection for 42 sectors of industry in 1968. One of the highest rates of effective protection was for textiles (120 percent of value-added), largely reflecting high profits, since the return at world prices on the book value of fixed assets was a respectable 17 percent. Increased excise duties or lower tariffs therefore would be possible. Similarly, high effective protection was found for metal goods (143 percent); but, here, competitiveness was lacking as the rate of return on capital, now around 45 percent, would decline to only 2 percent at world prices. When domestically produced steel replaces imported metal as a raw material some years hence, protection may have to be increased even further. The highest degree of protection is found in the assembly, furniture, glass products, radio and television industries (usually over 200 percent); the lowest, even negative protection, in export industries, which explains their difficulty in competing abroad.

Most industries appear to be highly profitable, operating near to capacity and essentially in a seller's market. The liberalization of imports in 1971 evidently reduced profits somewhat, but the current (1972/73) budget substantially increased the competitiveness of domestic industries relative to imports, as import duties on finished products were raised while those on raw materials were lowered. Excise duties on a range of domestic manufactures were also reduced by as much as 50 percent. While labor costs have increased considerably, they represent only 6 percent of total costs, and these, in turn, do not appear to have risen in relation to the value of sales.

Incentives and Promotion Policies

The time when foreign investment could enter and repatriate freely in an economy with abundant market potentials is ending and Nigerian participation is now given considerable emphasis. Accordingly careful analysis and project preparation will be necessary, particularly for investments in sectors where linkages need to be taken into consideration. Industrial incentives are of fairly recent date and the Pioneer Companies Relief is one of the most significant. These incentives grant tax relief for 3 to 5 years, related to the rate of expansion, standards of efficiency, training of Nigerian staff and the use of local raw materials. These tax reliefs are also granted to both foreign and indigenous industries, although the required initial investment for the former is a multiple of that for the latter. Other incentives have included refunds and concessionary import duties, the latter gaining in relative importance,[1] and accelerated initial and annual depreciation, with rates differing according to types of investments (mining expenditure, equipment, buildings). While this system has become less generous over time, the Plan suggests possibly increased rates, diversified according to national priorities. Small companies enjoy special income tax relief during their first 6 years of operation, provided that their profits are below £N1,000 each year and do not aggregate more than £N3,000.

Over the years, the administration of these incentives has improved, with better appraisal of applications and a noticeable reduction in arbitrariness. While the government has balanced its provision of incentives between indigenous and foreign applicants, it has used income tax relief

---

1. The Approved User Scheme was abolished in the 1972/73 budget.

grants judiciously to encourage Nigerian participation in predominantly expatriate industries. Between 1955 and 1968, there were 101 approved Pioneer Certificates which were effectively used (out of 179 granted). Import duty relief was provided in the form of refunds and by way of concessional tariffs. Accelerated depreciation, almost automatically available to any company subject to company income tax, was utilized by 700 new establishments. The estimated gross revenue foregone by the government on account of these concessions amounts to £N40 million, although, on a net basis only about £N32 million, less than 4 percent of all revenues over the period. A recent University of Ibadan survey highlights the relatively minor role of tax incentives in investors' decisions: an estimated 60 percent of investments benefiting from tax relief would have taken place anyway. Market conditions and government attitudes are generally considered more important.

In addition to gradually increasing tariffs, the government has employed quantitative restrictions on imports, notably during 1966-70. Their reduction in 1970 and 1971 is commendable, and previous windfall profits to holders of scarce import licenses will now accrue to the government in the form of additional tariff revenues.

The basic rate of the profit tax is 40 percent, although a temporary surtax of 15-25 percent imposed during hostilities has been levied until recently.[2] Its structure favors retention of profits in Nigeria, without acting as a disincentive to new foreign investment. Excise taxes tend to reduce tariff protection, since they do not apply to imported goods. With the rapid expansion of the commodity base, their importance in total revenues is measured. Excise taxes have been purposely introduced on domestic production to offset the high level of protection afforded by import tariffs.

The effective rate of protection derived from this structure may be characterized as follows:

(a) strong discrimination against export processing industries;
(b) a high average level of effective protection for new import substituting industries;
(c) greater protection for industries processing domestic inputs than for those using imported inputs; and
(d) discrimination against capital and intermediate goods in favor of consumer goods.

Its result has been a rapid growth of manufacturing, especially in import substitution where, although the limit has not yet been reached, further substitution may be costly in terms of scarce manpower, capital, and possibly additional revenue losses. The industrial structure remains little diversified: consumer goods industries have been preferred over intermediate and capital goods industries and export processing suffers from disincentives. Consequently, to diversify industrial growth, an overhaul of the tariff structure is needed, not only to increase protection on goods presently discriminated against, but also to enlarge the country's internal market. In this context, agricultural modernization and growth, accompanied by improved productivity and higher farm incomes is a key issue; a condition for more rapid growth of the domestic market is a reversal of the existing imbalance between rural and urban incomes.

It is unclear whether the government considers tax incentives an important tool of economic policy. The system needs reform away from general, uncoordinated and rather passive incentives toward a more diversified structure, which would then be employed as a major instrument of development policy. Other issues, such as industrial linkages, the promotion of export-oriented industries and improved treatment for intermediate and light capital goods industries, are also urgent. The present low ratio of value-added to gross output is a problem which also needs attention. Nigeria probably retains no more than 30 percent of the already low value-added in large-scale manufacturing because of low wages and substantial profit transfers abroad. However, since many products only survive behind tariffs of 50 percent or more on value-added, Nigeria, by manufacturing instead of importing some items, is probably losing foreign exchange on a net basis. Although there is no short-term cure for this, the training of Nigerians to replace expatriates may, in the longer run, reduce salary remittances abroad; the development of metal-using industries — depending on the size and growth of the market — may also gradually reduce imports of replacement machinery.

Past experience suggests that government investment in manufacturing should only be

----

2. The 1972/73 budget raised the profit tax rate to 45 percent for companies earning more than £N5,000, while providing tax exemption for firms earning less than £N3,000.

considered as a last resort, particularly in view of the probable high priority of other needs for public funds. In any case, the channeling of public capital to Nigerian private entrepreneurs is preferable to direct government investment in manufacturing. However, such a policy should not overlook the needs of the small entrepreneur for financial and technical assistance.

Education

Nigeria's educational system made modest progress during the 1960s. Primary and secondary school enrollment grew by about 2 percent and 1.5 percent annually, compared with an estimated 2.5 percent annual population growth. Technical and vocational school enrollment doubled and university enrollment tripled, both, however, from low base figures. Nigeria spent about 3.2 percent of GDP on education in 1970, a proportion that has remained almost constant since 1963 and is low compared with other African countries. This is not expected to increase during the present Plan period (1970-74). The states are primarily responsible for financing education, which accounted for an average 35 percent of their recurrent expenditures in 1970/71, but they receive federal government grants for part of their capital expenditures.

In 1970, the primary and secondary school enrollment ratios for the country as a whole were about 34 percent and 4 percent respectively, ranging from about 4 percent in some states to 70 percent in others at the primary level and 0.4 percent to 12 percent at the secondary level. The six northern states were at the lower end of both scales. Enrollment in technical and vocational schools was about 12,000 in 1968 (the latest year for which figures were available) and an estimated 16,000 students were enrolled in undergraduate courses at Nigeria's five universities in 1970/71.

The most recent statement of national educational policy is the government's Sessional Paper No. 3 of 1961 "Educational Development 1961-70" based on the Ashby Commission's Report "Investment in Education," published in 1960. The current Plan outlines proposals for capital investment during the period 1970-74 but does not purport to offer a coherent strategy for educational development. It is simply a statement of intent to restore facilities and equipment damaged or disrupted during the period of unrest and expand education at all levels to achieve higher enrollment ratios, improve quality, and educational equality between the states. Some £N139 million (13.5 percent) is allocated to education in the Plan's gross public sector capital investment program, £N49 million (8.8 percent) by the federal government and £N90 million (19.1 percent) by the states. About 45 percent is allocated to primary and secondary education, 9 percent each to technical education and teacher training, and 30 percent to university education; half of the federal government's planned expenditure is allocated to the universities and about 55 percent of the states' planned expenditure to primary and secondary education. The states' investment plans are very uneven, ranging from £N2.6 million in Kwara State to £N24.5 million in the Western State for the Plan period. While part of the disparity reflects population distribution between the states, it is not clear how these Plan allocations will help meet the objective of improving the balance of education opportunity within the country.

It is difficult to relate the Plan's objectives and financial targets to a comprehensive and specific program because of the inadequacies of educational and manpower planning, in particular the lack of data for such planning. Information on manpower development and utilization is meager and consequently it is virtually impossible, except for certain specialized categories, to match employment needs with educational outputs. More importantly, it is impossible at present to determine the relationship between projected economic growth and appropriate levels of future investment in education and, specifically, an optimum distribution of such investment within education. On the other hand, the short-term consequence of these difficulties is probably more apparent than real. In a country where, on the average in 1970, only 1 child in 3 of primary school age and only 1 in 25 of secondary school age was actually in school, even less in some states, the expansion of primary and secondary education is and should probably remain for some time primarily a function of social demand. This is not to say that the authorities must respond to any demand for education, however uninformed it may be. On the contrary, there is much that could be done, given appropriate information and sound planning, to improve and expand the existing educational system in a way that would better satisfy the aspirations of the population, contribute more directly to the country's developmental needs, and maximize presently planned investment in education.

Although the expansion of primary, and to a lesser extent, secondary education may properly proceed without direct reference to manpower requirements, all specialized and higher education and training should relate to some measure of anticipated needs. The importance of improving manpower data and educational planning at both federal and state levels, therefore, cannot be overstated. The federal government is currently involved in training educational planners in the states with Unesco assistance and it should seriously consider continuing and expanding its role in educational planning both nationally and in support of state governments. The federal government is also considering the establishment of a new national commission to study the educational system and recommend long-term national objectives. The mission supports this proposal with the reservation that the commission's work would be seriously impeded by the present inadequacy of educational and financial data.

Meanwhile, there are several priority areas where immediate qualitative improvement could be considered: industrial training, the reform of general secondary education curriculum and adult education. These issues, among others, are elaborated in the recent Unesco report.

Industrial Training. The contribution of the government trade schools to industrial training is small because of limited participation, if any, of employers in their programs and their inability to adjust quickly to changes in manpower demand. The state governments should therefore consider transferring the responsibility for trade training from Ministries of Education to autonomous state trade training boards under the aegis of Ministries of Labor, on which employers, the government and trade unions would be represented. Under this approach, industrial trade training would be directly linked to the specific needs of employers and employment opportunities for the students. The federal government proposes to establish an industrial training fund, which would probably be a suitable vehicle for financing the activities of the proposed trade training boards.

General Education. The Plan notes that, in expanding secondary education, both federal and state investment will concentrate on increasing facilities for the teaching of science and technical subjects. This emphasis is desirable because the existing secondary school curriculum is heavily biased toward academic subjects. Following the first three years of the course, which should be general in nature and common to all students, the last two years should be practical; science should be related to the local environment and the so-called academic studies should be adapted to emphasize the social, political and cultural development of the individual. Given the need for an external examination at the end of the course, its requirements should be broadened to include proof of practical skills. The overall objective would be to broaden the curriculum so as to improve the employment prospects of those students who do not proceed to higher education, improve their suitability for technical and on-the-job training, and better serve the country's manpower needs. In this connection, the structure and emphasis of teacher training would need to be changed.

Adult Education. The low productivity of Nigerian labor is probably attributable as much to the lower standard of education in early years as to the insufficient size of the present school system. Given the current weaknesses of Nigeria's administrative and executive capacity, government activity in rural extension services, administrative and management training is modest and could be improved.

While it is difficult to foresee what the level and composition of public capital investment on education should be after 1973/74, there is little doubt that Nigeria as a whole could make the necessary resources available to finance at least the present planned rate of annual expenditure of £N30 million to £N40 million, if this amount were needed and could well be used. On the other hand, the states which could best use resources to expand primary and secondary education may well be those with the least funds available. Federal grants for educational expenditures, both capital and recurrent, in those states will therefore probably have to be increased substantially if their educational objectives are to be achieved. In general, total capital expenditure will be affected largely by government decisions on university expansion, given its very high cost. These decisions can only be made on the basis of manpower studies yet to be undertaken.

Infrastructure

Transport and public utilities, the main public investment sectors, were in a critical position at the end of the civil war, owing to low investment, inadequate maintenance and war damage, particularly in the East Central, South Eastern and Rivers States. Since then, the private sector has recovered and there has been substantial, if not complete, restoration of overhead services. Before discussing policies and prospects for each sector, there are certain problems common to all, which are best dealt with in general terms.

First, there is the question of balance between major productive facilities and trunk connections, on the one hand, and distribution networks, on the other. The economy will probably respond more easily to the growth of the petroleum sector if the additional demand is widely distributed throughout the country. One approach would be to improve the supply of public and social services outside the main urban centers. This is not simply a welfare argument for public services. In some areas, the capacity of existing main roads and available electricity supply exceeds current demand, and their contribution to the economy could be increased if additional demand were created. Extending the distribution networks through, for example, rural electrification and feeder roads would be one way of achieving this.

Second there is the problem of centralized planning and operation in these sectors. Some statutory corporations need to decentralize by increasing the responsibility of operational units, for example in ports and railways, or transforming local operations into separate entities, for example in electricity distribution. On the other hand, in sectors which are state or federal/state concurrent responsibilities, strengthened planning capacity at the center seems to be necessary. This is most obvious in education and transport, and possibly water supply.

A third problem is the financing of infrastructure investment. Most new facilities are required in sectors presently the responsibility of state or local authorities, whose resources, compared with those of the federal government, are limited. Thus, apart from possible new conditions accompanying the statutory transfer of revenues from the federal government to the states, it may prove necessary in several sectors to provide that such transfers are associated with guidance, control and, if necessary, initiative in the preparation and implementation of investment programs. In principle, arrangements already exist, albeit on a small scale, for federal financing of certain state education and agricultural projects.

A fourth problem is management, training and technical know-how in these sectors. Even allowing for postwar difficulties, the performance of several public corporations has not satisfied the expectations of the federal government or public opinion and this situation has generated an atmosphere of crisis. This problem could be approached in several ways. The first would be to improve management methods within the corporations and especially to strengthen control. Top management can more easily delegate day-to-day decisions to middle management if these are made within the framework of a detailed budget and a system of frequent reporting. The second would be to upgrade middle management, especially those working away from the center. Although training is provided by the public corporations, its scope may be insufficient for the demands that will be placed on them in the future. Some training facilities are available abroad but these can provide at best only marginal assistance. The size of the problem in Nigeria would probably justify the public corporations' arranging with one of the universities for regular short courses for their professional and technical officers. With appropriate teaching staff, course material and facilities, such an institution could have substantial impact.

However, the management problems of the public corporations will not be solved quickly and, in some instances, the employment of expatriate advisory and operational personnel will continue to be necessary for some time. Moreover, given the prospective demand for skilled and professionally qualified people for the economy as a whole, the absolute number of expatriates in the country may well increase temporarily, although Nigerians should be able to secure an increasing share of these posts. In these circumstances, a forward policy of Nigerianization in the public sector, particularly in the public corporations, might risk starving the private sector of newly qualified Nigerians — a result which would be inconsistent with present policy and the long-run interests of the economy.

Transport

Nigeria's transport sector was severely affected by the internal unrest. These repercussions on transport were felt throughout the country and particularly severe damage was caused to roads and bridges not only in the East but elsewhere. Between 1965 and 1970, road transport rose by about 30 percent, rail transport declined by about 18 percent and water transport fell to a tenth of its prewar value. The modal allocation of freight transport in 1970 was estimated to be 77 percent by road, 22 percent by rail and 1 percent by water.

Roads. Serious attention was first given to road construction in Nigeria after 1918. By 1951, a total road network of over 27,000 miles had been constructed, of which 1,114 miles were paved. However, the paved roads lacked proper drainage and were poorly constructed and, as traffic volumes and axle-loads increased, they proved to be inadequate. Since 1951, when the need for better planning and improved construction was recognized, the network has developed rapidly in both total length and quality. By 1970, it amounted to about 55,000 miles, of which about 10,000 miles were paved. In general, the Federal Ministry of Works and Housing is responsible for the provision and maintenance of the main road network, and the 12 state governments and local authorities are responsible for all other roads. The quality of road maintenance and administration varies from state to state. Highway standards have deteriorated generally in recent years because of inadequate maintenance and the illegal use of large trucks.

Reliable vehicle statistics are not available, but it is estimated that in 1969 the number of vehicles in Nigeria was between 67,000 and 79,000 automobiles (including taxis), 28,000 to 30,000 trucks and buses, and 31,000 to 38,000 motorcycles. The geographical distribution of traffic is uneven with most vehicles concentrated in the South, particularly in and around Lagos, although many Lagos registered vehicles probably spend much of their traveling time outside the state. Nigeria has a vigorous road transport industry for both goods and passengers. Government controls are minimal, and there is currently free entry into the industry. A 1967 consultants' study suggested that, with the important exception of heavy trucks, Nigerian road users made an adequate contribution to highway costs.

Railways. The Nigerian Railway Corporation (NRC) was created in 1955 to manage and operate the railway system and to direct and control its expansion. As a statutory public corporation, it was expected to function commercially, although the government retained general powers of control over policies and rates.

NRC's route system includes 2,178 route miles of single lane track, all of 3'6" gauge. In 1971, its equipment included 89 diesel and 214 steam locomotives and 6,217 freight wagons, of which 35 percent had been in service for over 35 years. NRC is gradually replacing its steam locomotives with diesels. Although its wagon fleet increased markedly over the last decade in both number and capacity, this was not matched by increases in either passengers or goods carried.

The railways reached a peak of efficiency and profitability in 1963/64, when they carried almost 3 million tons of freight, and earned a net profit of £N34,000 from revenues of £N16.3 million. In 1964/65, however, tonnage carried declined by 5 percent, ton-miles by 13 percent, and operating revenues by 15 percent and NRC registered a loss of £N1.36 million before fixed charges and £N3.44 million after such charges. Between 1963/64 and 1964/65 average wagon turnaround time increased from 12.2 to 14.7 days, and net ton-miles per man employed fell from 50,747 to 41,400. In 1965 a Bank mission reported serious deficiencies in the railways and made detailed recommendations covering NRC's technical operations, management, staffing and investment. The government attributes the decline of the railways to defects in management, equipment and rate policies, and to competition from road transport.

The railways were hard hit by the civil unrest. The NRC lost about 6,000 employees of various skills and the eastern branch of the network was closed down. About one-third of NRC's rolling stock was tied up in the war zones and, consequently, deteriorated.

NRC operates under conditions of heavy traffic demand, long haul, easy terrain and spare track capacity which, given reasonable efficiency, should result in economic and profitable operation. But NRC is operating inefficiently, and is consistently in deficit. These deficits are growing and traffic demands are not being met. The government is anxious to get the railways running efficiently, so that they may meet their economic share of total transport demand and also cease being a burden on public funds. In order to achieve this, the government invited the Canadian National Railways to send a team of consultants to examine all aspects of the NRC's operations.

Inland Waterways. The Benue River is navigable for four months of the year to Yola (890 miles from the sea) and for two months to Garoua in the Cameroon Republic. The Niger River is generally navigable eight months of the year to Jebba, some 560 miles from the sea. The extended navigation season expected from the Kainji dam construction has not yet materialized and the Niger and Benue play only minor roles in the transport of goods and passengers. In the early 1960s, about 325,000 tons were moved annually from Garoua by commercially operated river fleets, but this traffic was interrupted and has not resumed. The potential for river transport in Nigeria is not at present clear. The government has asked its Transport Planning Unit to examine the merits of further investment in river transport.

Shipping. The Nigerian National Shipping Line (NNSL) was established in 1958 and became fully government owned in 1961. In 1971 it operated 12 ships with a total deadweight tonnage of 120,000 tons. Additional vessels are chartered when needed. NNSL has hitherto operated at a financial loss and its continued existence is dependent on government subventions. It is not known whether NNSL's foreign exchange earnings cover its economic costs. In the opinion of the government, NNSL's problems have been compounded by defective management and rapid turnover of personnel. To overcome these problems, an expatriate general manager has been appointed and an internal reorganization has taken place. The new management attempted to draw up an operational plan for 1971-72 which had some program budgeting basis in that it set output (tonnage carried) and net revenue targets based on physical capacity – after repairs and servicing – market prospects, etc.

Ports. The Nigerian Ports Authority (NPA) is an autonomous corporation charged with the operation and administration of the country's ports. The Authority directly controls the ports of Lagos, Port Harcourt, Calabar, Warri and Koko. In all, it operates 17 berths (including one that can be used for containers) in the port of Lagos, 8 in Port Harcourt and 3 in Calabar, 1 in Warri and 1 at Koko, as well as a large number of anchorages for vessels in all ports. In addition, the Authority undertakes pilotage and conservancy services and is responsible for dredging to maintain an adequate depth of water in the ports and their approaches.

The two main ports of Lagos and Port Harcourt are equipped with modern facilities including transit sheds and warehouses, modern cargo handling equipment consisting of fork lifts, mobile cranes of from 3 to 25 tons capacity, tractors, trailers, gantry cranes and floating cranes of 100 tons capacity. Lagos and Port Harcourt together handled about 70 percent of the country's imports and exports. The average tons-per-hour for imports was about 12, and for exports about 18, which compares favorably with standards in most modern ports.

Air. Scheduled services are provided to twelve airports, two of which (Lagos and Kano) are used for international flights. There are also 78 government and privately-owned landing strips. The main responsibility of the Aviation Department of the Federal Ministry of Transport is to provide safe and adequate facilities, including ground services, air traffic control, aeronautical communications and meteorological services, in addition to the general administration and regulation of air transport. Domestic air services are provided by Nigeria Airways, a government-owned corporation, and international services by Nigeria Airways and foreign airlines. Nigeria Airways' present fleet includes five F-27 Friendships, one F-28 leased from Fokker, one Boeing 707 leased from Ethiopian Airlines and one Piper Aztec, used as an air taxi. Audited accounts have not been published since 1966 but, following deficits in the 1960s there was a surplus of some £N0.51 million estimated for 1969/70. Air freight is still negligible.

Although most war damage has apparently been repaired, all twelve main airports require major improvements because, except for the runway extension at Lagos and repairs at Enugu, no major airport development has been undertaken in the past five years. The runways at Lagos and Kano airports are below international standards, and the Lagos terminal buildings are inadequate. The government considers that there is an urgent need for investment to improve the existing airport facilities.

Transport Administration

The Federal Ministry of Transport is chiefly responsible for developing and implementing transport policy. It is concerned with all transport modes except roads, which are the responsibility of the Federal Ministry of Works and Housing. The Federal Ministry of Transport is responsible for transport planning and coordination and exercises its powers by influencing budgetary allocations to the different transport modes (except road transport) and by making appropriate regulations. The Ministry of Economic Development, which has a transportation division, is responsible for coordinating transport with other sectors of the economy, and the Ministry of Finance is responsible for budgetary allocations.

Nigeria's twelve states also have ministries concerned with road maintenance (including the maintenance of federal highways on an agency basis) and with the construction of some secondary roads. There is no formal body to coordinate state/federal planning and the relationships between federal and state highway administrations are not clear. With the exception of roads and private transport, the provision of transport services is entrusted to statutory corporations such as the Nigeria Railways Corporation, Nigeria Airways and the Nigerian Ports Authority. The government is concerned that these bodies are inefficient, under-capitalized and not responsive to the changing needs of the growing Nigerian economy.

Transport coordination should be improved and the Ministry of Transport given the necessary power over all modes. A major coordination problem is the carriage of bulk export produce from the agricultural North to the southern ports. An increasing proportion of this traffic is carried by trucks too heavy for the roads and some could be carried at lower economic cost by an efficient railway system. The reasons for the diversion of long distance bulk produce from rail to road include: poor service offered by the railways and inflexibility in their tariff structure; laxity in enforcing road vehicle weight regulations; and insufficient road-user taxes on heavy vehicles, which do not pay for the full costs of the damage they inflict on the roads.

Transport Policy

Public policy in Nigeria has three main objectives, to: repair war damage and restore broken communications, particularly in the Rivers and East Central States; strengthen social and economic links between the country's diverse regions; stimulate economic growth and social development, particularly in rural areas.

To achieve these objectives the government is engaged in a program of rehabilitating damaged roads, railways and ports, and is planning to strengthen the primary road network.

The official basis of transport policy is still the "Statement of Policy on Transport" of 1965, which advocated the allocation of traffic between different modes on the basis of relative costs. However, it did not spell out the policies and regulations that should be introduced to improve traffic allocation. The government is concerned about "unhealthy competition" between road and rail and proposes to: regulate the maximum axle-loads permissible on the highways by prohibiting the importation of unsuitable vehicles; insure that road hauliers pay "a more equitable share" of the cost of providing road facilities; and see that the marketing boards employ the most rational mode of transportation in moving their commodities. The government is also concerned about the powers of the federal and state governments to plan and finance road construction and improvement. The consultants, KAMPSAX, have proposed the creation of a strong federal highway organization, responsible for both primary and secondary roads. The government has decided to establish a highway authority, but its functions and relationships with federal and state bodies have not yet been announced.

Special attention should be paid to improving coordination between different transport modes and infusing better management into the statutory corporations responsible for railways, ports, airways, and water transport. The government is strengthening the Ministry of Transport to prepare it for a more active role in policy formation and program planning. To this end, a new transport planning unit has been established in the Federal Ministry of Transport. The unit has done useful work but has only just started to concern itself with road planning in cooperation with the Federal Ministry of Works and Housing.

The need to improve the management of the statutory corporations concerned with transport is closely connected with the question of general policy. The government cannot evaluate the efficiency of the statutory bodies without first setting out performance targets and achievement yardsticks. It also has to establish a proper balance between commercialism and state control and to decide which activities should, and which need not, be operated at a financial profit. The government is aware of the need to tackle these questions and to take the necessary measures to insure that the affairs of the statutory bodies are entrusted to the best men available. In the cases of the Nigeria Airways and the Nigerian National Shipping Line, the government is considering hiring management expertise from outside as a temporary measure, pending the training of Nigerian managers.

Electricity ✓

Three separate entities own and operate facilities for production, transmission and distribution of electric energy in Nigeria: The Electricity Corporation of Nigeria (ECN), the Niger Dams Authority (NDA) and the Nigerian Electricity Supply Corporation Limited (NESCO), a private company, which supplies the mining industry on the Jos Plateau. Following the recommendations of consultants, the federal government has decided to merge ECN and NDA to form a single new corporation.

The three utilities operate an installed capacity aggregating 790 MW, 350 MW of hydro capacity, and 440 MW of thermal capacity. Whereas the hydro capacity is in good condition, the thermal capacity has seriously suffered from lack of maintenance and poor operation during the late 1960s.

Before hostilities the electric power industry was expanded at a very high rate. From 1950 to 1967 the compound rate of growth of consumption was 19 percent per annum. Despite this very high rate of growth, power consumption per capita is, and will remain for a long time, very low: 20 KwH/capita in 1970 increasing to an estimated 70 KwH/capita in 1980.

To meet the fast growing demand for power, considerable investment will be needed. The Plan allocates about £N45 million over the four years 1970/71 through 1973/74, but it now appears likely that actual capital expenditure in this sector will not exceed £N32 million during this period. After 1973/74, annual capital expenditure should be about £N20 million, increasing at between five and ten percent per year. A more rapid increase would be difficult to achieve because of limited executive capacity in this sector. In the longer term, toward 1980, a choice will have to be made between another relatively capital-intensive hydroelectric development at Jebba, and the installation of more thermal generating capacity. The decision will depend on the availability, cost and price of fossil fuels.

The government is preparing terms of reference for a survey that would include an inventory of energy resources and recommendations for the most advantageous use of the natural gas available.

The federal government recently authorized state governments to set up their own electricity companies, thus ending ECN's monopoly. This development reflects impatience in some states to have rural electrification programs, which ECN has been unable to carry out, and dissatisfaction with standards of electricity supply throughout the country. The Western State government is considering a project with bilateral assistance for small towns and villages in the state.

The federal government commissioned a study of rural electrification in 1970. This study considered the extension of the present transmission system to 137 small towns and villages not presently supplied. It is hoped that the provision of electricity in rural areas will encourage industrial and commercial development at the local level, assist in promoting economic growth, and reduce migration from rural to urban areas. The report proposed a phased program costing about £N28 million to be carried out over an eight-year period. In view of the overall financial resources available and the size of the electricity program as a whole, this is not an over-ambitious objective. The new national electricity corporation, together with any new institutions set up by state governments, should attach high priority to a program of this kind.

Water Supply and Sewerage ✓

The construction and operation of public water supply systems is a state responsibility in Nigeria. In most states there is a Water Supply Division within the Ministry of Works but, over the past few years there has been a trend toward the establishment of semi-autonomous water corporations or boards. The first water corporation was set up in the Western State in 1964 but did not become operational until 1968. The intention was that it should be commercially oriented, self-financing and free from government control in its day-to-day affairs. In practice, salaries and employment conditions are controlled by the Statutory Corporations Services Commission and water charges must be approved by the Executive Council. While commercial accounting methods are used, water charges are too low and their collection too inefficient for the organization to be financially self-sufficient. In fact, a government subsidy provides 60 percent of the operating income as well as financing capital charges. Water boards have recently been set up in the Mid-Western and North Central States, though not yet fully separated from the works ministries, and formation of such organizations has been considered in most other states.

The municipal councils and other local authorities seem to have the legal responsibility for operating public sewerage systems. However, very little has been constructed to date. These bodies are organizationally and financially weak and are thus unlikely to commit themselves to expensive sewerage projects.

Current Status of Water Supply. Data on water supply for Nigeria as a whole are scanty. About 200 cities and towns have public water supplies of which about 150 are in the South. Only an estimated 23 percent of the population have access to piped water, varying from 30 to 50 percent in the South to as little as 5 percent in some northern states.

Per capita consumption of water for some major cities varies from 2 to 44 gallons per day. Except in a few large cities, the majority of those with access to public water supplies are served by public standpipes or selling stations. Only about 10 percent of those with access to piped water are served by house connections. Before hostilities most systems gave 24-hour service, but the lack of new investment and war damage in some states has reduced the standard of service and even in parts of Lagos and Ibadan service is intermittent. Metering of commercial and industrial services is usual, but domestic metering is common only in the North.

Inadequate maintenance of facilities is a serious problem throughout the country. To some extent, this is attributable to the lack of spare parts and disruption during 1966-70, but the fact that the life of assets can be greatly prolonged by simple routine maintenance procedures is not fully appreciated. In many water works, most meters and recorders have ceased to function. Except in Ibadan, there was little construction in the five years prior to 1970, while in the Eastern states, much destruction and looting of water supply facilities took place. These factors, coupled with general neglect of maintenance, have caused demand to outstrip supply in most cities, Kano and Kaduna being notable exceptions. However, construction has now resumed in most states.

Financial Policies and Constraints. Little attention has been paid to the financial aspects of water supply. Many states realizing the budgetary implications of subsidies plan to put water supply on a more self-supporting basis, however. In most states revenues do not cover operations and maintenance costs. Pricing policies in some states involve serious inequities as the amounts paid are based neither on the amount of water consumed nor on ability to pay, as measured by income or property valuation. All states need to review their pricing policies and the level of charges. Those states which have formed corporations or boards will need to take steps to make these bodies financially self-supporting. In the war-damaged eastern states the lack of finance for rehabilitation is the most serious constraint. At least twenty water systems have yet to be restored and, except for some external assistance, the budgeted funds for this work have not been released. Elsewhere in the country the availability of finance is less critical than the shortage of manpower and of adequately prepared projects.

Several states are discussing or planning the formation of water corporations. However, this may not be the most appropriate organization for every state and the advantages and disadvantages need to be carefully weighed. Foreign assistance, particularly in management, could be valuable in setting up such bodies and in strengthening the existing water boards. There is a general feeling that some kind of coordinating body for water supply at the federal level is needed. State officials see this as a body which would draw the attention of foreign lenders to their projects and would channel financial assistance to the states. Federal officials generally would like to give this body executive authority to set priorities, direct state planning in water supply and determine the feasibility of projects. They visualize that this body might also handle technical matters such as standards. As such a body would have to be acceptable to both the federal and state governments, there is clearly a need for continuing discussion.

An alternative approach might be the creation of a lending agency, along the lines of a development bank, which would have staff qualified to appraise and evaluate the technical, financial and managerial aspects of projects submitted to it by the states. Such an agency could also examine the overall water supply and sewerage program of a state and assist in developing criteria for assigning priorities to individual projects within the program. It could also be the agency through which federal and external funds could be channeled for water and sewerage construction. ✓

Sewerage. No city is presently served by a sanitary sewer system. The federal government has built some small systems to serve its own establishments and a housing estate in Lagos, and some commercial and industrial firms have small private systems. The larger cities have night soil collection services, while the more affluent urban dwellers use septic tanks. Sewer systems are planned in a few cities. For example, a UNDP/WHO project for sewerage, drainage and refuse disposal in Ibadan is entering the final design phase and foreign assistance is being sought to execute the project. In Lagos, preliminary planning has been done for a very large project and it is proposed to construct the first stage of this under the current Development Plan.

The absence of a sewerage system is adding to the severe public problems of Nigeria. The incidence of waterborne diseases is high, often because of the use of polluted stream water. Construction of sanitary sewer systems with adequate sewage treatment facilities would do much to alleviate these problems. Development, however, is constrained by the low priority given to this service in most states.

Postal and Telecommunications ✓

The postal and internal telecommunications services of Nigeria are run by a federal government department, while international telecommunications are provided by Nigerian External Telecommunications, Ltd., which is owned by the government and a private company. The usual postal services are provided throughout the country. The service is not particularly efficient but its weaknesses can be largely attributed to the shortcomings of the transportation system, which have already been discussed, and to the problem of managing a large labor force in Nigeria. Postal services are subsidized through the federal government budget.

The inadequacies of the domestic telephone and cable services constitute a serious problem affecting the efficiency of public administration and of the economy as a whole. The demand for telecommunication services has far exceeded present capacity, and current expansion plans have been found to be insufficient to meet this demand. Implementation of the current Ten-Year Plan (1968-78) was delayed by internal strife and, furthermore, the new twelve-state political structure is creating a different pattern of demand for telecommunication services than that on which the current plans are based. In 1969 there was about one telephone per one thousand population, and apart from rehabilitation of some of the services in the war-affected areas, this ratio has probably not improved much since. However, the rapid recovery of economic activity in general has led to a sharp rise in the number of telephone calls made per connection, and the exchanges have become seriously overloaded, especially in the Lagos area.

Investments in telecommunications have been based on a survey conducted by a foreign manufacturing company in 1963. The government adopted a program which provided for the construction of a heavy micro-wave route from Lagos to the eastern parts of the country, for modern high-capacity cross-bar exchanges at Lagos, Enugu and Port Harcourt and for heavy, medium and light radio routes to interlink twenty-three of the main towns. Twenty-four new automatic exchanges were to be installed; countrywide subscriber trunk dialing was to be introduced. The last step of this program was to extend telephone services to a large number of rural locations. The development program also provides for a telex network and for an underground coaxial cable from Lagos to Kaduna to duplicate the radio telephone route which has already been installed.

The heavy radio route to the East of the country was completed in 1966 and is now being rehabilitated following war damage. The installation of cross-bar exchanges has been completed in Lagos, but they are not yet fully operational, whereas the radio routes to the northern states are expected to be completed in 1972. The last project accounts for the bulk of present capital expenditures in the sector which amounted to £N8.8 million in 1970/71.

The availability of both local and long-distance telecommunications facilities throughout the country is much below the demand for such facilities. The main bottleneck in the system is the inadequate capacity of the exchanges in the Lagos area, and a team of engineers has already been invited to review the situation within the city. Furthermore, a new plan for the development of telecommunications over the next five years is to be prepared to meet all the demands which will be placed on the system, and government has requested UNDP to finance the necessary studies which are to be carried out as a matter of urgency with ITU assistance.

The government has decided that the postal and telecommunications services should be managed by a public corporation, and this decision is to be implemented during the 1970-74 Plan period. The creation of such a corporation would be desirable in that it would facilitate the commercial operation of telecommunications services. It is possible that the organization and procedures of the future P&T Corporation should be studied in the context of the preparation of the long-term development plan so that when the new corporation is set up it may be technically and financially prepared to implement the very substantial development program which will emerge from these studies.

CHAPTER 8
OPTIONS AND IMPLICATIONS FOR LONG-TERM DEVELOPMENT

The Setting

The economic development of Nigeria during the last 20 years conforms in some respects to generally observed characteristics elsewhere, but deviates in others. The purpose of this chapter is to suggest a possible course of long-term development which appears feasible in terms of existing capabilities and constraints and which falls within the range of observed developments elsewhere under similar circumstances.

Nigeria shares with many other developing countries the common characteristics of low savings and investment rates, with a clear concentration of those efforts in the public sector. The dynamics of economic growth are often provided first by agricultural exports, gradually strengthened further by the expansion of domestic construction activity in infrastructure and the establishment of an industrial base concentrated on the manufacture of import substitutes. If industries are permitted to be established outside the public sector, private investment activity accelerates in this second stage of development. Simultaneously, imports of investment goods and of materials begin to rise faster than exports, the latter remaining rather undiversified and consisting largely of primary agricultural products. Consequent reductions in foreign exchange reserves and persistently rising balance of payments deficits may lead to import controls and higher tariffs, which provide additional incentives to import substitution. At this stage, balance of payments considerations become of overriding importance in development policy. Nigeria's growth through the late 1960s conformed to this pattern and it indeed began to experience serious foreign exchange problems which were subsequently accentuated by the civil disturbances.

The expansion of private investment and production combined with a growing demand for social services and an increasing need to finance the operating and maintenance costs of economic and social infrastructure tend to put strong pressures on government expenditure. The requirements of national administration after independence add to these pressures which are then less easily resisted. From a narrow and unbalanced tax base, it is difficult to raise the revenues to meet those demands, leading to erosion of the budgetary position. The difficulties of generating adequate resources are compounded by a lack of institutions capable of preparing and implementing public sector development programs and by insufficient skilled and experienced staff to build these institutions. In these respects, Nigeria like other developing countries has experienced problems both in terms of financial and of institutional resources.

New economic activities tend to concentrate in urban centers which appear to promise high incomes, although at high risk, for a poor rural population. Urban migration which is significant in Nigeria provides an added dimension to the problems of economic and social development.

Nigeria's exceptional circumstance is the rapid growth of its oil producing sector which, combined with price increases resulting from the recent oil agreements, has removed simultaneously balance of payments constraints and the problem of resource mobilization in the public sector. However, these developments do not remove the institutional weaknesses of the public sector nor the persistent pressure to increase current expenditure with little or no priority in terms of development objectives. Nigeria's medium-term development problems therefore relate mainly to the efficient allocation and use of the considerable resources that are now becoming available. The search for appropriate and efficient uses of the expected resources need not be limited to the public sector but could also include the private sector as well. This could include support for the government's indigenization policies through channeling some of its resources into participation in foreign-owned ventures.

The economy over the next decade and a half is likely to sustain a rate of growth considerably above that experienced during the 15 years before the outbreak of hostilities. In contrast to historical experience, the future growth of the economy will most certainly involve a substantial transformation of its structure. A favorable shift in the external terms of trade is also expected to account for a substantial increase in real income.

To gain some insight into the pattern and implications of these expected developments, a simulation model was used.

In Chapter 9 the structure of the model is described, followed by a presentation of the major sources of data used in the model. Variables are then defined and a complete set of equations is presented. Tables there summarize the macroeconomic projections.

The objective of the model was to stimulate a growth pattern of the economy over the 15 years with given allocations of the government's resources consistent with given developments in the agriculture and petroleum sectors. A priori, it is expected that the impact of these developments on the rest of the economy will be largely indirect, and differ considerably among different productive sectors and income groups. A highly disaggregated approach is therefore necessary and the model's specifications are fairly complex. The structure of the model, however, may be summarized as follows:

Developments in the agriculture and petroleum sectors are specified outside the model. Agricultural output projections made by a recent IBRD agricultural sector mission are relied upon as exogenous inputs to the model. However, some adjustments have been made to the projected output of some food crops (e.g., yams, cassava), the production of which is assumed to be determined primarily by demand conditions.

The growth of crude oil production and the resulting import requirements and income generated are also specified separately. Development in this sector is not likely to be affected by the rest of the economy, so that an independent projection seems to be reasonable.

Thus, these pre-specified developments in the agriculture and petroleum sectors represent the basic dynamic forces in the model. The overall growth of the economy is then assumed to be generated by the response of the remaining sectors to the increased income and consequent expansion of consumer and intermediate demand generated by these two sectors, and by the income and inter-industry multiplier effects arising from the interactions of the sectors with each other and with the household and public sectors. Specifically, the growth of manufacturing output is assumed to be determined by the expansion of consumer and intermediate demands for manufactures, including opportunities for import substitution. Output of public utilities and transport services is assumed to depend mainly on pre-specified public sector investment expenditure in these sectors and also on private investment efforts, which are functions of the overall growth rate of the economy. Finally, the growth of construction and other service sectors is determined by increases in investment expenditure and private and public consumption expenditure. In most sectors, the linkages between increased demand and increased production are indirect, increased demands stimulating investment expenditure which, in turn, generates increased output after a certain lag in time.

Exports, limited primarily to agricultural products and crude oil, are also pre-specified in the model. Imports are defined separately for a number of categories (by end-use) as the differences between domestic demand and production. This is based on the assumption that the unprecedented rise in consumer and investment demands expected over the next 15 years will not be matched immediately by increases in domestic production. In the manufacturing sector, however, import substitution is assumed to be generated whenever demands increase faster than production, and whenever domestic production is below a pre-specified proportion of domestic demand. The only exception is the machinery and equipment subsector in which import substitution is not considered to be feasible during the projection period. Time lags are introduced between demand and investment expenditure, and between investment expenditure and actual production.

Each type of government revenue is defined as a function of the source of revenues, i.e., petroleum profit taxes and royalties to crude oil production, import duties to imports by the non-oil sectors, export duties to agricultural exports, excise duties to manufacturing production, corporation income tax to value-added in the modern sectors and miscellaneous federal revenues as well as the states' own revenues to GNP. Except for revenues from petroleum which are computed independently, fixed coefficients are used, assuming constant tax rates. Government recurrent expenditure is pre-specified, the alternative assumptions reflecting possible uses of public resources as outlined earlier in this chapter.

Private income is defined as GNP (including the wages and salaries components of government recurrent expenditure) less government revenues plus subsidies and transfers from the public sector. Private consumer demand for different categories of goods is then related to private income through constant income elasticities, while demands for services are defined as the residual of total private consumption less expenditure on goods. On the assumption that agricultural income represents rural income, consumer demands are specified separately for the rural and urban sectors.

Intermediate demands are related to production activities by input-output coefficients taken from earlier studies.

Investment expenditure in the petroleum sector is specified exogenously, with the present projection limited only to investment in crude oil production. While investment in associated petroleum products (e.g., liquefied natural gas) may be possible during the projection period, estimates of the likely timing and magnitude are not feasible and the impact of these ventures on the economy is likely to be very small until the mid-80s (Chapter 6). Private investment expenditure outside the oil sector is assumed to be a function of demand growth, including import substitution possibilities. Public investment expenditure is specified and reflects the mission's assessment of the public sector's executive capacity.

All variables are defined in constant base-year prices and in current prices, except financial variables which are defined only in nominal terms. Price indices are pre-specified for agricultural products, other goods, services (wages) and imports as well as for all export products. Except for the export products, prices of domestic goods and services are presumed to follow the trend of exogenously-determined import prices after initial allowances are made for adjustments to peace-time conditions (e.g., wage increases as a result of the Adebo Award) and the recent change in the U.S. dollar exchange rate. In terms of foreign currency, this assumption is equivalent to the situation in which domestic prices move differently from international prices, but a constant purchasing power parity is maintained through changes in the exchange rate.

The model is initially formulated as a two gap model, with independent specifications of investment, saving, export and import functions. It is then found that the balance of payments surpluses (deficits) are consistently smaller (larger) than the excesses (shortages) of savings over investment. As surpluses are more evident over the projection period, it seems unlikely that imports would be restricted in order to generate surpluses as large as that indicated by the *ex-ante* saving surpluses. Therefore, it is assumed that actual savings would be equal to projected investment less the resource balance obtained from the current account projection. The implication is that *ex-ante* national savings in excess of domestic investment which are not linked to foreign capital (such as in most of the petroleum and manufacturing sectors) and for which foreign exchange is not available for investment abroad, would be diverted to consumption expenditure.

The Prospects

Expected developments in the two major sectors — agriculture and petroleum — serve as the main inputs of this analytical exercise. The overall growth of the economy is then assumed to be determined by the direct response of the remaining sectors to the increased income and expansion of demand generated by growth in these two sectors and by the income and inter-industry multiplier effects arising from the interactions of all the sectors. Some of the specific assumptions about the growth of agriculture and petroleum, the investment capacity of the public sector and, more generally, the outlook for the remainder of the current Plan period have all been dealt with in previous chapters. Other assumptions relating to the growth, balance of payments and budgetary prospects follow.

Initial crude projections indicate that savings will not be a constraint to growth. In fact, during most of the period for which projections are attempted, the savings potential of the economy will probably be larger than its capacity, in both the public and private sectors, to invest with adequate rates of return. This will be reflected in the balance of payments as current account surpluses may not be as substantial as domestic resources over investment. In other words, if estimates are made independently of savings and investment on the one hand, and of imports and exports on the other, the latter show smaller excess resources than the former.

As a possible pattern — and in line with the realities of most developing countries — one could begin from an assumed capacity to save under a particular set of policy conditions which relate to savings behavior. Such an assumption in Nigeria would imply that the resource balance in the economy is determined as the difference between the capacity to save and the (smaller) capacity to invest efficiently. This resource balance would then, combined with projected export receipts, determine directly the permissible import level. On any, even modest, assumptions about marginal savings rates, such projections inevitably lead to the untenable conclusion that an import policy should be excessively restrictive. Under the projected conditions of buoyant foreign exchange earnings, it is unlikely that the government would be willing or able to restrict imports solely for the purpose of increasing national savings which add to foreign exchange reserves, over and above such accumulations as are already projected without any policy to stimulate savings.

In the projections, the assumption is made that the balance of payments determines the distribution of domestic resources between consumption and savings. Consequently, no specific savings behavior for the economy is assumed; savings will simply meet whatever is the requirement for savings, defined as the difference between projected levels of investment and the resource balance obtained from the balance of payments. Consumption is assumed to absorb whatever part of disposable income does not need to be saved.

Fiscal Prospects and Options

The key assumption of the growth projections described in the following paragraphs is the growth rate of current public expenditures. As a first approximation – to be replaced by an alternative assumption at a later stage – some link with past trends can be established.

From 1961-66, public sector current expenditures (federal and regional together) increased on the average by 10.7 percent per year. Defense and security expenditure increased somewhat faster than the average; civilian current expenditure increased therefore at the slightly slower rate of 10.3 percent per year. During 1966/67-1971/72 the growth of civilian current expenditure was considerably more rapid at 16 percent per year, reflecting both a rapid increase in debt service charges and the more pronounced inflation during the period.

The first alternative, therefore, is based on the modest assumption that public current expenditure (at current prices), excluding defense and security, will grow by 12 percent per annum from 1971/72 through 1978/79 and by 10.4 percent per annum thereafter. In the earlier years, this provides for some of the wage and salary increases now being implemented, as a net addition to the historical rate of increase would again become equal to the prewar rate. Defense expenditures, which in 1971/72 accounted for 36 percent of total public sector current expenditure and about 7 percent of GNP, are projected independently. It is assumed at this stage that their volume (i.e., their amount in base year prices) will be maintained so that expenditure increases only reflect increases in prices. This assumption would reduce the defense component to 24 percent of total current expenditure by 1978/79, and to around 5.5 percent of GNP.

The present relationships between government revenues and the sources of revenues are assumed to remain constant during the projection period, except for petroleum revenues which are projected to rise by an average rate of 20 percent per annum from 1971/72 to 1975/76 (as discussed in Chapter 6) and by 7 percent per annum thereafter. The expansion of the oil-producing sector will then provide the major impetus to economic growth through increased revenues and income. The growing purchasing power of the economy will in turn lead to an expansion of investment and output in other sectors of the economy through increased private demand for goods and services.

In the aggregate, a projected rate of growth of GNP at an average of 7.8 percent per annum is found to be consistent with the presumed pattern of growth in the agriculture and oil sectors and in the government's budget. This rate of growth would be sufficient to increase per capita income from its present level of around £N39 to about £N70 (in constant 1970 prices) by 1983/84, i.e., a doubling of the average per capita income in about 14 years. The balance of payments would indicate throughout most of the period a possible accumulation of reserves; only small reductions would begin to appear in the mid-80s. Tax revenue shows a fairly high elasticity to GNP growth in the years through 1978/79 – about 1.20 as measured in current prices – largely because of the income from oil operations, but, in the following years, the growth of revenues becomes about equal to the growth of GNP, with a constant share of around 27 percent. This compares with an actual share in GNP of only 18 percent in 1970/71, which was already considerably above the level of the 1960s.

Under these circumstances and with projected investment expenditures as discussed in Chapter 3, the government would generate large and increasing surpluses (Table 8-1), both on current account and after investment expenditures are accounted for. These surpluses would be generated exclusively at the federal level, assuming for the moment that no changes were made in the existing revenue sharing system between the federal and state governments.

Table 8-1: GOVERNMENT ACCOUNTS PROJECTION ("Low" Expenditure Alternative)

(In Millions of Current £N)

	1971/72	1973/74	1978/79	1983/84	Annual Average Rate of Growth (%) 1971/72-1978/79	1978/79-1983/84
Current revenues	696	945	1,645	2,595	12.9	9.6
Current expenditures	525	665	1,005	1,520	9.3	8.6
Current surplus	161	280	630	1,075	21.1	11.3
Investment expenditures	164	255	460	735	16.2	9.9
Overall budget surplus	-3	25	170	340	–	–
ibid, % of GDP	–	0.7	3.7	5.3		

The prospect of very substantial surpluses – amounting to some 4 percent of GNP in the decade following the current Plan period – opens up a number of options for the government to further increase its role in the economy. Three such options might be: increased current expenditure for maintenance and operation of economic and social infrastructure; tax reductions and other incentives to private industry; and the reduction of the share of foreign capital in the private sector.

Future Expenditure on Economic and Social Services. In past years, the largest shortfall in federal and state government expenditures has occurred in the economic and social services, which represents the recurrent costs of maintaining and operating the country's social and economic infrastructure. These expenditures also declined as a proportion of total government spending; from 35 percent to 20 percent in 1970/71. As described in some detail later in this report, there is considerable scope for improving allocations for these purposes. Given projected public investment expenditure over the next Plan period, it would not be inconsistent with experience in other countries to estimate a possible additional expenditure of the order of £N100 million by 1978/79 above that indicated on the basis of the historical trend. This would allow for some reduction in the present backlog in such expenditure.

The present situation is also characterized by the inequality of these services, both in quantity and quality, among different parts of the country. Surveys indicate that, for example, per capita recurrent expenditures for education are closely related to per capita current revenues in each of the states. Because there are substantial differences in income levels and distribution between the states, there appears to be a tendency to provide fewer services in relatively poor areas of the country.

Most of these services are provided through the state governments; in 1970/71 their expenditures under this heading amounted to 83 percent of the total, the remaining 17 percent being the federal government's share (Table 4-2). It is, therefore, hardly realistic to expect increased allocations and expenditures to take place in future years if the present arrangements for revenue sharing are maintained. Nor would any purpose be served if present allocations to the states were increased in the same proportions as apply today. This would tend to perpetuate existing inequalities.

Very little is known about the costs of education, the maintenance of roads and bridges, the operating costs of health and community facilities or the existing water supply and sewerage facilities. Statistics of this nature are generally of poor quality and their collection is irregular and unsystematic. Given the inadequacy of current allocations, the staff and time that the government could spend on the collection of better and more comprehensive information would be well spent, if this led to a more accurate assessment of needs and, in turn, to a more adequate allocation of financial resources for the provision of these services. An effort of this kind would also make it possible to obtain more insight into regional disparities and could thus form the basis for a more equitable distribution of resources to the states,

Incentives for Agriculture and Private Industry. There is some difference of opinion about the relative importance of tax incentives and other factors in attracting private investment, notably in manufacturing industries. The Second Development Plan includes proposals for changes in the incentives system which would provide greater selectivity to stimulate investment in those industries which produce a relatively high value-added per unit of output.

Private investment in 1971/72 is estimated at some £N300 million, excluding investment in the oil-producing sector. For a rate of growth of income and product outside the oil sector of close to 8 percent per year during the next Plan period, it would be necessary to increase private non-oil investment in real terms by about 50 percent over those 5 years (1973/74-1978/79) or by 9 percent per annum. It would seem therefore, inadvisable to reduce the incentives to private investment,[1] particularly in view of the government's announced intention of increasing indigenous participation in foreign-owned enterprises and its apparent desire to restrict expatriate quotas.

Stronger tax incentives to private investment would in any case constitute only a small claim on public sector resources. Over the years 1958-68, it is estimated that the cost of tax relief averaged about £N5 million per year. Were this amount to be doubled or tripled during the current decade, the impact on total revenues would be insignificant although the effect of private investment could be considerable.

Reduction of the Share of Foreign Capital. The policy of the Nigerian Government is to indigenize foreign enterprise in the country over a period of several years, by means of varying degrees of participation in the public and private sectors, depending on the size and type of enterprise. Participation in existing manufacturing establishments will involve relatively small expenditures. Larger amounts could be involved in the construction and trade sectors, although even a crude estimate of their magnitude is impossible. Participation in the oil sector and in some of the major new industries presently contemplated (iron and steel, paper, petrochemicals and liquefied natural gas) could involve substantial financial commitments.

The policy of the government is to initiate and promote private Nigerian participation in existing foreign-owned industries. Forced participation could result in the diversion of Nigerian private resources (savings) away from new ventures — with relatively high risks — and into existing enterprises of proven profitability. This could reduce the overall level of private investment, particularly if former foreign owners transfer their receipts abroad rather than reinvest within Nigeria. Were the government to prohibit such transfers on some reasonable schedule, new foreign private investment would be discouraged. Therefore, it would seem advisable to permit these transfers, but at the same time to channel budget resources to the private sector to finance participation in order to avoid the diversion of the private sector's own savings away from new investments.

Also, the distribution of income and wealth could be affected if public funds were made available to private participating parties on the basis of their existing resource position. The suggestion of a "unit-trust" which would participate with public funds and, over time, sell shares to the public, therefore would be one way of potentially avoiding the concentration of wealth in the hands of too few.

Direct public-sector participation in the equity of the oil industry and in its future expansion (including petrochemicals and liquefaction of natural gas) could be an attractive option. Basically, it would amount to an exchange of current oil revenues which may be in excess of what could be used efficiently at present for a larger income stream in the future. Economically, this option is attractive so long as the rate of return on such investment is higher than on any alternative use of the oil revenues. The return on oil sector investment has been very high and may rise in the future. Given the limited capacity to prepare and implement projects in the public sector and the limited availability of capable management in the private non-oil sector at present, the marginal return on alternative uses of capital may well be considerably lower.

Each of these alternative uses could present a substantial claim on the surplus resources of the public sector. Additional expenditure for maintenance and operation of economic and social services could probably easily claim half of the available funds and the participation in existing and new private enterprises could well require the same amount of funds, although it is difficult to

---

1. Tax incentives are often considered unimportant by foreign investors because these are granted about equally in most countries. However, a reduction or abolishment of existing incentives could have adverse effects on private investment.

assess the impact of such additional expenditure in the absence of a more specific breakdown by types.

These alternatives are of course not exhaustive. For example, the option of foreign reserve accumulation also appears to be attractive, particularly in view of the likelihood that the country's longer-term balance of payments would be considerably less favorable than the short- and medium-term.

The following sections are an attempt at an alternative projection which distinguishes from the preceding one only in respect of the growth rate of public sector current expenditures. The alternative projection is based on the same assumptions with respect to the relation of government revenue to economic growth, combined with a rate of growth of non-defense current expenditure 3 percent per year above the preceding projection after the current Plan period; 15 percent per annum through 1978/79 and 13 percent thereafter. This is considerably above past rates of increase, reflecting in part the more comfortable resource position of the public sector; the projection of defense expenditure is maintained as described earlier. Table 8-1 describes the projected budget under this alternative.

Table 8-2: GOVERNMENT ACCOUNTS PROJECTION ("High" Expenditure Alternative)

(In Millions of Current £N)

	1970/71 Actual	1971/72	1973/74	1978/79	1983/84	Annual Average Rate of Growth (%) 1971/72- 1978/79	1978/79- 1983/84
Federal Government:							
Current revenues	378	646	880	1,555	2,550	13.3	10.4
Current expenditures	271	315	375	525	765	7.6	7.8
Transfers to States	143	176	220	410	700	12.8	11.3
Current surplus	-37	155	285	620	1,085	22.0	11.8
State Government:							
Own revenues	45	50	65	105	175	10.9	10.8
Federal transfers	143	176	220	410	700	12.8	11.3
Current expenditures	170	210	290	635	1,230	16.3	14.2
Current surplus	-18	16	-5	-120	-355	–	–
Total Government surplus	-19	171	280	500	730	17.5	7.9
Public investment	100	164	255	460	735	16.2	9.9
Overall budget surplus	-119	7	25	40	-5	–	–

The mission has not attempted to distinguish between federal and state capital expenditure because the distribution of responsibilities in several sectors of the economy may change over time. In any case, it is clear that considerable additional resource transfers to the states will be needed for current as well as capital expenditure financing. Moreover, the federal government will still have sufficient budgetary surpluses to permit this transfer of additional financial resources to the states, while at the same time retaining adequate means to finance its own expenditure.

Although the public sector is still projected to generate some overall surpluses in the years immediately after 1973/74, these are no longer so impressive as in the previous alternative. The relatively modest change in the assumptions about current expenditure have, therefore, a rather significant impact on the accounts of the public sector. This is sufficient demonstration of the fact that the resource prospects of the public sector, although quite satisfactory, do not allow much of a margin for additional spending beyond the levels projected earlier. Even taking account of possible net inflows of external capital, these conclusions still stand.

Macroeconomic Prospects

The projections indicate that a growth rate of the economy sufficiently high and sustained to double average per capita income in Nigeria within the next 12 years appears clearly feasible if economic policies are geared to the objective of economic growth. In constant 1970 prices, this would imply a growth rate of about 8.2 percent per year and about the same when the growth of the oil sector is excluded in the context of the higher alternative of public recurrent expenditure. In terms of time-phasing, the oil sector is expected to lead with very high rates of growth in the initial years and through the mid-1970s, but slowing subsequently to an expansion of some 3-4 percent per year. The other sectors of the economy will then take over the momentum of growth. The projections assume that agriculture, forestry and livestock output will only increase at a rate slightly above 3 percent per year, about equal to past trends. Thus, modern sectors of the non-oil economy – manufacturing, construction, transport and utilities – are expected to carry the momentum of growth increasingly over time with rates ranging between 12 and 15 percent per year.

The transformation of the economy which can reasonably be expected is demonstrated by the projected sector shares in the national product (Table 8-3). The years chosen for the presentation are those at the end of the current Plan and the last years of the presumed five-year plans to follow. By the end of the "fourth" plan, in 1983/84, the agricultural sector may not account for more than about one-quarter of the domestic product, half its relative importance in the base year 1970/71. Even excluding the oil-producing sector, value-added in manufacturing, other mining and construction may be of almost the same relative importance as agriculture by the end of the period covered.

Table 8-3: STRUCTURAL CHANGES IN GDP BY ORIGIN

(Percent)

	1970/71 Actual	1973/74	1978/79	1983/84
Total GDP at Factor Costs	100	100	100	100
Agriculture	50	42	33	27
Petroleum sector	11	15	15	12
Manufacturing, construction	13	16	20	24
Transport, public utilities	4	5	7	10
Other services	22	22	25	27

It is of some interest to note that the share of the oil producing sector reaches a peak soon after the end of the current Plan period (1973/74) and will fall thereafter. This is based on the assumption that present fields will remain in full production with some modest increase of output over the years but no major new discoveries nor any investments in the utilization of the vast natural gas resources of Nigeria will be made. Although plans and proposals to begin gas lique-faction on a large scale are presently being discussed, the time-phasing, costs and outputs are too uncertain at this time to take these into account. The projections therefore presuppose a declining trend in investment in the oil producing sector by 10-12 percent per year after 1973/74, which in fact may not be realistic if a liquefied natural gas complex is to be established.

The growth projections described above, with GDP at factor cost increasing at an average rate of 8.2 percent per annum between 1971/72 and 1983/84, are based not only on the expected impact on growth and resources originating in the oil-producing sector, but also on the assessment of the capability of the economy to invest these resources efficiently. Implementation capacity in the public sector has been assessed with some care by sectors, agencies and states. It is assumed that major efforts to strengthen the implementing agencies in the early years will pay off later and will allow a more rapid rate of growth of public investment than can reasonably be assumed for the earlier years. Combined with policies to stimulate both domestic and foreign private investment outside the oil-producing sector, the projection is derived from a feasible growth of non-oil investments of about 11 percent per year through the end of the "fourth" plan or about the same as in past years.

Declining investments in the oil sector and an increase of non-oil investment that is slightly more rapid than GNP growth will together maintain the overall investment level fairly constantly at about 20 percent of GNP throughout the 1970s and early 1980s. This estimate is arrived at from sectoral assessments of investment requirements which on the average result in an estimated incremental capital/output ratio around 2.80, in the same range as observed in the past. The average conceals, however, a considerable change in the composition of investments by sectors, as is shown in Table 8-4. The decline of the petroleum sector's share may not be realistic, as explained above, and may, in fact, stay at a considerably higher level.

Table 8-4: SECTORAL COMPOSITION OF INVESTMENT

(Percent)

	1971/72	1973/74	1978/79	1983/84
Total Fixed Investment	100	100	100	100
Agriculture	8	8	10	8
Petroleum sector	21	16	6	2
Manufacturing, construction	29	27	30	39
Transport, public utilities	21	24	27	27
Other services	21	25	27	24

Investment in agriculture remains low throughout the projection period (however, base-year data on non-monetized investment in this sector are very weak, and may be the source of a continuous underestimate in the projections), largely reflecting the lack of capacity to implement projects at the level of the states which carry the major responsibility in this sector. The heavy investments in the construction sector in the base year, 1971/72, inflate the share of manufacturing and construction. The increasing share of other services reflects substantial investments in public administration in the new states and in education and health facilities.

The changing composition of investment activities as projected can also be observed when comparing the growth of private and public sector investment. In the past, the resource constraint kept public sector investment at about 5 percent of GNP through the 1960s; in future, larger financial resources will allow this to increase.

Table 8-5: PUBLIC AND PRIVATE INVESTMENT

(As Percent of GNP at Market Prices)

	1971/72	1973/74	1978/79	1983/84
Private investment	15	16	13	14
Petroleum sector	4	4	1	
Other sectors	11	12	12	14[a]
Public investment	6	7	8	8
Total investment	21	23	21	22

[a]Less than 0.5 percent.

As shown in Table 8-5, the stability of the share of total investment in GNP (both measured in constant 1970 prices) conceals the assumed decline of oil investments and the growth of both private and public investment outside the oil sector. Private investment other than in the oil sector does not rise much as a proportion of GNP through the 1970s, although the base year level is exceptionally high.

In the past, growth of investment and output led to a considerable strain on the balance of payments. The rapid growth of oil exports, even if taken net of factor income payments abroad, will remove this constraint of growth for some time to come. But, by the end of the projection period in the early 1980s, the same problem may arise. This could be caused by oil exports which are projected to grow more slowly than import demands generated by the expansion of the economy from the 1980s onward.

Future import trends cannot be predicted with much confidence. The need for capital and intermediate products will depend largely on the future composition of output and investment. The demand for imported consumer goods will be related to such uncertain elements as agricultural growth and the rate of inflation in the domestic economy vis-a-vis that abroad. Thus, the growth of imports under less favorable circumstances than assumed here could well be significantly more rapid and the reappearance of a resource gap could arise earlier than projected below.

The growth of imports is linked in the projections to domestic demand by category of expenditure. Imports of consumer goods take account of further import substitution for manufactured products and of the possibility that domestic food production will not be adequate to meet demand. Intermediate goods imports are linked to the growth of output in the modern sectors of the economy; with allowance for anticipated import substitution capital goods imports follow the expansion of investment activity. The needs of the oil-producing sector for imported goods are treated as a separate category.

The postwar liberalization of imports led to major growth in merchandise imports in 1970 and 1971. It is expected that a marked slowdown will occur over the next few years and that, on the

Table 8-6: IMPORTS OF GOODS AND NON-FACTOR SERVICES

(In Millions of £N)

	1971/72	1973/74	1978/79	1983/84	% – Annual Rate of Growth 1971/72- 1978/79	1978/79- 1983/84
In 1970 prices:						
Total imports of goods	540	610	875	1,390	7.2	9.9
Petroleum sector imports	40	45	40	40	–	–
Consumer goods	140	160	255	490	9.0	13.8
Intermediate goods	150	160	205	205	4.6	–
Capital goods	210	245	375	655	8.7	12.0
Import price index (1970=100)	103	105	116	127	–	–
In current prices:						
Imports of goods, non-factor services	685	775	1,160	1,990	7.8	11.5
Total imports of goods	555	640	1,010	1,770	9.0	12.0
Non-factor services	130	135	150	220	2.0	7.7

average, the volume of imports of goods and non-factor services will not rise more than 6 percent per year through 1978/79. When excluding imports directly related to the oil-producing sector, remaining imports are projected to grow in volume-terms by about 7.7 percent or close to the rate of growth of GNP. In the 5 years which follow, through 1983/84, the projections indicate volume-growth rate of imports of 9.3 percent per year including oil sector imports and 9.7 percent excluding the latter. The implicit increase of the overall import elasticity between the first and second period reflects major increases of capital goods imports in line with accelerating investment expenditure. There is also a more pronounced growth of demand for imported consumer goods as the more obvious opportunities for import substitution are exhausted (Table 8-6).

Major efforts in import substitution can be observed in the intermediate goods category. The low growth rate of non-factor services in the first period reflects the large component of oil services, which are expected to decline along with oil investment.

The acceleration of import growth over time is not matched by a similar pattern of export growth. On the contrary, exports (in current prices) will rise on the average by 10 percent per year from 1971/72, to 1978/79, but only 6.5 percent per year thereafter. Again, it should be emphasized that this projection is based on conservative assumptions regarding developments in the oil-producing sector and ancillary industries. Following an average annual growth rate of 16.4 percent between 1971/72 and 1975/76, the growth rate of crude oil exports is projected to increase by 7 percent per annum thereafter on the assumption of a 4 percent volume growth combined with a 3 percent price inflation.

As a result of these differences in the projected development of imports and exports, the balance of payments is expected to show large and increasing surpluses in the years through 1975, declining surpluses from then until 1980 and deficits thereafter.

Table 8-7: BALANCE OF PAYMENTS PROJECTIONS

(Millions of Current £N)

	1971/72	1973/74	1978/79	1983/84
Exports of goods, non-factor services	805	1,020	1,565	2,145
Imports of goods, non-factor services	-683	-775	-1,160	-1,990
Resource balance	122	250	405	155
Net factor payments, transfers	-251	-315	-475	-635
Current account balance	-129	-65	-70	-480
Net medium-/long-term capital	210	175	160	150
Changes of reserves, short-term assets	+81	+110	+90	-330

The projections imply an increase of £N800 million in foreign exchange reserves during the 1970s from the end-1971 level of about £N100 million. By the end of the decade, reserves would be equivalent to nine months' imports. However, with the declines which set in thereafter, reserves fall to a projected level equivalent to only two months' imports by 1983/84. This decline would be considerably smaller if proposed liquefied natural gas operations are launched during the 1970s. It should be observed that the trends established during a period of abundant resources can easily lead to a major reversal of the development pattern if sufficient care is not taken well in advance to set targets of growth and investment in accordance with sound long-run balance of payments management. The projections do "overshoot" in this sense, but actual plans and policies should not follow that pattern, unless the prospects of export growth can be assessed more optimistically than postulated here.

Reserve accumulations of the magnitude and continuity projected clearly indicate a resource position which would permit much larger investments than are likely to take place. Domestic savings will exceed investment expenditures and the surplus will be invested abroad. Any net inflow of medium- and long-term capital, while being used for the financing of investment will also increase the surplus of domestic savings over investment and lead to larger accumulations of foreign exchange reserves.

Under these circumstances, it is not useful to discuss savings mobilization as an objective of development policy. The more important questions relate to the use of savings, i.e. the size and allocation of the investment program, the effectiveness of its implementation and the distribution of its benefits among the participants in the development process. The surplus of exports over imports equals the excess of domestic savings over investment expenditure. As total investment expenditure is projected to remain at about 20 percent of a (rapidly growing) GNP and as the resource surplus declines toward the end of the projection period, domestic savings also show a declining trend as a percent of GNP. Factor income payments are about the same proportion of GNP throughout most of the period but decline toward the later years. As a consequence, national savings as a proportion of GNP show a similar declining trend from a high level in 1973/74.

Table 8-8: INVESTMENT AND SAVINGS PROJECTION

(Millions of Current £N)

	1970/71 Actual	1971/72	1973/74	1978/79	1983/84
Gross fixed investment	450	595	730	1,205	2,135
Resource balance	-50	120	250	405	155
Gross domestic savings (1+2)	400	715	950	1,610	2,290
Net factor income payments and transfers	-70	250	-315	-475	-635
National savings (3+4)	230	467	635	1,135	1,655
As % of GNP:					
Gross fixed investment	19	20	20	19	21
Domestic savings	17	24	25	26	22
National savings	10	16	18	18	16

Part of these savings find their way to the financing of investment; assuming realistically that foreign medium- and long-term capital inflows and direct foreign investment are tied to specific programs. These inflows substitute for the country's own savings which then are added to foreign exchange reserves, i.e. they become investments outside Nigeria. The composition of national savings by origin and their use are shown in Table 8-9 distinguishing between government budgetary surpluses on the higher of the two expenditure alternatives and private savings, and taking account of the projected net capital inflows as an additional investment resource.

Table 8-9: NATIONAL SAVINGS BY ORIGIN AND USES

(Percent of GNP)

	1970/71 Actual	1971/72	1973/74	1978/79	1983/84
Government budget surplus	-2	6	7	8	7
Private savings	12	10	11	10	9
National savings	10	16	18	18	16
Less invested abroad	-3	3	2	2	-3
Invested in Nigeria	13	13	16	16	19
Net capital inflows	6	7	4	3	2
Total investment	19	20	20	19	21

It should be noted that the projections imply a considerable increase in the share of national savings which are invested in the Nigerian economy, or, conversely, a decline of savings invested abroad.

Implications of Alternative Assumptions

A comparison of the alternative projections not only demonstrated how vulnerable the projections of government budgets are to relatively small variations in expenditure estimates but, even more, how important fiscal policies will be for the pattern of growth and stability of the economy. With the lower of the two expenditure alternatives for the public sector, it would appear that balance of payments will continue to be in surplus throughout the 1970s, foreign exchange reserves accumulating by some £N1,250 million before the point is reached — in the middle 1980s — where small drawings on reserves will again become necessary. In the second alternative, which assumes that the government will increase its current expenditure slightly faster, reserves would still increase by about £N800 million, but the recourse to reserves would then occur several years earlier, in the late 1970s, and subsequently drawings would be such as to deplete reserves over a fairly short period. These differences in the balance of payments demonstrate the risks of high current expenditure growth rates in the public sector. It may also be observed that the considerably less favorable outlook in the second alternative is not compensated by any significantly higher growth of the economy. With the lower expenditure alternative, the economy expands by 7.8 percent per annum, compared with an 8.2 percent per annum with the higher alternative. The cost of this more rapid growth appears in the form of an early return of balance of payments constraints. Furthermore, the higher growth rate would raise consumption expenditure, particularly in the public sector, to a level which would be difficult to reverse when resource scarcities recur.

As stated earlier, the projections are based on assumptions which imply roughly the same marginal productivity of capital as in the past. Not much can be said with any degree of certainty, apart from the observation that this assumption may be optimistic for such rapid growth of investment as projected for this decade in Nigeria. As an alternative, a gradual increase of the marginal capital costs per unit of output can be assumed over time. If a one percent annual increase is assumed, well within any reasonable margin of uncertainty, the major changes in the growth pattern would occur in the balance of payments. The consequences with regard to overall economic growth would not be particularly impressive: the GNP growth rate would decline to about 7.7 percent per year (still with the high public expenditure alternative) or 0.5 percent less per annum. The accumulation of foreign exchange reserves would be further reduced to some £N600 million with drawdowns becoming necessary by the end of this decade. Reserves consequently would return to their present level or even less before 1983/84, if no other means were used to stem the rapid growth of import demand. A comparison of the balance of payments of the three alternatives discussed above is presented in Table 8-10.

Table 8-10: BALANCE OF PAYMENTS IMPLICATIONS OF ALTERNATIVE ASSUMPTIONS

(In Millions of Current £N)

	1978/79			1983/84		
	I	II	III	I	II	III
Import of goods and NFS	1,080	1,160	1,240	1,755	1,990	2,380
Resource balance	485	405	330	398	155	-230
Current account balance	15	-70	-140	-235	-480	-860
Charges of reserves, short-term assets	+175	+90	+20	-85	-330	-710

Note: Alternative I: Low recurrent expenditures, constant ICOR.
Alternative II: High recurrent expenditures, constant ICOR.
Alternative III: High recurrent expenditures, increasing ICOR.

Again, this demonstrates the vulnerability of the projected growth path to small changes in the assumptions which are well within the range of realistic values. Careful husbanding of public sector resources, therefore, remains a most important element of economic policy. The substantially larger share of the national income which the government will find at its command implies that fiscal policies, which in the past have had only limited effects on the economy, may in the future have a much deeper impact on the rest of the economy.

Distributive Implications

Earlier in this chapter, some possible long-term courses of development in Nigeria were sketched out. Some of the issues arising in that context have been mentioned or discussed in more detail. The projections do not pretend to constitute an accurate picture of the way things will happen but rather to suggest orders of magnitude for important growth indicators under reasonable assumptions. The same caveat applies to the conclusions and implications; while not precise, they are reasonable assumptions about the consequences of growth in Nigeria over the next 15 years.

An overall GNP growth rate of about 8 percent per year is a respectable acceleration over the past performance of the economy and would allow per capita income to double between 1971 and 1985, notwithstanding a 40 percent growth in population. Taking only those elements of national product and income which accrue as private income, growth over the same period would be around 8.3 percent per year.

The distribution of private income between urban and rural areas is, at present, without doubt very uneven — which is normal in most countries — although probably more pronounced at earlier stages of development. Although it is far from easy to analyze the income distribution issue, given the scarcity and unreliability of the data, it is nevertheless possible to take some readings from the sectoral origins of national income and product. There is very little else in terms of economic activity in the rural areas but agriculture and most other sectors are based in the urban centers. Although part of the urban income appears to be transferred to the rural areas, reducing inequalities to some extent, the impact on those inequalities may not be very significant.

If the simple assumption is made that all non-agricultural activities are urban, it would follow that in 1971/72 private income in the rural areas was about 55 percent of total private income. As urban centers probably contain only 20 percent of the population, it follows that urban per capita income on the average would be about 3.0 to 3.5 times the rural per capita income. This does not appear excessively high compared with other countries at similar stages of development. In fact, it may overstate the ratio because some incomes included as urban may accrue to the rural sector either because of the location of the activity (such as trade, construction or transport) or because of income transfers from urban centers to the rural areas.

The course of future events will depend not only on the growth of economic activity in urban versus rural areas, but also on migration trends toward the cities. Again, assuming that agriculture is the only source of rural income, and also considering what would happen if there were not migration over the period through 1984, it is found that the ratio between urban and rural income would rise to about 9, which is clearly unrealistic. Of course, such an assumption of zero-migration is not consistent with the projections of growth itself. The urban concentration of the modern sectors, which will generate the largest part of the rise in output, requires a substantial inflow of workers from the rural areas. Without additional supplies of labor, this growth of output would not be feasible.

The opportunities for higher urban income will attract migrants to the cities to a point where advantage and risk will balance and, although it is difficult to define that point, a range can be established. In analyzing past trends, the impression is that about 30 percent of the natural increase in rural population migrate to cities. If this trend is assumed to continue the projection would yield inequalities between rural and urban areas of twice the magnitude now existing over the course of the next 12 years. The average urban dweller would be 6 times better off than his rural counterpart. Only on the assumption that no less than 70-80 percent of the natural growth of the rural population migrate to the cities each year, would the degree of inequality remain in the same range as at present.

Migration of 70-80 percent of the increase in rural population to the cities would imply productivity growth (excluding petroleum) of 4 percent per year in the urban centers. Thus, about one-third of the increase of output in the modern sectors of the economy would be the result of additional output per employee, the remaining two-thirds being the result of increases in the numbers employed. This is in line with findings in other countries and although no information for such developments in Nigeria's economic history is available, may nevertheless fairly represent a feasible growth path. Concurrently, the outflow of population from the rural sector would imply a productivity increase of about 2.5 percent per year in agricultural activities even with modest projected increase in production.

The consequences of such population flows can only be imagined. The urban population would grow from about 14 million at present, to about 35 million to 40 million in 1984, accounting for about 35 percent of the total population. The strains on urban facilities such as housing, transport, water and sewerage would be extraordinary. Two major points emerge: first, the importance of emphasizing agricultural development and modernization as a means of increasing rural incomes faster than is assumed here, thus stemming the tide of migration to the cities; second, the urgent need to organize and strengthen the urban institutions which must plan for the growth of the cities which inevitably will take place. In the agricultural sector as well as in the urban areas those institutions are now very weak or non-existent.

Urban growth combined with a more rapid rate of increase of urban per capita income will also affect the balance in another way: through the growth of the market economy as compared to the relative size of the subsistence sector. Whereas little growth of agricultural production is needed to meet the needs of the rural subsistence sector, the supplies of agricultural produce for the urban sector may have to triple over the next 10-12 years. Although there is hardly any doubt that such quantities can be produced in Nigeria, assuming appropriate price and tax policies for farm produce, the tasks of transporting, storing and marketing will be very large. The inadequacies of the present system, demonstrated by the recent inflation of food prices in major cities, imply that the investments in moving agricultural products from the producer to the consumer need to be very large, not only to keep up with urban growth, but even to meet present minimum needs.

A large part of those investments will have to take place in the rural sector of the economy, in the form of feeder and access roads, storage facilities and agricultural credit. In due course, an increasing degree of processing of agricultural products may also be efficiently done in the smaller rural centers, close to the producing areas. Many of these investments will, directly or indirectly, provide additional income opportunities in the rural areas. Thus, they will not only provide better market outlets and improved urban supplies, but also contribute to the objective of a more equal income distribution in the country and improvements of employment possibilities outside the urban centers.

These trends and priorities deserve considerable attention in the government's plans for future development. The changing consumption patterns which urbanization and higher incomes generate will be more flexible, compared with those of a predominantly subsistence economy. The possibilities of substituting imported goods for scarce and expensive domestic supplies are now considerably greater and the inadequacies of domestic marketing channels will not only deprive the rural sector of the potential growth of its income, but also increase the demand for imports beyond levels projected here. In that way, the growth of foreign exchange reserves may be considerably reduced and the points where deficits in the balance of payments recur may be reached earlier. The projections have already demonstrated that even under optimistic assumptions, the balance of payments will probably show increasing deficits from the end of this decade. Failure to pay adequate attention to agriculture will shorten this period and thus leave less time and resources to establish a sound foundation for long-term economic growth, including the development of the rural infrastructure which will allow the agricultural sector to develop in harmony with the modern sectors of the economy.

Foreign Aid

Despite the large absolute and percentage increase in foreign earnings that Nigeria can reasonably look forward to over the next 5 years, the country will continue to belong to the group of the world's lowest income countries. In the short run, the expansion of the petroleum sector is providing revenues to sustain public and private consumption and simultaneously to undertake those investment projects which will in the future maintain economic growth. One of the country's most pressing needs is to develop additional investment projects in both the public and private sectors. Nigeria needs assistance in these areas as well as in the implementation of invest-ment decisions. New investment activity specifically needs to be undertaken and generated in agriculture and manufacturing. Into these sectors and supporting infrastructure, a greatly expanded volume of investment resources must be directed if agricultural and industrial output is to rise fast enough to maintain the momentum of growth which is now generated by the growth of crude oil output.

The overriding conclusion with respect to Nigeria's economic prospects is that the oppor-tunity now exists to achieve a significant improvement in the standard of living within the relative-ly short time span of 10-12 years. Over this period, economic growth need not be hampered by savings or foreign exchange constraints. Nevertheless, the absence of financial restraints will be shortlived. Projections show that, by the end of this decade, constraints may arise again, albeit at a time when considerable improvements above the present standard of living should be evident.

During the next ten years, the country could enjoy uninterrupted development, providing a sound basis for further growth thereafter. However, it is essential that, during this period, policies and strategies be adopted to improve the balance between urban and rural growth, between the development of agriculture and the modern sectors and between the different regions of the country in terms of economic and social infrastructure. The distribution of vastly increased government resources between different uses and claims can in the process of planning and spend-ing, contribute to the establishment of institutions capable of carrying the main responsibility for development during the 1970s and thereafter. Foreign aid in the public and the private sectors, both in the form of technical assistance and capital, can be of great value in a period when the opportunities for development appear to be well in excess of the country's capacity, in terms of domestic organization and skills to make full use of these opportunities.

The Nigerian economy has recovered with remarkable resilience from the stresses and costs arising from a serious internal conflict, and is now launched upon the task of providing a rising income for all its people by exploiting its mineral resources for exports and then by building up its own means of production.

CHAPTER 9

LONG-TERM PROJECTION MODEL OF THE ECONOMY

The economy over the next decade and a half is likely to sustain a rate of growth considerably above that experienced during the fifteen years before the outbreak of hostilities. In contrast to historical experience, the future growth of the economy will most certainly involve a substantial transformation of its structure. A favorable shift in the external terms of trade is also expected to account for a substantial increase in real income.

This chapter describes the mission's attempt to construct an analytical framework within which some insights may be gained as to the pattern and implications of these expected developments. The results and findings of this exercise are described in the relevant chapters of this book; this chapter is limited to a description of the simulation model used for this purpose.

The structure of the model is described, followed by a presentation of the major sources of data used in the model. Variables are then defined and a complete set of equations is presented. Tables 1, 2, and 3 summarize the macro-economic projections.

Structure of the Model

The objective of the model now described is to simulate a growth pattern of the economy over the next fifteen years with given allocations of the government's resources consistent with given developments in the agriculture and petroleum sectors. A priori, it is expected that the impact of these developments on the rest of the economy will be largely indirect, and differ considerably among different productive sectors and income groups. A highly disaggregated approach is therefore necessary and the model's specifications are fairly complex. The structure of the model, however, may be summarized as follows.

Development in the agriculture and petroleum sectors is specified outside the model. Since the determinants of agricultural growth are not easily amenable to the simplification necessary for a macro-economic model and the mission's knowledge of the sector is very limited, agricultural output projections made by the recent IBRD agricultural sector mission are relied upon as exogenous inputs to the model. However, some adjustments have been made to the projected output of those food crops (e.g., yams, cassava) the production of which is assumed to be determined primarily by demand conditions.

The growth of crude oil production and the resulting import requirements and income generated are also specified separately. Development in this sector is not likely to be affected by the rest of the economy, so that an independent projection seems to be reasonable.

Thus, these pre-specified developments in the agriculture and petroleum sectors represent the basic dynamic forces in the model. The overall growth of the economy is then assumed to be generated by the response of the remaining sectors to the increased income and consequent expansion of consumer and intermediate demand generated by these two sectors, and by the income and inter-industry multiplier effects arising from the interactions of the sectors with each other and with the household and public sectors. Specifically, the growth of manufacturing output is assumed to be determined by the expansion of consumer and intermediate demands for manufactures, including opportunities for import substitution. Output of public utilities and transport services is assumed to depend mainly on pre-specified public sector investment expenditure in these sectors and also on private investment efforts, which are functions of the overall growth rate of the economy. Finally, the growth of construction and other service sectors is determined by increases in investment expenditure and private and public consumption expenditure. In most sectors, the linkages between increased demand and increased production are indirect, increased demands stimulating investment expenditure which, in turn, generates increased output after a certain lag in time.

Exports, limited primarily to agricultural products and crude oil, are also pre-specified in the model. Imports are defined separately for a number of categories by end-use as the differences between domestic demand and production. This is based on the assumption that the unprecedented rise in consumer and investment demands expected over the next fifteen years will not be matched immediately by increases in domestic production. In the manufacturing sector, however, import substitution is assumed to be generated whenever demands increase faster than production, and whenever domestic production is below a pre-specified proportion of domestic demand. The only exception is the machinery and equipment subsector in which import substitution is not considered to be feasible during the projection period. Time lags are introduced between demand growth and investment expenditure, and between investment expenditure and actual production.

Each type of government revenue is defined as a function of the source of revenues, i.e., petroleum profit taxes and royalties to crude oil production, import duties to imports by the non-oil sectors, export duties to agricultural exports, excise duties to manufacturing production, corporation income tax to value added in the modern sectors and miscellaneous federal revenues as well as the states' own revenues to GNP. Except for revenues from petroleum which are computed independently, fixed coefficients are used, assuming constant tax rates. Government recurrent expenditure is pre-specified, the alternative assumptions reflecting possible uses of public resources as discussed in Chapter 8.

Private income is defined as GNP (including the wages and salaries components of government recurrent expenditure) less government revenues plus subsidies and transfers from the public sector. Private consumer demand for different categories of goods is then related to private income through constant income elasticities, while demands for services are defined as the residual of total private consumption less expenditure on goods. On the assumption that agricultural income represents rural income, consumer demands are specified separately for the rural and urban sectors. Intermediate demands are related to production activities by the usual input-output coefficients.

Investment expenditure in the petroleum sector is specified exogenously, with the present projection limited only to investment in crude oil production. While investment in associated petroleum products (e.g., liquefied natural gas) may be possible during the projection period, estimates of the likely timing and magnitude are not feasible and the impact of these ventures on the economy is likely to be very small until the mid-80s (Chapter 6). Private investment expenditure outside the oil sector is assumed to be a function of demand growth, including import substitution possibilities. Public investment expenditure is specified and reflects the mission's assessment of the public sector's executive capacity.

All variables are defined in constant base-year prices and in current prices, except financial variables which are defined only in nominal terms. Price indices are pre-specified for agricultural products, other goods, services (wages) and imports as well as for all export products. Except for the export products, prices of domestic goods and services are presumed to follow the trend of exogenously-determined import prices after initial allowances are made for adjustments to peacetime conditions (e.g., wage increases as a result of the Adebo Award) and the recent change in the U.S. dollar exchange rate. In terms of foreign currency, this assumption is equivalent to the situation in which domestic prices move differently from international prices, but a constant purchasing power parity is maintained through changes in the exchange rate.

The model is initially formulated as a two gap model, with independent specifications of investment, saving, export and import functions. It is then found that the balance of payments surpluses (deficits) are consistently smaller (larger) than the excesses (shortages) of savings over investment. As surpluses are more evident over the projection period, it seems unlikely that imports would be restricted in order to generate surpluses as large as that indicated by the *ex-ante* saving surpluses. Therefore, it is assumed that actual savings would be equal to projected investment less the resource balance obtained from the current account projection. The implication is that *ex-ante* national savings in excess of domestic investment which are not linked to foreign capital (such as in most of the petroleum and manufacturing sectors) and for which foreign exchange is not available for investment abroad, would be diverted to consumption expenditure.

Table 9-1: SUMMARY OF MACROECONOMIC PROJECTIONS IN CONSTANT PRICES

In constant (1970) prices and exchange rates:

(percent)

	(£N Million)				Average annual rate of growth			Shares of GNP			
	1970/71	1973/74	1978/79	1983/84	1970/71-1973/74	1973/74-1978/79	1978/79-1983/84	1970/71	1973/74	1978/79	1983/84
Gross Domestic Product (at factor cost)	2,346	3,120	4,604	6,741	10.0	8.1	8.0	99.4	98.7	96.3	93.5
Agriculture, forestry, fisheries	1,174	1,296	1,506	1,794	3.4	3.0	3.6	49.7	41.0	31.5	24.9
Petroleum production	253	466	675	811	23.0	7.7	3.7	10.7	14.7	14.1	11.2
Manufacturing, other mining, quarrying	205	309	583	1,082	14.7	13.5	13.2	8.7	9.8	12.2	15.0
Construction	102	195	327	507	24.0	10.9	9.2	4.3	6.2	6.8	7.0
Public utilities, transport	93	142	337	667	15.1	18.9	14.6	3.9	4.5	7.1	9.3
Public administration, defense	140	188	285	436	10.5	8.6	8.9	5.9	5.9	6.0	6.0
Other services	379	525	891	1,444	11.5	11.1	10.1	16.1	16.6	18.6	20.0
Indirect Taxes (net of subsidies)	204	249	453	785	6.9	12.7	11.6	8.6	7.9	9.5	10.9
Gross Domestic Product (market prices)	2,550	3,369	5,057	7,526	9.7	8.5	8.3	108.0	106.5	105.8	104.4
Net Factor Payments from Abroad	-170	-207	-279	-320	6.8	6.1	2.8	-8.1	-6.5	-5.8	-4.4
Gross National Product (market prices)	2,380	3,162	4,778	7,206	9.9	8.6	8.6	100.0	100.0	100.0	100.0
Imports of Goods and services	726	941	1,277	1,876	9.0	6.3	8.0	30.5	29.8	26.7	26.0
Petroleum sector goods imports	28	45	40	40	17.1	-2.2	—	1.2	1.4	0.8	0.6
Consumer goods	120	160	257	492	10.1	9.9	13.9	5.1	5.1	5.4	6.8
Intermediate and capital goods	271	405	526	861	14.3	5.3	10.4	11.0	12.8	11.0	11.9
Non-factor services	137	124	125	163	-3.4	—	5.5	6.2	3.9	2.6	2.3
Net factor payments	170	207	279	320	6.8	6.1	2.8	8.1	6.5	5.8	4.4
Total National Resources (5 + 6)	3,106	4,103	6,055	9,082	9.7	8.1	8.4	123.6	129.8	120.9	121.6
Exports of Goods and services	506	742	1,008	1,217	13.6	6.3	3.8	21.4	23.5	21.1	16.9
Petroleum and products	293	500	729	881	19.5	7.8	3.9	12.4	15.8	15.3	12.2
Other goods	188	217	254	311	4.9	3.2	4.1	8.0	6.9	5.3	4.3
Non-factor services	25	25	25	25	—	—	—	1.1	0.8	0.5	0.3
Investment Expenditures	450	670	992	1,592	14.2	8.2	10.0	19.1	21.2	20.8	22.1
Public investment	100	227	380	548	31.0	10.9	7.6	4.2	7.2	8.0	7.6
Private investment	350	443	612	1,044	8.2	6.7	11.3	14.8	14.0	12.8	14.5
Consumption Expenditures	2,150	2,691	4,054	6,273	7.8	8.5	9.1	91.1	85.1	84.8	87.1
Public	303	383	577	880	8.1	8.5	8.8	12.8	12.1	12.1	12.2
Private	1,847	2,308	3,477	5,393	7.7	8.5	9.2	78.3	73.0	72.8	74.8
Resource Balance (8 - 6 - 4 = surplus)	-50	8	10	-339							
Current Account Balance (11 + 4)	-220	-208	-269	-659							

Table 9-2: SUMMARY OF MACROECONOMIC PROJECTIONS IN CURRENT PRICES

In current prices:

	(£ N Million)				Average annual rate of growth (percent)			Shares of GNP			
	1970/71	1973/74	1978/79	1983/84	1970/71-1973/74	1973/74-1978/79	1978/79-1983/84	1970/71	1973/74	1978/79	1983/84
Gross Domestic Product (at factor cost)	2,346	3,756	6,147	9,928	17.0	10.3	10.1	99.9	100.1	98.5	95.6
Agriculture, forestry, fisheries	1,174	1,422	1,799	2,344	6.6	4.8	5.4	49.7	38.1	28.8	22.6
Petroleum production	253	746	1,230	1,710	43.0	10.5	6.8	10.7	20.0	19.7	16.5
Manufacturing, other mining, quarrying	205	339	702	1,442	18.2	15.7	15.5	8.7	9.1	11.3	13.9
Construction	102	232	429	736	30.0	13.1	11.4	4.3	6.2	6.9	7.1
Public utilities, transport	93	169	442	968	22.1	21.2	17.0	3.9	4.5	7.1	9.3
Public administration, defense	140	223	374	633	16.8	10.9	11.1	5.9	6.0	6.0	6.1
Other services	379	625	1,171	2,095	18.2	13.4	12.3	16.1	16.8	18.8	20.2
Indirect Taxes (net of subsidies)	204	282	567	1,088	11.4	14.0	13.9	8.6	7.6	9.1	10.5
Gross Domestic Product (market prices)	2,550	4,037	6,713	11,017	16.5	10.7	10.4	108.1	108.2	107.6	106.1
Net Factor Payments from Abroad	-170	-307	-476	-633	22.0	9.2	5.8	-8.1	-8.2	-7.6	-6.1
Gross National Product (market prices)	2,380	3,731	6,238	10,383	16.2	10.8	10.7	100.0	100.0	100.0	100.0
Imports of Goods and services	726	1,078	1,635	2,627	14.1	8.7	10.0	23.6	28.9	26.2	25.3
Petroleum sector goods imports	28	46	42	44	18.0	-1.7	0.9	1.2	1.2	0.7	0.4
Consumer goods	120	168	298	631	11.9	12.1	16.2	5.1	4.5	4.8	6.1
Intermediate and capital goods	271	425	668	1,102	16.2	9.5	10.5	11.0	11.4	10.7	10.6
Non-factor services	137	135	150	217	—	2.1	7.7	6.2	3.6	2.4	2.1
Net factor payments	170	307	476	633	22.0	9.2	5.8	8.1	8.2	7.6	6.6
Total National Resources (5 + 6)	3,106	4,808	7,871	13,010	15.7	10.3	10.6	123.6	128.9	126.2	125.3
Exports of Goods and services	506	1,021	1,565	2,147	26.0	8.9	6.5	21.4	27.4	25.1	20.7
Petroleum and products	293	800	1,326	1,859	40.0	10.6	7.0	12.4	21.4	21.3	17.9
Other goods	188	193	178	253	0.9	-1.5	7.2	8.0	5.0	2.9	2.4
Non-factor services	25	28	31	35	3.9	2.1	2.5	1.1	0.7	0.5	0.3
Investment Expenditures	450	732	1,206	2,135	17.6	10.5	12.1	19.1	19.6	19.3	20.6
Public investment	100	248	462	735	35.0	13.2	9.7	4.2	6.6	7.4	7.1
Private investment	350	484	744	1,400	11.4	9.0	13.5	14.8	13.0	11.9	13.5
Consumption Expenditures	2,150	3,055	5,100	8,728	12.4	10.8	11.3	91.1	81.9	81.8	84.1
Public	303	444	740	1,246	13.6	10.7	11.0	12.8	11.9	11.9	12.0
Private	1,847	2,611	4,360	7,482	12.2	10.8	11.4	78.3	70.0	69.9	72.1
Resource Balance	-50	250	406	153							
Current Account Balance	-220	-57	-70	-480							

Table 9-3: SUMMARY OF MACROECONOMIC PROJECTIONS, PRICE INDEX

	(1970/71 = 100)			Average annual rate of increase		
	1973/74	1978/79	1983/84	1970/71-1973/74	1973/74-1978/79	1978/79-1983/84
Gross Domestic Product	120	134	147	6.4	2.1	2.0
Agriculture, forestry, fisheries	110	120	131	3.1	1.7	1.9
Petroleum production	157	182	211	16.2	3.8	3.0
Manufacturing, other mining, quarrying	110	120	133	3.1	1.9	2.1
Services	119	131	145	6.0	2.0	2.0
Gross National Product	118	131	144	5.7	2.1	2.0
Imports of goods	105	116	128	1.7	2.0	2.0
Total national resources	117	130	143	5.4	2.1	2.0
Export	137	155	176	11.1	2.5	2.6
Petroleum and products	157	182	211	16.2	3.0	2.2
Others	91	75	86	-3.2	-3.9	2.8
Investment expenditures	109	122	134	3.0	2.2	2.0
Consumption expenditures	113	126	139	4.3	2.1	2.0

LIST OF VARIABLES AND BASE-YEAR VALUES

Symbol	Definition	Value in FY 1970/71 (in LN million except where otherwise indicated)
	Value-added	
YAec	Agriculture, export crops	107.00
YArc	root crops	290.00
YAcg	coarse grains	296.00
YArw	rice and wheat	23.00
YAmc	miscellaneous crops	170.00
YAft	forestry	63.00
YAlv	livestocks and fisheries	225.00
YA	Agriculture, total	1,174.00
YP	Petroleum, mining	253.00
YMN	Mining, non-petroleum	8.00
YQR	Quarrying	10.00
YMcf	Manufacturing, crafts	27.00
YMpf	processed food	42.00
YMtx	textiles	36.00
YMoc	other consumer goods	50.00
YMig	intermediate goods	32.00
YM	Manufacturing, total	187.00
YCT	Construction	102.00
YWT	Utilities	11.00
YT	Transportation and communication	82.00
YPA	Public administration	140.00
YHE	Health and education	72.00
YOS	Other services	307.00
	National Accounts	
Y	Gross domestic product, at factor cost	2,346.00
GNP	Gross national product, at market prices	2,380.00
Ggnp	Growth rate of GNP	0.12
	Investment	
IA	Agriculture, forestry and fisheries	40.00
IP	Petroleum	115.00
IMNQ	Mining and Quarrying	4.00
IMcf	Manufacturing, crafts	0.20
IMpf	processed food	18.00
IMtx	textiles	18.00
IMoc	other consumer goods	30.00
IMig	intermediate goods	22.00
ICT	Construction	51.00
IUT	Utilities	8.00

Symbol	Definition	Value in FY 1970/71 (in LN million except where otherwise indicated)
ITg	Transportation, government	33.00
ITp	Transportation, private	35.00
IHEg	Health and education, government	18.00
IHEp	Health and education, private	10.00
IPA	Public administration	7.00
IOS	Other services	41.00
I	Total fixed capital formation	450.00
	Exports	
Ep	Exports of petroleum products	293.00
Enp	Exports, non-petroleum	188.00
E	Total exports of goods	481.00
ENFS	Exports of non-factor services	25.00
	Imports	
Mp	Imports by petroleum sector	28.00
Mcr	Imports, cereals	9.00
Mof	other foods	25.00
Mtx	textiles	21.00
Moc	other consumer goods	65.00
Mig	intermediate goods	119.00
Mme	machinery and equipment	108.00
Mte	transport equipment	44.00
M	Total import of goods	419.00
MNFnp	Imports of non-factor services, non-petroleum	56.00
MNFp	Imports of non-factor services by petroleum sector	81.00
MNF	Total imports of non-factor services	137.00
T	Transfers and net interest payments	17.00
FPp	Net factor payment by petroleum sector	134.00
FKS	Foreign capital stock, non-petroleum	300.00
FPnp	Net factor payment by non-petroleum sector	53.00
	Government Revenues	
Rm	Import duties	117.00
Rep	Export duties	21.00
Rec	Excise duties	66.00
Rd	Direct taxes and other income of federal government	59.00
Rs	States' revenues	39.00
Rpf	Petroleum revenues accruing to federal government	86.00
Rps	Petroleum revenues accruing to state governments	30.00
RST	Non-petroleum federal revenues transferred to state	113.00
RRF	Revenues retained by federal government	236.00

Symbol	Definition	Value in FY 1970/71 (in LN million except where otherwise indicated)
RRS	Revenues received by state governments	182.00
	Private Income	
Npr	Private income, rural sector	1,174.00
NPu	Private income, urban sector	942.00
NP	Private income, total	2,116.00
	Consumption and Government Recurrent Expenditure	
CGfg	Federal general recurrent expenditure	54.00
CGsg	State general recurrent expenditure	163.00
CGd	Defense recurrent and capital expenditure	173.00
CGft	Federal government transfers to private sector	50.00
CGst	State governments' transfers to private sector	22.00
C	Total consumption	2,150.00
CP	Private consumption	1,847.00
	Consumer and Intermediate Demand	
CRrc	Consumption of root crops, rural	232.00
CRcg	Consumption of coarse grains, rural	251.00
CRrw	Consumption of rice and wheat, rural	15.00
CRmc	Consumption of miscellaneous crops, rural	133.00
CUrc	Consumption of root crops, urban	58.00
CUcg	Consumption of coarse grains, urban	45.00
CUrw	Consumption of rice and wheat, urban	17.00
CUmc	Consumption of miscellaneous crops, urban	37.00
Crc	Consumption of root crops, total	290.00
Ccg	Consumption of coarse grains, total	296.00
Crw	Consumption of rice and wheat, total	32.00
Cmc	Consumption of miscellaneous crops, total	170.00
Cptx	Consumption of textiles, private	95.00
Cpom	Consumption of other manufactures, private	200.00
Ctx	Consumption of textiles, total	103.00
Com	Consumption of other manufactures, total	220.00
Dp	Demands for local goods and services by petroleum sector	50.00
Dig	Demands for intermediate goods	200.00
	Prices	
Pae	Price index, export crops	1.00
Pao	other agricultural products	1.00
Pp	Export price index of petroleum (realized price)	1.00
Pg	Price index of domestic goods	1.00
Ps	Price index of services (wages)	1.00

Symbol	Definition	Value in FY 1970/71 (in LN million except where otherwise indicated)
Pm	Price index of imported goods and services	1.00
Pgdp	GDP deflator	1.00
Pynp	Non-petroleum GNP deflator	1.00
Pct	Price index of construction	1.00
	Population	
Gp	Natural growth rate of population	2.6 percent
GR	Migration rate (defined as the proportion of the natural increases in rural population that remains in the rural sector)	30 percent
PP	Total population	68 million
PPr	Rural population	54 million
PPu	Urban population	14 million
Grp	Growth rate of rural population	1 percent
Gup	Growth rate of urban population	9 percent
	Savings	
S	National savings	230.00
Sfg	Current surplus of the federal government	-36.00
Ssg	Current surplus of the state governments	-3.00
Sp	Private savings	269.00
	Capital Inflows	
Kp	Foreign capital inflows, petroleum sector	115.00
Knp	Foreign capital inflows, non-petroleum	48.00

System of Equations

All the following variables refer to year t except where otherwise noted. Symbols with *prime* refer to variables in current prices; all others are in constant base-year (1970) prices.

Value added

in 1970/71 prices:

YAec	=	exogenous
YArw	=	exogenous
YArc	=	exogenous
YAcg	=	exogenous
YAmc	=	exogenous
YAft	=	exogenous
YAlv	=	exogenous
YA	=	YAec + YArw + YArc + YAmc + YAft + YAlv
YP	=	exogenous
YMN	=	YMN_{t-1} x 1.03
YQR	=	0.09 x YCT
YMcf	=	$YMcf_{t-1}$ x 1.01
YMpf	=	$YMpf_{t-1} + IMpf_{t-1}/2.5$
YMtx	=	$YMtx_{t-1} + IMtx_{t-1}/2.5$
YMoc	=	$YMoc_{t-1} + IMoc_{t-1}/3.5$
YMig	=	$YMig_{t-1} + IMig_{t-1}/4.00$
YM	=	YMcf + YMpf + YMtx + YMoc + YMig

YCT	=	0.47 [0.88IA + IMNQ + 0.48IMtx + 0.48IMoc + 0.53IMig + 0.39IMpf
		     + 0.18ICT + 0.63IUT + 0.35IT + 0.95IHE + IPA + 0.95IOS + 0.12CGd
		     + 0.07CGg + 0.45Dp]

YUT	=	$YUT_{t-1} + IUT_{t-2}/5.0$
YT	=	$YT_{t-1} + ITp_{t-1}/4.0 + ITg_{t-3}/6.0$
YPA	=	0.30CGg + 0.48CGd
YHE	=	$YHE_{t-1} + IHEp_{t-1}/4.0 + IHEg_{t-2}/10.0$
YOS	=	$YOS_{t-1} + IOS_{t-1}/1.5$
Y	=	YA + YMN + YQR + YM + YCT + YUT + YT
GNP	=	Y - [FPp'/Pp] - [(Fpnp' - Rm' - Rep' - Rec')/Pynp]
Ggnp	=	GNP/GNP_{t-1} - 1.0

in current prices:

$YAec'$	=	$YAec \times Pae$
YA'	=	$YAec' + [YAec]Pao$
YP'	=	exogenous
YMN'	=	$YMN \times Pg$
YQR'	=	$YQR \times Pg$
YM'	=	$YM \times Pg$
YCT'	=	$YCT \times Ps$
YUT'	=	$YUT \times Ps$
YT'	=	$YT \times Ps$
YPA'	=	$YPA \times Ps$
YHE'	=	$YHE \times Ps$
YOS'	=	$YOS \times Ps$
Y'	=	$YA' + YP' + YMN' + YQR' + YM' + YCT' + YUT' + YT' + YPA' + YHE' + YOS'$
GNP'	=	$Y' + Rm' + Rep' + Rec' - FPp' - FPnp'$

Investment

IA	=	exogenous
IP	=	exogenous
IMNQ	=	$2.5[YMN + YQR - YMN_{t-1} - YQR_{t-1}]$
IMcf	=	$YMcf - YMcf_{t-1}$
IMpf	=	$2.50YMpf[Cpf + Cpf_{t-1})/(Cpf_{t-1} + Cpf_{t-2}) - 1.0]$

IF $2.37YMtx < 0.90Ctx$:

$IMtx = 2.50Mtx[(Ctx + Ctx_{t-1})/(Ctx_{t-1} + Ctx_{t-2}) - 1.0]$
$\qquad + 2.50[0.025Ctx_{t-1}/2.27]$

      IF $2.27YMtx \geqslant 0.90Ctx$:

        $IMtx = 2.50YMtx[(Ctx + Ctx_{t-1})/(Ctx_{t-1} + Ctx_{t-2}) - 1.0]$

IF $3.1YMoc < 0.80Com$:

$IMoc = 3.50YMoc[(Com + Com_{t-1})/(Com_{t-1} + Com_{t-2}) - 1.0]$
$\qquad + 3.50[0.025Com_{t-1}/3.1]$

      IF $3.1YMOC \geqslant 0.80Com$

        $IMoc = 3.50YMoc[(Com + Com_{t-1})/(Com_{t-1} + Com_{t-2}) - 1.0]$

IF $2.54YMig < 0.80Dig$

$IMig = 4.00YMig[(Dig + Dig_{t-1})/(Dig_{t-1} + Dig_{t-2}) - 1.0]$
$\qquad + 4.00[0.03Dig_{t-1}/2.54]$

      IF $2.54YMig \geqslant 0.80Dig$

        $IMig = 4.00YMig[(Dig + Dig_{t-1})/(Dig_{t-1} + Dig_{t-2}) - 1.0]$

ICT	=	$1.25\ [/CT - YCT_{t-1}]$
IUT	=	exogenous
ITg	=	exogenous
ITp	=	$ITp_{t-1}\ [1.65Ggnp_{t-1} + 1.00]$
IHEg	=	exogenous
IHEp	=	$IHEp_{t-1}\ [1.50Ggnp_{t-1} + 1.00]$
IPA	=	exogenous
IOS	=	$1.50YOS\ [1.20Ggnp_{t-1} + 1.00]$
I	=	IA + IP + IMNQ + IM + ICT + IUT + ITg + ITp + IHeg + IHEp + IOS + IPA
I'	=	[MME + Mte] Pm + [I - Mme - Mte] Pct

Exports

Ep	=	exogenous
Enp	=	exogenous
Ep'	=	exogenous
Enp'	=	exogenous
E'	=	Ep' + enp'
ENFS'	=	exogenous

Imports

Mp	=	given
Mcr	=	Ccg + crw - YAcg - YArw
Mof	=	$Mof_{t-1}\ [NP/NP_{t-1}]$
Mtx	=	Ctx - 2.27YMtx
Moc	=	Com - 3.10YMoc
Mig	=	Dig - 2.54YMig
Mme	=	0.12IA + 0.50IMN + 0.53IMtx + 0.53IMoc + 0.47IMig + 0.61IMpf + 0.82ICT + 0.37IUT + 0.04IHE + 0.04IOS + 0.13CGd
Mte	=	0.65IT
M	=	Mp + Mcr + Mof + Mtx + Moc + Mig + Mme + Mte
M'	=	M x Pm
MNFnp	=	$MNFNP_{t-1}\ [Ggnp + 1.0]$
MNFnp'	=	MNFnp x Pm
MNFp'	=	exogenous
MNF'	=	MNFnp' + MNFp'

T'	$=$	exogenous
FPp'	$=$	exogenous
FKS'	$=$	$[0.9FKS'_{t-1} + K'np_{t-1}]\ [Pynp/Pynp_{t-1}]$
$FPnp'$	$=$	$0.15FKS' + T'$

Government Revenues and Private Income

Rm'	$=$	$0.28M'$
Rep'	$=$	$0.11[E' - Ep']$
Rec'	$=$	$0.16[2.27YMtx + 3.09YMoc + 2.54YMig + 2.31YMpf]$
Rd'	$=$	$0.041\ [YM' + YCT' + YT' + YOS'] + 0.013GNP'$
Rs'	$=$	$0.016GNP'$
Rpf'	$=$	exogenous
Rps'	$=$	exogenous
RST'	$=$	$0.35Rm + Rep' + 0.50Rec'$
RRF'	$=$	$Rpf' + Rm' + Rep' + Rec' + Rd' - RST'$
RRS'	$=$	$Rs' + Rps' + RST'$
Npr	$=$	YA
NPu	$=$	$GNP - [Rm' + Rep' + Rec' + Rd' + Rs')/Pynp] - [Rpf' + Rps'/Pp]$ $+ 0.40CGg + CGtf' + Cgts' - NPr$
NP	$=$	$Npr + NPu$

Consumption

$CGfg$	$=$	exogenous
$CGsg$	$=$	exogenous
CGd	$=$	exogenous
CGg	$=$	$CGfg + Cgsg$
$CGft'$	$=$	exogenous
$CGst'$	$=$	exogenous
$CGfg'$	$=$	$[0.79Ps + 0.14Pg + 0.07Pct]\,CGfg$
$CGsg'$	$=$	$[0.79Ps + 0.14Pg + 0.07Pct]\,Cgsg$
CGd'	$=$	$[0.65Ps + 0.23Pg + 0.12Pct]\,CGd$
C'	$=$	$YMP' - I' - E' - ENFS' + M' + MNFS'$
CP'	$=$	$C' - 0.60[CGfg' + CGsg'] - Cgd'$

Consumer and Intermediate Demands

rural consumer demands

$CRrc$ = $CRrc_{t-1}[Grp + 1.0]$

$CRcg$ = $Crcg_{t-1}[0.60(NPr/NPr_{t-1} - Grp - 1.0) + Grp + 1.0]$

$CRrw$ = $CRrw_{t-1}[0.20(NPr/NPr_{t-1} - Grp - 1.0) + Grp + 1.0]$

$CRmc$ = $CRmc_{t-1}[0.50(NPr/NPr_{t-1} - Grp - 1.0) + Grp + 1.0]$

urban consumer demands

$CUrc$ = $CUrc_{t-1}[-0.20(NPu/NPu_{t-1} - Gup - 1.0) + Gup + 1.0]$

$CUcg$ = $CUcg_{t-1}[0.40(NPu/NPu_{t-1} - Gup - 1.0) + Gup + 1.0]$

$CUrw$ = $CUrw_{t-1}[1.00(NPu/NPu_{t-1} - Gup - 1.0) + Gup + 1.0]$

$CUmc$ = $CUmc_{t-1}[0.50(NPu/NPu_{t-1} - Gup - 1.0) + Gup + 1.0]$

rural and urban

Crc = $CRrc + CUrc$

Ccg = $CRcg + CUcg$

Crw = $CRrw + CUrw$

Cmc = $CRmc + CUmc$

$Cptx$ = $Cptx_{t-1}[1.80(NP/NP_{t-1} - Gp - 1.0) + Gp + 1.0]$

$Cpom$ = $Cpom_{t-1}[2.35(NP/NP_{t-1} - GP - 1.0) + Gp + 1.0]$

Ctx = $Cptx + 0.04CGg$

Com = $Cpom + 0.10CGg$

Intermediate

Dp = exogenous

Dig = $0.014YA + 0.14[YMN + YQR] + 0.13YMpf + 0.27/Mtx + 0.27YMoc + 0.69Ymig + 0.53YCT + 0.49YUT + 0.27YT + 0.05[YPA + YHE + YOS] + 0.10CGd$

Prices

Pae = exogenous

Pao = exogenous

Pp = exogenous

Pg = exogenous

Ps = exogenous

Pm = exogenous

$Pgdp$ = Y'/Y

Pynp	=	$[Y' - YP']/[Y-YP]$
Pct	=	$0.47Ps + 0.52Pm$

Population

Gp	=	given
GR	=	exogenous
PP	=	$PP_{t-1}[1 + Gp]$
PPr	=	$PPr_{t-1}[1 + GR \times Gp]$
PPu	=	$PP - PPr$
Grp	=	$PPr/PPr_{t-1} - 1.0$
Gup	=	$PPu/PPu_{t-1} - 1.0$

Savings

S'	=	$GNP' - C'$
Sfg'	=	$RRF' - CGfg' - CGd' - CGft'$
Ssg'	=	$RRS' - CGsg' - CGst'$
Sp'	=	$S' - Sfg' - Ssg'$

Capital accounts

Kp'	=	IP'
Knp'	=	exogenous

CHAPTER 10
AGRICULTURE

The share of agriculture in gross domestic product has been declining constantly since 1958/59. At constant factor cost, the share of agriculture, forestry and fishing stood at 66 percent in 1958/59; by 1966/67 it was down to 55 percent, and is estimated to be about 50 percent in 1970/71. Part of this decline in the share of GDP can be attributed to the high growth rates of manufacturing and petroleum. But value-added in agriculture itself stagnated from 1963/64 to 1966/67, after growing at an average rate of nearly 6 percent per annum from 1958/59 to 1963/64. Statistics on agriculture during the war years 1967/68 to 1969/70 show some fluctuations because of the varying geographical coverage and the disruptions in productive activity caused by the hostilities.

The only major export commodities not related to agriculture and forestry are petroleum and tin metal. The agricultural sector accounted for almost all of Nigeria's exports until the early sixties. With the growth of petroleum, the share of agricultural commodities in the total value of exports dropped to 61 percent in 1966 and 38 percent in 1970. This trend will probably continue, with agricultural products providing less than 12 percent of gross export proceeds by 1975.

However, agriculture must continue to be a major focus of development activity in Nigeria, as about 72 percent of the labor force derive their income from the agricultural sector. The sector also has considerable untapped development potential. The following review of the agricultural sector is based to a large extent on the survey undertaken by the IBRD early in 1971.

If immediate steps are taken to improve price incentives, the supply of farm inputs and transportation to restore production in the East, agricultural production could achieve an average growth rate of about 3 percent through 1975, provided the weather is favorable and food output responds to the pressures of demand. This is still less than the average annual increase of 3.3 percent achieved from 1958/59 to 1966/67. In the longer run, provided appropriate steps are taken to overcome the development constraints discussed here, the annual rate of growth could reach 5 percent by 1980.

Table 10-1: PRODUCTION OF MAJOR EXPORT CROPS

(Thousand Tons)

	Average 1959/60-64/65	Average 1965/66-70/71	1974/75	Projections 1979/80	1984/85
Groundnut	625	728	1,100	1,400	2,100
Cocoa	203	226	265	285	330
Palm oil[a]	504	406	515	560	800
Palm kernel[a]	404	285	425	425	470
Rubber[a]	65	60	79	72	95
Seed Cotton	126	154	240	320	560

[a]Calendar years

Source: Statistical Annex Table 36. Projections are IBRD estimates.

An analysis of trends for individual agricultural products shows that the constraint on expansion has almost always been supply rather than demand, even for export crops. The rate at which domestic demand may grow in the years ahead make it likely that this will continue to be true for a number of important crops. The shortage of supply is not so much a consequence of constrained production potential, but is rather a result of the lack of infrastructure and organization. Those involved in production and distribution are not able to respond promptly and effectively to changes in the market situation, and more specifically, to increase in demand.

Investment programs alone cannot create conditions in which an adequate supply response is assured. There is no doubt that improved roads, and specifically access and feeder roads which would end the isolation of traditional agriculture from the modern sector, must play an important role. The promotion and use of modern inputs and the provision of improved plant material through the revamping of an entirely inadequate extension service is equally important, as are the provision of marketing channels and storage facilities. All this, and maybe more, can become a wasted effort if it is not made a part of a coherent and consistent strategy of the government for rural and agricultural development, embracing not only direct investment and the input of more and better trained manpower, but also including proper pricing policies and realistic recognition of the role of the private sector in agricultural marketing and distribution.

Such a strategy, adequately geared to realistic domestic demand forecasts and the need to maintain reasonable price stability should be devised. The lack of, or weakness of existing institutions, the uncertainty of the role of the federal government in agricultural development, the peculiar relation between prices paid to agricultural procedures and the revenues of the states and uncertainty regarding future federal/state financial relations all tend to go together in hampering the effective implementation, or even the formulation, of a sound strategy.

The main emphasis here is on the description and analysis of present patterns of production, marketing and input use, the market prospects for major export crops and the identifiable constraints to development. It summarizes those parts of the IBRD's agricultural sector survey and does not venture into the major policy issues in this part of the economy which are discussed in Chapter 1.

Crops and Livestock

Nigerian agriculture is marked by considerable diversity of output. There is fairly sharp regional specialization in the production of cash crops, based on ecological characteristics. Groundnuts and cotton are grown in the North; the tree crops (cocoa, palm oil and rubber) in the South. In the center of the country is the food crop belt which produces yams, cassava, maize and rice as cash crops. But virtually every farm family, even in areas specializing in other cash crops, also grows food for its own subsistence. Millet, sorghum (guinea-corn) and cowpeas are the staple foods in the groundnut and cotton belts; yams, cassava, cocoyams, maize and rice are grown in the tree crop belt. The tree crop belt is the major food deficit area, partly because it contains the main urban centers. A small surplus of cowpeas is shipped South from the northern states. In aggregate, however, no more than 20 percent of food production enters commercial trade, most of it from the food crop belt to the deficit areas in the South.

Cereals and starchy roots and tubers are the principal items in the average Nigerian diet. Although little reliable data are available, the National Agricultural Development Committee placed the average daily per capita intake at 2,200 kilo calories in 1968/69, which is approximately equal to the estimated requirement. Protein, of which animal protein probably was less than one-third, was only about one-tenth of the total intake. Diets vary considerably between the northern states — where millet and sorghum predominate — and the southern states, which depend mainly upon cassava, yams and cocoyams. Maize is eaten in all areas. Cattle provide the main course of meat in the Muslim North, while the South also relies heavily on goat, sheep, pork and fish. Goats, sheep and various domestic and wild animals are consumed throughout the country.

Groundnuts. The northern states produce 10 percent of world output of groundnuts and supply over 30 percent of world exports. The major part of production is exported, most of it as kernels. Before the growth of petroleum exports since 1969, groundnut products contributed over 20 percent of Nigeria's export earnings. Domestic processing capacity is only half of marketing board purchases. Total production was over a million tons in 1966/67 but has since declined. One of the major causes of this decline was the shift to cotton cultivation in response to a change in relative producer prices. Recently, output has also been adversely affected by climatic conditions.

Domestic demand is projected to double by 1985 to a level of about 0.5 million tons. World export demand is projected to grow at about 2.5 percent per annum. World demand for Nigerian groundnuts is estimated at between 1 million and 1.4 million tons of kernels by 1985. Prices are expected to decline in the next few years because of a relatively rapid increase in world supply.

The northern states will be able to expand production sufficiently to meet a projected demand of 1.5 million to 2.0 million tons by 1985. It is estimated that acreage will increase by

1.75 percent per annum and yields by 2.7 percent per annum.

Cocoa. In the decade before 1970, cocoa contributed 18 percent of Nigeria's export earnings with an annual average output of 210,000 tons. In 1970/71, excellent growing conditions resulted in a record crop of about 310,000 tons, but the world price dropped from U.S.45.7c per pound in 1969 to U.S.29c in 1970.

World demand for cocoa is expected to grow at about 3.5 percent per annum. Because of production limitation, it is unlikely that Nigeria will be able to maintain its present share of 20 percent of world exports. It is estimated that production will be 265,000 tons in 1975, the share in world production dropping to 14 percent by 1985.

Palm Oil. Palm oil is grown predominantly in the eastern states and production was disrupted during hostilities. Production in 1970 was estimated at about 480,000 tons of oil and 295,000 tons of kernels. These levels are still below the production of 1966. Exports of palm oil, £N11 million in 1966, have now been completely displaced by domestic demand. Projections of demand, therefore, depend largely on assumed population growth rates in Nigeria. Domestic consumption could well reach about 800,000 tons of palm oil consumption by 1985. This demand can be met without imports if about 0.5 million acres are replanted in 10-12 years. This is a substantial task, since 90 percent of the present production comes from semi-wild groves covering 3 million acres.

Exports of palm-kernels are estimated to rise to about £N13 million in 1985, still below the average of £N22 million from 1960 to 1966.

Rubber. Production and exports of rubber were maintained at a fairly stable level until 1966 but suffered a set-back because of hostilities. Looking ahead, production rather than world demand will limit exports of rubber.

Taking account of the technological possibilities of substitution between synthetic and natural rubber, it is expected that natural rubber will maintain its 40 percent share of the world market. In 1965, Nigeria had a 3 percent share of world production of natural rubber. Being a price-taker, Nigeria could expand its export substantially without affecting world price. However, production prospects are not bright. In the Mid-Western state which produces 80 percent of Nigeria's rubber, half the acreage will be out of tapping by 1973/74. There has been very little rehabilitation of small holdings and increases in production can be expected only from farm settlements and large plantations. In 1975, production is expected to be 79,000 tons, only slightly higher than production in 1964; by 1980, production will have dropped to 72,000 tons. However, the underlying conditions are favorable to the production of rubber and Nigeria can profitably undertake sizable investment to rehabilitate small-holdings, improve yields and raise the quality of rubber produced.

Cotton. Cotton is second to groundnuts as a cash crop in the northern states. The bulk of raw cotton is consumed in Nigeria, but there is no domestic processing of cottonseed. With textile demand rising at about 6.1 percent per annum, demand for seed cotton is expected to increase four-fold in fifteen years, to a level of 445,000 tons in 1985. Provided there is no shift in the relative prices offered for groundnuts and cotton, this demand can be met from domestic production. It is anticipated that yields will grow at an average of 5 percent per year and acreage at 2.5 percent per year. At these rates of expansion, there will be no difficulty in exporting all available supplies of cottonseed, since Nigeria supplies only 4 percent of world trade in this commodity.

Livestock. Although the livestock sector accounts for only 5 percent of GDP, it is important as a source of protein. Estimates of livestock vary widely but there are approximately 8 million cattle, 23 million sheep and goats, 38 million poultry and 300,000 pigs. The six northern states have nearly all the cattle and two-thirds of the sheep, poultry and goats.

Consumption of meat in 1970 was 154,000 tons of carcasses, of which 26 percent was imported. With rising population and per capita income, the demand for beef at current relative prices is estimated to increase at about 5.7 percent per annum to 271,000 tons of carcasses by 1980. Since it is unlikely that supplies from other West African countries will rise above present levels, this represents a sizable increase in demands on domestic production potential.

It is unlikely that production will increase at more than 3 percent per annum and an upward price trend seems inevitable. Rangeland is insufficient and deteriorating, due in large part to uncontrolled grazing by nomadic herds and encroachment of cultivation. Tsetse fly infestation is widespread, covering an estimated 80 percent of the land area at the end of the rains. Rapid extension of tsetse fly eradication to the middle belt is not practical since techniques to be used in relatively high rainfall areas have not been fully established. Unless the program for tsetse fly eradication is stepped up substantially, with a much greater input of technical manpower, it is unlikely that more than 40,000 square miles will be cleared by 1980. This represents less than 60 percent of the need for the new grazing land.

While tsetse fly eradication is the most important element in a long-term program, an early increase in the supply of meat can be obtained by fattening existing stock prior to slaughter and by encouraging semi-intensive production of pigs and poultry. The major constraint in accomplishing this is the inadequate supply of reasonably priced feed such as sorghum and corn, which can be overcome in the short-run by importing concentrated feedstuffs.

Forestry. Of Nigeria's total land area, 39 percent is classified as forest land and 12.6 percent (45,000 square miles) form the current forest estate. The most valuable area is the high forest, nearly all of which lies in the Western, Mid-West and South Eastern States, and which supplies 75 percent of production on a cutting cycle of 50 years.

During 1960-66, timber exports realized an average of £N7.7 million a year, but this has since dropped to £N4.5 million. The outlook for exports of forestry products is not very promising over the short term because of rising production costs. However, Nigeria is geographically well placed to meet Western European demands. With proper forest management it should be possible to export 20 million cubic feet by the year 2000.

Fuel wood comprises 95 percent of domestic needs for forestry products, but there is a growing demand for sawn wood, poles and paper. The value of industrial wood used locally is estimated at between £N15 million to £N20 million annually and is conservatively estimated to double in the next 30 years.

At present rates of exploitation, resources outside the high forest estate are expected to be exhausted within the next two decades and all natural forest in the high forest estate will have been logged over shortly after the turn of the century. However, forestry output can be expanded substantially by using existing forests more intensively, establishing plantations of quick-growing trees and by establishing integrated industries using existing hardwood forests, and pulp and paper mill complexes based on quick-growing plantations.

Development Constraints and Needs

Land. The total land area of Nigeria is 228 million acres of which 84 million acres are judged to be of medium and high productivity and reasonably suitable for agriculture. This figure does not include areas that might be suitable for range farming. Applying modern technology and making needed improvements, this area could potentially be increased to about 179 million acres.

The degree of utilization of these land resources is still very low. The area presently cropped represents only 25-35 percent of the suitable 84 million acres and only 11-16 percent of the land potentially suitable for agriculture. With traditional shifting cultivation practiced widely, much of the land farmed at any time is in bush fallow. There are also large areas which are not farmed at all.

Although in aggregate land is relatively abundant, population pressures have become serious in the tree crop belts in the South and in the groundnut and cotton belts in the North. Fallow periods under shifting cultivation have become too short to restore fertility in some areas. The original cropping cycle of 10-15 years in large segments of the tree crop belt has already been reduced to five years. In the North, extension of cultivation has reduced the grazing area for nomadic herds, resulting in over-grazing and erosion.

An area which is still under-populated and under-farmed is the vast middle belt covering an area of approximately 75 million acres. Very little has been done to date toward developing this area, which could become the mixed farming area *par excellence* of Nigeria. The major obstacle is the prevalence of the tsetse fly, but its elimination can be economic in the middle belt provided the area is brought into continuous and intensive use.

Techniques. Production is carried out almost entirely by small farmers with holdings of three to seven acres growing a variety of crops, usually including their subsistence needs of food crops. In 1963, about 40 percent of farmers in the northern states and over 60 percent in the southern states held less than 2.5 acres. Ninety percent of the output of palm oil comes from small semi-wild groves.

The implements used in farming are hoes, cutlasses and other primitive hand tools. Use of ox-drawn implements is limited by climatic conditions such as the tsetse fly and the shortage of fodder. Use of power equipment and machinery is almost nil.

Input. The use of improved inputs is extremely limited. Use of chemical fertilizers of all types reached a peak of 65,000 tons in 1967 for a harvested acreage of about 29 million acres. This represents an average of only 5 lbs. per acre. There is no local production of fertilizer, and very little private sector participation in distribution. Fertilizer is imported in bulk and distributed through the extension services and local agents. However, adequate supplies are frequently not available when farmers need them.

The supply of suitable planting materials is seriously deficient for tree crops. Seed production is inadequate even for present needs of cocoa planting and for any large expansion of rubber and palm oil. The distribution facilities for cottonseed and groundnuts will have to be expanded drastically to cope with the rising demand for improved planting materials. Supplies of improved materials for food and feed crops scarcely extend beyond those used for research and experimentation.

Insecticides and other farm chemicals are particularly important for cocoa, palm oil, rubber and cotton, and projected increases in output will require a vastly improved supply network. Further study is also required to assess technical and economic feasibility and possible harmful effects on the environment.

Irrigation. Annual rainfall ranges from 20 inches in the North to about 160 inches in the southeastern region of Nigeria. About 30 percent of the country receives less than 40 inches per annum. Only 36,000 acres are now irrigated, mostly in the North Western, North Eastern and Kwara States and more irrigation is probably necessary to achieve projected expansion in the output of wheat, sugarcane and rice. The Second Development Plan seeks to increase the irrigated area to 160,000 acres by 1974 and 610,000 acres by 1980.

The major problem in expanding irrigation is the absence of basic data to plan projects. Hydrologic data are meager or non-existent; topographic and soil and land surveys are yet to be accomplished; cropping programs need to be established and crop soil acceptances and crop husbandry procedures need to be investigated. These will require considerable time, making it very unlikely that Plan targets, even if found to be justified, will be met. On a very optimistic estimate, no more than 500,000 acres could be brought under irrigation by 1985, contributing an increase in agricultural output of only 3 percent. The same result can be achieved with much less investment by extending the area cropped under rain fed cultivation — currently only 30 million acres out of a possible 80 million acres of arable land.

Tenure. Land tenure systems vary among ethnic groups but a common feature is the absence of individual ownership. In the coastal states, land is regarded as the joint property of the community and the right to cultivate is given to individuals by the traditional head of the community. In the fallow period, land reverts back to the community, although trees are regarded as the property of the man who plants them. Such a system discourages individual investment in conservation, and improvement of land makes it difficult for a farmer to obtain loans using his land for security. In the northern states, land is owned by the state and tenure is on the basis of customary usufruct, a system that leads to friction between herders and farmers.

In many parts of the country the system is already in transition. While there is no need for a major program of land reform, there is need for changes in local legislation that will help the transition to individual tenure and for policies to promote improvement of commercial grazing areas.

Marketing. State marketing boards constitute the exclusive ultimate purchasers of cocoa, groundnuts, cotton, palm produce and a number of minor commercial crops. The major commodities not controlled by marketing boards are rubber and food crops.

Although the original objective in establishing the marketing boards was to stabilize prices earned by farmers and to improve the marketing organization, they have been used during the sixties as a convenient instrument for taxing agriculture. The emphasis on raising revenues has resulted in producer prices being set at roughly half the unit value of exports. Consequently, the return to the farmer engaged in production of export crops is low. At current producers' prices, the gross return per man-day of labor is less than 4 shillings in groundnut and cotton production;

the return on the investment required to establish a nucleus plantation of palm oil is only about 5 percent.

In recent years producer prices have risen substantially: cocoa by 57% from £N96 per ton in 1968/69 to £N151 in 1970/71; groundnuts by 36 percent from £N43 to £N55 per ton in 1968/69. The producer prices of palm products have risen slightly in 1970/71, from £N41 to £44 per ton for palm oil and from £N29 to £N30 per ton for palm kernel. Maintenance of these producer prices will necessarily involve a reduction in revenues generated by marketing boards since world prices of cocoa, groundnuts and cottonseed are all expected to drop slightly over the next five years.

The marketing board system has also been criticized for inefficiencies in opeation. The major items of expense are the buying allowances to the licensed buying agents, transport costs and general and administrative expenses. These amount to about £N20.5 per ton for groundnuts, £N18.6 per ton for cocoa and £N11.7 per ton for palm kernels. It has been estimated that determined efforts to improve efficiency might reduce expenses by 20 percent.

The system of licensed buying agents has also come in for criticism. There is some evidence that the allowances paid to them are excessive and, further, the marketing boards have no effective control over the prices paid to the farmer by the licensed buying agents. There is considerable scope for licensed buying agents to short-change producers on weight and grade of produce purchased.

The marketing of products not controlled by the marketing boards is handled by a traditional, fragmented system. Various studies on the marketing of foodstuffs have concluded that, given the existing infrastructure, traders were reasonably efficient and achieved a considerable degree of inter-market coordination. The infrastructure, however, is inadequate. Poor transport links tend to cause seasonal price variations in small isolated markets. Storage costs are as high as 2½–3 percent of the value of produce stored per month. Lack of adequate wholesale market facilities inhibits the inflow of perishable foodstuffs into the cities, widening the spread of prices between urban and rural centers. The high cost of distribution of foodstuffs has probably contributed to the increase in urban food prices.

Transport. Transport is the principal component of marketing costs. It accounts for 30–40 percent of total marketing costs for cotton, 35–55 percent for groundnuts and about 20 percent for cocoa. The transport network and the main arterial roads are in poor condition because of vehicle overloading and inadequate maintenance. These roads are vital in moving export crops to the ports. The railways have been unable to service traffic demand adequately, resulting in increased transport costs. For example, from 1967 to 1970 the number of cattle moved by rail halved both in absolute numbers and as a percentage of total cattle moved. The alternative modes of transport, road and hoof, involve higher direct costs and higher mortality rates.

Since there is little animal transport, a farm family's marketed output is limited largely to the amount of goods which can be moved by human power unless there is an adequate network of feeder roads. Greater attention will have to be given to the development of feeder roads to facilitate the distribution of farm inputs, and evacuate produce economically.

Credit. Lack of agricultural credit is increasingly singled out as a major handicap. Institutional credit has been available to farmers for the past two or three decades but has not been successful. The only institutions now in operation in the Western and Mid-Western states do not have active credit programs and are concerned only with collecting old debts. Commercial banks have extended credit to some large-scale plantations but not to small farmers. Agricultural cooperatives reach less than 5 percent of the farming population. They have limited financial programs, most of which go to marketing and they provide negligible credit for production purposes.

Improved income for farmers and the modernization of agriculture will bring forth a rising demand for credit. On the basis of present plans for replanting of cocoa, rubber, and palm oil alone, annual credit needs are estimated at about £N11 million by 1980. Credit needs for production of cotton and groundnuts could exceed £N5 million by 1980.

The absence of a federal institution is being remedied by the establishment of a National Agricultural Credit Bank. The bank will lend money for credit projects which would be administered by the states or state institutions. The Second Development Plan has earmarked £N6 million for the bank over the next five years. Since farmers now incur interest charges somewhere between 24 percent and 50 percent, the Credit Bank should be able to charge interest rates high enough to cover expenses.

Research. Research has been conducted in a number of semi-autonomous institutions situated in the various ecological regions in the country. Export crops have received the main emphasis while food and feed crops have been comparatively neglected. The best prospects of immediate application are for tree crops, groundnuts and cotton, where experimental yields have been two to three times higher than present yields. By the mid-seventies suitably high-yielding varieties of sorghum, maize and rice should be available for multiplication. There are possibilities for increasing yields of yams and cassava but further work needs to be done to develop disease-resistant varieties and improve farming practices.

Much of the problem in research has been the absence of overall direction. The Agricultural Research Council has recently been set up to remedy this. Another drawback has been that research has sought technical optima for individual crops instead of focusing on the total farming system and on integrating improvements within that system.

There is inadequate agro-economic data on basic economic limitations, such as the shortage of labor at key periods in the cropping year, to provide complete guidance for re-orientation of technical research programs. There is urgent need for more studies of the type now being carried out by the Rural Economic Research Unit at the Institute of Agricultural Research.

Manpower and Coordination. Inadequate overall planning and coordination at the federal level is an impediment to agricultural development. Unitl recently, the principal responsibility of the Federal Ministry of Agriculture and Natural Resources was limited to research. The links between the federal and state ministries of agriculture are weak, making it difficult to monitor the implementation of projects in the Development Plan. The present system also tends to discourage regional specialization based on comparative advantage.

Moves to strengthen the state ministries have come up against the shortage of suitably qualified personnel, necessitating consideration of large-scale outside assistance.

Perhaps the most serious restraint on agricultural development is the shortage of qualified personnel for planning and project preparation as the state level. With few exceptions, state staffs have no more than one year's experience in planning or project work. Present training facilities are inadequate. In the long run, an increased supply of manpower should be forthcoming from the educational system. What is urgently needed is the establishment of ad hoc, in-service training centers to solve the short-term problem.

CHAPTER 11

FISCAL TRENDS AND PROSPECTS

From the 1971/72 fiscal year the budgetary outlook in Nigeria has totally changed. Whereas during the whole of the decade of the sixties the state governments in Nigeria faced serious financial difficulties, the outlook for the next five years appears to be one of large budgetary surpluses substantially increasing over time. The overall budget surplus of the federal government will increase from 14 percent of all government (federal and state) revenues in 1971/72 to 46 percent in 1975/76, a substantial part of this being realized in the next two years or so.

The financial difficulties of the sixties were largely the result of the inelasticity of the existing tax structure, inadequate tax effort and rapidly increasing recurrent expenditure, especially on administration, defense and public debt charges. The emergence and expansion of the petroleum sector in recent years has improved the fiscal situation. The rest of the tax system, however, remains substantially unchanged.

When the Second National Development Plan was formulated in 1970 the "radical transformation" of the budgetary situation resulting from the long-run prospects of oils was foreseen. Nevertheless, finance was considered the most serious bottleneck during the present Plan period. Consequently, the government appears to have been caught somewhat unprepared for the revenue surpluses it has enjoyed in more recent months. Not having planned for the "optimum" utilization of these unanticipated revenues, the government has started retiring the short-term indebtedness it accumulated with the banking system during hostilities.

Over the longer term the government has a number of options, and, therefore, must make a number of decisions, regarding the disposition of those resources accruing to it in excess of *planned* amounts.

First, the government can continue to retire short-term debt in the interest of economic stability. (In the long run, it would also be desirable to lengthen the maturity structure of the public debt and encourage the non-public holdings of government indebtedness.) The limit to which budgetary surpluses could be used for this purpose should be determined by the debt service burden, the needs of the money and capital markets for financial assets, and the effect on income distribution, as well as the *returns* on alternative uses of budgetary resources. On the whole it appears that the scope of this policy option will remain limited.

Second, the government could expand its recurrent expenditure on economic, social and community services. The absolute level of the federal government recurrent expenditure on these services in 1969/70 was exactly the same as in 1961, and such increases as the state governments achieved during the past decade were inadequate. The share of recurrent expenditure of all governments on these essential services declined from 52 percent in 1961 to 32 percent in 1970/71. Besides improving the overall availability of essential public services, the government could also attempt to overcome the large inter-state disparities in the levels of public services. This is one of the stated priorities of the Second Plan. However, since development services are provided by the state governments and local authorities, the finances of these entities will have to be strengthened. The existing heavy dependence of the states on the central government suggests that, at least in the short run, any solution will involve increasing federal revenue transfers to the states. In the medium and long run, the state governments will have to expand their own tax base and make a greater tax effort. Their past performance in this respect leaves much to be desired. In recent years, the federal government has seriously attempted to expand statutory appropriations to the states and, in the interest of balanced development, to divorce revenue allocations from the controversial "derivation" principle. If the state governments are to avoid severe financial difficulties (and the recent Adebo Award has added to their financial problems), the revenue allocation system will have to be kept under constant review.

While it would be desirable to increase recurrent expenditure on development services (and simultaneously to reduce government expenditure on general administration, defense and internal security), this should be accompanied by an improvement in the overall quality of public services. A general expansion of the government wage bill, resulting from salary revisions and larger employment, will not insure an adequate volume of essential public services. There should also be a significant increase in the proportion of recurrent expenditure on goods and services devoted to developmental services.

Third, the government can revise its Plan investment targets and expand the scale and composition of capital expenditure. The constraint here seems to be the lack of adequate executive capacity both at the federal and state levels. Optimum utilization of existing capacity may require revisions in the level and pattern of federal capital grants provided to the states in the short run. In the medium and long run, the government will have to invest in the future expansion of executive capacity itself.

Fourth, the government can encourage private investment in industry and agriculture through fiscal and non-fiscal incentives. The government has recently revised its policies on tax incentives for industrial development; it plans to narrow the scope of existing tax incentives and to make them more selective. The problem of fiscal incentives to agricultural development is particularly complicated. The taxation of agricultural exports is directly related to state finances, and a reduction of the tax burden on agricultural exports, were it to be considered essential, would probably have to wait until there had been a more general resolution of the whole question of state finances. So far as the traditional agricultural sector is concerned, fiscal incentives must operate from the public-expenditure side. Since agriculture is primarily a responsibility of the state governments, this will involve aiding the state governments for purposes of agricultural development. The government can also provide many non-fiscal incentives for both agricultural and industrial development but these are not discussed in this chapter.

These are some of the policy options which the government has for the use of its budgetary surpluses and each is subject to its own constraints. The federal-state financial relations is the one factor which emerges as *crucial* to all policies involving an *optimum* use of likely budgetary surpluses.

Any revisions which might be undertaken must recognize the fact that there is a substantial taxable capacity which the state governments are not presently exploiting. This exists specifically in the areas of personal income taxation, property taxation, sales taxes and certain specific rates. The problems of the state governments' tax collections and administrations is another subject which requires close attention. These and many other tax reforms appear necessary not only to resolve the financial problems of the state governments, and to reduce their dependence on the federal government, but also in the interest of controlling excessive demand, mitigating inflationary pressures and reducing the inequalities of incomes and wealth, including specifically the rural-urban disparities.

While formulating an overall strategy for the utilization of the budgetary surpluses, the government should also look into the scope for improving the profitability of statutory corporations through financial and non-financial means.

The emergence of budgetary surpluses provides a propitious opportunity to examine and revamp various aspects of fiscal policy, which, in any event, the government had planned to do during the Second Plan period.

Budgetary Developments and Projections

The fiscal year 1971/72 marks a dramatic transition from a period of rising deficits to a situation of overall budget surplus which is expected to remain a feature of public finance for some years to come. The fiscal development of the sixties was marked by a gradual erosion of initially substantial annual current surpluses in the federal government budgets. These virtually disappeared around the middle of the decade. The defense expenditures associated with the disturbances of 1967-70 created serious financial difficulties for the federal government and resulted in mounting internal debt and severe cutbacks in civil expenditures, particularly government expenditures on essential economic and social services. The sharp increase of revenue originating in the petroleum producing sector since 1970 is expected to continue for several years to come and is markedly changing the situation.

In this chapter, which discusses in detail the developments and issues outlined in Chapter 1, Nigeria's past and present performance is described and analyzed, and major issues which are expected to be important in the future are identified. Fiscal developments in the past ten years are analyzed for three distinct periods with the civil war providing the dividing lines. A discussion of fiscal performance between 1961 and 1966 is followed by an account of the financing of the civil war (1966-70) and by an analysis of current developments. In the latter part, the consequences of the recent salary adjustments in the public sector stemming from the report of the Adebo Commission are emphasized. The next section discusses the fiscal prospects of Nigeria through the mid-1970s. The emphasis is on revenue projections and the provision of a forecast of current expenditures, assuming policies similar to those of the past years.

Certain topics have been selected for discussion because of their relevance to Nigeria's fiscal outlook. The present government debt and the levels and composition of current expenditures are two of those topics. The distribution of resources between different levels of government is discussed under current expenditures. The capital expenditure prospects are assessed with the issues of providing adequate financial resources to state and local governments and the statutory agencies. Sections on tax incentives to private investment and on the needs and scope for tax reforms follow.

Fiscal Developments, 1961-66

When Nigeria became independent in 1960, it inherited, like other less-developed countries, a tax structure which was neither very productive nor very balanced. Government revenues (of federal and regional governments) were 11.5 percent of GDP at factor cost in 1961. This cannot be considered unduly low for a country with as small a per capita income as Nigeria at that time. About 60 percent of these revenues were from foreign trade taxes. Import duties alone accounted for 45 percent of total government revenues.

In Nigeria, a federation, much of the federal government's revenues from import, export, and excise duties have been returned to the regions or states from which they were derived. In 1961, for example, about 30 percent of recurrent revenues of the federal government were returned to regional governments. Since the federal government's own recurrent expenditure was small, there was still a current surplus exceeding 38 percent of retained revenues (Table 11-1).

The First Development Plan (1962-68) identified the need for increased tax effort, both at the federal and regional government levels, to generate adequate resources to finance public investment programs. The Plan contained few specific objectives and targets on ways to improve the tax structure between direct and indirect taxes and between domestic and foreign trade taxes. Little attention was given to the generation of resources to finance increased current expenditures on economic and social services needed to maintain and operate the country's expanding economic and social infrastructure.

Actual fiscal developments during the First Plan period were not encouraging. The revenue ratio (i.e., ratio of federal and regional governments' revenues to GDP at factor cost) which stood at 11.5 percent in 1961 increased to 12.3 percent in 1966/67. The receipts from foreign trade taxes declined from a share of 60 percent to 58 percent of total revenues over this period. However, the regional governments claimed an increasing share of the federal government's current revenues, increasing from 30 percent in 1961 to 40 percent in 1966/67. These larger transfers improved the revenue position of the regional governments, but also adversely affected the revenue retentions of the federal government. However, the revenues raised by the regional governments, mainly from the personal income tax, produce purchase and sales taxes, licenses and fees, showed little improvement (remaining almost constant at £N30 million) during these years (Table 11-2).

Between 1961-66, the recurrent expenditure (Table 11-3) of the federal government increased by 83 percent, close to 13 percent per annum (Table 11-3) while revenues rose only 37 percent. The current surplus of the federal government dwindled from 34 percent of its retentions in 1961 to a current deficit in 1966 (Table 11-1). The largest increase in expenditure took place in general administration, defense, and public debt charges. (Amortization payments are included in recurrent expenditures. Separate data on interest and repayments are not readily available.) A quadrupling of debt charges, a doubling of general administration expenditure, and an 80 percent increase of defense outlays almost preempted the entire increase of retained federal government resources (Table 11-3).

In contrast to the rapid growth of general administration, defense expenditures and debt charges during 1961-66, the increase of federal expenditures on essential economic, social and community services was only 20 percent (Table 11-3). However, regional expenditures in these categories, especially education, increased much faster over this period, so that total outlays for

Table 11-1: FEDERAL GOVERNMENT FINANCES, 1961-66

					(In Millions of £N)	
	1961	1962	1963	1964	1965	1966
Recurrent revenues (of which taxes on	111.8	119.4	124.5	138.6	160.5	153.2
international trade)	(73.7)	(71.5)	(74.8)	(90.7)	(100.6)	(72.8)
Revenues transferred to Regions	33.4	36.0	37.8	56.5	65.4	60.7
Revenues retained by the Federal Government	78.4	83.4	86.7	82.1	95.1	92.5
Federal recurrent expendi- tures (including defense and internal security capital expenditures)	51.7	57.6	64.3	78.8	85.4	94.4
Current surplus/deficit (+/–)	+26.7	+25.8	+22.4	+3.3	+9.7	-1.9
Capital expenditures[a]	34.7	43.5	36.7	35.5	43.0	47.7
(of which loans/grants to Regions)	(4.5)	(17.4)	(9.0)	(5.2)	(10.2)	(14.6)
Overall budget deficit (–)	-8.0	-17.7	-14.0	-32.2	-33.3	-49.6

[a]Excluding capital expenditure on defense and internal security.
Source: Based on Statistical Annex, Tables 24 and 25.

Table 11-2: REGIONAL GOVERNMENT FINANCES, 1961-66

					(In Millions of £N)	
	1961	1962	1963	1964	1965	1966
Recurrent revenues (of which transfers from	58.6	65.2	67.7	84.9	97.0	90.6
Federal Government)	(33.4)	(36.0)	(37.8)	(56.5)	(65.4)	(60.7)
Recurrent expenditures	57.8	69.1	63.7	71.9	83.8	86.1
Current surplus/deficit (+/–)	+0.8	-3.9	+4.0	+13.0	+13.2	+4.5
Federal capital loans/grants	44.5	117.4	9.0	5.2	10.2	14.6
Capital expenditures	28.4	28.1	27.8	31.3	20.5	32.0
Overall budget deficit (-)	-23.1	-14.6	14.8	-13.1	-7.1	-12.9

Source: Based on Statistical Annex, Tables 25 and 26.

Table 11-3: GOVERNMENT RECURRENT EXPENDITURES, 1961-66

(In Millions of £N)

	1961	1966	Annual % change
Federal Government	51.7	94.4	12.9
General Administration	10.8	21.7	15.0
Defense and Internal Security[a]	12.9	23.2	12.6
Debt Charges	5.1	22.6	34.6
Economic & Social Services	18.2	21.9	3.8
Other	4.7	5.0	1.3
Regional Governments	57.8	86.1	8.4
General Administration	12.6	18.1	7.5
Economic & Social Services	37.5	58.4	9.3
Others	7.7	9.6	4.5
Total Federal/Regional Governments	109.5	180.5	10.7

[a]Includes capital expenditures on defense and internal security.
Source: Based on Statistical Annex, Tables 25 and 26.

economic and social services nevertheless showed significant growth, although still much less than other current expenditures.

Defense and internal security not only absorbed an increasing share of the federal government's current budget, but also of its capital budget. Federal government capital expenditures on defense and internal security increased from £N3.3 million in 1961 to £N7 million in 1965 (Table 11-1). While defense absorbed 7.5 percent of all government expenditures (and 1.1 percent of GDP) in 1961, its share was close to 9 percent (and 1.5 percent of GDP) in 1966/67.

Despite the country's commitment to a Development Plan, federal government capital expenditures (excluding loans on-lent and grants to the regions and defense expenditures) remained almost stationary, increasing from £N29 million in 1961 to £N33 million in 1966 (Table 11-1). The federal government invested large amounts of capital in transport and communications, especially in roads. Roads accounted for about 60 percent of all federal government capital expenditures in 1961 and over 52 percent in 1966.

Capital expenditures by the regions, like those of the federal government, remained more or less static around £N30 million between 1961 and 1966 (Table 11-2). Their investment in agriculture increased from £N1 million in 1961 to £N8 million in 1966. This was perhaps because the regional governments' finances were closely linked to agriculture – both through taxes and the surpluses of the marketing boards. Other regional capital expenditures declined.

While the re-lent funds from the federal government provided an expanding source of regional government capital receipts, the marketing board surpluses continued to provide a major share – at times equivalent to a third or one-half of their overall budget deficits.

To summarize: during the First Plan (1962-68) public finances of the federal and regional governments lacked buoyancy. The chief characteristics of the fiscal situation were a relatively low revenue effort,[1] heavy dependence on foreign trade taxes, rapidly growing administrative and defense expenditures, low levels of absolute capital expenditures and relatively slow growth in the modest economic and social services. The share of recurrent and capital expenditures on developmental services in GDP at factor cost remained around 8.2 percent between 1961 and 1966. The

1. Cf. A.O. Phillips, "Nigeria's Tax Effort," *The British Tax Review* (May-June 1970), pp. 180-194 and V.P. Diejomaoh, "Tax and Revenue Allocation Policies," paper presented at the *Conference on Integration and National Unity*, University of Lagos, December 15, 1970, pp. 6-9.

low tax effort was perhaps partly because the First Development Plan anticipated substantially more foreign aid than, in fact, materialized. Also, there was a heavy reliance by the federal government on customs duties which increased only modestly. The regional governments became more dependent upon federal transfers, on-lent funds, and marketing board surpluses.

While the federal government apparently attached low priority to recurrent and capital expenditures on essential public services — focusing on general administration and defense — the regional governments concentrated primarily on education, agriculture and health. Other economic and social services, e.g., water supply and feeder roads, were almost ignored. The stagnating levels of federal and regional government capital expenditures added to the apparent lack of effort to improve basic economic and social facilities. As for the tax effort, this may have resulted from planned over-dependence on foreign aid during the First Plan. At the same time this could also be a reflection of the lack of executive capacity, now singled out as a major constraint in the Second National Development Plan (1970-74) of Nigeria.

Declining current budgetary surpluses led the federal government to rely increasingly on internal borrowing to finance its capital expenditure. Public debt as a percent of GDP at factor cost increased from 7.4 percent in 1961 to 15.1 percent in 1966/67 (Statistical Annex Table 32.) The regional governments relied largely on marketing board surpluses and federal relending to them. Thus both levels of governments in Nigeria financed a stationary amount of capital expenditures aided by substantial growth in internal borrowings.

Financing the Civil War, 1967-1969/70

The war, which broke out during 1967, aggravated the fiscal situation further. Planned economic development halted completely from 1967 to 1969. Federal government's defense and internal security expenditures on recurrent account grew from £N18.2 million in 1966/67 to £N136.1 million in 1969/70 and defense capital expenditure rose from £N5.6 million to £N56 million (Statistical Annex Table 25). Together, the share of defense expenditure in total government expenditure increased from 9 percent in 1966/67 to 41.7 percent in 1969/70, and as a proportion of GDP at factor cost from 1.5 to 12 percent over these years.

While the federal government's revenues increased substantially, largely from import duties which rose from £N56.9 million in 1966/67 to £N80.7 million in 1969/70, they proved totally inadequate for defense needs. The federal government cut both recurrent and capital expenditures on economic social and community services during the war years. Total government expenditure on these services fell from 8.2 percent of the GDP in 1966/67 to 5.9 percent of the GDP in 1968/69, recovering however to 7.7 percent in 1969/70 (Statistical Annex Tables 24 and 25.) During the same years, the federal government current surplus of £N1.2 million was converted into a current deficit of £N167.9 million (Table 11-4).

Resources required to finance the civil war could not be obtained by cutting government expenditures on economic and social services alone. Substantial internal borrowing became necessary and, consequently, the amount of internal debt outstanding increased from £N173.2 million in 1966/67 to £N468.9 million in 1969/70. The ratio of public debt to GDP at factor cost increased from 11.1 percent in 1964/65 to 34.7 percent in 1969/70 (Statistical Annex Table 32). The pressures of defense were so large that even federal grants and re-lending to the state governments and statutory corporations had to be reduced — from £N20.4 million in 1966/67 to £N10.7 million in 1969/70. This might not appear to be a large cut in absolute terms, but was quite significant compared to the already meager capital resources of the state governments.

The development of state finances cannot be analyzed as the available data exclude the finances of the eastern states in some years and only incomplete information is available for several states recently. Yet, the existing data demonstrate that state governments' capital expenditures fell sharply between 1967 and 1969 and investments in economic and social services were severely cut.

General administration and defense were largest among the few expenditure categories which grew unabated over the sixties. Both of these tend to be only upwardly flexible. This, therefore, poses a continuing threat to the generation of adequate development resources. The debt service burden continued to grow (in 1969/70 it absorbed 15.2 percent of government current revenues - Table 11-9), as did the proportion of public debt to GDP. Neither of these growth rates are alarming, however.

Table 11-4: FEDERAL GOVERNMENT FINANCES, 1966/67-1971/72

(In Millions of £N)

	1966/67	1967/68	1968/69	1969/70	1970/71	1971/72 (Est.)[a]
Recurrent revenues (taxes	169.6	150.1	149.9	217.9	377.8	646.0
on international trade)	(70.9)	(68.6)	(73.1)	(99.9)	(137.1)	(176.0)
(oil revenues)	(21.3)	(23.1)	(13.5)	(34.8)	(102.8)	(320.0)
(other)	(77.4)	(58.3)	(63.3)	(74.1)	(115.6)	(150.0)
Transfers to the States	68.6	61.4	53.0	89.7	143.4	176.0
Revenues retained	101.0	88.7	96.9	128.2	234.4	470.0
Recurrent expenditures	99.8	126.0	161.5	296.1	271.4	315.0
(defense and internal security)[b]	(23.8)	(61.8)	(91.5)	(192.0)	(172.8)	(182.0)
Current surplus/ deficit (+/-)	+1.2	-37.3	-64.6	-167.9	-37.0	+155.0
Capital expenditures[c]	46.8	35.2	37.3	31.5	42.0	56.0
Overall budget Deficit (+/-)	-45.6	-72.5	-101.9	-199.4	-79.0	+99.0

[a]Mission estimates.
[b]Includes capital expenditures on defense and internal security.
[c]Excludes defense and internal security but includes capital transfers to states.
Source: Based on Statistical Annex, Tables 24 and 25.

Although the fiscal performance of the past has not been adequate from a development viewpoint, it is nevertheless remarkable that a country which had limited public sector resources and which fought a difficult and costly war for several years has been able to emerge from this period without serious financial problems. Oil revenues now accruing to the federal government do, to an extent, mask the true impact of war financing on the more recent budgets, but even in the immediate postwar period revenues were high and rising, external borrowing had not been a factor in the financing of the war, and internal borrowing, although substantial, was not of a magnitude which could not be overcome in the course of subsequent years. This achievement of the government under serious financial pressures is a factor of some importance in judging the performance of the Nigerian fiscal authorities.

Budgetary Position, 1970/71-1971/72

The major development since the war has been the appearance of substantial and increasing federal government revenues from the petroleum sector. These revenues rose from £N34 million in 1969/70 to over £N300 million in 1971/72. While the government revenues from mining rents and royalties more than doubled, petroleum profits taxes increased even more from £N12 million in 1969/70 to £N230 million in 1971/72. This increase resulted from three factors: increased oil production — from 52 million barrels in 1968 to an estimated 560 million barrels in 1971; an increase in the posted price of oil from £N0.78 per barrel before March, 1971 to £N1.15 per barrel thereafter; and a rise in the tax rate from 50 percent to 55 percent in April 1971.

Government revenues, other than those from oil, are also buoyant. The liberalization of imports initiated in 1970/71, accompanied by certain adjustments in import duty rates, should cause significant increases in import duty receipts. Assuming an "average" import duty rate of 30 percent[2] and a merchandise import level of £N540 million, import duty receipts may have reached a level of £N162 million in 1971/72. The mission's estimate of £N155 million is more conservative, and accounts for refunds to the oil companies. This would still mean a doubling of import duty receipts since 1969/70.

Excise duty receipts have also begun to improve, largely as a result of resumption of production and reconstruction following the civil war. Although there have been some increases in excise duty rates, e.g., beer, in 1971/72, they have been partly offset by reductions elsewhere, e.g., butter and margarine. Excise receipts, which increased from £N39 million in 1969/70 to £N65.9 million in 1970/71, are likely to have increased further to £N82 million in 1971/72.

Thus, total federal government tax revenues were probably about £N646 million during 1970/71 compared to an original budget estimate of £N385 million and actual revenues of £N378 million in 1970/71 (Table 11-4). Larger tax receipts of the federal government would also imply larger revenue transfers to the state governments. States should receive about £N176 million of the federal revenues against £N143.4 million in 1971. This should help some states though not eliminate the overall budget deficits of all states (Tables 11-14 and 11-15).

While federal government revenues, and particularly those from oil, improved substantially in 1971/72, recurrent expenditures should increase. Assuming that: (a) public debt charges (including repayments) and other transfers will be close to £N50 million, as estimated in the budget; (b) defense and internal security expenditure, on current and capital account, will increase from £N173 million in 1971 to £N195 million in 1972 because of general price increases and possible wage increases; and (c) all other recurrent expenditures, budgeted at £N62 million, will be exceeded by about £N8 million largely as a result of the implementation of the Adebo Award and the general price increases, the recurrent expenditure of the federal government is likely to be £N315 million in 1971/72 compared with £N296 million in 1969/70 (Table 11-4).

Wages and Salaries: The Adebo Award

The Salaries and Wages Review Commission was appointed in April, 1970, under the chairmanship of Chief S.O. Adebo to examine the existing pay scales at all levels of public service, including statutory public corporations and state-owned companies. The cost of living and remuneration levels in the private sector, and requirements for the rapid development of the national economy were considered. The commission submitted its final report in August, 1971, and recommended the increases in the wages and salaries of both monthly-rated and daily-rated staff shown in Table 11-5.

The federal government implemented the salary increases recommended by the Adebo Commission effective September 1, 1971. The Adebo Award did not apply to the Armed Forces or to the Police. For these the government has (or will shortly) set up separate study groups whose recommendations will be considered soon.

The Adebo Award will increase the wages and salaries of all non-defense personnel of the federal government by 12 to 30 percent per year. As most employees are in the salary range of £N500 or below, the average increase of the government wage bill will be about 25 percent. In 1971/72, non-defense recurrent expenditure (excluding public debt charges) was budgeted at £N62 million. Assuming that 50 percent of this amount represented the wage bill,[3] the annual cost

---

2. Import duty collections of £N75.8 million and £N109 million on merchandise imports of £N232.3 million and £N368.9 million for 1969 and 1970 respectively, yielded "average" import duty rates of 32.6 and 29.5 percent in these years. The 1971/72 budget raised the import duties on consumer items such as coffee, flour, tomato puree and paste, unbleached fabrics and certain other textile intermediates, but reduced those on industrial machinery and parts. Concessionary import duties have been introduced for certain intermediate products.

3. Cf. the economic classification of federal current expenditures given in *Annual Abstract of Statistics, 1969,* Table 11.5, p. 121.

Table 11-5: ADEBO COMMISSION RECOMMENDATIONS ON
SALARY INCREASES

State(s)	Revised Wage Rate
1. Daily-Rated Workers	
Lagos	10-0 per day or £N13-0-0 per month
Kwara, North Eastern and North Western	7-0 per day or £N9-2-0 per month
All others	8-9 per day or £N10-0 per month

2. Established and Monthly-Rated Staff

Existing Salary Levels Per Annum		Award
£N200 or below		30 percent of the salary of £N36 whichever is higher
£N200	£N500	£N60
£N500	£N1,000	£N120
£N1,000	£N2,000	£N180
£N2,000	£N2,500	£N240
Over £N2,500		£N300

Source: Federal Republic of Nigeria, *Second and Final Report of the Wages & Salaries Review Commission, 1970-71* (Lagos, 1971) p. 84.

of the Adebo Award to the federal budget could be about £N7 million to £N8 million. Because the Adebo Award applied for only six months of the fiscal year, its cost to the recurrent budget would be around £N4 million in 1971/72.

This, however, does understate the impact of the Adebo Award on the federal current budget. It does not take account of the federal government's wage bill for defense and police. If this part of the wage bill rose as much as the Adebo Award, it could add another £N9 million to current expenditures in 1971/72. Assuming that 50 percent of the government's defense (and internal security) expenditure of £N145 million represents the wage bill, an average 25 percent increase in salaries of defense and police personnel would increase the defense expenditure by £N18 million per annum or £N9 million over the six-month period. More importantly, the Adebo Award is also applicable to employees of the statutory public corporations, federally-owned companies, state governments, and local authorities and their corporations. The federal government recognizes the inability of many of these agencies to meet the financial costs of the Adebo Award. The major statutory corporations are already suffering losses (Table 11-20). The financial difficulties of the local authorities as well as of many state governments are recognized by the federal government.[4] Undoubtedly, this additional burden will largely be passed on to the federal government budget,

4. Federal Government of Nigeria, *White Paper* on Adebo Commission report, 1971, paragraph 9 (iv).

although estimates now cannot be made easily. Assuming that the federal government employs some 40 percent of the civilian public sector manpower and the remaining 60 percent are employed by state governments, local authorities, and public corporations,[5] and that the average salaries in the non-federal public sector are not markedly different from those in the federal government, the cost of the Adebo Award to the rest of the public sector could be about 2/3 times the cost for the civilian staff of the federal government. The additional cost involved could be about £N18 million per year or £N9 million for the last six months of 1971/72.

The White Paper on the Adebo Commission Report notes that "the total effect of the acceptance of the Report on various levels of the public sector is far-reaching". The cost to the federal current budget could be at least £N14 million in 1971/72, or, under the most unfavorable assumptions, could be about £N25 million. After the following fiscal year, it would be at least £N20 million, but could rise to around £N50 million. The lower or upper limits depend upon whether the federal government decides to transfer revenues to the non-federal public sector to finance the Adebo Award. If the upper estimate is reached, the Adebo Award would absorb a large part of the current surplus and serious inflation could result.

The buoyant revenues in 1971/72 should have been more than adequate to absorb the budgeted growth in recurrent expenditure as well as the known cost of the Adebo Award. The federal government is likely to have realized a larger current surplus despite a larger expenditure on economic and social services than in 1970/71. Nigeria's current public finance problem is not the presence of constraints on the mobilization of current revenues to finance public sector outlays, but rather the character of those revenues and the impact of public spending on the economy. The government's oil revenues originate in a sector which adds no goods and services directly to the domestic economy, and very few indirectly. Inflationary impact of government spending financed with oil revenues can only be avoided if these revenues are spent on imports or used in ways which simultaneously create additional output of goods and services.

Capital Expenditure

The federal government's capital expenditures in 1971/72 should be close to £N50 million to 60 million as compared to £N42 million in 1970/71 (excluding capital expenditure on defense and internal security). If capital transfers to states were excluded, these amounts would be £N40 and £N34 respectively. These are about 40 percent of the budgeted levels. These shortfalls partly reflect the delays in 1970/71, and to some extent in 1972, to get actual spending and implementation underway. To a degree it also reflects inadequate project preparation and the lack of executive capacity, rather than any shortage of finances. The estimates of the 1971/72 fiscal year indicate that the federal government should have an overall budgetary surplus of almost £N100 million in 1971/72 representing about 20 percent of retained recurrent revenues (Table 11-4).

While the federal government would experience an overall budget surplus, the state governments are likely to face financial difficulties. According to their budget estimates, the states would have had an overall deficit of some £N122 million in 1971/72, after allowing for an expected £N16 million from relending and grants of the federal government and another £N6 million from the marketing boards (Statistical Annex Table 28). However, state governments are likely to receive larger federal receipts than their budgets show; probably £N176 million against £N126 million budgeted. Their realized capital expenditure would be lower so that the difference would more than offset the remaining estimated current deficit. All the same, they would have a substantial overall deficit (Table 11-6). A detailed account of the investment program of the public sector and its implementation is given in Chapter 1. The main issue – to be discussed separately – with respect to financing of capital expenditures is the contrasting positions of the federal and state governments. The tight situation facing the latter is very different from the substantial surpluses being generated by the federal government.

---

5. An estimate of 10 percent and 80 percent is given by the Secretary of the National Manpower Board, Mr. F.I. Oduah in his paper "Meeting the Nigerian Manpower Requirements for the Successful Implementation of the 1970-74 Plan (Public Sector)." See Federal Republic of Nigeria, *Report of the Seminar on the Second National Development Plan,* 1971 (Lagos: Federal Ministry of Information, 1971), p. 67. These estimates appear to be too low for the federal government: the assumption used above is however purely arbitrary.

Fiscal Prospects, 1972/73-1975/76

The mission's projections of the federal government's budget for 1972-76 are illustrative and should not be considered as forecasting public sector financing. The purpose is to estimate the future resource position to review expenditure alternatives. Increased production rather than a higher posted price is the main reason for the estimated increase in oil revenues.

Other assumptions are that:

a. import duties will grow nominally at the same rate as total imports.[6]

b. Export duties will remain more or less constant, in accordance with projected non-oil export values.

c. Excise duties will grow nominally at the same rate as production of manufactured goods.[6]

d. Corporation income tax will grow nominally at the same rate as projected for value-added in modern manufacturing.

e. Revenues transferred to the states will continue to be determined by the existing revenue allocation formula. The state governments will receive approximately 35 percent of import duties, 50 percent of excise duties, 100 percent of export duties, and 95 percent of mining rents and royalties.

f. Ordinary recurrent expenditures will grow 15 percent per year. This is based on the 1960-66 growth rate of recurrent expenditures. (See also the later section on Problems of Recurrent Expenditure.) The Second Development Plan also assumes that the average growth in general government consumption will be 15 percent yearly over the Plan period.[7] This, however, could be an underestimate if the federal government should decide to finance the full cost of the Adebo Award for the entire public sector. In this case, the annual growth rate of recurrent expenditure during the next few years could be around 20 percent.

g. Recurrent expenditure on defense and internal security is assumed to increase during 1971/72 and 1972/73 primarily due to the wage and salary increases parallel to the Adebo Award as well as general price increases. Lacking contrary evidence, it is assumed that there will be no major demobilization before 1976 (before the expected return of civilian rule). Recurrent expenditures on defense and internal security have, therefore, been assumed to remain constant in real terms and increase only by the inflation factor.

h. Public debt charges and other transfers are assumed to remain constant over the next few years. They could decline slightly if the federal government continued to redeem some of its short-term internal indebtedness.

i. Public investment is assumed to grow approximately 20 percent yearly. The availability of financial resources would permit a higher actual growth rate, but further acceleration without undue efficiency losses would require major efforts to eliminate constraints on executive capacity at the federal and state levels.

The projections demonstrate that, according to the liberal assumptions given above, the federal government will accumulate large and increasing current surpluses. The federal government would still have substantial overall budgetary surpluses growing from about £N100 million in 1971/72 to £N270 million in 1975/76, even after achieving optimistic levels of federal capital expenditures (Table 11-7). These estimates concern only the federal government. If the financial (both current and capital) needs of the state governments were also considered, the overall budgetary surpluses would be substantially smaller (Tables 8-1 and 8-2). Also, as Chapter 1 indicates, a modest change in the assumption about recurrent expenditure of the federal and state governments would have a significant impact on the public sector accounts.

The availability of such large budgetary resources implies the need to formulate policies to assure the effective use of these resources and to review planned investment targets. The govern-

---

6. Adjustments have been made for changes in the import and excise duty rates announced in the 1972/73 Budget.

7. See *Second National Development Plan, 1970-74*, Table 16, p. 58.

ment is now beginning to consider this major issue. Meanwhile, the government has begun to use this year's surplus to redeem short- and medium-term debt. The need to formulate and implement a rehabilitation program have so far stood in the way of planning beyond the current Plan (ending 1974).

Much thought is now being given to using budget surpluses to finance participation in the foreign-owned oil sector. Potential needs for and means of channeling funds to the private sector to finance the Nigerianization of foreign-owned enterprises outside the oil sector are also being studied. Longer-term sectoral planning has started in some areas but they need to have wider scope and intensity if sound programs are to be ready for implementation by the time financial resources are available.

Table 11-6: STATE GOVERNMENT FINANCES, 1967-1971/72

					(In Millions of £N)
	1967[a]	1968[a]	1969/70[b]	1970/71[b]	1971/72[c]
Recurrent Revenues (transfers from Federal Government)	58.9 (42.9)	55.9 (38.5)	125.8 (89.7)	188.4 (143.4)	224.0 (176.0)
Recurrent Expenditures	63.5	52.3	111.6	170.0	210.0
Current Surplus/Deficit (+/-)	-4.6	+3.6	+14.2	+18.4	+14.0
Capital Receipts from Federal Government	11.8	0.6	9.0	8.4	16.0
Loans from Marketing Boards	5.9	6.2	8.7	8.8	6.0
Capital Expenditures	25.4	12.1	41.7	54.0[c]	100.0[c]
Overall Budget Deficit (-)	-12.3	-1.7	-9.8	-18.4	-64.0

[a]Excluding eastern states.
[b]Partly budget estimates and provisional data from the Central Bank of Nigeria.
[c]Tentative estimates made by the mission.
Source: Central Bank of Nigeria, *Economic and Financial Review* (June 1970, and Statistical Annex, Table 23.

The federal government has a variety of options for using the projected surplus resources:
a. the redemption of internal short-term and medium-term indebtedness could be continued. The merits of this alternative (although not an end in itself) and the magnitude of budgetary surpluses that it could absorb must be analyzed;
b. the federal government could expand recurrent expenditure for economic, social and community services which apparently lagged in the past. This may involve also a revision of methods of allocating revenues to the states. State governments are responsible for many essential development services;
c. the federal government could opt for higher federal and state capital expenditure programs; and
d. the federal government could use its budgetary resources to provide larger tax incentives to the private sector, especially in manufacturing and agriculture.

An analysis of the implications and existing constraints of these various policy alternatives is made later in the chapter. It must be stressed that while the state governments in Nigeria may not consider tax reform essential to increase tax revenues, since the probable revenue effects would be only marginal in relation to the anticipated oil revenues, some fiscal reforms might be necessary to control inflation. Inflation is already serious and is likely to be further accentuated by the recent

Table 11-7: FEDERAL GOVERNMENT FISCAL PROJECTIONS, 1971/72-1975/76[a]

(In Millions of £N)

	1970/71 (A)	1971/72 (E)	1972/73 (P)	1973/74 (P)	1974/75 (P)	1975/76 (P)
Current Revenues	379	646	745	880	1,000	1,120
Oil Revenues	102	320	400	500	580	655
Import Duties	117	155	160	170	180	190
Export Duties	21	21	20	20	20	20
Excise Duties	66	82	85	100	120	140
Corporation Income Tax and Others	73	68	80	90	100	115
Less Revenues Transferred to States	143	176	195	220	250	280
Oil Revenues		60	75	85	105	125
Non-Oil Revenues		116	120	135	145	155
Revenues Retained by the Federal Government	236	470	550	660	750	840
Federal Recurrent Expenditures	271	315	355	375	395	420
Ordinary[b]	53	70	85	100	115	135
Defense and Internal Security[c]	173	195	215	220	225	230
Others (e.g.,financial transfers, etc).	45	50	55	55	55	55
Revenues Available for Capital Expenditure	+35	+155	+195	+285	+355	+420
Federal Capital Expenditures[d]	46	60	95	105	130	150
Over-all Budgetary Surpluses (+)/ Deficits (−)	+75	+95	+100	+180	+225	+270

A = Actual; E = Mission Estimate; P = Projection.

[a]The projections are only illustrative and, therefore, the data have been rounded.
[b]Includes government expenditures on general administration, social and community services and economic services.
[c]Including capital expenditures on defense and internal security.
[d]Excluding capital expenditures on defense and internal security but including capital expenditures of federal corporations (see Table 3-1).

Adebo Award,[8] despite the government's best intentions to control prices, to improve local food production and distribution to increase imports of essential commodities, to control house rents, etc. Tax reforms may also be necessary to influence income distribution. The scope and possibilities of tax reforms in the light of these considerations are discussed briefly in a later section on this subject.

Government Indebtedness

Levels and Composition of Public Debt

Government indebtedness increased significantly during the sixties — first due to inadequate financial resources for the Development Plan and later due to the civil disturbance. The total government indebtedness increased from £N42 million in 1959/60 to £N715 million in September 1971 (Table 11-8). The ratio of public debt to GDP at factor cost rose from 3.8 percent in 1959/60 to 34.7 percent in 1969/70. The largest increase in government indebtedness in absolute terms took place after 1967/68. For the six years between independence and the beginning of the war, about 9 percent of both capital and recurrent expenditures of federal and regional governments were financed by net internal borrowing. In the following six years, total expenditures were almost twice as large in absolute terms and about 20 percent were financed from internal borrowing. Thus, the increase of internal indebtedness since the beginning of the war was about four times the level of the preceding six years.

As Table 11-8 indicates, a very large part of the federal government debt is internal: in September 1971, it was close to 87 percent. The hostilities were entirely financed with internal borrowing; the major part of this was short-term. In 1970/71, short-term debt formed more than 50 percent of the total internal debt as opposed to less than 30 percent in 1965/66.

A large part of the budget was financed during this period by short-term internal borrowing from the banking system which held 45 percent of the internal debt in 1966/67. The banking system held no less than 58 percent of a much larger internal debt in 1970/71. From 1968-71 the banking system financed 70-80 percent of the overall budget deficits of the federal government.

Contributions from non-bank sources to the federal government's domestic borrowing have never been large. These contributions are usually in the form of long-term development stocks (with a maturity period exceeding 5 years) held by savings-type institutions such as the National Provident Fund, pension funds, marketing boards, and state and local governments. Individuals hold negligible amounts of total internal debt.

The National Provident Fund

The contribution of the National Provident Fund (established in 1962) to non-bank public borrowing for the federal government has been valuable and represented 8 to 10 percent of total internal debt. It was designed to provide sickness benefits, a lump sum payment on reaching the age of 55 years, and payments on the death of a contributor. Membership to the Fund is limited to non-pensionable employees of the federal and state governments, statutory public corporations and companies, and staffs of private firms with ten or more employees.

The fund is completely self-supporting and has already reimbursed the federal government for the initial grant of £N144,000 it received in 1962. It is presently financed by contributions from members and their employers. It also earns income on its investments. Each member is required to contribute 5 percent of his wages up to a maximum of £N24 yearly; employers are required to

---

8. Government measures to control inflation are indicated in the *White Paper* on the Adebo Commission Report. The Adebo Award will not only expand the wage outlay of the public sector, but will also affect wages in the private sector. The government has stipulated that the Adebo Award should be fully paid to employees in the private sector whose annual incomes do not exceed £N500. For employees earning over £N500 per year, the government has indicated that trade unions and employers should make necessary adjustments (*White Paper*, p. 8). The Federal Manpower Board estimates that the present Adebo Award would cost the public sector about £N28 million per year, and another £N20 million if defense personnel are also to be covered. The total increase in wage incomes in the economy, could amount to £N90 million annually.

Table 11-8: FEDERAL GOVERNMENT PUBLIC DEBT, 1959/60-1970/71

		1959/60	1964/65	1969/70	Sept. 1971
Internal:		17.5	116.2	468.9	616.9
	Treasury Bills,				
	Certificates	8.2	35.0	306.0	436.0
	Development Stock	7.1	69.0	150.4	178.4
	Other	2.4	12.2	12.6	12.6
External:		24.9	46.5	88.3	88.0
	Total	42.4	162.7	557.2	714.9
Of which: re-lent to Regional/State Govt's, Statut. Corporations		(18.7)	(61.9)	(110.7)	(128.7)
Public Debt Outstanding as % of GDP (at factor cost)		3.8	11.1	34.7	32.0

Source: Based on Statistical Table 32.

match these contributions. The contributions are credited to each worker's account and earn 4 percent interest annually. The number of employees registered with the fund increased from 457,000 at the end of 1964 to 734,000 at the end of 1969. Their contributions increased from £N10.3 million in December 1964 to £N30.4 million in December 1969 — a yearly increase of about £N4 million. After paying benefits and deducting operating expenses, the Fund invests the balance of its income and receipts in Federal Government Development Stock. The National Provident Fund is currently the largest single purchaser of Development Stock, having invested £N49 million in these securities since its establishment. It holds about 38 percent of the long-term internal indebtedness of the federal government.

The National Reconstruction and Development Savings Scheme

This scheme was initiated in January 1968 by the federal military government as a wartime measure and as a one-year compulsory savings scheme. It embraced all Nigerian workers including pensioners. As originally decreed, all workers earning about £N50 yearly were required to contribute 5 percent of their gross monthly income while those whose annual incomes were below £N50 were required to pay 10s. once during the contribution period. The scheme was subsequently modified to give some relief to workers who participated in the National Provident Fund. Under the scheme, all funds collected were to be loaned to the federal government at 3 percent simple interest, both capital and interest to become repayable after ten years. Government bonds were issued to contributors showing the total amount collected at the end of the contribution period. These bonds are not redeemable until 1977, although they will become negotiable in January 1973. By March 31, 1970, this plan had collected £N5.1 million. No contributions are expected in the future. This scheme represents all of the holdings of internal debt by individuals.

In summary, the main features of government indebtedness in Nigeria are: (a) large internal and small external indebtedness; (b) relatively large short-term indebtedness; (c) relatively large holdings of domestic debt by the banking system; (d) relatively large contributions of the National Provident Fund in long-term Development Stocks, and (e) a negligible role of individual holdings in total government securities.

The federal government has started retiring its short-term indebtedness, largely held by the banking system, to offset the large budgetary surpluses which have accrued during the last few months. An important question is whether the federal government should adopt a policy of retiring its indebtedness in the next few years. The most immediate considerations in weighing the merits of this option would be the: seriousness of the debt service burden on the federal budget; impact of existing government indebtedness and its retirement on income distribution; and limit to which internal debt can safely be retired, given the need for financial instruments to operate in the money and capital markets and the liquidity requirements of the banking system.

Debt Service Burden

Table 11-9 presents indications of the burden of public debt charges in relation to the current budget of the federal government. Public debt charges as a percent of federal current revenues (and of federal recurrent expenditures as well) have increased tremendously during 1969-71. However, as government current revenues increase in the near future, the debt service burden will be reduced. In fact, this decline began in 1970/71.

Table 11-9: FEDERAL GOVERNMENT DEBT SERVICE BURDEN, 1959/60-1970/71

Year	Public Debt Charges as Percent of:		GDP at Factor Cost
	Federal Recurrent Expenditures	Federal Current Revenues	
(1)	(2)	(3)	(4)
1959/60	1.1	0.9	0.1
1964/65	5.5	4.5	0.5
1969/70	15.3	15.2	1.9
1970/71	17.4	10.7	2.0

Source: Budgets of the Federal Government and *Annual Abstract of Statistics.*

In appraising the debt service burden, one must remember that the percentages given in Table 11-9 are "gross" ratios for the federal government. Substantial sums are always re-lent to the state governments and statutory public corporations who take over the debt service cost from the federal government (Table 11-8). The proportion of re-lent funds in government indebtedness declined during hostilities when the federal government defense needs grew rapidly.

Federal-State Relations in Borrowing

Public debt is almost exclusively the responsibility of the federal government. Under the Federal Constitution, only the federal government can borrow for federation-wide plans, but the regions (now states) can borrow internally for their own purposes and are permitted to borrow overseas for not longer than 12 months on the security of assets outside Nigeria.

At the first meeting of the Loans Advisory Board (January, 1958), the regions agreed that between 1958-60 only the federal government would raise loans internally. This was because the regions appreciated that internal borrowing was intimately connected with general control over monetary policy and because the local loan market was limited and had to be heavily supported by the Central Bank. The federal government agreed to make internal loans available to the regions on the terms on which they were raised. This arrangement has continued with the creation of the twelve states in 1967. The states have not exercised their constitutional jurisdiction over public borrowing for their own use.

The distribution of the receipts from loans between the federal government and the regions was originally resolved by the Loans Advisory Board and later by an annual conference of the

Finance Ministers from the federal and regional governments. Since the creation of the states, meetings of the Commissioners of Finance from the federal and state governments have distributed loan receipts.

In the past, the proceeds of the long-term (Development Stock) borrowings were shared between the federal and state governments on a 50/50 basis. From the 1971/72 fiscal year onward, this ratio has been changed to 40/60 in favor of the state governments. Half of the states' share is allocated between them according to their populations, while the other half is equally distributed among them. In case any state government does not want its share, its allocation is dispersed among the remaining states. This principle would apply to the federal government as well, i.e., if the federal government does not want to borrow, as might be the case in the future, all development loan proceeds would be shared among the states.

Whatever the merits of this procedure, a large amount of funds borrowed initally by the federal government is re-lent to the state governments on the same terms at which they have been initially raised. This implies a reduction in the *net* debt service cost to the federal budget. For example, in 1970/71 the *net* debt service burden as a percent of federal current revenues was 9.9 percent as compared to a *gross* figure of 10.7 percent.

It is, however, more appropriate to measure the *net* debt service burden on the federal government against the revenues retained, rather than against those collected by the federal government. On that basis, the *net* debt service burden in 1969/70 amounted to 21 percent, declining to 15.6 percent in 1971/72. Thus, the debt service charges as a proportion of revenues of the federal government have already begun to decline. As federal revenues expand in the next few years, the debt service ratio will fall rapidly. For example, the *gross* debt service burden could fall from 10.7 percent in 1970/71 to 4-5 percent in 1975/76. Thus, unless the total indebtedness of the government increases rapidly in the next few years, there is little cause for concern.

In Nigeria, most domestic debt is held by the banking system, financial institutions, and state and local governments, rather than by individuals. Therefore, the government does not need to be concerned with early debt retirement as a means to change income distribution.

The major problem of government indebtedness in Nigeria is the large amount of short-term debt. During hostilities, the Treasury Bills Act was repeatedly amended by the federal government to enable increased borrowing to meet defense needs. Under the original Treasury Bills Act (1959), the maximum issue of Treasury Bills was 50 percent of the federal government's estimated current revenue. This was amended in 1968 to 85 percent; in 1969, to 100 percent; and in 1970, to 150 percent of the estimated revenue retained by the federal government and the gross revenues of the states. Based on 1971/72 revenue levels, the maximum issue is about £N810 million as opposed to an issue of £N308 million of Treasury Bills as of September 30, 1971.

To finance the civil war, the federal government issued Treasury Certificates in December 1968 with a one or two-year maturity and a higher interest rate than Treasury Bills. While the Treasury Bills (maturity 91 days) bear 4-1/2 percent interest, Treasury Certificates (maturity 1/2 years) bear 4-5/8 percent to 5 percent interest. The interest rate on National Development Stocks (maturity 6/25 years) varies between 5 and 6 percent. Initially the maximum value of certificates which could be issued was 50 percent of the estimated current revenues of the federal government but, in June 1969, this limit was raised to 60 percent. These certificates, which form a part of the unfunded debt, increased from £N50 million in 1968/69 to £N128 million in 1970/71.

The federal government has started retiring Treasury Bills and Treasury Certificates and under present budgetary circumstances could continue to do so. The government could retire a limited number of them soon. However, the needs of the money and capital markets for financial instruments as well as to meet legal portfolio requirements will have to be provided for.

There is both a limited need and a limited scope for retiring government debt. The government should continue, in the interest of price stability, to reduce its short-term debt, held largely by the banking system. The use of future budgetary surpluses for this policy option could not, and should not, be very substantial.

Problems of Recurrent Expenditure

Recurrent expenditure of the federal government grew rapidly during the sixties — about 15 percent yearly before hostilities. Between 1967/68 and 1969/70, it grew more than 75 percent a year mainly because of the growth in defense and defense-related expenditures, and to a lesser extent because of a rise in public debt charges. In 1970/71, defense and internal security absorbed about 60 percent of federal government recurrent expenditure; public debt charges, another 19 percent.

Level of Development Services

Recurrent expenditures on economic, social and community services have always lagged. The absolute level of the federal government's recurrent expenditure on these services in 1969/70 was the same as in 1961, and rose only slightly in 1970/71. The actual federal expenditures on social and community services were, in fact, lower in 1970/71 than in 1961.

Table 11-10 presents the disbursed federal budgets as a percent of approved federal budgets for the years 1966/67 and 1970/71. As expected, during hostilities, the only recurrent items consistently exceeding budgeted amounts were defense and internal security and public debt charges. Generally, there were shortfalls in most recurrent expenditures for social, community and economic services in addition to the severe cuts that were already implicit in the budget estimates. This implied an actual decline in federal public services such as higher education, trunk road and bridge maintenance, teaching hospitals, preventive health measures, social welfare, and other public services.

The states' performance has been somewhat better. Their recurrent expenditures on social and economic services increased by about 85 percent between 1961 and 1969/70. This could hardly offset the declines in public services affected at the federal level. Recurrent expenditures on social and community services as a percentage of total government recurrent expenditures fell from 35.4 percent in 1961 to 27.6 percent in 1966/67; and further, to 20 percent in 1970/71. Similarly, the share of recurrent expenditures on economic services in total government recurrent expenditures fell from 17 percent in 1961 to 16.3 percent in 1966/67 and 11.8 percent in 1970/71. This indicates a need for larger allocations and uses of government resources in these fields.

The low level of public service expenditures has been unequally divided in terms of quantity and quality among the different regions/states. Although sometimes recognized,[9] this has seldom been substantiated partly because of the lack of data and partly because of the 1967 break-up of the regions into states and the disruption of the civil war. The latest year for which some indicators are available is 1966; these are presented in Table 11-11. It appears that the northern states were behind other states in 1966 and that Lagos State was leading. The Western and Mid-Western States were above average in education and per capita income while the eastern states were above average in roads and health facilities.

Table 11-12 summarizes the financial position of each individual state for the years 1968/69-1971/72. Lagos State has the best budgetary performance: large revenues, a substantial current budget surplus and an overall budget surplus. In contrast with Lagos, most of the other states have financial difficulties. They have either recurrent deficits or negligible recurrent surpluses, and most of their overall budgets show large deficits. The availability of public services from the state governments is closely related to their current revenues. The Unesco Mission, for example, observed that the level of per capita recurrent expenditure on education in the states was largely determined by the level of per capita recurrent revenue.[10]

As was observed earlier, the state governments depend heavily on receipts from the federal government, both for revenue appropriations and capital receipts. In 1961, the regional governments financed 44 percent of all their expenditures with funds from the federal government; this dependence increased to 66 percent in 1965. Although lower in recent years, this level remained well above 60 percent between 1968 and 1971/72 (Table 11-13). The degree of dependence varies between states. It was fo nd that states as Benue Plateau, Kano, Kwara, North Western and Rivers have higher than average ratios of federal statutory appropriations to total current revenues.

9. E.g., A. Adedeji, *Nigerian Federal Finance* (London: Hutchison Educational, 1969); V.P. Diejomaoh, "Tax and Allocation Policies," paper presented at the *Conference on Integration and National Unity,* University of Lagos, December 15, 1970, esp. pp. 28-30.

10. Unesco, *Education in Nigeria* (September, 1971).

Table 11-10: FEDERAL BUDGET EXECUTION AS % OF APPROVED FEDERAL BUDGET, 1966/67-1970/71

(Percent)

Expenditure Category	1966/67		1967/68		1968/69		1969/70		1970/71	
	Current	Capital	Current	Capital	Current	Capital	Current	Capital	Current	Capital
Administrative Services	78.2	71.8	121.9	89.5	190.7	79.3	314.5	88.2	204.0	79.5
Social and Community Services	128.7	34.1	125.5	46.3	85.9	42.8	116.9	43.2	93.7	12.3
Economic Services	97.4	39.0	87.5	44.3	93.8	40.0	90.5	37.5	109.3	30.1
Public Debt/Financial Obligations		100.0		112.5		170.4		135.0		97.1
Statutory Appropriations to State Governments/Capital Grants and Loans re-lent to State Governments	87.9	107.0	90.6	40.6	97.2	70.6	94.9	65.7	124.3	36.8
Total	94.9	53.8	95.6	71.9	124.7	63.1	177.9	91.1	144.9	48.1

Recently, the Mid-Western and Western States joined this group. Lagos depended the least on federal receipts.

Federal-State Relations in Current Revenues

Under the Nigerian Constitution, the federal government has the exclusive power to impose and collect import, export, and excise duties; corporation income tax including the petroleum profits tax; and mining royalties and rents. The federal government retains all revenues derived from the corporation income tax, petroleum profits tax, import duties on alcoholic beverages and certain export duties. The state governments, on the other hand, have exclusive jurisdiction over personal income tax, property tax, personal (poll) tax, produce sales/purchase taxes, motor licensing fees, court fees and fines, licenses and some other minor taxes. The federal government shares with the state governments the revenues of general import duties (excepting those on tobacco and motor spirits), all excise duties, and mining rents and royalties. The present basis of federal and state government shares in the revenues of individual taxes are given in Table 11-14.

The state governments receive two kinds of allocations. One part of statutory payments is allocated to states on the basis of the "derivation principle," i.e., on the basis of the state of origin or consumption or to states where those revenues were derived. In the past, most of the federal government revenues were shared between the regions/states on this basis. As this method was controversial,[11] it is used less frequently today. All import duties on tobacco and motor spirits, most of basic export duties on agricultural produce, and about half of mining rents and royalties

Table 11-11: INDICATORS OF REGIONAL LEVELS OF PUBLIC SERVICES, 1966

	Northern	Eastern	Western	Mid-Western	Federal Territory of Lagos	All Nigeria
Road Mileage per 10 square miles of land area	0.76	6.17	3.15	3.90	76.67	1.55
Hospital beds in all medical establishments per 1,000 population	0.25	0.92	0.44	0.53	4.0	0.49
Primary school pupils per 1,000 population	17.0	100.0	72.0	153.0	214.0	54.0
Secondary school pupils per 1,000 population	0.6	5.5	8.0	11.2	21.2	3.8
Per capita GDP, 1965 (£N)	19.0	20.0	25.0	31.0	123.0	22.0

Source: O. Teriba and O. A. Phillips, " Income Distribution and National Integration," *Nigerian Journal of Social and Economic Studies XIII,* (March 1971): 81-83, based on *Annual Abstract of Statistics, 1967.*

11. Cf. "the principle of derivation bedevilled the development of a rational and equitable system of revenue allocation in Nigeria, it has poisoned inter-governmental relationships and has exacerbated inter-regional rivaling and conflict . . .," A. Adedeji, *Nigerian Federal Finance,* (1969), p. 254.

are still shared between the states on the *derivation* basis.

A Distributable Pool Account (DPA), created in 1959, is the second type of allocation to the states. Over time, larger tax revenues have been placed in the DPA. The DPA today covers 35 percent of the general import duties, 100 percent of import surcharges, 50 percent of excise duties, and 50 percent of the mining royalties and rents (Table 11-14). Funds are allocated on the basis of population and balanced development. Half the DPA money is equally divided between the states and the other half is distributed according to the 1963 estimated population. The presently operative distribution formula and its basis are shown in Table 11-15.

An increasing part of the federal revenues is now equally distributed among the states or distributed according to population. The part which is distributed on the *derivation* basis has declined, but remains at about two-thirds of all distributed revenues. The distribution formula (Table 11-15), which has operated since April 1969, departs from past methods in many ways. It expanded the size of the Distributable Pool by allocating a larger proportion of *unspecified* import duties, mining rents and royalties than before.[12] This was done by reducing the federal government's share in these taxes. The Distributable Pool Account was expanded at the cost of statutory payments allocated according to the *derivation* principle, in the case of mining rents and royalties. Before 1969/70, 50 percent of mining rents and royalties were distributed according to *derivation*, this percentage was reduced to 45 percent. The allocation of the DPA among the states was revised significantly. Before 1968/69, the six northern states got 42 percent of the DPA; they now get approximately 52 percent. In fact, all the northern states except Kwara have increased their relative shares of the Distributable Pool. The share of the East Central State was reduced from 17.5 percent to 10.6 percent and that of the Western State from 18 percent to 12.7 percent.[13]

State governments depend so heavily on federal receipts that the allocation of revenues to the DPA as well as the arrangements for the allocation between states have been and will remain, a major issue. The federal government has said that the existing arrangements will be studied by a Constituent Assembly, to be convened before 1976.[14] Pressures by the state governments and by academicians for early revisions can be noted.[15]

The state governments have been under severe financial strains recently as their budgets have expanded and tax efforts have lagged. Lagos State is an exception because the federal government is located there yielding high personal income taxes. Federal revenue shares have financed most state government expenditures. State governments have been hurt by slow or inadequate releases of federal funds because they cannot raise ways and means advances to cover short-run financial difficulties.

At present, *statutory payments* for each state are calculated when the federal budget is prepared and are specified, tax by tax, in the recurrent estimates of the federal government. The payments to the states are then made on a pro rata basis monthly (sometimes twice a month) on mutually arranged dates. Adjustments are made every quarter for actual revenue collections by the federal government and the states receive the adjusted amounts, or are required to refund if actual revenue collections are short of the budget figures.

Many state governments feel that the federal government has been underestimating the statutory appropriations due to the state governments, thus severely curtailing the flow of revenues to them during the fiscal year. For 1969/70 and 1970/71, the actual receipts from some of those taxes which the federal government shares with the state governments have substantially exceeded

12. In April 1970, 40 percent of the one-third of the export duties were also transferred from "Statutory Payments" to DPA.

13. O. Teriba and O.A. Phillips, "Income Distribution and National Integration," *Nigerian Journal of Economic and Social Studies (NJESS),* Vol. 13 No. 1 (March, 1971), p. 112.

14. Cf., for example, the following statement: reflecting on the cost of the Adebo Award to state governments, the *White Paper* said, "As the Federal Government is anxious to develop and maintain a true spirit of federalism, a new formula for assisting the states will have to be evolved when considering Revenue Allocation principles in the future." (p. 5).

15. See, for example, O. Aboyade, "The Role of the Federal Government in the Development of the States" in the *Report of the Seminar on the Second National Development Plan, 1971* (Lagos: Federal Ministry of Information, 1971) especially p. 42.

Table 11-12: FINANCIAL POSITION OF THE STATES, 1968/69-1971/72

(In Millions of £N)

	Current Surplus (+)/Deficit (–)				Overall Surplus (+)/Deficit (–)			
	1968/69	1969/70	1970/71[b]	1971/72[b]	1968/69	1969/70	1970/71[b]	1971/72[b]
Benue Plateau	-1.0	+0.9	-0.2	+0.4	-1.4	-0.8	-5.9	-0.1
East Central[a]	–	–	-15.4	-5.1	–	–	-31.9	-5.1
Kano	+0.1	+0.8	+0.1	+5.0	-0.6	-3.7	-14.1	-7.6
Kwara	-0.3	-0.7	-0.6	+0.1	-0.3	-0.7	-6.1	-8.5
Lagos	+6.3	+6.7	+0.5	+0.3	+6.2	+6.2	-4.1	-10.7
Mid-Western	+0.4	+1.2	+6.2	+6.2	-3.4	-5.0	-3.0	-6.6
North Central	+0.7	+2.5	+0.1	+0.1	+0.3	+0.8	-9.1	-12.0
North Eastern	-1.1	+1.2	-0.6	–	-1.5	-2.7	-9.8	-12.7
North Western	-0.7	+1.0	–	+0.7	-1.0	-2.1	-9.7	-10.3
Rivers	+0.2	-5.3	-0.6	-0.1	+0.2	-5.3	-12.6	-15.4
South Eastern	-3.8	-3.0	-0.5	+1.1	-3.8	-14.0	-12.9	-13.1
Western	+0.2	-0.6	+2.2	+0.1	-4.8	-10.2	-11.3	-11.4
Total	+5.5	+4.2	-8.8	+8.8	-5.6	-37.5	-130.4	-122.5

[a]Not available for 1968/69 and 1969/70.
[b]Budget estimates.
Source: Based on Statistical Annex, Table 22.

Table 11-13: STATES' DEPENDENCE ON FEDERAL GOVERNMENT, 1961-1971/72

(In Millions of £N)

Year	Revenue Appropriations	Loans on-lent and Grants	Total Federal Receipts	Current Expenditures	Capital Expenditures	Total Expenditures	Total Federal Receipts as a Percent of Total Expenditures
1961	33.4	4.5	37.9	57.8	28.4	86.2	44.0
1962	36.0	17.4	53.4	69.1	28.1	97.2	54.9
1963	37.8	9.0	46.8	63.7	27.8	91.5	51.1
1964	56.5	5.2	61.7	71.9	31.3	103.2	39.8
1965	65.4	10.2	75.6	83.8	30.5	114.3	66.1
1966	60.7	14.6	75.3	86.1	32.0	118.1	63.8
1967[a]	42.9	11.8	54.7	63.5	25.4	88.9	61.5
1968[a]	38.5	0.6	39.1	52.3	12.1	64.4	60.7
1969/70	89.7	9.0	98.7	111.6	41.7	153.3	64.4
1970/71[b]	115.3	8.4	123.7	163.0	105.2	268.2	46.1[c]
1971/72[b]	126.0	16.0	142.0	183.2	131.3	314.5	45.2[d]

[a]Excludes Eastern states.
[b]Budget estimate.
[c]Revenue appropriations in 1970/71 were actually close to £N143 million while the states' capital expenditure was close to £N78 million. Taking these into consideration, this ratio is a gross underestimation. Actual percentage works out close to 63 percent.
[d]Mission estimates that the revenue appropriations for 1971/72 would be close to £N176 million, current expenditures £N221 million and capital expenditures £N73 million. This would yield the actual percentage of 65 percent.
Source: Central Bank of Nigeria.

Table 11-14: PRESENT ARRANGEMENTS FOR REVENUE ALLOCATION, 1971

(Percent)

Category of Tax	Retained by the Federal Government	"Statutory Payments" to States Allocated by Origin or Consumption	Allocations to Distributable Pool Account
Import Duties			
Alcoholic beverages	100.0	—	—
Tobacco, motor spirits, diesel oil	—	100.0	—
Unspecified	65.0	—	35.0
Surcharge on Imports of Petroleum Products (Tariff No. 27.09/10)	—	—	100.0
Export Duties			
Agricultural Produce, hides and skins [a]	—	86.7	13.3
Unspecified	100.0	—	—
5 Percent Surcharge levied on Cotton, Cocoa, etc. (Customs Tariff Order, 1969)	—	60.0	40.0
Excise Duties			
Cigarettes, motor spirit, diesel oil	50.0	—	50.0
Unspecified [b]	50.0	—	50.0
Mining Royalties and Rents	5.0	45.0	50.0

[a] Prior to 1st April 1970, 100 percent of these export duties were allocated to states of origin. Since then 40 percent of one-third of these export duties are allocated to Distributable Pool Account.
[b] This revenue is allocated to the states in the same proportion as the Distributable Pool Account but does not form a part of that account.

Source: Decree No. 13 of 1970 and Federal Ministry of Finance.

Table 11-15: ALLOCATION OF DISTRIBUTABLE POOL ACCOUNT – PRESENT ARRANGEMENT, SINCE APRIL 1969

State	Area (square miles)	Population[a] (in thousands)	Distribution of 50 Percent Pool by Population Percent	Distribution of 50 Percent Pool in Equal Shares Percent	Distribution Formula[b] Based on (4) and (5) Percent
(1)	(2)	(3)	(4)	(5)	(6)
Benue Plateau	38,929	4,009	7.2	8.3	7.8
East Central	11,548	7,228	13.0	8.3	10.6
Kano	16,630	5,775	10.4	8.3	9.3
Kwara	28,672	2,399	4.3	8.3	6.3
Lagos	1,381	1,444	2.6	8.3	5.5
Mid-Western	14,922	2,536	4.6	8.3	6.4
North Central	27,108	4,098	7.4	8.3	7.8
North Eastern	105,300	7,793	14.0	8.3	11.3
North Western	65,143	5,734	10.3	8.3	9.3
Rivers	6,985	1,545	2.8	8.3	5.6
South Eastern	10,951	3,623	6.5	8.3	7.4
Western	29,100	9,488	17.0	8.3	12.7
Total	356,669	55,670	100.0	100.0	100.0

[a]Figures are from 1963 Census.
[b]Calculated as [(0.50) x (Population Percent) + (0.50) x (Equal Shares Percent)].
Source: Annual Abstract of Statistics, 1969 and Federal Ministry of Finance.

Table 11-16: FEDERAL BUDGETARY PERFORMANCE, 1966/67-1970/71

(In Millions of £N)

	1966/67			1967/68			1968/69			1969/70			1970/71		
	Budget Estimate	Actual	Difference	Budget Estimate	Actual	Difference	Budget Estimate	Actual	Difference	Budget Estimate	Actual	Difference	Budget Estimate	Actual	Difference
Recurrent Revenues of which:	185.1	169.6	-15.5	161.1	150.1	-11.0	147.7	149.9	+2.3	186.8	218.0	+21.2	278.5	377.8	+99.3
Import Duties	84.1	56.9	-27.2	52.1	53.6	+1.5	54.7	58.2	+3.5	54.7	80.7	+26.0	69.8	115.5	+45.7
Export Duties	13.7	14.0	+0.3	13.2	15.0	+1.8	13.1	14.9	+1.8	13.3	19.2	+5.9	22.0	20.5	-1.5
Excise Duties	35.1	35.8	+0.7	38.5	24.8	-13.7	29.3	28.2	-1.1	33.5	39.0	+5.5	54.2	65.9	+11.7
Mining Rents & Royalties	17.0	18.4	+1.4	20.4	16.9	-3.5	11.5	10.9	-0.6	30.5	22.9	+7.6	40.5	36.4	-4.1
Recurrent Expenditures of which:	178.3	169.3	-9.0	160.7	153.7	-7.0	146.1	182.3	+36.2	186.1	331.1	+145.0	274.2	396.2	+122.0
Statutory Appropriations to State Governments	78.0	68.6	-9.4	67.7	61.4	-6.3	54.4	52.9	-1.5	73.4	91.0	+17.6	115.3	143.4	+27.9
Capital Expenditures of which:	97.4	52.4	-45.0	95.8	68.9	-26.9	109.9	69.4	-40.5	96.0	87.5	-8.5	146.5	68.0	78.5
Loans on-lent and extending grants to governments	15.8	16.9	+1.1	18.7	7.6	-11.1	17.0	12.0	-5.0	13.7	9.0	-4.7	22.8	8.4	-6.7

Source: Budgets of the Federal Government and Official Gazettes.

the budgeted amounts (Table 11-16
governments in the budget were lowe

Finances of Local Authorities

In addition, to the federal gover
local authorities in Nigeria. These au
formerly comprising the Northern Re
Government Councils in the other S
primary education, medical and healt
and maintenance of local roads. They
nary, maintenance of libraries and re
native courts, etc.

The main sources of revenue for
munity and then apportioned by the c
between 3 shillings to 7 shillings 6 p
education), special rates on buildings
and fines (collected in the courts, in

Table 11-17: FINANCES OF LOC

(In Millions of £N)

	1962/63	Percent	1963/64	Percent
Current Revenues	28.6	100.0	25.6	100.0
Tax Revenues	16.6	58.3	17.8	69.5
(i) Direct Taxes	(10.8)	(37.8)	(11.5)	(45.1)
(ii) Cattle Tax	(1.4)	(4.8)	(1.0)	(3.8)
(iii) Local Rates	(4.5)	(15.7)	(5.2)	(20.6)
Income from Property[a]	0.3	0.8	0.3	1.2
Transfers from Federal/Regional Governments	6.9	24.3	3.3	13.1
Other Transfers[b]	0.1	0.4	0.1	0.3
Other Revenues[c]	4.6	16.2	4.1	15.9
Current Expenditures	23.2	100.0	20.9	100.0
Personal Emoluments	12.5	53.7	12.6	60.0
Maintenance of Roads and Buildings	2.3	9.8	1.3	6.3
Other Goods and Services	6.6	28.7	6.3	30.2
Interest on Debt	0.6	2.6	0.1	0.4
Payments and Grants to Others	1.2	5.2	0.6	3.1
Current Surplus	+5.4		+4.7	

[a]Includes rent and interest.
[b]Includes transfers from marketing boards.
[c]Includes earnings, sales, fines, fees and licenses.

Source: Federal Office of Statistics.

16. G. O. Orewa, *Local Government Finance in Nigeria* (1966).

orities also share the personal income tax and poll (or
. In most states, they receive grants-in-aid from the state
ts for road maintenance, water supply and agriculture, unit
health centers, and certain block and equalization grants.
and expenditures of local authorities are available only for the
64 (published by the Federal Office of Statistics in 1969). As it is
and expenditures have not changed significantly in recent years, a
s provided in Table 11-17. Current expenditure of local authorities were
current expenditures at all levels of government in Nigeria. Current revenues
centage of revenues of all levels of government.

ation of twelve state administrations the relative importance of local authorities
Nigeria. The federal government is now responsible for prisons which were former-
by local governments. Local authority police forces have also been merged with the
police. Primary education has been partially removed from local authority jurisdiction and
controlled by boards of education responsible to the state Education Ministries. Simulta-
ously, the states have increased their share of the most important taxes collected by the local
authorities. Under the Personal Tax Law of 1962 the states were to be paid 12-1/2 percent of the
revenue from the community and cattle taxes leaving 87-1/2 percent for the local authority which
assessed and collected these taxes. Now in almost every state, the state share of these taxes has
been increased to 15 percent, 20 percent or even 25 percent. At the same time, the tax base for
the local authorities has been reduced as the State Income Tax Departments have extended their
assessments. For example, in the northern states, all persons paying income tax under a Pay As
You Earn (PAYE) system are exempt from local personal taxes. In recent years, the local authorities have thus tended to become the local arm or subordinate agent of the state governments
and have come to depend heavily on grants received from the state governments, especially for
health and education.

Summarizing the trends and composition of recurrent expenditures, it appears that the federal
government's own recurrent expenditures on social and economic services have lagged throughout
the sixties. The federal government is now able to utilize some of its future budget surpluses to
improve the balance in federal recurrent expenditures between developmental and non-
developmental services. This would be even more feasible if defense spending were contained. The
Adebo Award will increase the cost of these services, which would both justify and require more
emphasis on improving the quality of public services.

In the past, the federal government's recurrent expenditure was growing at about 15 percent
annually, partly because of increased civil employment (at a rate close to 7 percent yearly)[17] and
because of normal salary increments (at 4 percent to 5 percent yearly),[18] salary revisions based on
cost of living increases (which have normally taken place about every five years),[19] price increases
and increased purchases of goods and services. The Adebo Award will add about 20 percent to 25
percent to the government's wage bill from 1973 onward, and significantly more by way of
subventions to other parts of the public sector. Continued growth of recurrent expenditures, material as well as personnel, at these rates cannot be sustained in the long run. A careful assessment of
priorities is needed; first, between direct spending by the federal government and additional transfers to state governments. As state governments have most of the responsibility for the maintenance and operation of economic and social services, including the major functions of education
and agriculture, high priority must be given to state expenditures. Resources retained for use by
the federal government also must be allocated according to priorities and effectiveness levels, and
based on careful analysis of their impact on income distribution and the maintenance of price
stability.

17. The established civilian staff of the federal government (excluding daily paid workers) increased
from 39,560 in 1960 to 68,691 in 1971 (see *Federal Civil Service Manpower, 1970*). This excludes the defense
personnel whose number has increased significantly during the civil war. It also excludes the daily-rated workers.

18. For the salary structure of federal government employees, see *Recurrent Estimates of the Government of the Federal Republic of Nigeria, 1971-72.*

19. Cf. *Second National Development Plan, 1970-74* pp. 72-73.

The recurrent exp[...]
amounts were allocated [...]
roads, etc., and these rec[...]
their new administrative [...]
be underrated and new w[...]
improved and state reven[...]
expenditures. Their proble[...]
collects and retains revenue[...]
revenue allocation arrangem[...]
principle and to expansion o[...]
allocate funds to the states ac[...]
public services should be red[...]
viability of the federation. Fir[...]
effort of the individual states to[...]

An alternative to this could [...]
important state government func[...]
would, however, create serious adr[...]
which cannot be ignored in any cor[...]

Local authorities in Nigeria per[...]
expenditure obligations have declin[...]
fectiveness was reduced. There is a l[...]
sibilities effectively. Obviously, their [...]
public services expanded. The state-l[...]
financial problems as are federal-state [...]
the state governments.

There is no doubt that increased [...] ...ns of [...] specific purposes at all government levels in Nigeria are essential. Th[...] ...ation and proper use requires judicious
decision-making. Proper use of resources [...] ...res a conscious and deliberate policy to contain administration and defense expenditures as well as the wage demands of government employees. The
Second Plan enumerates several elements of recurrent expenditures which have a bearing on this
issue. The demobilization of Armed Forces personnel,[20] the use of part of the military as task
forces for reconstruction and development[21] and the target of containing prices within an annual
1.5 percent increase[22] all appear to have specific implications which require a thorough analysis as
to their impact on the budget.

Prospects of Capital Expenditure

Recent Trends in Capital Expenditure

Both the federal and state governments' capital expenditures were substantially below the
Plan estimates in 1970/71 (Table 11-18). The shortfalls were most striking for social, economic
and community services.

While in the past, the shortfall in federal capital expenditure might have been caused by the
lack of finances, in more recent years the inadequacy of executive capacity and project preparation is becoming the major constraint on the capacity of the government to expand its capital
expenditure.[23] The Second Plan allows for a shortfall of actual capital expenditure in the public

20. *Second National Development Plan, 1970-74*, p. 91.

21. *Ibid*, p. 90.

22. *Ibid*, p. 40.

23. Cf. the remark "Finance is no longer the critical factor in the implementation of the Second
National Development Plan . . . (while) . . . inadequate executive capacity in the traditional sense (is)". A.A.
Ayida, "Financing the Second National Development Plan, 1970-74" in *Report of the Seminar on the Second
National Development Plan, 1971*, p. 21.

162

NIGERIA: OPTIONS [...]

sector from the Plan targets of about 20 percent, mainly [...]
Efficient use of capital expenditure allocations can only [...]
of those constraints; thus only limited growth can [...]
federal government may therefore not be in a p[...]
for purposes of direct investment.

Federal Statutory Corporations

The statutory corporation[...]
The major federal statutor[...]

Table 11-1[8]

ue to the lack of executive capacity.[24]
y be maintained if due cognizance is taken
be achieved in federal capital expenditure. The
osition to utilize all expected budgetary surpluses

account for a very large part of federal government investment.[25]
corporations are public utilities: Electricity Corporation of Nigeria

: GOVERNMENT CAPITAL EXPENDITURES

(In Millions of £N)

| | 1970/71 | | 1971/72 (six months) | |
	Federal	States	Federal	States
Economic	34.8	29.8	17.0	21.9
Agriculture	2.4	5.9	1.4	4.7
Industry	0.4	4.6	—	6.8
Fuel and Power	5.6	0.4	1.7	0.1
Transport	20.8	16.2	11.6	7.9
Communications[a]	2.3	—	0.7	—
Resettlement and Rehabilitation[a]	2.4	—	1.3	—
Social	1.7	19.0	0.7	19.0
Education	1.4	8.6	0.3	7.1
Water and Sewerage	—	4.6	—	3.9
Administration	28.3	5.0	0.9	5.9
General administration	0.4	5.0	0.9	5.9
Defense and Security	27.9	—	5.7	—
Financial	6.8	—	6.7	—
Total	71.7	53.9	31.0	46.9
Less Transfers	5.0	—	0.7	—
Total	66.7	53.9		
		120.6		77.2

[a]These figures are incomplete.

Source: First Progress Report on the Second Development Plan.

24. *Second National Development Plan, 1970-74,* p. 267.

25. In 1965/66, for example, they accounted for some 63 percent of federal government capital expenditure. See A.R. Prest, "Public Utilities in Nigeria: Economic and Financial Aspects" *Administration,* Volume II No. 4 (July 1968), p. 199.

(ECN), Nigeria Railways Corporation (NRC), Nigeria Airways Corporation (NAC), Nigerian Ports Authority (NPA), Niger Dams Authority (NDA), Nigerian Coal Corporation (NCC), and Nigerian Broadcasting Corporation (NBC).

Reliable data on the performance of these corporations are not readily available. Table 12-20 provides summary data on the financial operations of the statutory corporations over the past decade. While the NRC, ECN and NDA have been making increasingly large losses in the past, only the NPA has been increasing its profits. However, excluding interest payments, ECN's operating revenues have increased from £N308,000 in 1969/70 to an estimated £N4.6 million in 1971/72 while NDA's operating revenues rose from £N2.2 million to £N2.9 million over the same period. The operating losses shown in the table have been derived without allowing for depreciation; hence they understate the magnitude of the corporations' financial problems.

The statutory corporations' losses have been studied for several years. The Working Party on Statutory Corporations and State-Owned Companies appointed in April 1966 concluded that the losses and inefficiency of many of these corporations are the result of political influences, wrong pricing policies, their public-oriented goals, lack of adequate executive and technical personnel, and inadequate policy coordination. As the Second Plan stresses, "The actual performance of many of the public enterprises in Nigeria, however, leaves very much to be desired . . . Some do not possess the tools of translating into reality the hope of successful commercial operations. The level and quality of personnel are sometimes mediocre and reflect the worst traditions and rigidities of the civil service . . . Many of them suffer from over-capitalization and poor managerial effectiveness . . . The principle of insulation from partisan political pressure and sectionalism is more remarkable for its breach than for its observance."[26]

The major problems of the Electricity Corporation of Nigeria (ECN) are frequent breakdowns in generating units or transmission lines and lack of maintenance personnel.[27] The Nigerian Railway Corporation (NRC) has been incurring losses since 1959/60, and its major problems relate to operations, equipment, staffing, and investment decisions and rate policy,[28] the last one is particularly serious.[29] Besides, NRC also faces acute competition from the road system which has been greatly improved by substantial investments of the federal and state governments. Recently, the railways were severely affected by hostilities — the eastern branch of the network was closed down and about one-third of the rolling stock was immobilized and deteriorated. The railways are operating with over-aged equipment and physical facilities and need considerable modernization. Railways could probably absorb large capital investments, but this cannot be undertaken until its management and pricing problems are resolved.

The Nigerian Airways Corporation (NAC) suffers from the problems of operating modern aircraft, lack of adequate ground equipment, and perennial management problems. The losses of the Niger Dam Authority (NDA) in the past reflected the fact that its major revenue source, the Kainji Hydroelectric Scheme, was still under construction. The NDA has already started making profits and its financial position should improve in the future. The Nigerian Coal Corporation (NCC), set up in 1951, has been showing operating losses since 1960/61 because some of its major customers have shifted to other energy sources. The Nigerian National Shipping Line (NNSL), established in 1958, is over-capitalized due to bad investment decisions and poor management.[30]

On the whole, the major problems of statutory corporations are inadequate management, inefficient rate structures, bad investment decisions and faulty capitalization, and the inherent difficulty of achieving an operational balance between financial soundness and public accountability.[31] The scope for expanding their investment programs financed from the federal government

26. *Second National Development Plan, 1970-74*, pp. 75-76.

27. *Ibid*, p. 158.

28. *Ibid*, p. 182.

29. A.R. Prest, *op. cit.*, p. 200-201.

30. *Second National Development Plan, 1970-74*, p. 184.

31. *Ibid*, p. 186.

budget will be limited for some time unless their operations undergo structural reforms.

Capital Receipts and Expenditure of State Governments

Capital expenditures of many state governments also fell short of budget estimates in 1970/71. The most critical states in this respect were East Central, Kwara, North Eastern and Rivers. Only Lagos State and Western State show substantial improvements over their budgets. Otherwise, all states show shortfalls. One of the major reasons for the shortfall of state government expenditures, besides the lack of executive capacity, is the inadequacy of current budget surpluses, as stressed earlier. In the past, the state governments have relied very heavily on loans re-lent from the federal government, capital grants from the federal government and marketing board surpluses.

The limit to which any state government can depend upon loans re-lent from the federal government is determined by the general monetary conditions, the federal government's own borrowing needs, and the formula for the allocation of public borrowings among different states.

Federal Grants to State Governments

Federal grants are given for specific purposes in the context of the Plan. The Second Plan, for example, provides for about £N37 million in federal capital transfers to the states over the four years of the Plan, largely for education, agriculture, and infrastructure. The largest grants are for agricultural development – £N17 million for seed multiplication schemes, improvement of extension services, provision of fertilizers, pesticides, tractors, and other agricultural equipment [32] and £N3 million for special agricultural schemes which cut across state boundaries, expand the output of industrial raw materials, or promote import substitution. The education sector is allocated £N9.8 million, mainly for primary schools. Other major grants totaling £N5 million are to be given for the construction of secretariat buildings in the nine new states.

The Second Plan did not specify criteria for allocation of these grants to the states and left the decision to the respective federal ministries. Only about £N2 million of agricultural grants have been distributed to the states out of £N8 million allocated for the first two years of the Plan. The state governments have apparently been hurt by the delays in releasing these funds.

In the future, the federal government may not need to raise loans to finance its own capital budget and therefore a larger part of federal and borrowed funds can be re-lent to the states. The fact remains that in the past, state governments' resources to carry out their capital expenditure programs have been limited. They have, of necessity, tried to obtain as much money as possible from marketing boards.

Loans and Grants from the Marketing Boards

The relative dependence of the state governments on marketing boards varies from state to state. Unfortunately, the more recent data on the trading profits of the boards and their disposal are not available. Some published data up to 1967 are available and are summarized in Table 11-21. The data reveal that between 1954 and 1967, out of the accumulated surplus of £N171 million, £N72 million (or 42 percent) was used for capital grants to the state governments, and another £N12 million (or 7 percent) was loaned to the state governments. The Western State, especially, made extensive use of its marketing boards to obtain additional revenues. The marketing boards also provided another £N15 million (or 9 percent) to state development and finance companies and grants to various ministries of the state governments.

The marketing boards have contributed in certain years as much as 30 to 40 percent of some states' capital expenditures. The Second Plan anticipated that the marketing boards would contribute £N64 million (or 14 percent) towards financing state capital expenditures of £N470 million over the Plan period.[33] As this type of resource generation postulates specific produce price policies conducive to the creation of surpluses by the marketing boards, the implications of

32. *Ibid*, p. 112.

33. *Second National Development Plan, 1970-74*, p. 198.

Table 11-19: SHORTFALL IN GOVERNMENT CAPITAL EXPENDITURES, 1970/71

(In Millions of £N)

Government	Plan Estimates Nominal Capital Program[a]	Plan Estimates Effective Capital Program[b]	Actual Expenditure 1970/71	Actual as Percentage of Effective Capital Program
Federal	132.4	107.5	66.7	62.0
Benue Plateau	4.8	3.3	3.5	106.1
East Central	15.9	12.3	2.6	21.1
Kano	11.2	9.2	8.1	88.0
Kwara	4.0	3.7	2.1	56.8
Lagos	3.9	3.2	1.9	59.4
Mid-Western	8.1	6.6	8.1	122.7
North Central	7.8	6.5	2.5	38.5
North Eastern	7.0	5.1	4.3	84.3
North Western	6.5	5.2	3.4	65.4
Rivers	6.0	5.2	1.0	19.2
South Eastern	6.9	5.3	2.7	50.9
Western	22.2	16.9	13.6	80.5
Total	236.8	190.0	120.5	63.4

[a]Inclusive of transfers and assumed underspending.
[b]Exclusive of transfers and assumed underspending.

Source: First Progress Report on the Second Development Plan.

this for agricultural incentives and farmer's incomes could be adverse (see Section on Taxation of Agriculture).

At present, the sources of capital receipts of the state governments are constrained for several reasons. While it is true that state governments could, and should, generate larger current surpluses through their own tax efforts and economy in recurrent expenditures, the scope of this increase appears to be small. If the state governments have to expand their development efforts, particularly in economic and social services, it is essential that their financing pattern and the availability of capital resources be reviewed.

At all levels of government considerable efforts will be required to overcome the limitations of executive capacity for expansion of the country's development. This also applies to the weak statutory corporations, whose profitability and management need to be improved. In order to insure the effectiveness of new investments in or by these corporations, structural reforms are necessary for improving their efficiency.

Tax Incentives for Private Investment

The federal government has the option of using available financial resources for encouraging private enterprise. This can be done in several ways: through the fiscal instruments of tax incentives, through the non-fiscal instrument of cheaper and liberal credit, by way of technical assistance, education and training of management and labor, or channeling of funds to the private sector either by direct venture participation or the funding of development banks. Only the scope of tax incentives for private investment will be explored in this chapter.

Tax Incentives for Industry

Only the federal government has the authority to enact laws relating to tax incentives for industrial investment. Similarly, the levy and collection of corporation income tax and custom tariffs, under which most of the tax incentives are given to industry, are under federal jurisdiction. The tax incentives given to industry are embodied in five Acts[34] – the Industrial Development (Income Tax Relief) Act, 1958; the Industrial Development (Import Duty Relief) Act, 1957; the Customs Duties (Dumped and Subsidized Goods) Act, 1958; the Customs (Drawback) Regulations, 1959, and the Income Tax (Amendment) Act, 1959. These are discussed in detail in the Manufacturing Industry Section.

Judging by the opinions expressed in government and academic circles, existing tax incentives are viewed as fairly liberal.[35] It is also felt that the present tax incentives are indiscriminate and should be made more selective. Tax concessions reduce the effective rates of taxation significantly[36] and cause substantial revenue loss. According to one estimate, 148 companies (out of approximately 1,000 medium and large-scale firms) benefited from pioneer tax holidays between 1958 and 1968. Their investment in 1968 was approximately £N75 million. The cost of tax relief from 1958-68 is estimated at £N6.6 million. In addition, these companies (as well as others) enjoyed import duty reliefs reducing tax revenues by another £N45 million during those ten years.[37]

While it is difficult to evaluate the overall effectiveness of incentive measures on investment in the past,[38] it appears that the government has started to reduce the existing tax incentives. The increase of capital expenditure limits for eligibility to pioneer companies tax relief, the reduction of the rates of tax depreciation allowances and of initial investment allowances are some of the changes that have already been introduced.

The future policy of the government on tax incentives is defined in the Second Plan. The Plan states "that what is important for purposes of influencing the amount of foreign investment in Nigeria today is not the battery of incentives . . ." The Plan, therefore, proposes "a shift in emphasis and the adoption of more selective measures." It also emphasizes that "during the Plan period, 'Pioneer Status' will gradually give way to a system of 'Priority Status' which will depend on the value-added potential of proposed industries . . . Another incentive which will be manipulated . . . is the granting of initial and annual capital allowances . . . capital allowances would further be granted so as to discriminate among industries; and within each individual industry, between different activities."[39] Thus, it is clear that the emphasis of future government policy would be on a reduction in tax incentives and on selectivity in granting them. The government appears not to intend to use additional resources to finance fiscal incentives to private industrial investment.

This strategy is certainly appropriate if tax incentives are not important to private investment

34. A detailed survey of these incentive legislations is given in S.A. Aluko *Fiscal Incentives for Industrial Development in Nigeria* (1967).

35. Cf., for example, A. Adedeji, *Nigerian Federal Finance* (1969), p. 204, Ben W. Lewis, *Incentive for Industrial Development in Nigeria* (unpublished, 1962), *Second National Development Plan, 1970-74*, pp. 284-285, and I.O. Dina, "Fiscal Measures" in *Reconstruction and Development in Nigeria* (1971), pp. 386-389.

36. See O.A. Phillips, 'Nigeria's Companies Income Tax" *Nigerian Journal of Economics and Social Studies*, Vol. X, No. 3 (November 1968), pp. 321-338.

37. S.A. Aluko, "Incentive Policies for Industrial Development in Nigeria," paper presented at the *Interregional Seminar on Incentive Policies for Industrial Development* at Vienna (UNIDO 10 March-21 March 1969), pp. 21-25. In 1969, eight more companies received pioneer status.

38. Some writers have argued that in the Nigerian context, tax incentives play a minor role in investment decisions. See A.N. Hakam, "The Motivation to Invest and the Locational Pattern of Foreign Private Industrial Investment," *Nigerian Journal of Economic and Social Studies* (March 1966). Also see P. Kilby, *Industrialization in an Open Economy: Nigeria, 1945-1966* (1969).

39. *Second National Development Plan, 1970-74*, pp. 285-286.

Table 11-20: FINANCIAL OPERATIONS OF MAJOR FEDERAL STATUTORY CORPORATIONS, 1960/61-1970/71

(In Millions of £N)

	1960/61	1961/62	1962/63	1963/64	1964/65	1965/66	1966/67	1967/68	1968/69	1969/70	1970/71
Nigerian Railway Corporation											
Revenues	13.2	15.2	14.9	16.3	14.2	14.6	13.1	11.1	12.0	11.6	12.0
Operating Expenses (including interest)	15.6	16.3	15.9	16.3	17.7	18.8	17.6	14.5	15.7	16.8	18.2
Operating Profits (+)/Losses (–)[a]	-2.4	-1.1	-1.0	—	-3.5	-4.2	-4.5	-3.4	-3.7	-5.2	-6.2
Electricity Corporation of Nigeria											
Revenues	5.7	6.9	8.1	9.6	11.1	12.6	14.0	11.1	12.3	14.6	18.5
Operating Expenses (including interest)	4.5	6.0	7.3	9.1	10.0	12.2	13.9	14.2	16.0	19.9	20.2
Operating Profits(+)/Losses(–)[a]	+1.2	+0.9	+0.8	+0.5	+1.1	+0.4	+0.1	-3.1	-3.7	-5.3	-1.7
Nigerian Port Authority											
Revenues	6.9	7.7	7.7	8.9	10.6	12.3	10.4	8.5	9.5	13.6	22.7
Operating Expenses (including interest)	NA	6.7	7.1	7.6	8.5	9.4	8.8	8.1	8.2	9.7	18.9
Operating Profits(+)/Losses(–)[a]	NA	+1.0	+0.6	+1.3	+2.1	+2.9	+1.6	+0.4	+1.3	+3.9	+3.7
Nigeria Airways Corporation											
Revenues	4.4	4.3	4.1	4.7	4.9	5.4	5.7	5.1	5.2	6.1	6.0
Operating Expenses (including interest)	3.9	3.9	4.5	4.9	5.4	5.8	5.9	6.0	5.1	5.7	5.7
Operating Profits(+)/Losses(–)[a]	+0.5	+0.4	-0.4	-0.2	-0.5	-0.4	-0.2	-0.9	+0.1	+0.4	+0.3
Nigerian Coal Corporation											
Revenues	1.4	1.5	1.6	1.6	NA	NA	NA	NA	NA	NA	NA
Operating Expenses (including interest)	1.6	1.6	1.7	1.7	NA	NA	NA	NA	NA	NA	NA
Operating Profits(+)/Losses(–)[a]	-0.2	-0.1	-0.1	-0.1	NA	NA	NA	NA	NA	NA	NA

Nigeria Dam Authority											
Revenues	—	—	—	—	—	—	—	—	—	5.2	NA
Operating Expenses (including interest)	—	—	(Neg)	(Neg)	0.6	0.7	1.2	1.8	3.2	3.0	NA
Operating Profits(+)/Losses(−)[a]	—	—	—	—	−0.6	−0.7	−1.2	−1.8	−3.2	+2.2	NA
Posts & Telegraphs Department											
Revenues	4.4	4.7	5.2	5.3	6.1	6.8	7.9	5.8	5.4	5.9	NA
Operating Expenses (including interest)	5.0	5.3	5.7	5.6	6.3	6.8	8.5	6.6	6.2	6.9	NA
Operating Profits(+)/Losses(−)[a]	−0.6	−0.6	−0.5	−0.3	−0.2	—	−0.6	−0.8	−0.8	−1.0	NA
Nigeria External Telecommunication Ltd.											
Revenues	—	—	—	0.9	0.9	1.1	1.1	1.1	1.2	1.5	1.7
Operating Expenses (including interest)	—	—	—	0.6	0.6	0.7	0.7	0.7	0.6	0.7	0.9
Operating Profits(+)/Losses(−)[a]	—	—	—	+0.3	+0.3	+0.4	+0.4	+0.4	+0.6	+0.8	+0.8
Nigerian Broadcasting Corporation											
Revenues	1.2	1.2	1.4	1.3	1.1	1.3	1.6	1.9	1.8	2.0	2.1
Operating Expenses (including interest)	1.1	1.1	1.1	1.1	1.2	1.2	1.5	1.6	1.8	1.7	1.8
Operating Profits(+)/Losses(−)[a]	+0.1	+0.1	+0.3	+0.2	−0.1	+0.1	+0.1	+0.3	—	+0.3	+0.3

[a]Not accounting for depreciation.

Source: Central Bank of Nigeria.

Table 11-21: ACCUMULATIONS AND USES OF FUNDS OF REGIONAL MARKETING BOARDS, 1954-67

	Eastern Region	Northern Region	Western Region	Total
				(In Millions of £N)
Accumulations				
Transfer from Commodity Marketing Boards, 1954	11.5	32.6	42.9	87.0
Net Trading Surpluses, 1954-1961	10.8	–3.2	14.3	21.9
Excess of Other Income over Expenditure, 1954-1961	1.7	2.5	5.3	9.5
Net Accumulations, 1962-1967	1.6[a]	10.6	40.5[b]	52.7
Total, 1954-67	25.6	42.5	103.0	171.1
Utilization of Accumulated Funds				
Cumulative Grants to Regional Governments	7.5	—	64.3	71.8
Cumulative Grants to Regional Development and Finance Corporations	2.8	1.9	0.9	5.6
Other Cumulative Grants and Expenditures (e.g. extension services, produce inspection, research institutes, feeder roads improvements, input subsidies, etc.)	0.2	6.1	2.8	9.1
Loans outstanding to Federal Government	1.8	5.7	—	7.5
Loans outstanding to Regional Governments	—	11.8	—	11.8
Loans outstanding to Regional Development and Finance Corporations	0.5	0.7	3.6	4.8
Equity Investment in Nigerian Private Companies	3.5	2.6	17.4	23.5
Loans Outstanding to Nigerian Private Companies	—	1.0	2.8	3.8
United Kingdom Securities	3.2	4.6	—	7.8
Federation of Nigeria Securities	—	6.1	—	6.1
Total, 1962-67	19.5[c]	40.5[c]	91.8[c]	151.8[c]

[a]Data not available for 1963-1967.
[b]These accumulations are up to 1968 instead of 1967.
[c]This is not a complete listing; for example, it excludes working capital and fixed assets of the Marketing Boards.

Source: G.K. Helleiner, *Peasant Agriculture, Government and Economic Growth in Nigeria,* (Richard D. Irwin, Inc., Yale, 1966), p. 175 and E.O. Obayan, "The Marketing Board and Economic Development," paper presented at the International Conference on the Marketing Board System (March 29-April 3, 1971), Tables 2 and 3, pp. 15-16.

decisions.[40] The evidence, although not fully conclusive, does point in that direction. The use of other incentives to support private investment activity and the provision of adequate credit and loanable funds from budget resources therefore acquires added importance. These are especially important when account is taken of the substantial private funds that may be needed for full implementation of the government's indigenization policy.

Taxation of Agriculture

The possibility and desirability of tax incentives to agriculture, and more specifically to agricultural exports, is a difficult issue. The present taxation of agricultural exports is an important component of state government finances; therefore decisions cannot be made by the federal government alone. The trading profits of the marketing boards which have contributed significantly to state finances are directly related to the producer prices given to farmers. The degree to which existing prices constitute a disincentive to production and exports must be analyzed.

Exports of agricultural produce are taxed twice: through export duties and by the produce purchase/sales tax. Export duties are levied by the federal government (in consultation with the state governments) and also collected by it, but the proceeds are fully passed on to the state governments (Table 11-14). The produce purchase/sales taxes are levied, collected, and retained by the state governments. Unlike import duties, the rates of export duties have not been changed frequently. Up until 1950, export duties were *specific* with effective rates generally below 5 percent of value. At present, a basic 15 percent export duty is levied on agricultural exports whenever their price is below a certain specified minimum. Whenever export prices exceed these limits, the rate of export duty goes up by 1/10 percent for every £N or part thereof, with some exceptions. The maximum duty is 20 percent. Some specific rates are applied to relatively minor exports such as animals, birds, reptiles, bananas, cattle hides and skins, peanuts, sheep, fur, wood and timber.

The rates of produce purchase/sales tax have been revised even less frequently — in fact, only once for some commodities and never for others — since the tax was first imposed in 1954/55 (Table 11-22). The tax is limited to cocoa, groundnuts, palm oil, cotton, benneseed, and soybeans and is based on the volume of produce. Produce tax is referred to as Produce Purchase Tax in the eastern States and Produce Sales Tax in all other states. Under the provisions of these taxes, the tax is payable at the time of sale to the boards' licensed buying agents and the boards are accountable to the state governments for the tax collected.

While nominally the rates of the two export taxes do not appear very high, yet, taken together with the trading profits of the marketing boards, the average tax burden on agricultural exports is substantial. Table 11-23 gives some estimates, although they are not up-to-date. Two observations can be made about tax on agricultural produce. First, there is a substantial difference in the average tax burden on different export crops. Taxes on palm kernels and cocoa absorb almost one-third of the world price. Second, the average tax burden on all products fell substantially during 1954-61. Though it has risen in the sixties, the level is still not close to that which existed during 1947-54. The fluctuations in the average tax burden, despite the relative stability of rates of export duties and produce purchase/sales tax, are the result of fluctuations in world prices as well as the varying effort used by marketing boards to collect trading surpluses over the years.

Producer Prices

The trading profits of the marketing boards are directly related to the ratio of producer prices to world prices. Table 11-24 shows how producer prices have fluctuated from one period to another and how the ratio of producer prices to world prices have changed widely over the years. The range of fluctuation is much wider for cocoa than for other crops. This is because the Western State has utilized the marketing board as a fiscal device much more than the other states. In any case, the producer prices for all products were fairly depressed in the last few years and have been raised in the last year or so.

If export farmers are to be given tax incentives, either the rates of export duties and produce

40. Cf. A.O. Phillips, "Nigeria's Experience with Income Tax Exemption — A Preliminary Assessment," *Nigerian Journal of Economic and Social Studies,* Vol. X, No. 1 (March 1968).

purchase/sales taxes have to be reduced and/or the producer prices have to be raised (which is another way of saying that the taxes hidden in the marketing boards' trading profits have to be reduced). A reduction of the burden of *explicit* and *concealed* taxes on the farmers could increase farmers' incomes and reduce the flow of labor from the land to the urban areas. This in itself may be an important factor as most exports come from small farmers. Higher agricultural incomes could enlarge markets for industrial products and provide the necessary impetus for industrialization. However, if higher producer prices would not result in higher farm production, but only increase private trade profits, this could well prove to be inflationary. A reduction in export taxes, which would lead to higher farm incomes, could also reduce the relative profitability of food crops as compared to export crops and have serious implications for the supply of domestically produced staple foods.

Despite much literature on the subject, opinion is divided about the adequacy of existing producer prices. Yet the Second Plan does state that agricultural exports suffer from relatively low producer prices and that over the Plan period farmers will have to be given *fair* and *better* producer prices.[41] The state governments depend very heavily on export taxes although the level of dependence varies. In sum, the states have depended on export taxes to the tune of 20 to 25 percent of their current and capital receipts in the past (Table 11-25). It will be extremely difficult to ignore this dependence in reviewing the question of tax incentives to agriculture. Unless revenue losses of the states can be offset by increased taxes and/or additional transfers the proposition of lower tax burdens on agriculture may be difficult for the states to accept.

While the government has virtually decided that the level of existing tax incentives to industry is too high and must be reduced, the question of taxation of agriculture is quite controversial. There are more hypotheses than evidence on this subject and it will not be easy for the government to make a decision in the near future. The decision-making on this issue is further complicated by the fact that the fate of state government finances is directly involved in it. The question can, therefore, only be tackled in the context of a comprehensive review of state finances.

Table 11-22: RATES OF PRODUCE PURCHASE/SALES TAXES, 1954/55-1971/72

		(In £N per Ton)
Commodity	1954/55– 1960/61	1961/62– To date
Cocoa	4–0–0	4–0–0
Groundnuts	1–0–0	1–10–0
Palm Oil	4–0–0	4–0–0
Palm Kernels[a]	2–0–0	2–0–0
Cotton[b]	1–10–0	3–2–0
Benneseed[c]	0–1–0	1–0–0
Soybeans	0–2–6	0–5–0

[a]The rate of the tax in the northern states and Western State is £ N1 per ton.

[b]Tax is levied per pound of cotton sold to the boards' licensed buying agents. The rates are equivalent to £N0–18–8 and £N2–8–0, respectively for cottonseed and cotton lint.

[c]The rate of the tax in the eastern states remained unchanged at £N0–10–0.

Source: Marketing board annual reports, 1954/55 onwards.

41. *Second National Development Plan, 1970-74*, pp. 105-106, 291 and 198. It is difficult to reconcile this statement of the Plan with its target of generating large resources through the marketing boards to finance capital expenditure of the state governments.

Table 11-23: AVERAGE TAX BURDEN ON AGRICULTURAL
EXPORTS, 1947-67

Commodity	Total Withdrawals as a Percent of Potential Producer[a] Income		
	1947-1954[b]	1954-1961[b]	1961-1967[c]
Cocoa	39.4	26.1	29.4
Palm Kernels	29.2	27.1	32.3
Groundnut	40.0	14.9	16.5
Cotton	42.3	11.2	15.3

[a]Includes export duties, produce purchase tax and marketing board trading surpluses but excludes the operating expenses of marketing boards.
[b]G.K. Helleiner, *Peasant Agriculture, Government and Economic Growth in Nigeria,* p. 163.
[c]E.O. Obayan, "The Marketing Board and Economic Development," paper presented at the International Conference on the Marketing Board System (March 29-April 3, 1971), Table 1, p. 14.

Tax Reforms

This section will discuss the short-run goals of tax reform — inflation control and improvement of state finances — rather than the longer-range aims of creation and maintenance of a tax system which will serve the ultimate development objectives of the country. Indeed, the longer-range goals of employment, income redistribution, improvement in resource allocation, etc., would also be served by the short-run measures. The dangers of inflationary pressure which can be expected to remain for several years need to be avoided. Also a sound financial arrangement is needed for adequate contribution to development by the state governments. The Second Plan repeatedly stressed the need by all levels of government, especially the states, to improve their internal revenue collection and tap additional sources of revenue.[42]

The following analysis is an attempt to highlight important factors in tax reform. At the federal level, the existing taxes which may need particular attention appear to be excise and import duties; while at the state level, the important factors are improvement and extension of the personal income tax and property tax. The state governments might also explore the possibilities of levying a general sales tax.

Excise Duties. The list of commodities subject to federal excise duties has been expanded over time. Today about forty-eight items are subject to excise. The most important are: textiles, cement and paint, soap, household utensils and auto tires. There are very few exemptions from excise duties, the main ones being the head of the state, diplomats, and the defense departments. Many rates are specific, while those which are *ad valorem* range between 5 percent and 15 percent (except cigarettes, jewelery and certain oils).[43]

The excise duties have not been raised for most items since 1965. The system of excise taxation was revised in 1964/65 in order to compensate for the loss of import duties when tariff levels were sharply raised to protect local industries. Similar changes on a small scale were made in 1969/70. The significant increases in the customs tariffs during those years were not matched by increases in excise duties. An examination of the coverage and rates of excise duties may help to determine the scope for additional revenues and lead to review of desired levels of effective protection for domestic industry.

Import Duties. The data on the collection of import duties are not available by suitable commodity categories. Therefore, it is not possible to estimate average effective import duties for broad classes of goods. It appears that the overall incidence of import duties has been significantly raised over time.

42. *Second National Development Plan, 1970-74,* especially pp. 65 and 198.

43. The 1972/73 Budget significantly reduced the rates of many excise taxes.

Table 11-24: PRODUCER PRICES IN RELATION TO WORLD PRICES, 1948-70

Mean Averages	Cocoa		Palm Oil		Palm Kernel		Groundnut	
	Producer Price (£ per ton)	Producer Price as Percent of World Price	Producer Price (£ per ton)	Producer Price as Percent of World Price	Producer Price (£ per ton)	Producer Price as Percent of World Price	Producer Price (£ per ton)	Producer Price as Percent of World Price
1948 - 1952[a]	117.4	49.2	46.8	61.8	28.2	60.9	22.6	35.1
1953 - 1957[a]	178.0	70.0	47.4	62.0	32.2	59.2	37.6	47.8
1958 - 1962[a]	134.4	65.9	41.4	52.1	29.4	53.3	39.6	62.3
1963 - 1967[a]	98.0	64.3	40.5	55.5	27.6	50.2	41.4	67.8
1968/69[b]	96.0	37.6	41.0	67.2	29.0	43.0	25.0	41.4
1969/70[b]	146.0	42.1	41.0	62.5	29.0	52.3	30.0	40.0
1970/71[b]	151.0	60.3	44.0	46.8	30.0	48.0	34.0	41.2

[a]D. Olatunbosun and S.O. Olayide, "The Effect of the Marketing Boards on the Output and Income of Primary Producers," paper presented at the International Conference on the Marketing Board System (29th March-3rd April 1971), p. 17 and p. 21.
[b]Central Bank of Nigeria.

Table 11-25: RELATIVE DEPENDENCE OF REGIONAL
GOVERNMENT FINANCES[a] ON EXPORT PRODUCE,
1955/56-1965/66

Year	Western Nigeria	Eastern Nigeria	Northern Nigeria
1955/56	30.7	24.8	21.8
1956/57	57.5	20.6	27.3
1957/58	25.5	18.6	26.7
1958/59	30.0	17.2	29.9
1959/60	45.1	18.0	26.5
1960/61	60.5	18.1	15.6
1961/62	7.2	27.8	21.0
1962/63	33.5	14.1	21.3
1963/64	21.9	17.5	21.3
1964/65	19.0	13.1	22.4
1965/66	24.4	15.9	23.2

[a]Receipts from Export Duties, Produce Sale Tax, marketing boards' grants as a
percent of recurrent and capital receipts of regional governments.

Source: O. Teriba and O. Olakanpo, "Fiscal, Monetary and Investment
Implications of the Marketing Boards," paper presented at the International
Conference on the Marketing Board System (29th March-3rd April 1971),
Table 7, p. 17.

Nigeria began as a relatively open economy in 1960; most imports entered duty-free or with very low duties. By the middle sixties, however, import duties, measured as a *weighted average* tariff, had risen to 48 percent for all commodities. Recently, nominal tariffs continued to rise for foodstuffs and other consumer articles. Further increases and the introduction of a surcharge in 1967 raised the average overall nominal tariff rate to about 62 percent in 1968. The liberalization of imports since the end of the war has been accompanied by some further tariff increases. This increase occurred despite the reduction in the general import surcharge from 7-1/2 percent to 5 percent in April, 1970, and some selective reductions in duty rates. These ad hoc revisions of import duties may have created a tariff structure which may no longer be economically rational in terms of protection and domestic price policy. While there may not be an urgent need to revise the import duties on raw materials and capital goods, the rate structure affecting the food items and consumer durables (which in 1970 accounted for one-third of total imports) deserves examination especially in relation to their potential effectiveness for the control of urban demand and prices.

Personal Income Tax. In most developing countries, personal income tax is a federal or central government subject, in Nigeria it is under the jurisdiction of the state governments. This has created considerable diversity of tax rates, allowances, etc., despite the efforts of the federal government to create a uniform conceptual, procedural and administrative framework of personal income taxation under the Income Tax Management Act of 1961. Table 11-26 gives an impression of the diversity of personal income tax structures in different parts of the country.

The tax rates presented may appear to be fairly steep, but in fact the generous allowances granted taxpayers reduce the effective rates.[44] Moreover, except in Lagos State, various forms of income, e.g., rental income, dividends, capital gains, income in-kind and foreign income, are excluded from the income tax base. In addition, the state governments lack the necessary collection machinery; tax evasion and avoidance appear substantial among the middle and upper in-

44. See A. Adedeji, *Nigerian Federal Finance* (1969), p. 192 and V.P. Diejomaoh, "Tax and Revenue Allocation Policies," paper presented at the *Conference on Integration and National Unity,* University of Lagos, December 15, 1970.

Table 11-26: AVERAGE AND MARGINAL INCOME TAX RATES IN STATES

Lagos State

Total Chargeable Income £N	Marginal Rate[a] Percent
First 1,000	12.50
1,000 - 1,400	17.50
1,400 - 1,800	22.50
1,800 - 2,800	30.00
2,800 - 3,800	37.50
3,800 - 4,800	46.25
4,800 -10,000	57.50
£N10,000 and above	75.00

Northern States

Total Chargeable Income £N	Marginal Rate[b] Percent
Income not exceeding £400	
First 500	6.25
500 - 1,000	8.75
1,000 - 1,500	15.00
1,500 - 2,000	20.00
2,000 - 3,000	25.00
3,000 - 4,000	32.50
4,000 - 5,000	40.00
£N5,000 and above	50.00

Mid-Western States

Total Chargeable Income £N	Marginal Rate[c] Percent
First 500	6.25
500 - 700	6.67
700 - 900	7.50
900 - 1,100	12.50
1,100 - 1,500	17.50
1,500 - 2,300	22.50
2,300 - 3,300	27.50
3,300 - 4,300	37.50
£N4,300 and above	47.50

Western States

Total Chargeable Income £N	Marginal Rate[c] Percent
First 500	6.25
500 - 700	7.50
700 - 900	10.00
900 - 1,100	12.50
1,100 - 1,500	17.50
1,500 - 1,900	22.50
1,900 - 2,300	27.50
2,300 - 3,100	32.50
3,100 - 3,900	37.50
3,900 - 4,900	45.00
4,900 - 6,900	52.50
6,900 -10,000	62.50
£N10,000 and above	75.00

Eastern States

Total Chargeable Income £N	Average Rate Percent
50	1.00
100	3.00
200	4.00
300	5.00
400	5.20
500	5.60
600	6.00
700	6.00
800	6.25
900	6.50
1,000	7.25
1,100	8.00
1,200	8.50
1,300	10.00
1,400	10.50
1,500	11.00
2,000	15.00
4,000	25.00
6,000	32.50
8,000	35.00
10,000	37.50

aIn addition to income tax, there is in Lagos an income rate payable by every taxable individual resident. The rates vary between a minimum of 10/-and a maximum of £N5 for any one year.

Total Income	Amount of Income Rate		
	£N	s:	d
Income not exceeding £N100	=	10:	=
Exceeding £N100 but not exceeding £N200	1	=	=
£N201	1	10:	=
£N202	2	=:	=
£N203	2	10:	=
Exceeding £N203 but not exceeding £N300	3	=:	=
£N300 but not exceeding £N400	4	=:	=
£N400	5	=:	=

bAll income earners whose incomes exceed £N400 are expected to pay 6d. in the £N on the first £N400 in addition to tax paid on the chargeable income.
cThe rates include development contributions of 6d. in the £N, paid by all individuals who earned over £N50 per annum; these contributions have now been done away with.

Source: Central Bank of Nigeria and A. Adedeji, *Nigerian Federal Finance* (1969).

come groups.[45] As a consequence income taxation in Nigeria tends to be regressive: while every taxpayer pays the basic rate (flat poll tax), the middle and high income taxpayers enjoy substantial exemptions and allowances from the personal income tax. Poll tax is an essential element of personal income taxation in the states. Every male person who is sixteen years of age or more and is not pursuing full-time studies or apprenticeship is presumed to have a minimum income. Such a person, whether gainfully employed or not, pays a poll tax at a flat rate, which varies from state to state. In the northern states it takes the form of a community tax.

The collection and retention of poll tax is generally left to the local authorities who, in Western and Mid-West States, also assess, collect and substantially retain taxes on incomes in the range of £N51 to £N300 from self-employed persons and those who come under the PAYE scheme. This involvement of local authorities in personal income taxation is also considered one of the major defects in the Nigerian income taxation,[46] as the administration of the income tax is inhibited by inefficiency and political consideration. The evasion of both the poll tax and the personal income tax is a serious problem, and the lack of administrative capabilities of the state and local authorities are important factors.[47]

If personal income tax is to become an effective tool of fiscal policy, it is essential that the regressivity of the tax for the middle and upper income groups be corrected. Moreover, the tax should be made uniform and simpler to administer. The tax base could also be expanded to cover various other elements of income besides wages and salaries. In recent years, many state governments have reduced the rates of income tax. The Western and Mid-Western States, for example, reduced their poll tax rate from £N3 to £N2 in 1969/70. They also removed the *development contribution* of 6d. per pound (£N) of chargeable income in 1970/71. Lagos State reduced the personal income tax rates for incomes below £N300 in 1970/71. Although some of these measures may have made the system more progressive, such reductions during a period of considerable inflation appear to have accomplished little more than an erosion of the present tax base.

Certain states have property taxation but only in rudimentary form, while others do not have any at all. Nowhere is the property tax integrated with effective taxation of capital gains,[48] rental income, dividends and inheritance and gift taxes. The agricultural sector does not pay a property tax because of the traditional direct (poll and cattle) taxes levied on it and the heavy burden of export taxation. Although the legal basis exists for property taxation in the states, there is, in fact, a notable absence of effective property taxation in Nigeria. In all of Nigeria, only 15 cities,[49] with less than half of the urban population, levy the tax and the bulk of the tax revenue is generated by Lagos State alone, largely because of the non-residential properties of statutory corporations. Even there the average effective tax rate on capital values is about one percent, though the statutory rate appears high.

Properties are reassessed infrequently, unimproved lands are generally not taxed, and there is an unusually long delay (generally 2/3 years) in adding new properties to the valuation list. There is a high delinquency rate in the payment of property taxes — in Lagos State it is estimated at 20 percent. The legal structure does not permit the seizure of property for tax delinquency, so that property tax arrears are a serious problem everywhere. The northern states have never shown much interest in property taxation on the ground that the existing community tax is essentially a

45. The extent of tax evasion and lack of adequate coverage can be seen from the fact that in the West State only 840,000 persons out of a population of over 10 million paid personal income tax in 1970/71. Cf. G.O. Orewa, *Taxation in Western Nigeria* (1962), Chapter 2. The major reason for the widespread tax evasion is the lack of adequate administrative and tax collection machinery at the state levels.

46. A. Adedeji, *op. cit.,* p. 199.

47. Milton C. Taylor, "The Relationship Between Income Tax Administration and Income Tax Policy in Nigeria," *The Nigerian Journal of Economic and Social Studies,* Vol IX, No. 2 (July 1967), pp. 203-215.

48. A capital gains tax was levied by the federal government in 1967/68 at a flat 20 percent rate but the tax is generally ineffective. See A.O. Phillips, "Nigeria's New Capital Gains Tax". *Administration,* Vol. III, No. 2 (January 1969), pp. 125-137.

49. These cities are Lagos, Kano, Jos, Zaria, Kaduna, Enugu, Port Harcourt, Aba, Umahia, Calabar, Abeokuta, Ibadan, Sapele, Benin and Warri. The property tax rates vary between 2-4 shillings on a £N of annual rental value in the eastern cities and 10 shillings on a £N of annual rental value in Lagos.

tax which takes into account the wealth of an individual at the time of apportionment. Ibadan in Western State, the most important urban area in the country after Lagos, does not levy the tax at all.[50] In summary, the need for and the scope of improving property taxation is substantial in Nigeria,[51] and this is especially so when the state and local governments are finding it hard to meet the costs of rapid urban development.

Sales Tax. Under the Constitution, the state governments are authorized to levy a sales tax only on agricultural produce. Recently however the Joint Tax Board authorized the states to levy a general sales tax and it is hoped that the states will soon take action. At present none of the states levies such a tax, nor does the federal government. The revenue potential of this tax should be substantial, but it could also create serious inter-state commerce problems especially if the tax rates are not aligned.

Other Taxes. The water rates collected in the urban areas are too low and in many areas, especially in the Western State, take the form of a per capita (poll) special rate rather than being a function of property valuation or metered use. Only the eastern states appear to be recouping revenues from water rates at levels close to maintenance costs. In most other states, even maintenance costs are not covered by revenues, let alone longer-run overhead and capital costs. The state and local authorities can also levy license fees on marriages and registration of births. They can also levy taxes on the transfer of ownership of motor vehicles and other properties.

The main scope for tax reforms lies in the area of personal income taxation, property and wealth taxation and sales taxation. All these could not only make the existing tax system of Nigeria more balanced, but would also help reduce the financial problems of state and local governments. They should make the tax system a more potent instrument of public policy especially in controlling purchasing power in the hands of the public.

50. Many of these problems of property taxation in Nigeria are highlighted in the papers presented at the *Third National Conference on Local Government* held at Benin (December 7-12, 1970).

51. Cf. V.P. Diejomaoh, *op. cit.,* pp. 21-22.

CHAPTER 12
EDUCATION AND TRAINING

The Present System

The administration of primary and secondary education is the responsibility of the state governments.[1] The federal government operates a few national secondary schools and assists the expansion of education in states with less well developed school systems. Universities are a concurrent responsibility of the federal and state governments. Since independence, four universities have been created in addition to the one at Ibadan. Although the federal government is under increasing pressure to permit the creation of university level facilities in each state, the high cost of these institutions and the concentration of new resources in the federal budget imply that the National Universities Commission should have increasing influence over university expansion. It is important that the size, composition and distribution of additional universities be centrally controlled to prevent duplication of effort and inefficient use of scarce resources.

The structure of the present educational system is illustrated in Chart 1. The quality of data for the states' educational systems is uneven and in places very poor; statistics for the six northern states have been incomplete for several years and for the period of unrest in the three eastern states. The Federal Ministry of Education is sponsoring training courses for state educational planners and this should lead to improved data over the next few years.

A very striking feature of the school system is the large disparity in enrollment ratios between the northern states and the rest of the country. Table 12-1 gives approximate enrollment ratios. The abnormally high ratios for the war-affected eastern states reflect a backlog of overage students. The disparities in secondary education are even greater.

An alternative measure of these disparities is shown in Table 12-2, where enrollment per million population is expressed as a percentage of the figure for Mid-Western State, which is taken as having the highest enrollment ratios. This table shows, for example, that first year enrollments in both primary and secondary education are about 15 times higher in the Mid-Western State than in Kano State as compared with their population.

The marked differences in primary Grade I enrollments are later reflected in Grade VI enrollments, which influence the size (and quality) of initial enrollments in secondary schools. University enrollments, which in some states are inhibited by low enrollments in the terminal years of secondary education, show even wider differences.

A special situation exists in the three eastern states, which before hostilities had well developed school systems that suffered considerably both from population movements and from damage to buildings. Although some buildings are now in use again with minimal facilities and others are being rehabilitated and reconstructed, the disruption caused has affected the quality of education provided. It may be some time before the educational system in these states recovers fully and adjusts to the changing employment opportunities in the economy. The conversion of secondary education to comprehensive schools is one step in this direction, particularly insofar as it gives the secondary graduate wider employment opportunities in the private sector.

One of the government's educational objectives is the attainment of a national minimum enrollment ratio of 50 percent in primary education by the mid-seventies. When the Plan was being prepared, educational data did not allow the implications of this objective to be fully determined; it is now clearly impossible and attempts to attain it in some states may lead to a serious decline in the quality of primary education. The southern states have such a large lead that the objective of national equalization will only be attained in primary education when all states approach complete enrollment at entry to primary education. For example, the North-Western State's education plan has adopted a target of 15 percent primary enrollment by 1974 as against 8 percent in 1970. While the actual enrollments ratio may be understated because of uncertainty on state population figures, they are equivalent to approximately tripling total primary enrollment between 1970 and 1974/75. On the other hand, the existing stock and prospective output of primary teachers would

1. In preparing this chapter, the mission has benefited from the report of the Unesco Project Identification Mission which visited Nigeria in February 1971. *Education in Nigeria: Educational Projects for External Aid* (Paris: Unesco, September 1971).

Table 12-1: PRIMARY GRADE I ENROLLMENT RATIOS

State	Percent
North Eastern	10
North Western	11
North Central	20
Kano	9
Kwara	34
Benue Plateau	27
Western	86
Lagos	107
Mid-Western	95
East Central	171
South Eastern	129
Rivers	119
All Nigeria	66

Source: Unesco, *Education in Nigeria: Educational Projects for External Aid* (Paris: September 1971), p. vii.

not allow any improvement in the proportion of fully qualified (Grade II) teachers during the same period, presently at 42 percent. This constraint would be even more acute after 1975. The Mid-Western State is at the opposite extreme; primary enrollments are projected to rise from 84 percent to 95 percent during 1970/74, which would imply complete enrollment of the first year primary age group by 1974. This prospect emphasizes the importance of accurate demographic statistics and careful siteing of additional schools to insure local balance of facilities. It also emphasizes the magnitude of the task of equalization of opportunities and the time it will take to achieve. During the Plan period, other states in southern Nigeria can be expected to approach full enrollment at entry to primary education.

Efficiency of the Education System

The available data concerning the costs and benefits of the educational system are inadequate to assess its efficiency in detail. Enrollment data are incomplete and no state provides information about the numbers of pupils repeating classes and the frequency of overage students. Unit cost data are also incomplete in that in most states they do not cover voluntary agencies' contributions, and are probably not comparable between states.

Table 12-3 illustrates the crude flow rates for primary and secondary education in nine states. This shows the number of students enrolled in the final year of primary and secondary education for every 1,000 students enrolled in the corresponding first year. Compared with many other educational systems, the numbers completing primary and secondary education in the six northern states suggest satisfactory performance of these educational systems. The situation in Lagos primary education is also not untypical of urban school systems with high enrollment rates. However, in the Mid-Western and Western States the performance of the primary school systems, with less than 450 of every 1,000 pupils left in class after 5 years' school, is indicative of the problems which often result from very rapid expansion of first year enrollments. The performance of the secondary school system in these two states is also apparently less efficient than those of the much smaller secondary school systems in most northern states. It is usually found that, when allowance is made for pupils repeating classes and for overage pupils entering above the first grade, the actual efficiency of the school system is less than that indicated by the crude flow rates.

Table 12-2: ENROLLMENT INDICES (about 1970)

(Mid-Western State: 100.0)

State	First-year enrollment per million population		
	Primary	Secondary[a]	University
Benue Plateau	21.6	15.2	9.4
East Central[b]	155.1	n.a.	n.a.
Kano	6.9	6.5	4.0
Kwara	27.1	40.2	38.8
Lagos	85.1	115.2	28.6
Mid-Western	100.0	100.0	100.0
North Central	16.4	10.5	5.4
North Eastern	9.4	7.6	4.0
North Western	8.6	7.6	3.6
Rivers[b]	106.0	56.2	18.8
South Eastern[b]	115.5	21.7	28.6
Western	62.2	96.0	83.0

[a]Including grammar, commercial, trade, etc.
[b]The data on enrollments is not comparable because of the backlog of students entering primary school following the civil war.
n.a.=not available

Source: Unesco, *Education in Nigeria,* p. 12.

Financing Education

The historical development of educational expenditure has been well documented.[2] Total recurrent expenditure rose from £N31.94 million in 1965/66 to £N32.54 million (excluding the eastern states) in 1968/69. By 1970/71, total estimated current expenditures were £N64.55 million. The corresponding capital expenditures were £N7.7 million in 1965/66 and £N4.20 million in 1968/69 reflecting the general decline in capital expenditure during the crisis. By comparison, planned capital expenditures on education during 1970/74 is about £N30 million annually.

Table 12-4 gives the composition of 1970/71 budgeted current expenditures. The federal government accounts for only one-sixth of total expenditure overwhelmingly allocated to the National Universities Commission. Primary education accounts for half the expenditure of the states and 42 percent overall.

As an indication of perceived priorities, Table 12-5 presents the composition of Plan allocations for capital expenditure on education. These figures give an incomplete picture of Plan allocations. It is known that present educational capital expenditures are not proceeding at the rate envisaged in the Plan. During 1970/71, implementation of the university program had barely begun and several states encountered difficulties in carrying out school building programs at both primary and secondary levels. The distribution of investment among states is uneven. The Western State alone accounts for one-third of primary allocations and the four largest northern states together account for little more than the Western State's Plan taken by itself. It is not evident from the Plan's overall financial allocations that the balance of educational opportunity within the country will be improved. The southern states are spending most of their primary allocations on repair of existing buildings and on keeping up with population growth, while the northern states are expanding their primary systems. Secondary education is being expanded rapidly throughout the country and it is not clear whether existing disparities are being reduced. In principle, places are available to students irrespective of their state of origin but all the universities are largely filled with students from the areas they serve. In practice, enrollment of northern students is inhibited

2. A. Callaway and A. Musore, Unesco: *Financing of Education in Nigeria;* IEEP, (Paris; 1968).

Table 12-3: CRUDE FLOW RATES: NUMBERS OF PUPILS ENTERING FINAL YEARS OF PRIMARY AND SECONDARY EDUCATION PER 1,000 ENTERING CORRESPONDING FIRST GRADE[a]

State[b]	Primary Education After 5 years	After 6 years	Secondary Education After 4 years
Benue-Plateau	802	766	836
Kwara	680	697	856
Kano	886	920	886
North Central	793	763	892
North Eastern	848	835	780
North Western	915	918	725
Lagos	1,019	—	497
Mid-Western	432	—	694
Western	447	—	750

[a]The weighted average of the crude flow rate from grade to grade is calculated from the latest statistics, and the rates thus found are compounded to form a theoretical typical sequence indexed to 1,000 in the initial year.
[b]The available statistics for East Central, Rivers and South Eastern States do not allow this type of analysis.

Source: Unesco, *Education in Nigeria,* Annexes 20 and 31.

Table 12-4: COMPOSITION OF RECURRENT EDUCATION BUDGETS 1970/71

(In Millions of £N)

	Federal	States	Total
Total	10.25	54.30	64.55
Percent	100.0	100.0	100.0
Primary Education	—	49.9	42.0
Secondary Education	5.0	18.5	16.3
Technical/Vocational	3.4	1.7	1.9
Teacher Training	1.1	7.7	6.7
Higher Education	81.9	8.9	20.5
Adult Education	—	0.2	0.2
Administration and Inspectorate	2.1	7.3	6.5
Other (Including Scholarships)	6.5	5.8	5.9

Source: Federal and state governments' estimates 1970/71. Compiled by Unesco in *Financing of Education in Nigeria* (Paris: 1968), Annex 85.

more by the lack of qualified secondary school graduates than by lack of facilities. To allow for more rapid expansion of university enrollment in the northern states it would be necessary first to improve sixth form facilities and to expand secondary education as a whole at the same time as maintaining, if not improving its quality.

Longer-Term Investment Requirements

The existing plan for capital expenditure on education appears to be based on the accumula-

Table 12-5: PLANNED EDUCATION CAPITAL EXPENDITURE, 1970/71-1973/74

(In Millions of £N)

	Federal	States	Total
Total	49.1	89.8	138.9
Primary	6.5	27.5	33.9
Secondary	7.0	21.4	28.4
Technical	2.6	9.7	12.3
Teacher training	2.0	11.2	13.2
University	25.5	15.5	41.0
Other	5.5	4.5	10.1

Source: Plan, p. 246.

tion of the proposed investment programs of the states. It probably is not being carried out and it is not clear how the existing Plan contributes to national objectives in education. It is therefore difficult to project what the level and composition of public capital expenditure on education should be beyond 1973/74. Nationally, resources could certainly be made available to finance the present planned rate of expenditure of £N30 million to 40 million a year if it was required and could be well used. However, the states which could best use resources to expand primary and secondary education may well prove to be those least able to pay for it. Federal grants for educational expenditures in these states will probably have to be increased rapidly if their educational objectives are to be met. This is as true, if not more so, for recurrent as for capital expenditures. Total capital expenditures will be very much affected by decisions regarding university expansion. These can only be taken on the basis of manpower studies yet to be undertaken.

Educational Planning

Educational planning is concerned, among other things, with the determination of educational objectives in relation to the economy as a whole and with the coordination of the educational system to achieve these objectives. At present, neither function is being fulfilled entirely satisfactorily. The weaknesses of information on manpower requirements have been referred to above and it is important that this be rapidly improved within. the framework of the existing but strengthened Manpower Board. If expansion of primary and secondary education is to proceed with respect to considerations other than manpower requirements, all specialized and higher education and training must be related to some measure of anticipated need.

However after educational priorities are determined, they must be carried out and it is at this level that the lack of information and planning is most acute, both at the federal and state levels. Although state governments are primarily responsible for education, the fact that there *are* national educational objectives and that the federal government is involved in financing education implies that educational planning should be a federal responsibility at the national level. The one area in which the federal government has been active in this respect is the training of educational planners in state governments with Unesco assistance. The importance of this work for the long-term efficient development of the educational system is critical, and the federal government should consider continuing and expanding its role in educational planning, both at the national level and in support of the state governments.

The federal government is also considering a proposal to set up a national commission to study the educational system and to recommend long-term national objectives. An important feature of the commission's work could be to suggest improvement in the present system of collecting educational and financial data.

Quality of General Education

The proposed removal of vocational education from the formal system and the fact that existing primary education is poor and secondary education is heavily biased in favor of academic subjects raises the question of change in the content of the mainstream of first and second level education and improvement of its quality.

Currently, curriculum development activities are scattered and uneven. The Unesco mission recommended that a network of educational developmental activities be created, based on a National Institute for Educational Development and training units. These units would experiment with and develop integrated programs for primary and adult education. The institute would serve as the central focal point of all educational development activities carried out by the units, the university institutes of education, associations of subject teachers and others. Integrated with the development work would be the instruction of teacher trainers and educational administrators, supervisors and planners for the whole federation.

The curricula of primary, secondary and adult educational programs need review and modernization. The first two or three years of the secondary course should be of a general nature, common for all students; the latter years should concentrate on developing skills and attitudes which will help to prepare its students for employment. The Unesco mission recommended that examination requirements be broadened so that each candidate be expected to show some practical skill and that universities, especially the science-based faculties, should also require evidence of practical skills as a qualification for entry.

These proposals have implications for teacher training. The current structure of teacher training encourages students to concentrate on public examinations associated with general or grammar education rather than their training as teachers.

The number and quality of primary school teachers could be improved if primary teacher training were progressively changed to a two-year post-school certificate course. The course would be almost exclusively pedagogical but include oral and spoken English and basic environmental-based science. This change should be implemented in each state as quickly as the growth of school certificate holders from secondary schools will allow.

The Unesco mission also pointed out the need for upgrading the existing primary teacher force as well as improving the quality of new entrants. They did not support the present school inspection system, because it is too superficial and is not succeeding in providing professional supervision for the teachers. It is suggested that the inspection system be expanded and integrated into a system of educational supervision. The supervisors would be associated with the development centers and units and should be sufficiently numerous to be able to visit their teachers three or four times a term. The additional cost of this measure would be fully justified by the improved teaching in the primary schools. The Unesco mission's main suggestion affecting secondary teaching is the training of teachers of practical subjects in the advanced teachers' training colleges in view of the prospective expansion of these subjects in secondary education.

Industrial Training

A discussion in Chapter 7 identifies the very limited role of government trade schools in industrial training. This problem was studied by the Unesco team, which concluded that their weaknesses could be attributed to the limited participation, if any, of employers in their programs and to the potential difficulty that these schools would have in adjusting rapidly to changes in current and emerging manpower demands. A training program that can count less on long-range manpower estimates and more on current labor market signals such as wage movements in the private sector, the experience of recent trainees in locating jobs, and annual establishment surveys, and that can react quickly to signals of changing demand is required. The duration of training should also be more flexible. It is suggested, therefore, that state governments might consider transferring the responsibility for trade training to trade training boards, consisting of representatives of the government, trade unions and employers.

Employers in the modern sector do provide some in-employment training but its extent and standard remains unknown. The federal government has established an Industrial Training Fund to finance industrial training. This would appear to be a suitable vehicle for the financing of the activities of the proposed industrial training boards.

Technician Training

For several years there has been no national plan for technician training. There is apparently no agreement as to the level at which this should be carried out and little evidence of interest on the part of students mainly due to inadequate salaries paid to technicians by industry.

Technician education is carried out in five polytechnic schools with both full- and part-time students. Full-time courses are at two levels leading to the London City and Guilds Ordinary Technician Diploma and the Higher Technician Diploma. The Unesco mission concluded that an annual output of 2,500 technicians should be reached by the end of the 1970s. Approximately 75 percent of the students would receive ordinary diplomas and 25 percent would receive higher diplomas. Plans to achieve this objective include the improvement of the quality of training, particularly by strengthening part-time courses to upgrade skilled workers and by providing balanced courses for secondary school graduates which include industrial experience as well as theoretical and practical training. The Unesco mission recommended that the expansion in capacity, where it is justified, should be concentrated on the five existing polytechnic schools.

However, if industry is to have a supply of well trained technicians, their salaries will have to be commensurate with their responsibilities. Existing salary scales for technicians suggest that most are recruited from among skilled craftsmen; experience elsewhere suggests that, however desirable this may be, it may not provide the cadre of properly trained technicians required to fulfill satisfactorily the needs of developing industry.

Agricultural Training

Perhaps the most serious constraint on agricultural development is the shortage of agricultural personnel at the technician levels for planning and project preparation in the state governments. With few exceptions, the agricultural staff in the states have little more than a year or two of experience in planning or project work and even less in the implementation of agricultural projects. In the long-run, an increased supply of manpower should be forthcoming from the educational system but meanwhile present training facilities are inadequate and ad hoc in-service training centers are urgently required to solve the short-term problem.

In most states, the immediate prospects of meeting establishment schedules are not good. It may be misleading, however, to discuss staff requirements in terms of posts created but not filled. This is because the numbers of posts required have often been determined by subjective rule of thumb ratios for the number of farmers per extension worker, or of technicians per graduate supervisor.

Output of agricultural graduates has been rising rapidly from a low base: 55 people graduated from Nigerian Universities in agricultural subjects in 1968. By 1970, the figure was 160 even though the University of Nigeria had no graduates during these years. Of these, 112 graduated in general agriculture, 33 in veterinary science and 15 in forestry. About half the agricultural graduates in recent years have not gone into public agricultural employment and there are probably less than 200 agricultural graduates currently employed in the private sector. Although shortages currently exist, it is likely that the current capacity of the Nigerian universities' agricultural faculties are almost sufficient to meet long-term demands for agricultural graduates assuming that the University of Nigeria quickly recovers its pre-1967 capacity. Only limited expansion of university agricultural education would, therefore, appear justified. The overall adequacy of capacity makes certain regional imbalances. For example, the northern states encounter severe shortages of local agricultural graduates. In one of the southern states the supply of agricultural graduates is more than adequate and there are already examples of graduates in agriculture taking posts as science teachers in secondary schools. A somewhat similar picture is apparent at the technician training level.

There is a shortfall between the numbers of sub-professional staff for which training facilities are available and the needs of the various agricultural services. The present capacity for training is equivalent to about 740 technicians annually of whom 550 would be junior technicians. Training capacity for forestry technicians is only 32 per year. In view of the extensive nature of the forestry service and the scope for development in this area, this facility is clearly inadequate. A Unesco mission suggested that forestry training at technician level has high priority and that a forestry school of capacity of about 300 is urgently required. In other areas, existing capacity for senior and junior technicians are probably sufficient to meet the long-term demands.

A possible exception in this respect is the training of technicians to supervise farmers benefiting from irrigation projects. Some of the northern states have initiated pre-investment programs which may well lead to substantial investment for irrigation of farmers' lands over the coming years. Initial experience suggests that adequate staffing of the irrigation services will be crucial if these investments are to be successfully implemented. The size of training requirements has not yet been determined, but it is suggested that pending more detailed information at least one irrigation school at technician level will be required.

Adult Education

Improving the quality of the labor force is not just a question of expanding formal education, which only affects new entrants. It should also involve the re-education of the existing labor force, where the low productivity of the labor force may be due to the much lower standard of education which prevailed in earlier years, rather than the insufficient size of the present school system. Government activity in this area is modest. In rural areas, the extension service is the main vehicle for adult education and certain states operate adult literacy programs. The training needs of the Federal Civil Service have been studied[3] and the federal government operates two federal training centers with a total budget of about £N150,000. Short courses are also provided at the institutes of administration for civil servants from the state governments.[4] However, most adult training is undertaken by the private industrial firms. Through the Industrial Training Fund, the government will help to finance an expansion of these activities and the kind of training to be provided will be one of the main preoccupations of the controlling board. Management education is also organized by the larger firms, the Institute of Management, and the Continuing Education Center at Lagos University.

3. Federal Republic of Nigeria, *Training Needs of the Federal Civil Service* (Nigeria: Ministry of Information, 1968).

4. Except that the Institute of Administration in the East Central State is presently not serviceable.

CHAPTER 13

TRANSPORTATION AND POWER

At the end of hostilities, many of Nigeria's infrastructure facilities were in a critical position. Low investment during the war had created a backlog of requirements, inadequate maintenance had led to deterioration of existing facilities and much of the infrastructure in the East Central, Rivers and South Eastern states was out of commission by war damage. Since the end of hostilities, private sector activity has rapidly recovered, aggravating in many respects the strains on infrastructure that were, in any case, bound to emerge. Meanwhile, there has been substantial, if not complete, recovery in public services.

The first general issue regarding infrastructure facilities concerns the balance between the major productive facilities and trunk connections on the one hand, and the distribution networks on the other. The economy will respond more easily to growth opportunities now generated by the petroleum sector if the increase in economic activities could be widely distributed throughout the country rather than being concentrated in urban areas. The various ways in which this could be done are discussed elsewhere in this report, but one way would be to improve public and social services outside the principal urban centers. In some areas the capacity of main roads and the electricity supply are in excess of current demand, and the contribution to the economy of these existing investments could be raised if additional demand were created. Extending the distribution networks through, for example, village electrification and feeder roads, would be one way of doing this.

Second, there is the question of the degree of centralization of the planning and operation of these sectors. In certain statutory corporations there is a need to decentralize either by increasing the responsibilities of the operational units in ports and railways, or by delegating responsibility for local operations to separate entities, as is being tried for electricity distribution. On the other hand, in areas of state or concurrent responsibilities, a strengthened planning capacity at the center is called for to assist the states. This is most clear for education and transport, and possibly in water supply.

A third question concerns infrastructure investment. Much of the new facilities have to be provided in sectors which are now in the province of the state governments or their local authorities which, in general, have limited resources compared with those of the federal government. In some sectors or states it may prove necessary to make arrangements whereby the transfer of capital funds from the federal government is associated with guidance, control and, if necessary, initiative in the preparation and implementation of investment programs. Such arrangements already exist in principle, if on a small scale, for federal financing of certain education and agricultural projects at the state level.

A fourth question concerns management, training and technical knowhow in these sectors. Even allowing for postwar difficulties and the exceptional demands which have arisen, the performance of several public corporations has not come up to the expectations of the federal government or the public.

The problem could be approached in several ways. The first would be to improve management methods within the corporations and especially to strengthen financial control. Top management could more easily delegate day-to-day decisions to middle management if they were made within the framework of a detailed budget and a frequent reporting system. The second would be the upgrading of middle management in these corporations, especially those working away from the center. Although training activities are carried on by the public corporations, their present scope may be insufficient for the future demands that will be placed on these corporations. While some training opportunities are available abroad from time to time, these can provide at best only marginal assistance and the size of the problem would probably justify the public corporations' making continuing arrangements with one of the universities for regular short courses for their professional and technical officers. With appropriate teaching staff, course material and facilities, the institution thereby created could have a substantial impact over time.

It is not suggested that the management problems of the public corporations can be solved quickly. In certain circumstances, it will for the time being be necessary to employ expatriate advisory and, in more serious cases, operational personnel. This is at best a temporary expedient.

In the economy as a whole, the prospective demands for skilled and professionally qualified people will almost certainly exceed anything that has been experienced before. While Nigerians should be able to secure an increasing share of these posts, the absolute numbers of expatriates in the country may well increase in the short term. In the circumstances, a forward policy of Nigerianization in the public sector, and particularly in the public corporations, might risk starving the private sector of newly qualified Nigerians.

Transportation

Road Transport Industry

There are a few large firms operating in road transport. The largest are the urban bus companies, followed by the trucking firms involved in specialized transport and contract hauling. However, as in many developing countries, most of the firms operate less than ten vehicles. Bus and taxi services flourish in the main cities and rural areas. The city councils also provide public transport services. On the whole, the supply of public transport does not meet the demand. This is not so much reflected in high fares (which are regulated by city councils—and by public opinion), but by long queues at bus stops, crowded vehicles and irregular services to and from rural communities.

One possible reason is the cumulative effect of several years' import controls leading to a deterioration in the vehicle fleet, which has not yet been restored. A second reason may be inadequate credit facilities for the small firms operating in the road transport industry. A third may be that fares are too low—particularly in the cities. A further reason which would apply particularly to rural communities is the poor condition of the roads. Rural demand for transport services is difficult to determine before roads and vehicles become available, but the substantial price differentials which exist for agricultural produce over quite short distances in rural areas suggest that transport may be an important bottleneck.

The unsatisfied demand for transport services is also indicated by the very short period over which the investment in a truck can, barring accidents, be recovered by the owner, because of the very high rates for general haulage; and by the large numbers of old vehicles which are retained in service. A further indication is that Nigeria has one of the lowest ratios of vehicles to length of paved roads in the world (7 vehicles per kilometer of paved road, compared to 14 in Ghana, 20 in Niger, 28 in Tanzania and 39 in Ivory Coast).

The rapid growth of bulk transport by very heavy vehicles is largely a result of the inadequate service provided by the railway and of the transport policies of some of the marketing boards. The use of these vehicles in turn causes damage to the roads and high maintenance costs. The government proposes to introduce restrictions on the import and local assembly of vehicles designed to carry excessive axle loads in order to protect the roads. The improvement of railway services and appropriate policies by main shippers (principally the marketing boards and the petroleum distribution companies) should lead to a reduction in the demand for this kind of road transport, as would the implementation of proposals to increase the taxation of heavy vehicles.

The Road System

Road transport is by far the most important element of the transport system, both in terms of traffic and investment. It accounts for 77 percent of freight ton-mileage and roads have been allocated 69 percent of public capital investment in transport under the current four-year Plan.

These figures show the concentration of vehicles in the southern part of the country, and particularly in Lagos with its high number of private cars. In part, they reflect the distribution of wealth and economic activity, though they may overstate the significance of Lagos since many vehicles registered there ply on routes all over the country.

Roads outside the immediate influence of the main urban areas are generally lightly traveled. In the northern states only the most important roads carry traffic volumes in excess of 500 vehicles per day (vpd) with a strong seasonal influence. The main Lagos-Ibadan road, with traffic in excess of 3,000 vpd, is the busiest inter-urban road in the country. A few roads in the East and West carry around 1,000 vpd, but on most trunk roads volumes range between 100 and 300 vpd.

Table 13-1: DISTRIBUTION OF VEHICLES IN NIGERIA

	Vehicles[a] per 1,000 people	Vehicles[a] per mile of road	Vehicles[a] per sq. mi. of area
All Nigeria	1.4	1.5	0.24
Lagos	13.8	106.8	16.00
Northern States	0.6	0.9	0.07
Western State	1.4	1.6	0.52
Mid-Western State	2.0	1.6	0.38
Eastern States	1.7	1.3	0.62

[a]Private and commercial vehicles only.

These figures are mainly impressionistic; traffic counting and use of traffic data has largely broken down but the government has plans to reinstitute it. This gap in information limits assessment of traffic growth rates for different parts of the country. Scattered evidence suggests, for example, that on the main Western States roads, automobile traffic has risen at about 8 percent per annum in recent years and truck traffic at 4 percent per annum. Toll figures at the new Sapele bridge indicate a traffic increase of 75 percent because of the recovery of the economy in the area and Warri's new importance as a base for oil company operations. This latter case, however, is not representative of general trends.

The condition of the present road network of federal ("Trunk A") roads ranges from good quality, 24'-wide roads (Kaduna-Zaria; Benin-Warri; Onitsha-Enugu) to extremely poor stretches between Kabba and Ilorin that are little better than tracks. Surfaces are generally poor and inadequately maintained. Some important links (Jos-Makurdi, for example) are cut entirely in the rainy season. Calabar has a very poor road connection with the rest of the country, but can be reached by a ferry from Oron.

It is against this background that one has to assess the current investment program and the prospects for development of the road system. Work is to be carried out under three headings. First, a few *continuing projects* which were started before 1970/71, are being completed. Some have been completed already (Benin-Warri, Maiduguri-Beni Sheik, Bauchi-Gombe-Numan-Yola, Calabar-Ikom) whereas the others are either under way or have not yet been designed (Benin-Auchi-Lokoja).

The main thrust of the present road improvement effort is being made through *rehabilitation projects*. Some of these projects were initiated in 1968 as an emergency measure to facilitate produce evacuation during hostilities, and the Ilorin-Jebba rehabilitation was completed on this basis at a cost of £N12,000 per mile. However, during the course of the preparation and approval of the Plan, the number of rehabilitation projects grew until they represented a major program. Also, it has proved increasingly difficult for the Federal Ministry of Works and Housing (FMWH) to interest contractors in these projects at prices below £N30,000 per mile, and the resulting works amount in many cases virtually to full reconstruction, the economic justifications of which are sometimes doubtful.

The third element of the federal program is *new projects* to be undertaken during the Plan period. Engineering work for these projects is either under way or has been completed, but little actual investment can be expected before the end of the Plan period. The three main projects are the Kontagora-Yelwa-Jaredi road, the Ibadan-Ife road and the Lagos-Ibadan motorway. The former will improve north-south access to Sokoto and North Western State.

The Lagos-Ibadan motorway will serve the route with Nigeria's densest traffic and link of the two largest centers in the country. It may cost £N19 million. The phasing of the construction will depend on, *inter alia*: the traffic levels anticipated on different segments of the motorway, the capacity of the existing road after rehabilitation and progress on the complementary urban road systems. Adequate accesses are required to the motorway through the congested city of Lagos and around Ibadan.

The fourth component of the program consists of *state road projects*. Existing projects and commitments of the former regional governments have, by and large, been taken over by the new states. For example, the bulk of the Western, Mid-Western and Benue Plateau programs are of this nature. The East Central State program is mainly concentrated on rehabilitation, but several of the new projects are carryovers. In other cases, the creation of states from the old regions has necessitated the review of investment priorities. The South Eastern State is an example where the immediate concern is to provide satisfactory access to the whole state from Calabar. The state is fortunate insofar as distances are short and the main links are federal roads, so that it can concentrate its own resources on its minor roads.

The North Eastern and North Western States are not so fortunate. Previously located at the extremes of the East-West extensions of the northern road system, these states' programs are primarily designed to provide a basic North-South axis within each state. Great distances, high construction costs and the rather high standards to which roads are being designed, together with low population density and incomes, may well put these projects beyond the states' investment budgets during this Plan period. The standards adopted for much of the states' programs are often higher than necessary, and both the budgetary burden and the economic return to these investments could be improved through greater attention to economic construction standards.

Before discussing the federal road pre-investment program, a review of the existing basis for national planning of roads is in order. In 1968, the government received the report of a Trunk Road Study for the Federation.[1] The report made recommendations for developing the road system, and indicated the roads likely to be affected by the recommendations. The financial implications of these recommendations, also discussed in the report, are now out of date.

The recommendations of the report have not yet been formally accepted by the federal government, but they have clearly had a considerable influence in the choice of long-term road development priorities, and are the best available indication of the direction highway planning can be expected to take. The authors of the report carried out cost/benefit estimates to show the order of priorities under which this program should be implemented.

The government did accept the report's recommendations for the creation of three East-West and three North-South *heavy primary* axes. To these it added a fourth North-South axis to connect Maiduguri with the port of Calabar. Of these axes, the Kaduna-Benin and Jebba-Akwanga branches do not exist as main roads. The others are based on upgrading existing main roads. This major grid would be supplemented by *light* primary roads and by secondary roads.

It is expected that most of the feasibility studies mentioned in the current Plan will be initiated in the very near future. The only major difference between these studies and the proposed grid is that Jebba-Kaduna is to be retained as a heavy primary road. This is realistic insofar as Lagos is likely to remain the principal port serving Kano and Kaduna for the foreseeable future. To the extent that these feasibility studies cover sections that are being upgraded under the Sokoto-Ileya, Benin-Asaba, Kaduna-Kano, Kano-Katsina. A feasibility study of Kano-Daura will also be of limited interest in view of existing studies for Kano-Babura and the rehabilitation of Kano-Katsina.

The proposed grid would have the advantage that it would improve the access of the six northern states to ports other than Lagos and would provide main road services to areas of the middle belt that are currently inaccessible.

The pre-investment program also includes study of new river crossings at Jebba, Makurdi, Katsina-Ala, Lokoja and Numan/Yola. The optimal siteing of these crossings should, of course, be an integral part of the feasibility studies described above. Among them, the Makurdi bridge probably has lowest priority because of the good condition of the existing road/rail structure. In some cases, improved ferries may be more appropriate than new bridges.

The economic viability of some of these major road and river-crossing projects has yet to be

---

1. Highway Survey in Nigeria 1967, Trunk Road Study. Kampmann Kierulff and Saxild A/S (KAMPSAX), Copenhagen. Draft Final Report, December 1967; Final Report, October 1970.

demonstrated. Insofar as the middle belt areas are relatively under-developed, the economic justifications for the proposed roads (Kaduna-Lokoja; Jebba-Akwanga; Aliade-Yola) would depend largely on potential agricultural development. Chapter 7 highlighted the priority of agricultural development with particular reference to foodcrops, and the opening of these areas is a necessary first step. However, there is as yet no clear evidence of the degree to which the lack of transport facilities is presently constraining agricultural development. Further studies in this connection are needed, probably on a case-by-case basis and including studies at farm level which could assist in identifying the necessary actions for agricultural development. For example, the area between the Jebba-Akwanga road and the Niger-Benue valley could be considered as one region to be served by the two new proposed roads. Also, the area northeast of the Katsina-Ala river to be served by the proposed Katsina-Ala bridge and the road to Yola could form the basis for a second study of the local agricultural economy and the impact of transportation upon it.

While steps have already been taken to define the next federal road plan, the situation in the states is less well advanced, and few states have a continuing pre-investment program. The state plans after 1973/74 will most probably include whatever carry-over remains from the existing programs, some of which are not easy to justify by economic or development criteria. The most urgent projects identified by the UNDP Western Region study are to be financed with the participation of the IBRD. In the northern states, the UNDP-financed road development survey concluded that the federal "A" trunk roads had the greatest shortcomings, and that the majority of the state "B" roads were adequate for their current purposes, and for traffic likely to develop by 1977. A UNDP regional survey of the area comprising the East Central, South Eastern and Rivers States was also completed before hostilities but, pending a review in the present context, it is not known to what extent this survey can still be used as a basis for long-term investment planning.

The only state currently initiating a new pre-investment study is the Mid-Western State where a transport survey is to be undertaken to identify priorities for road and river transport, and to carry out project feasibility studies. The study will assist the federal and state authorities to formulate policies and programs for the development of transport in the midwest area.

The administration and financing of roads raises difficult questions, particularly in regard to federal/state relationships. An appropriate long-term strategy might be for the federal government to build up the capacities of the state highway bodies so they may eventually take over construction, maintenance and detailed project planning functions for trunk roads. The federal government could formulate broad policy and strategic planning functions, determine design and other standards, provide all or part of the funds, enforce traffic regulations and retain general construction and maintenance control.

Any changed relationship among federal and state highway authorities would require changes in the broad system of highway financing, independently of the question of road-user charge levels. At present the federal and state governments are one hundred percent responsible for financing their own roads; the state governments have little or no say on the standards or timing of construction for federal roads passing through their states, although benefits to intrastate traffic may be the most important factor in improvement justification. Decisions on construction timing and design standards are taken by the federal authorities which, meanwhile, have little concern with state roads, except in a residual way by limiting allocations in the National Development Plan or approving foreign-financed schemes. The federal authorities may be building trunk roads while no corresponding effort is being made to develop appropriate feeders.

In a number of countries the central or federal government participates in the financing of roads by means of matching grants. This enables the central authority to control road standards and ease the financial problems of local authorities, while leaving in their hands considerable initiative in the preparation of projects. It is possible that some such arrangement would also be beneficial to Nigeria.

The federal government should use its financial leverage to encourage the economic use of scarce resources in investment decisions concerning state road projects and should continue to strengthen its own planning staff with a view to developing its capacity to assess the economic priorities of state investment programs.

There is no accepted basis for relating a given main road to corresponding feeder road requirements, but prospective expansion and upgrading of the main road system may possibly lead to an imbalance in this respect. On the one hand, the planning and the technical capacity of the local authorities could not be more modest. On the other hand, their financial resources are limited in the extreme. Furthermore, the state governments themselves are typically straining their technical and financial resources to carry out their own road programs. Current inflation in the costs of their larger projects is also adding to their difficulties. Small wonder then to find that taking the state government plans together, the allocation for *minor improvements, minor roads*, or *feeder roads* is only 9 percent of their total road plans. Excluding the South Eastern State, it is 7 percent. (The South Eastern State has hardly any main roads which are not federal roads. State resources can, therefore, be concentrated on the minor roads.) As a proportion of actual expenditure, it is probably even less.

It is as yet unclear how much is likely to be invested in roads during the 1974-78 period. The program of feasibility studies included in the 1970-74 Plan may give rise to investments of about £N15-20 million a year, assuming that most of the projects are found justified and/or are carried out. The Ministry of Transport is undertaking a national transport demand study, which should provide information about future transport needs.

Railways

The railway system owned and operated by the Nigerian Railway Corporation (NCR) consists of two main lines from Lagos to Kano (702 miles) and from Port Harcourt to Maiduguri (897 miles) connected by the main line, Kaduna-Kafanchan. There are five branch lines, the main ones linking Kaura in the northwest, Nguru in the northeast and Baro on the Niger. The railway system should be suitable for the long distance haulage of exports from the North, and raw materials and manufactured goods from the main ports and industrial areas in the South. The line on the whole is in good condition and trackwork is limited to increasing rail weights, re-sleepering and some minor realignments. A short section in urban Lagos is to be doubled to facilitate commuter traffic.

Goods traffic declined from 2.5 million tons in 1963/64 to 1.5 million tons in 1970/71; whole ton-miles declined from 1,462 to 692 million. Passenger traffic declined from 526 million passenger miles in 1963/64 to 302 million passenger miles in 1970/71. The government attributes the railway's decline to defects in management, equipment and rate policies, and to competition from road transport. It is hoped that improved efficiency and modernization will enable the railways to regain goods traffic, but the loss of passenger traffic may be irrecoverable.

The most urgent investment is the complete replacement of steam locomotives by diesels. This program was deferred during hostilities, but is now proceeding. Replacements for some rolling stock might be needed, but there is some doubt as to the specific requirements as one of the main problems is the inefficient use of existing rolling stock.

The capacity of the track is far greater than actual traffic, and the marginal costs of long distance traffic could be lower than those of road transport if the railways were reasonably efficient. The railways should concentrate on hauling bulk cargos over long distances and leave short-haul traffic to road transport. However, increasing competition from roads, which may well become more severe as the road network is improved, has taken an increasingly large share of railway traffic. For example, the proportion of goods arriving at Apapa by rail (including a large proportion of long-distance hauls) fell from about 50 percent in 1966/67 to about 40 percent in 1969/70.

The National Development Plan envisages investment of some £N22 million in NRC for rolling stock, track and other facilities. NRC in its latest examination of requirements and current price levels anticipates that some £N28 million will be needed to fulfill the railway section of the Plan. The major part of the increase relates to a decision to expedite the completion of dieselization. This decision is reasonable and has been accepted by the government; financing has been arranged with Canada and Japan on favorable terms.

The investment program is subject to several uncertainties. Delivery times for locomotives are long, and actual expenditures for these may be deferred. Also, precise wagon requirements are presently being worked out for NRC by consultants, so the present estimate may change. The investment program assumes there will be no closures and no line extensions. Several branch lines have little prospect of economic operation and their future should be reviewed, but the mission considers that until the transport system has recovered from the crisis, it would be premature to close any lines. The first candidate would probably be Minna-Baro, but until it is clear whether river transport will recover, this line should not be closed.

There can be no doubt that a reasonably efficient railway system could perform an important service for the whole economy, but this does not mean that its traffic pattern or position with respect to competing transport modes should remain unchanged. Embarking on a far-reaching rehabilitation program without clear decisions about the railways' role and task might place a heavy burden on their future freedom of action and on the government's ability to set targets and priorities for the transport sector as a whole. Until the means and information are available to take the far-reaching decisions which are required, and until the railways show that they can use their existing equipment efficiently, railway investment should be confined to the minimum necessary to move traffic safely and effectively, and first priority should be given to organizational improvements.

Ports

The main ports are at Lagos (Apapa) and Port Harcourt. Calabar and Warri also have a couple of berths each and there are several smaller ports in the Niger delta, such as Sapele, Koko and Burutu. In 1970/71, Lagos port handled about 3.2 million tons of dry cargo (68 percent imports) while Port Harcourt handled 0.3 million tons, nearly all imports. Before hostilities, Port Harcourt was handling 0.8/0.9 million tons of dry cargo annually. Lagos also handles some groundnut oil exports (about 100,000 tons) and some imports of petroleum products. The latter amounted to 600,000 tons in 1969/70, but have been declining since then because of rising domestic production of refined products.

The development of the ports has been the subject of a recent major study.[2] The long-term development of ports has to take into account two major uncertainties. First, Port Harcourt has not yet recovered its pre-war role because of the still limited effective demand from the East Central State, the poor road and rail service to the Benue Plateau and the North Eastern States, and the continuing problem of getting skilled labor from Rivers State to staff the port. After four years' inactivity in Port Harcourt, importers and exporters are used to dealing through Lagos. The

Table 13.2: PROJECTION FOR LAGOS PORT TRAFFIC

			(In Millions of Tons)
	Imports	Exports	Total
General Cargo			
Conventional	1.23	.48	1.71
Containerized	.32	.23	.55
Dry Bulk			
Normal	.17	.33	.50
Pelletized	–	.19	.19
Grab	.22	–	.22
Liquid	–	.17	.17
Logs (midstream)	–	+	+
Total	1.94	1.40	3.34

2. *Development of the Ports of Nigeria, 1970-90,* NEDECO, (The Hague, February, 1971).

problem is to restore full service at the existing six berths in Port Harcourt so that it can recover its share of the export/import trade. The second uncertainty is the future techniques to be used (e.g., containerization) in developing Nigeria's ports and their investment requirements.

The Plan envisages construction of four berths, four transit sheds and four warehouses at Apapa between 1970/71 and 1973/74 at a cost of £N6.6 million. Planning, especially engineering and site acquisition, has been delayed. It is evident, therefore, that the planned projects cannot be completed on schedule. In addition, because of construction cost increases, it is likely that the cost figures in the plan will prove to be low.

On the basis of their study, including a discounted cost minimization analysis to determine an optimum distribution of traffic by ports, NEDECO (Netherlands Engineering Consultants) arrived at the 1980 projection for Lagos shown in Table 13-2.

On this basis and using assumptions as to the speed of containerization and productivity levels in handling conventional general cargo, NEDECO concluded that all the capacity necessary could be provided, not by the conventional berths/transit sheds/warehouses solution as envisaged in the Plan, but by the following investments:

Table 13-3: PROPOSED INVESTMENTS FOR LAGOS PORT

(In Millions of £N)

	1971-75	1976-80	Total
Container Berth	0.84	5.09	5.93
Dry Bulk Terminal	0.21	—	0.21
Liquid Bulk Terminal	—	0.37	0.37
Total	1.05	5.46	6.51

The Nigerian Ports Authority's view of this change in the nature of proposed investments is that containerization will not be introduced as rapidly as assumed; and NEDECO has assumed productivity rates in handling general cargo which are about 25 percent above what might normally be achieved at Lagos (150,000 tons per annum per berth as compared with the NPA's best estimate of 120,000 tons) and developments in palletization and groundnut oil milling for which there is inadequate evidence in terms of domestic investments currently taking place or scheduled.

Accordingly, to avoid the shortage of berth capacity that seems likely later this decade, NPA has begun detailed planning and engineering for at least three of the four berths envisaged in the Plan. Initially, plans should cover building the quay walls and dredging the channel. It is unlikely that the NPA will have to commit itself firmly to the type of berth —conventional or container— until the end of 1973, by which time the pattern of traffic may be clearer and a more accurate forecast possible. The berths could be designed for conversion to containerization should this proceed at a faster rate than currently envisaged by leading shipping companies serving the country. A decision as to whether to construct berths in 2x2 increments or some other combination can be taken in the light of further developments.

The investment program in the minor ports is secondary to the basic decisions required for Lagos and Port Harcourt. Permanent facilities for the petroleum industry are required at Burutu or Warri. At Warri, the oil industry is presently utilizing most of the existing port facilities. The effects of this on the port's ability to handle general imports should be investigated. The hinterland of Calabar is being extended by federal and state road programs, and at least one new berth is required there. A certain amount of equipment will be required at all ports in the normal course of events but apart from specific container equipment, most of this can be provided on the basis of quite short-term plans.

Shipping

The Nigerian National Shipping Line (NNSL) was established as a joint venture but is now fully government-owned. It operates twelve ships with a registered net tonnage of 46,000 tons. The line carries about three-quarters of a million tons of goods a year (1970/71).

The line is currently operating at a substantial loss and any new investment would have to be financed by the government. The Development Plan provides for replacement of four of the fleet at a cost of £N3.5 million, but, since the major shipping lines may decide to invest increasingly in container fleets, additional expenditure on freighters might not be wise at this time. In any event, before undertaking new investments, NNSL should concentrate on improving its organization and profitability.

Inland Waterways

The coastal lagoons and delta creeks are navigable from Dahomey to Opobo, East of Port Harcourt. The Niger and Benue Rivers are navigable for barges all the year round as far as the confluence, and seasonally upstream. However, river traffic which accounted for more than 300,000 tons of exports annually in the early 1960s is now negligible, in spite of investments in locks and navigational aids under the last Plan.

The war closed the delta ports, maintenance of navigational aids ceased, and the private shipping companies have withdrawn from the business following the nationalization of their port facilities. The present situation calls for a fresh appraisal of the place of river transport in the economy. In the first place, it would be necessary to restore navigational aids; secondly, the shipping service would have to be renewed; and thirdly, the improvements that have been made to the rapids section between Jebba and Kainji on the Niger do not seem to have been adequate. If these difficulties can be resolved, there should still be substantial scope for water transport. Costs are lower than any other mode,[3] which gives an advantage for bulk transport of produce and petroleum products. Investment requirements are modest, and can lead to savings in other modes. If produce can be taken off the roads, investment in vehicles and maintenance can be reduced. Also, direct trans-shipment and bulk handling would be facilitated in the ports.

Federal policy is as yet unclear. However, some of the states are backing river transport. Three states, Mid-Western, East Central and Benue Plateau, have recently created a jointly-owned river transport company. The progress of this initiative is a matter of considerable interest as other states may also consider participating in the company. The North Western State is counting on river transport services reaching the proposed new port at Yelwa upstream of Kainji; the state government's road program is designed to feed the Yelwa port.

The country's inland waterways are not ideal for navigation, but they remain a valuable natural asset, and their potentialities should be realized to the fullest extent, especially in the context of present problems affecting other transport modes.

Civil Aviation and Nigeria Airways

Domestic air services are still not well developed, given the size and population of the country. There is substantial unsatisfied demand for domestic passenger services. The distribution of government among twelve states and the existence of several industrial centers suggest that demand may rise significantly in the future. Most domestic passenger traffic is generated by government and business activities, since there is little tourism. Poor mail and telephone communications and time-consuming road transport result in considerable demand for air travel.

Some fifteen international air lines provide services to Ikeja airport, and the facilities there are inadequate to handle the traffic. In 1970, total passenger movements at all airports were 576,000, compared with 436,000 in 1965, of which about 100,000 were domestic passengers.

The civil aviation investment program in the National Development Plan provides for rehabilitation of Lagos, Kano, and twenty-two other airports, and for the Lagos terminal. Landing aids will be installed at Lagos and Kano. Apart from the extension of the Lagos runway, where work is now

---

3. But apparently no longer low enough to cover trans-shipment costs from the railway at Baro.

proceeding, little work has begun. The Enugu project is about to be undertaken but the necessary studies of the other airports have yet to be completed.

Feasibility studies have been prepared for improvements of airports at all the state capitals and a few secondary centers. The Lagos airport project is likely to absorb about £N5.0 million before the end of the current Plan, and some £N15-20 million during the next Plan period. The planned improvements to the other airports will cost some £N20 million as well. Only £N3/4 million of this amount is likely to be spent during the current Plan period (Enugu, Ilorin, Kaduna). The minor airports can be expected to feature in the next Plan.

Nigeria Airways' investment program has not been finally determined. The Plan provides for one long-haul jet aircraft and two medium-haul aircraft. To replace the existing leasing arrangements, a Boeing 707 has recently been purchased, at a cost of about £N4.5 million, and two medium-haul aircraft (Boeing 737/200 or DC9/30) would cost about the same. Nigeria Airways is also considering expanding capacity of short-range aircraft. An F28 has been recently leased, and two may be purchased.

During the 1975-80 period, studies indicate that it may be appropriate to expand further the medium-haul capacity and to use the F27/F28 planes for feeder services. A third long-haul aircraft may also be purchased. Taken together, Nigeria Airways' investment in aircraft during the next Plan period may be of the order of £N10 million, with, say, another £N1 million for ancillary services.

Power

Three separate entities own and operate facilities for production, transmission and distribution of electric energy in Nigeria: the Electricity Corporation of Nigeria (ECN), the Niger Dams Authority (NDA) and the Nigerian Electricity Supply Corporation Limited (NESCO). NDA was created in 1962, essentially to construct and operate the Kainji Dam. It also constructs and operates the high voltage transmission lines. ECN is a statutory corporation responsible for thermal generation transmission and distribution. NESCO is a private company, which supplies the mining industry on the Jos Plateau.

The existence of two governmental agencies with overlapping and, to some degree conflicting, duties and functions has brought about serious problems of coordination. These problems have contributed to power failures, delays in grid system extension and a serious operating deficit. The government appointed consultants to study the power supply industry and make recommendations to improve its management. Following the consultants' report,[4] the federal government has decided to merge ECN and NDA in the near future to form a single new corporation.

The three public utilities operate with a total installed capacity of 790 MW. It consists of 350 MW of hydro capacity, and 440 MW of thermal capacity. The hydro capacity is composed of 320 MW at Kainji and 30 MW spread over several small hydro stations operated by NESCO. The thermal capacity, belonging to ECN, is, for the most part, installed in five large power stations: Ijora, Ughelli, Aram, Oji River and Kaduna, totalling 340 MW.

Whereas the hydro capacity is in good condition, the thermal capacity has seriously suffered from lack of maintenance and poor operation during the late 1960s. Much of it must be discounted as obsolete, unreliable or uneconomic to run. The capacity to be scrapped is not known exactly, but could be estimated at 120 MW. The remaining 320 MW would consist of the 300 MW representing the total capacity of the five large interconnected thermal stations to be retained, and of 20 MW representing the total capacity of the isolated diesel stations.

A 330/132 kV transmission network connects Kainji to the five thermal stations mentioned above. It stretches from Lagos in the southwest to Aba in the southeast and to Kano in the north. From the 330 kV substations, 132 and 33 kV transmission lines supply 76 centers with electricity. The remaining 29 of the 105 electrified Nigerian centers are supplied by isolated diesel or small hydro stations.

Before hostilities, the electric power industry expanded at a very high rate. From 1950 to 1967, the compound rate of growth of consumption was 19 percent per annum. Due to the unrest, there was a decrease in demand in 1967 and 1968; but since 1969, growth has resumed at an even

4. *The Electricity Supply Industry of Nigeria,* Shawmont, Montreal 1971.

higher level than before. The annual rate of increase is now over 20 percent and is expected to remain at this level for a few years to come. It is then likely to taper off gradually to about 15 percent toward the end of the 1970s. Despite this very high rate of growth, power consumption per capita is, and will remain for a long time, very low: 20 KWh/capita in 1971/72 increasing to about 70 KWh/capita in 1980/81.

During recent years investments in the power sector have been much below the Plan allocation. Financial difficulties and management problems prevented ECN and to some degree NDA, from starting most of the projects provided in the Plan. Whereas the Plan allocates £N45 million to be spent over four years, 1970/1971 through 1973/74, recent studies indicate that the sector capital expenditures will hardly exceed £N32 million.

Table 13.4: ESTIMATED CAPITAL EXPENDITURES FOR ELECTRICITY

(In Millions of £N)

Year Ending March 31:	1971	1972	1973	1974
Total	2.6	2.8	10.7	16.3
Generation	–	–	0.4	0.9
Transmission	1.1	0.5	2.1	3.3
Distribution	–	0.9	4.6	8.3
Rehabilitation	1.0	1.4	2.0	1.1
Other	0.5	–	1.6	2.7

Source: IBRD estimates.

After 1973/74, annual capital expenditure will be about £N22 million per year, increasing at between five and ten percent per year. A more rapid increase would be difficult to achieve, not because of a slackening demand but because of the limited executive capacity in this sector.

Whereas the installation of the fifth and sixth units at Kainji is the most economic generation addition for 1975/76, the selection of the next block of generation, required for service in 1977/78 is not as clear cut. There are basically two solutions to the problem:

(a) installation of the seventh and eighth units at Kainji and extensive operation of the Afam, Ughelli and Ijora thermal stations; or,

(b) construction of a new 200 MW thermal station, which could be gas, oil or even coal-fired.

The choice between (a) and (b), and the selection of the type of fuel for case (b) will depend on the opportunity costs of the three possible fuels. It will also, as far as the future power entity is concerned, depend on the price of these fuels. However, since it is very likely that for several years natural gas will still be flared in very large quantities, the least-cost solution for the Nigerian economy will probably be the construction of a 200 MW gas-fired power station. Such a station would be located near the oil fields. This solution would also be the most attractive alternative for the power entity if the price of gas is realistic.

In the longer term, toward 1980, the problem will be to choose between another relatively capital-intensive hydroelectric development at Jebba and the installation of more thermal generating capacity. Again, the decision will depend on the availability, cost and price of fossil fuels.

The foregoing observations point out the need for, and the urgency of, a comprehensive survey of the energy resources of Nigeria. The government is preparing terms of reference for a survey that would include an inventory of the energy resources and recommendations for the most advantageous use of the natural gas available.

The federal government recently authorized state governments to apply for franchises to set up their own electricity companies, thus ending ECN's monopoly. To be franchised, such undertakings must conform to strict economic and physical standards laid down by the federal government. It is intended that they will eventually be taken over and operated by ECN. This develop-ment reflects the impatience in some states to have village electrification programs which ECN has not been able to carry out, despite financing made available by the state governments, and the dissatisfaction which prevails with the standards of electricity supply throughout the country.

Although there is considerable capacity for increasing the supply of electricity at low cost, annual per capita non-industrial consumption remains very low at 10 kWh and the prospective increase is modest. Furthermore, the Lagos area accounts for 51 percent of total consumption in Nigeria and of 87 percent of non-industrial consumption.

The federal government recognized this problem and commissioned a study of rural electrification.[5] The study considered the extension of the present transmission system to 137 small towns and villages not now supplied. The authors of the study based their priorities on the establishment of administrative services and infrastructure in the new states, on the creation of employment, and on balanced development. The provision of electricity in rural areas should en-courage industrial and commercial development at the local level, assist in promoting economic growth, and reduce migration from rural to urban areas.

The report proposes a phased program which would cost about £N28 million which could be carried out over an eight-year period. The program might be initiated during the current Plan period, but the main part would be carried out during 1974/75 - 1978/79. In view of the overall financial resources available and the size of the electricity program as a whole, this would not be an over-ambitious objective. The new national electricity corporation, together with any new insti-tutions set up by state governments, should attach high priority to a program of this kind.

5. *Nigerian Rural Electrification Study*: T. Ingledow Associates, Vancouver, December 1970.

STATISTICAL ANNEX
SOURCES OF DATA

The economy must rank as one of the most intensively studied economies in the world, by researchers both within and outside the country. Unfortunately, these research efforts apparently have not led to a consistent set of basic economic data for a reasonable time period. On the contrary, the multitude of experienced economists, both Nigerian and non-Nigerian, who have worked on problems of the economy has evidently led to a vast volume of economic data which are neither consistent with each other, nor sufficiently reliable, nor covering a long enough period to represent a firm indicator of long-term trends. For the year 1958, for example, for which most developing countries would be satisfied with any macroeconomic indicators at all, Nigeria is "endowed" with no less than *three* GDP estimates, and *five* estimates of gross fixed capital formation — the highest of which is some 35 percent higher than the lowest. In the use of economic data on Nigeria, therefore, it is necessary to rely a great deal on personal judgment and experience of other developing countries at similar stages of development.

The major sources of data used in the estimation of the model's parameters are listed here. Ordinary least square regression has been used whenever time series data exist, with the R_2 taken as the sole criterion for choice of equation.

Increment Capital-Output Ratio. Unpublished research of Professor Vielrose of the Nigerian Institute of Economic and Social Studies (NISER); Peter Clark's study on *Planning Import Substitution* (North-Holland Publishing, 1970) which includes ICOR's derived from a number of industrial census and feasibility studies in Nigeria; and data from other developing countries.

Consumption Elasticities. For manufactured goods, private consumption estimates in Okigbo, *Nigerian National Accounts 1950-57;* for food products, FAO agricultural study of Nigeria and unpublished research papers of Dr. Olatunbosun and Dr. Olayide of NISER.

Private Saving Functions. G. Helleiner's time series of savings and income from 1950 to 1960 (given in *Peasant Agriculture, Government and Economic Growth in Nigeria,* Yale, 1966) and the official national account series of the Federal Office of Statistics (FOS).

Input-Output Coefficients and Capital-Output Coefficients. N. Carter's input-output table (published in W. Stolper's *Planning Without Facts,* Harvard, 1966) and the Clark study cited above.

Sectoral Growth Elasticities. Okigbo's national account estimates for the 1950s and the current official series by the Federal Office of Statistics.

The tables are in three parts: base year data, the set of relationships used in the model of the economy, and a set of projections derived from the model and the base year information.

List of Tables

Table 1: POPULATION – URBAN AND RURAL, ACTUAL AND PROJECTED TO 1985

Year	Population			Percent Urban	Annual Rate of Increase (%)			Urban-Rural
	Urban	Rural	Total		Urban	Rural	Total	
1950	4,742	29,589	34,331	13.81	—	—	—	—
1955	6,055	32,186	38,241	15.83	5.01	1.70	2.18	3.31
1960	7,668	35,279	42,947	17.85	4.84	1.85	2.35	2.99
1965	9,830	38,846	48,676	20.20	5.09	1.94	2.54	3.15
1970	12,535	42,539	55,074	22.76	4.98	1.83	2.50	3.15
1975	16,098	46,924	63,022	25.54	5.13	1.98	2.73	3.15
1980	20,772	52,012	72,784	28.54	5.23	2.08	2.92	3.15
1985	26,878	57,822	84,700	31.73	5.29	2.14	3.04	3.15

Source: Urban and Rural population 1950-1985, ESA/P/W.P.33/RW1 September 22, 1970, United Nations.

Table 2: PROJECTED POPULATION BY AGE, 1965–85

Ages	1965	1970	1975	1980	1985
All ages	48,676	55,074	63,022	72,784	84,700
0–4	9,055	10,102	11,799	13,828	16,241
5–9	6,932	7,990	9,037	10,688	12,672
10–14	5,826	6,615	7,661	8,703	10,336
15–19	5,072	5,637	6,419	7,456	8,493
20–24	4,409	4,876	5,438	6,213	7,237
25–29	3,764	4,207	4,672	5,230	5,996
30–34	3,111	3,574	4,013	4,475	5,030
35–39	2,553	2,934	3,388	3,823	4,282
40–44	2,097	2,387	2,760	3,204	3,633
45–49	1,688	1,941	2,224	2,587	3,022
50–54	1,318	1,539	1,782	2,056	2,407
55–59	1,024	1,171	1,379	1,610	1,872
60–64	759	870	1,007	1,199	1,415
65–69	521	600	700	822	992
70 +	547	629	742	889	1,076

Source: Urban and Rural population 1950-1985, ESA/P/W.P.33/RW1 September 22, 1970, United Nations.

Table 3: POPULATION AND LABOR FORCE ESTIMATES AND PROJECTIONS
BY SEX, 1950–85

(in thousands)

| | | Population | | | Labor Force | |
	Male	Female	Total	Male	Female	Total
1950	17,322	17,009	34,331	9,334	6,711	16,045
1955	19,302	18,939	38,241	10,199	6,971	17,170
1960	21,685	21,262	42,947	11,249	7,273	18,523
1965	24,579	24,097	48,676	12,500	7,951	20,451
1970	27,686	27,387	55,073	13,803	8,731	22,534
1975	31,577	31,445	63,022	15,242	9,652	24,895
1980	36,381	36,403	72,784	16,905	10,702	27,607
1985	42,269	42,432	84,701	18,988	11,986	30,974

Annual Rate of Increase (%)

1950-55	2.2	2.2	2.2	1.8	0.8	1.4
1955-60	2.3	2.4	2.4	2.0	0.9	1.5
1960-65	2.5	2.5	2.6	2.1	1.8	2.0
1965-70	2.4	2.6	2.5	2.0	1.9	2.0
1970-75	2.7	2.9	2.6	2.0	2.0	2.0
1975-80	2.9	3.0	2.9	2.1	2.1	2.1
1980-85	3.0	3.1	3.1	2.4	2.3	2.3

Source: ILO, *Labor Force Projections* (1971), Part II.

NOTES

Nigeria has a centralized statistical organization consisting of the Federal Office of Statistics (FOS), located in Lagos, and 18 regional offices. The largest part of the staff (about 1,800) is located in the center, and the field staff consists of about 800 persons. On the average, one field office has about 45 staff members covering a population of 3 million people. Transport facilities are meager and calculating equipment is scarce; much of the equipment needs replacement. The office's capacity for processing and printing statistics is inadequate and there is need for additional equipment to handle the existing backlog in publishing statistics and to avoid future recurrence of delays.

These weaknesses in the statistical organization are clearly reflected in the scarcity of adequate and timely information on overall and sectoral economic performance and problems. Such information is vital to the formulation of economic plans and to the monitoring of development activities.

The poor state of demographic statistical information is most striking. The last population census, held in 1963, reported the total population at 55.67 million. It is widely recognized that this probably overstated the population by a wide margin. The UN Division of Population estimates the 1963 population at 46.32 million. This is based on the 1952 census and an assumed rate of growth of 2.5-3% per year since then. The first six tables present the UN estimates and projections. In the body of the report, however, the official estimates (68 million in 1970) have been used, since these estimates evidently form the basis of part of the official National Income estimates.

The following points should also be noted:

a. Because of the disruptions, national accounts estimates for all years after 1966/67 are highly unreliable (Tables 7-11).

b. As is usual in most developing countries, official estimates of fixed capital formation are based on estimates of capital goods imports and surveys of domestic construction activities. However, the very substantial amount of construction work undertaken by foreign contractors for the petroleum exploration companies has apparently not been included in the official estimates. The mission has, therefore, added the estimated payments by oil companies to foreign contractors (derived from the Central Bank's balance of payments estimates) to the official estimates of fixed capital formation (Table 9).

c. The Central Bank's balance of payment estimates for the oil sector are based on financial transactions of the oil companies. Estimates of investment income paid abroad and direct investment are therefore not suitable for national accounting purposes. The mission has attempted to estimate a consolidated national income and balance-of-payments accounts for the oil sector, based primarily on data provided by the Central Bank. Production costs were estimated on the basis of estimated per barrel production costs while investment expenditures were estimated by subtracting production costs from estimated total expenditures of oil companies (imports of goods and non-factor services plus local expenditures). Investment income paid abroad was then derived as a residual item, defined in the national income account as income not accounted for elsewhere, and in the balance of payments account as proceeds not remitted to Nigeria and not used as payments for imported goods and non-factor services. (These estimates of investment income were derived for the purpose of economic analysis only, and do not represent actual payments of dividends, interests on profits.) The results of the mission's calculations are presented in Table 46 and are also incorporated in the oil sector's balance of payments estimates in Table 18. It should be noted that the overall balance in Table 18 remains the same as the official Central Bank estimates.

Table 4: LABOR FORCE ESTIMATES AND PROJECTIONS, BY AGE GROUPS, 1950–85

(in millions)

		1950	1955	1960	1965	1970	1975	1980	1985
Males	10–14	.74	.72	.69	.68	.66	.65	.61	.63
	15–19	1.17	1.26	1.37	1.48	1.52	1.61	1.74	1.87
	20–24	1.40	1.56	1.74	1.95	2.08	2.23	2.50	2.87
	25–65	5.72	6.34	7.13	8.05	9.18	10.35	11.62	13.12
Subtotal	15–64	8.28	9.17	10.24	11.48	12.78	14.20	15.86	17.85
Total	10–65+	9.33	10.20	11.25	12.50	13.80	15.24	16.91	18.99
Females	10–14	.53	.53	.52	.52	.51	.50	.45	.47
	15–19	1.04	1.07	1.10	1.16	1.23	1.30	1.38	1.45
	20–24	.95	.99	1.02	1.11	1.21	1.35	1.50	1.69
	25–64	3.97	4.17	4.43	4.93	5.52	6.23	7.06	8.02
Subtotal	15–64	5.96	6.23	6.54	7.20	7.96	8.87	9.94	11.16
Total	10–65+	6.71	6.97	7.27	7.95	8.73	9.65	10.70	11.99
Total	10–14	1.27	1.25	1.21	1.20	1.17	1.15	1.06	1.10
	15–19	2.21	2.33	2.46	2.64	2.75	2.91	3.11	3.33
	20–24	2.35	2.55	2.76	3.06	3.29	3.58	4.00	4.56
	25–64	9.68	10.52	11.56	12.98	14.69	16.58	18.68	21.33
Subtotal	15–64	14.24	15.39	16.78	18.68	20.74	23.07	25.79	29.22
Total	10–65+	16.05	17.17	18.52	20.45	22.53	24.90	27.61	30.97

Source: ILO, *Labor Force Projections* (1971).

Table 5: ESTIMATED GROWTH OF LABOR FORCE BY AGE AND SEX, 1950–85

(percent)

		50–55	55–60	60–65	65–70	70–75	75–80	80–85
Males	15–19	7.7	8.4	7.9	3.2	5.9	7.9	7.6
	20–24	11.4	11.7	12.6	6.5	7.2	11.9	14.9
	25–65	10.8	12.4	12.9	14.0	12.8	12.3	12.8
Subtotal	15–64	10.7	11.7	12.1	11.3	11.1	11.7	12.6
Total	10–65+	9.3	10.3	11.1	10.4	10.4	10.9	12.3
Females	15–19	2.9	2.5	6.0	5.9	5.4	6.1	5.7
	20–24	4.2	3.1	9.1	9.2	11.0	11.4	12.6
	25–64	5.0	6.1	11.3	12.0	12.9	13.3	13.6
Subtotal	15–64	4.5	5.0	10.1	10.6	11.5	12.0	12.4
Total	10–65+	3.9	4.3	9.3	9.8	10.5	10.9	12.0
Total	15–19	5.4	5.7	7.1	4.4	5.6	7.1	6.8
	20–24	8.5	8.4	11.0	7.5	8.6	11.7	14.1
	25–64	8.7	9.9	12.3	13.2	12.8	12.7	14.2
Subtotal	15–64	8.1	9.0	11.3	11.0	11.2	11.8	13.3
Total	10–65+	–	7.0	7.9	10.4	10.2	10.5	10.9

Source: ILO, *Labor Force Projections* (1971).

Table 6: EMPLOYMENT BY INDUSTRY, 1966–68

The columns headed "Professional and Managerial", "Clerical", "Skilled and Semiskilled" and "Unskilled" refer to Nigerians. In 1966 the "Number of Establishments" figure for Misc. chemical products (20) is bracketed together with Petrochemical products.

Industries	Estab. 1966	Prof. & Mgr. 1966	Clerical 1966	Skilled & Semiskilled 1966	Unskilled 1966	Non-Nigerians 1966	Total Employed 1966	Estab. 1967	Prof. & Mgr. 1967	Clerical 1967	Skilled & Semiskilled 1967	Unskilled 1967	Non-Nigerians 1967	Total Employed 1967	Estab. 1968	Total Employed 1968
Meat products	11	23	134	576	330	22	1,085	11	18	125	570	285	23	1,021	11	1,206
Dairy products	4	8	40	171	145	7	371	4	8	44	155	127	7	341	5	385
Fruit canning	3	1	32	33	114	2	182	3	2	17	61	142	1	223	4	203
Grain mill products	4	21	94	231	259	33	638	4	14	104	262	260	37	677	4	682
Bakery products	28	34	175	788	604	19	1,620	30	33	187	814	522	14	1,570	32	1,630
Sugar and spirit distillery	3	119	119	513	1,890	31	2,672	3	40	38	254	176	18	526	3	569
Sugar confectionery	5	28	42	210	613	30	923	6	24	98	198	846	34	1,200	7	1,462
Misc. food prepar. & tobacco	8	64	432	723	1,221	40	2,480	8	72	437	877	1,105	38	2,529	9	2,627
Beer brewing	4	56	474	798	521	74	1,923	4	60	485	600	642	68	1,855	4	1,884
Soft drinks	6	22	73	399	221	28	743	7	37	125	332	352	19	865	6	868
Textiles	30	91	767	7,094	3,422	316	11,690	38	189	958	11,416	3,774	447	16,784	38	17,587
Footwear	11	38	104	1,046	189	47	1,424	13	27	137	836	489	43	1,532	10	1,476
Wearing apparel	12	6	23	375	80	14	498	12	4	22	376	79	17	498	13	735
Made up textile goods	6	4	33	607	964	31	1,639	7	4	33	735	800	33	1,605	8	1,707
Sawmilling	39	41	158	1,572	1,005	8	2,784	52	80	450	2,166	3,568	80	6,344	58	6,572
Furniture and fixtures	38	50	318	1,694	689	49	2,800	41	50	349	2,003	1,128	57	3,587	35	3,327
Paper products	9	14	79	328	383	25	829	10	37	106	623	193	28	987	9	842
Printing	41	174	998	2,502	853	56	4,583	47	171	1,068	3,018	860	48	5,165	55	5,645
Tanning	6	7	40	76	376	17	516	7	14	41	185	308	17	565	6	551
Travel goods	3	2	25	131	146	7	311	3	5	22	231	61	6	325	4	394
Rubber	8	21	176	577	228	46	1,048	21	48	306	928	1,039	61	2,382	24	6,372
Basic industrial chemicals	3	8	93	66	34	15	216	5	11	66	105	29	11	222	3	282
Vegetable oils	10	18	194	706	1,487	43	2,448	13	20	210	977	1,463	51	2,721	14	3,536
Paints	5	25	75	133	101	25	359	5	28	83	139	98	25	373	6	384
Misc. chemical products	20	89	762	1,206	1,014	82	3,153	26	116	941	1,433	959	105	3,554	23	4,279
Petrochemical products		4	31	386	222	23	666	12	12	42	521	349	26	950	18	1,865
Bricks, pottery and glass	8	23	262	1,048	696	68	2,097	10	39	228	1,051	596	69	1,983	14	1,176
Cement and concrete products	11	97	451	3,323	1,865	227	5,963	35	98	532	3,561	1,776	232	6,199	8	1,895
Basic metals and metal products	29	14	49	192	6	7	268	4	16	44	189	7	6	262	52	8,411
Machinery (non-electric)	4	20	176	335	215	16	762	11	22	63	312	149	13	559	7	511
Electrical equipment	9	11	377	958	239	56	1,641	5	17	405	947	162	49	1,580	14	817
Motor vehicle assembly	6	158	1,570	2,771	1,085	230	5,814	80	181	1,721	2,960	1,125	220	6,207	4	1,475
Motor vehicle repairs	67	23	136	554	388	25	1,126	18	26	185	534	422	37	1,204	72	4,884
Miscellaneous manufactures	13														16	976
Total	**464**	**1,314**	**8,512**	**32,122**	**21,605**	**1,719**	**65,272**	**555**	**1,523**	**9,672**	**39,369**	**23,891**	**1,940**	**76,395**	**596**	**87,213**

Source: Federal Office of Statistics, *Industrial Surveys*, 1966, 1967 and 1968.

Table 7: GROSS NATIONAL PRODUCT AT CONSTANT (1962/63) PRICES, BY ECONOMIC ACTIVITY

(millions of £N)

	1958/59	1959/60	1960/61	1961/62	1962/63	1963/64	1964/65	1965/66	1966/67	1967/68[a]	1968/69[a]	1969/70[a]	1970/71[b]
Agriculture, forestry and fishing	672.2	704.5	799.9	776.9	804.8	870.8	866.7	870.9	869.5	696.7	706.2	767	894
Petroleum	1.5	2.9	5.5	11.6	15.8	19.8	35.9	69.3	102.4	45.6	59.4	140	282
Mining, other than petroleum	8.7	9.3	10.3	10.8	11.0	11.7	12.1	14.0	13.4	11.1	10.4	11	14
Manufacturing and crafts	45.3	52.0	57.0	63.8	75.9	76.8	88.9	103.7	113.4	107.3	121.9	143	165
Public utilities	2.8	3.5	4.2	5.2	6.0	7.3	8.1	9.2	10.1	7.8	8.9	10	11
Building and construction	35.3	47.0	55.4	57.9	57.5	66.0	65.0	80.0	81.3	63.7	57.3	61	96
Distribution	127.9	136.1	154.7	155.5	161.1	180.9	194.9	202.7	200.9	178.5	180.4	198	235
Transport and communication	41.4	45.2	53.9	60.0	61.9	69.2	68.9	66.3	64.7	56.2	60.5	63	75
General Government	31.4	38.7	39.9	38.6	38.8	38.9	44.8	48.4	51.1	46.0	56.5	111	114
Education	26.1	30.6	32.1	35.1	38.9	41.4	46.6	48.7	55.1	44.7	48.2	51	54
Health	4.9	5.6	6.3	7.1	8.4	8.9	10.0	11.5	12.5	9.2	10.1	11	14
Other services	21.8	22.7	25.3	28.1	28.2	27.9	30.7	36.2	41.4	34.4	38.8	39	42
Gross Domestic Product, at factor cost	1,019.3	1,098.1	1,244.5	1,250.6	1,308.3	1,419.6	1,472.6	1,560.9	1,615.8	1,301.2	1,358.6	1,605	1,996
Indirect taxes less subsidies	70.7	79.8	92.5	97.7	96.8	101.5	125.9	125.6	119.7	96.7	102.6	135	174
Gross Domestic Product at market prices	1,090.0	1,177.9	1,337.0	1,348.3	1,405.1	1,521.1	1,598.5	1,686.5	1,735.5	1,397.9	1,461.2	1,740	2,170
Factor payments and transfers, net[c]	-0.6	-5.5	-8.0	-8.0	-12.5	-22.2	-38.8	-78.8	-88.1	-29.8	-51.8	-114	-145
Gross National Product at market prices	1,089.4	1,172.4	1,329.0	1,340.3	1,392.6	1,498.9	1,559.7	1,607.7	1,647.4	1,368.1	1,409.4	1,626	2,025

[a] Excluding Eastern States.
[b] Provisional.
[c] Mission estimates, derived from current price estimates in Table 8.

Source: GNP 1958/59–1968/69: Federal Office of Statistics, Nigeria. GDP 1969/70–1970/71 and GNP: Federal Ministry of Economic Development.

Table 8: GROSS NATIONAL PRODUCT AT CURRENT PRICES, BY ECONOMIC ACTIVITY

(millions of £N)

	1958/59	1959/60	1960/61	1961/62	1962/63	1963/64	1964/65	1965/66	1966/67	1967/68[a]	1968/69[a]	1969/70[a]	1970/71[b]
Agriculture, forestry and fishing	630.0	642.0	708.8	728.3	804.8	837.5	839.0	845.9	892.2	783.8	818.0	936	1,174
Petroleum	0.6	0.9	3.5	10.6	15.8	16.5	27.6	59.5	68.0	21.8	40.2	142	253
Mining, other than petroleum	6.9	7.9	9.5	10.7	11.0	11.5	13.2	14.8	13.7	12.6	12.1	13	18
Manufacturing and crafts	40.5	46.9	54.0	61.4	75.9	78.9	92.9	109.0	119.2	112.9	128.2	154	187
Public utilities	2.7	3.6	4.8	5.8	6.0	7.7	8.8	9.3	9.9	7.2	8.0	9	11
Building and construction	30.3	38.7	47.4	53.1	57.5	61.4	63.2	80.6	82.7	65.5	59.8	63	102
Distribution	108.6	116.8	141.8	146.4	161.1	191.0	208.2	216.4	216.1	191.4	193.9	214	259
Transport and communication	33.7	38.3	50.1	59.7	61.9	70.9	72.3	69.6	68.1	59.1	63.5	67	82
General Government	25.3	32.7	37.2	38.4	38.8	39.8	46.9	50.7	53.5	48.2	29.2	117	140
Education	21.8	27.3	31.6	35.1	38.9	41.3	47.9	50.1	56.6	46.0	49.6	53	57
Health	3.9	4.7	5.8	7.1	8.4	9.1	10.5	12.1	13.1	9.7	10.6	12	15
Other Services	16.3	18.3	22.4	24.7	28.2	31.1	35.4	40.3	45.8	38.1	43.4	44	48
Gross Domestic Product at factor cost	920.6	978.1	1,116.9	1,181.3	1,308.3	1,396.7	1,465.9	1,558.3	1,638.9	1,396.3	1,486.5	1,824	2,346
Indirect taxes less subsidies	63.9	71.1	83.0	92.3	96.8	99.9	125.3	125.4	121.4	103.8	112.3	153	204
Gross Domestic Product at market prices	984.5	1,049.2	1,199.9	1,273.6	1,405.1	1,496.6	1,591.2	1,683.7	1,760.3	1,500.1	1,598.8	1,977	2,550
Factor payments and transfers, net[c]	-0.5	-4.9	-7.2	-7.6	-12.5	-21.8	-38.6	-78.7	-89.4	-32.0	-56.7	-129	-170
Gross National Product at market prices	984.0	1,044.3	1,192.7	1,266.0	1,392.6	1,474.8	1,552.6	1,605.0	1,670.9	1,468.1	1,542.1	1,848	2,380

[a]Excluding Eastern States.

[b]Provisional.

[c]Mission estimates, based on calendar year's balance of payments estimates (Table 18).

Source: GDP 1958/59 – 1968/69: Federal Office of Statistics, Nigeria. GDP 1969/70 – 1970/71 and GNP: Mission estimates based on Table 7.

Table 9: GROSS FIXED CAPITAL FORMATION BY TYPE OF CAPITAL GOODS

(millions of £N)

	1958/59	1959/60	1960/61	1961/62	1962/63	1963/64	1964/65	1965/66	1966/67	1967/68[a]	1968/69[a]	1969/70[a]	1970/71[b]
At Current Prices													
Land and agriculture development	14.2	11.6	11.0	30.2	25.6	33.4	33.0	36.7	35.8	26.1	23.1		
Buildings	35.7	43.2	45.5	45.9	55.2	55.8	58.0	63.9	58.2	40.3	43.6		
Civil engineering works	23.8	28.0	28.1	29.7	34.2	37.2	38.0	47.5	52.4	37.4	35.7	237	381
Plant, machinery and equipment	24.0	31.2	33.1	35.4	36.3	39.3	54.0	68.9	76.8	79.6	89.4		
Vehicles	11.5	8.7	11.5	11.1	6.6	13.8	22.0	24.3	19.4	15.0	15.4		
Payments to foreign oil contractors[c]	n.a.	n.a.	n.a.	n.a.	2.0	4.0	10.0	20.0	30.0	25.0	28.0	38	69
Total	109.2	122.7	129.2	152.3	159.9	183.5	215.0	261.3	272.6	223.4	235.2	275	450
(of which petroleum)[c]	n.a.	n.a.	n.a.	n.a.	4.0	8.3	22.7	44.0	63.4	45.0	36.0	61	115
At Constant 1962/63 Prices													
Land and agriculture development	16.1	13.7	12.5	31.3	25.6	32.9	31.7	36.2	35.3	25.8	22.7	n.a.	n.a.
Buildings	41.8	52.4	52.6	50.3	55.5	52.2	55.5	60.3	55.5	38.4	41.6	n.a.	n.a.
Civil engineering works	27.3	33.5	31.9	31.3	34.2	36.3	37.3	46.2	51.0	35.7	34.9	n.a.	n.a.
Plant, machinery and equipment	27.9	38.3	38.3	38.3	36.3	38.0	50.9	65.3	72.6	75.9	84.5	n.a.	n.a.
Vehicles	13.6	10.3	13.0	11.8	6.6	13.3	21.3	23.5	18.8	14.5	14.9	n.a.	n.a.
Payments to foreign oil contractors[c]	n.a.	n.a.	n.a.	n.a.	2.0	3.8	9.6	19.2	28.8	24.0	26.8	n.a.	n.a.
Total	126.7	148.2	148.3	163.0	159.9	176.5	206.3	250.7	262.0	214.3	225.4	257	406
(of which petroleum)[c]	n.a.	n.a.	n.a.	n.a.	4.0	8.0	21.8	42.2	60.9	43.2	34.5	57	104

[a]Excluding Eastern states.
[b]Provisional.
[c]Mission estimates, based on estimated petroleum sector accounts (Table 46).
Note: n.a. = not available.

Source: 1958/59–1968/69: Federal Office of Statistics, Nigeria.
1969/70, 1970/71: Federal Ministry of Economic Development, Nigeria, and mission estimates.

Table 10: GROSS NATIONAL PRODUCT BY TYPE OF EXPENDITURE, AT CONSTANT (1962/63) PRICES

(millions of £N)

	1958/59	1959/60	1960/61	1961/62	1962/63	1963/64	1964/65	1965/66	1966/67	1967/68[a]	1968/69[a]	1969/70[a]	1970/71[b]
Consumption	1,009.2	1,093.4	1,280.4	1,232.1	1,290.9	1,375.8	1,450.9	1,447.4	1,455.8	1,213.4	1,266.0	1,485	1,780
Public	56.4	69.3	79.5	81.4	85.2	87.9	102.0	117.9	114.9	123.0	145.0	218	202
Private	952.8	1,024.1	1,200.9	1,150.7	1,205.7	1,287.9	1,348.9	1,329.5	1,340.9	1,090.4	1,121.0	1,267	1,578
Gross Fixed Capital Formation	126.7	148.2	148.3	163.0	159.9	176.5	206.3	250.7	262.0	214.3	225.4	257	406
Public	57.8	74.6	70.6	64.5	64.5	61.0	65.3	80.4	87.4	79.9	82.1	n.a.	90
Private	68.9	73.6	77.7	98.5	95.4	115.5	141.0	170.3	174.6	134.4	143.3	n.a.	316
Exports of goods and NFS	149.9	156.1	151.4	184.9	181.7	209.0	223.3	272.3	303.4	223.7	238.6	312	448
Less imports of goods and NFS	195.8	219.8	243.1	231.7	227.4	240.2	281.7	283.9	285.7	253.5	268.8	314	467
GDP at market prices	1,090.0	1,177.9	1,337.0	1,348.3	1,405.1	1,521.1	1,598.5	1,686.5	1,735.5	1,397.9	1,461.2	1,740	2,167
Net factor payments and transfers	-0.6	-5.5	-8.0	-8.0	-12.5	-22.2	-38.8	-78.8	-88.1	-29.8	-51.8	-114	-144
GNP at market prices	1,089.4	1,172.4	1,329.0	1,340.3	1,392.6	1,498.9	1,559.7	1,607.7	1,647.4	1,368.1	1,409.4	1,626	2,023

[a]Excluding Eastern states.
[b]Provisional.

Source: Mission estimates, based on Tables 7, 9, and 11.

Table 11: GROSS NATIONAL PRODUCT BY TYPE OF EXPENDITURE, AT CURRENT PRICES, 1958/59–1970/71

(millions of £N)

	1958/59	1959/60	1960/61	1961/62	1962/63	1963/64	1964/65	1965/66	1966/67	1967/68[a]	1968/69[a]	1969/70[a]	1970/71[b]
Consumption	911.8	970.5	1,138.9	1,164.1	1,290.9	1,353.3	1,443.7	1,447.2	1,501.5	1,326.4	1,400.3	1,714	2,150
Public	51.0	61.5	70.7	76.9	85.2	86.5	101.5	117.9	118.4	134.5	160.4	252	244
Private	860.8	909.0	1,068.2	1,087.2	1,205.7	1,266.8	1,342.8	1,329.3	1,382.1	1,191.9	1,239.9	1,462	1,906
Gross fixed capital formation[c]	109.2	122.7	129.2	152.3	159.9	183.5	215.0	261.3	272.6	223.4	235.2	275	450
Public	49.8	61.8	61.5	60.3	64.5	63.4	68.0	83.8	90.9	83.3	85.7	n.a.	100
Private	59.4	60.9	67.7	92.0	95.4	120.1	147.0	177.5	181.7	140.1	149.5	n.a.	350
Exports of goods and NFS	155.4	167.0	177.3	191.2	181.7	214.4	239.6	296.0	309.0	236.7	264.3	349	506
Less imports of goods and NFS	191.9	211.0	245.5	234.0	227.4	254.6	307.1	320.8	322.8	286.4	301.0	361	556
GNP at market prices	984.5	1,049.2	1,199.9	1,273.6	1,405.1	1,496.6	1,591.2	1,683.7	1,760.3	1,500.1	1,598.8	1,977	2,550
Net factor payments and transfers	-0.5	-4.9	-7.2	-7.6	-12.5	-21.8	-38.6	-78.7	-89.4	-32.0	-56.7	-129	-170
GNP at market prices	984.0	1,044.3	1,192.7	1,266.0	1,392.6	1,474.8	1,552.6	1,605.0	1,670.9	1,468.1	1,542.1	1,848	2,380

[a]Excluding Eastern states.
[b]Provisional.
[c]Including adjustments for oil companies' payments to foreign contractors. See Table 9.

Source: 1958/59-1960/61: Federal Ministry of Economic Development.
            1969/70-1970/71: Federal Ministry of Economic Development and mission estimates.

Table 12: VALUE OF EXPORTS BY MAJOR COMMODITIES, 1958–71

(million of £N, f.o.b.)

	1958	1959	1960	1961	1962	1963	1964	1965	1966	1967	1968	1969	1970	1971[a]
Groundnuts	27.0	22.5	22.9	32.2	32.4	36.6	34.3	37.8	40.8	35.4	38.0	35.8	21.7	12.1
Groundnut oil	3.7	4.6	5.3	5.0	6.2	6.5	8.1	10.0	10.0	7.2	9.5	10.9	11.6	6.4
Groundnut cake	1.2	1.7	1.6	1.9	2.5	2.7	4.6	5.3	4.7	4.2	4.9	5.0	5.5	3.4
Cocoa	26.7	38.3	36.8	33.7	33.4	32.4	40.1	42.3	28.3	54.7	51.5	52.6	66.5	71.6
Petroleum crude oil	1.0	2.7	4.4	11.5	16.7	20.2	32.1	68.1	92.0	72.1	37.0	130.9	254.9	476.5
Palm kernels	20.5	26.0	26.1	19.9	16.9	20.8	21.0	26.5	22.4	7.8	10.2	9.8	10.9	13.0
Rubber	7.6	11.6	14.2	11.0	11.4	11.8	12.2	11.0	11.5	6.3	6.3	9.6	8.8	6.2
Raw cotton	7.8	7.3	6.2	11.1	5.9	9.5	6.1	3.3	5.2	6.5	3.3	3.4	6.6	5.5
Hides and skins	2.6	4.2	4.5	4.1	3.8	4.2	4.6	4.6	5.8	4.4	4.0	4.2	2.9	2.4
Palm oil	12.7	13.8	14.0	13.2	8.9	9.4	10.8	13.6	11.0	1.3	0.1	0.4	0.6	1.7
Tin metal	–	–	–	–	–	–	–	–	15.4	13.0	13.7	13.9	16.6	12.4
Timber and plywood	6.3	7.4	8.3	7.9	7.0	8.0	8.5	7.2	6.8	4.3	4.3	5.2	4.0	3.5
Other exports	15.7	20.4	21.3	18.6	18.9	22.8	28.1	33.5	24.8	20.9	23.7	32.9	27.9	25.7
Total exports	132.8	160.5	165.6	170.1	164.0	184.9	210.5	263.2	278.7	238.1	206.5	314.6	438.5	640.4

[a]Provisional.

Source: Federal Office of Statistics.

Table 13: QUANTITY AND UNIT VALUE OF PRINCIPAL EXPORT COMMODITIES, 1958–71

	1958	1959	1960	1961	1962	1963	1964	1965	1966	1967	1968	1969	1970	1971[a]
(Quantities in '000)														
Groundnuts (tons)	513	497	332	494	530	614	544	512	573	520	638	517	287	134
Groundnut oil (tons)	40	48	47	45	63	69	80	91	108	71	109	100	89	42
Groundnut cake (tons)	58	61	53	75	88	85	139	113	133	131	171	168	160	98
Cocoa (tons)	87	143	154	184	195	175	197	255	190	242	206	171	193	267
Petroleum oil (tons)	245	538	828	2,224	3,368	3,695	5,783	13,020	18,945	14,774	6,890	26,867	50,883	70,570
Palm kernels (tons)	441	430	418	411	367	398	394	416	394	163	159	176	182	238
Rubber (tons)	41	53	57	55	60	63	72	68	70	48	52	56	58	50
Raw cotton (tons)	34	37	27	46	23	40	25	14	23	33	14	14	28	22
Cotton seed (tons)	n.a.	n.a.	n.a.	n.a.	n.a.	n.a.	n.a.	n.a.	66	63	29	42	95	96
Palm oil (tons)	171	184	183	165	118	126	134	150	143	16	3	8	8	20
Tin metal (tons)	n.a.	n.a.	n.a.	n.a.	n.a.	n.a.	n.a.	n.a.	11	10	11	10	11	8
Timber and plywood (cu. ft.)	18,075	22,086	24,983	23,258	19,318	23,077	24,858	19,555	18,896	11,598	11,353	12,133	8,478	7,876
Hides and skins (cwt.)	200	230	230	240	215	185	180	172	163	150	144	144	102	77
(Average Unit Value)														
Groundnuts (£/tons)	52.5	55.3	68.9	65.2	61.18	59.6	63.0	73.8	71.2	68.1	59.5	69.2	75.8	90.3
Groundnut oil (£/tons)	93.7	96.4	113.2	110.9	98.05	94.9	101.7	110.0	92.8	101.2	86.6	109.6	131.1	152.4
Groundnut cake (£/tons)	20.3	27.7	29.4	25.7	27.86	32.2	33.3	46.5	35.4	32.2	28.7	29.8	34.6	34.7
Cocoa (£/tons)	306.5	267.8	238.8	183.4	171.01	184.9	203.6	167.4	148.6	223.9	251.7	307.8	345.1	268.2
Petroleum oil (£/tons)	4.0	5.0	5.3	5.2	4.97	5.5	5.5	5.2	4.9	4.9	5.4	5.0	5.0	6.8
Palm kernels (£/tons)	46.4	60.4	62.3	48.4	46.01	52.3	53.2	63.8	56.9	48.0	64.0	55.4	59.6	54.6
Rubber (£/tons)	185.1	217.5	248.8	200.0	190.43	186.7	168.8	161.9	163.3	132.6	121.6	171.0	150.5	124.0
Raw cotton (£/tons)	232.8	198.0	230.1	239.7	252.07	238.1	241.2	243.8	231.3	197.3	232.6	239.2	235.8	250.0
Cotton seed (£/tons)	n.a.	n.a.	n.a.	n.a.	n.a.	n.a.	n.a.	n.a.	28.4	29.9	31.0	24.1	22.2	32.3
Palm oil (£/tons)	74.1	75.0	76.4	80.2	75.74	74.3	80.3	90.6	76.6	76.5	42.6	54.2	75.4	85.0
Tin metal (£/tons)	n.a.	n.a.	n.a.	n.a.	n.a.	n.a.	n.a.	n.a.	1,342.0	1,255.2	1,215.8	1,377.0	1,547.0	1,550.0
Timber and plywood (£/cu. ft.)	0.35	0.32	0.33	0.34	0.36	0.34	0.36	0.38	0.35	0.36	0.37	0.42	0.47	0.41
Hides and skins (£/cwt)	n.a.	n.a.	n.a.	n.a.	17.7	30.2	34.6	35.5	35.3	29.1	27.8	29.0	28.5	31.2

[a]Provisional.

Source: Federal Office of Statistics.

Note: n.a. = not available.

Table 14: DIRECTION OF TRADE, 1967–71

Countries	Imports Value 1967	Imports Value 1968	Imports Value 1969	Imports Value 1970	Imports Value 1971	Imports % 1967	Imports % 1968	Imports % 1969	Imports % 1970	Imports % 1971	Exports Value 1967	Exports Value 1968	Exports Value 1969	Exports Value 1970	Exports Value 1971	Exports % 1967	Exports % 1968	Exports % 1969	Exports % 1970	Exports % 1971
United Kingdom	64.6	59.9	86.3	116.0	172.1	28.9	31.0	34.7	30.7	31.9	70.3	61.9	86.8	124.8	140.3	29.5	30.1	27.6	28.4	21.9
India	3.2	1.8	1.8	3.0	6.8	1.4	0.9	0.7	0.8	1.3	0.2	..	..	..		0.1	..	..	..	..
Hong Kong	2.6	2.3	2.4	5.4	8.7	1.2	1.2	1.0	1.4	1.6	0.1	0.3	0.5	0.9	2.0	..	0.1	0.2	0.2	0.3
Ghana	0.4	1.1	0.3	0.2	0.5	0.2	0.6	0.1	0.1	0.1	0.7	0.5	1.3	0.3	4.2	0.3	0.2	0.4	0.1	0.7
Other countries[a]	7.2	6.8	9.1	9.9	9.8	3.2	3.5	3.7	2.6	1.8	9.8	6.5	10.8	28.4	36.2	4.1	3.1	3.4	6.5	5.6
Total Commonwealth countries	78.0	71.9	99.9	134.5	197.9	34.9	37.2	40.2	35.6	36.7	81.1	69.2	99.4	154.4	182.7	34.1	33.5	31.6	35.2	28.5
United States of America	27.9	22.3	29.2	54.8	75.7	12.5	11.5	11.8	14.5	14.0	18.5	16.0	38.9	50.4	112.8	7.8	7.7	12.4	11.8	17.6
Japan	18.8	7.2	9.4	23.7	45.5	8.4	3.7	3.8	6.3	8.4	4.2	3.7	3.3	3.4	8.7	2.6	1.8	1.1	0.8	1.4
EEC countries																				
Western Germany	25.2	21.2	26.4	49.3	65.7	11.3	11.0	10.6	13.0	12.2	25.2	17.9	19.3	29.6	35.3	10.6	8.7	6.1	6.8	5.5
Italy	10.7	13.8	13.5	18.0	20.4	4.8	7.2	5.4	4.8	3.8	14.1	13.1	14.5	19.0	28.3	5.9	6.3	4.6	4.3	4.4
France	9.4	7.2	8.0	12.6	22.0	4.2	3.7	3.2	3.3	4.1	22.4	11.5	31.8	37.3	95.2	9.4	5.6	10.1	8.4	14.9
Belgium and Luxembourg	2.9	3.3	3.2	8.1	9.1	1.3	1.7	1.3	2.1	1.7	3.2	5.9	5.0	3.4	3.1	1.3	2.9	1.6	0.7	0.5
Netherlands	9.3	7.8	11.6	13.4	18.6	4.2	4.0	4.7	3.5	3.4	30.8	27.0	42.4	74.5	88.0	12.9	13.1	13.5	16.9	13.7
Total EEC countries	57.5	53.3	62.7	101.4	135.8	25.7	27.6	25.2	26.7	25.2	95.7	75.4	113.0	163.8	249.9	40.2	36.5	35.9	37.1	39.0
Norway	4.6	2.1	1.4	2.5	3.3	2.1	1.1	0.6	0.7	0.6	0.5	0.1	2.4	4.7	7.9	0.2	0.5	0.7	1.1	1.2
Iceland	1.0	0.1	0.2	0.3	0.1	0.4	0.1	0.1	0.1	..					–					
China (Mainland)	6.3	3.7	5.5	7.0	10.1	2.8	1.9	2.2	1.8	1.9	0.9	0.2	..	0.4	0.2	0.4	0.1	..	0.1	..
Eastern Europe[b]	8.0	8.1	8.7	14.3	16.8	3.6	4.5	3.5	3.8	3.1	6.2	9.4	10.6	12.4	18.4	2.6	4.6	3.4	2.8	2.9
Israel	1.1	0.9	1.1	1.5	2.1	0.5	0.5	0.4	0.4	0.4					–					
Other countries	18.5	21.1	28.7	36.3	50.3	8.3	10.9	11.5	9.6	9.3	29.1	31.6	47.0	49.0	59.8	12.1	15.3	14.9	11.1	9.4
Total Non-Commonwealth countries	143.7	118.8	146.9	241.8	339.7	64.3	61.8	59.1	63.9	62.9	157.0	137.3	215.2	284.1	457.7	65.9	66.5	68.4	64.8	71.5
Total all countries[c]	223.6	192.6	248.7	378.2	539.5	100.0	100.0	100.0	100.0	100.0	238.1	206.5	314.6	438.5	640.4	100.0	100.0	100.0	100.0	100.0

[a]Excludes South Africa.
[b]Comprising Czechoslovakia, Eastern Germany, Finland, Hungary, Poland and USSR.
[c]Includes parcel post.

Source: Federal Office of Statistics *Review of External Trade,* 1971.

Table 15: COMPOSITION OF IMPORTS BY SITC SECTIONS, 1958–71

(millions of £N)

SITC Sections	1958	1959	1960	1961	1962	1963	1964	1965	1966	1967	1968	1969	1970	1971[a]
0. Foods	18.2	20.8	23.9	22.7	23.5	21.9	20.6	23.0	25.8	21.3	14.2	20.9	28.8	44.0
1. Beverages and tobacco	5.6	5.8	6.2	6.1	4.7	2.9	2.9	2.0	2.3	1.8	1.2	0.8	2.0	2.2
2. Crude materials	2.0	2.1	2.1	2.5	2.4	3.1	3.7	6.6	7.2	5.8	5.3	5.7	8.3	10.3
3. Fuels	8.9	10.4	11.3	13.4	14.1	15.5	19.5	17.4	3.8	8.8	14.6	15.6	11.0	4.5
4. Animals and vegetable oils	0.1	0.1	0.1	0.1	0.1	0.1	0.1	0.2	0.2	0.2	0.3	0.4	0.5	0.4
5. Chemicals	8.3	10.1	12.2	12.6	12.3	14.5	17.1	20.2	20.8	21.4	22.4	30.2	44.2	61.3
6. Manufactured goods	65.9	65.9	81.1	87.5	73.1	74.2	89.6	90.0	79.3	72.3	54.7	72.0	113.0	159.7
7. Machinery and transport	39.4	42.7	51.6	50.5	48.3	50.6	74.9	92.4	95.5	71.6	59.9	73.2	141.3	214.4
8. Miscellaneous manufactured items	15.5	17.8	23.9	23.8	21.7	21.3	22.5	20.5	18.8	17.4	14.0	13.4	19.8	35.4
9. Other	2.4	2.7	3.5	3.3	3.0	3.5	3.0	2.9	2.7	3.0	6.0	16.5	9.3	7.7
Total imports	166.3	178.4	215.9	222.5	203.2	207.6	253.9	275.2	256.4	223.6	192.6	248.7	378.2	539.5

[a]Provisional.

Source: Federal Office of Statistics, *Economic Indicators* – 1966, 1970.

Table 16: IMPORTS BY ECONOMIC USE, 1959—71

(millions of £N, c.i.f.)

	1959	1960	1961	1962	1963	1964	1965	1966	1967	1968	1969	1970	1971
Consumer goods	96.1	122.4	121.4	105.0	103.0	109.5	112.3	98.4	93.6	65.5	73.8	108.9	174.7
Non-durable:	83.6	104.2	104.6	90.4	89.2	92.1	93.4	82.3	78.0	58.0	64.4	89.8	138.5
Food	27.6	31.0	29.8	29.4	25.6	24.3	25.8	29.3	24.0	16.1	21.8	31.1	46.6
Textiles	27.2	37.1	39.4	27.9	29.2	32.0	32.0	21.0	25.5	16.0	15.2	19.5	29.1
Others	28.8	36.1	35.4	33.1	34.4	35.8	35.6	32.0	28.5	25.9	27.4	39.2	62.8
Durable:	12.5	18.2	16.8	14.6	13.8	17.4	18.9	16.1	15.6	7.5	9.4	19.1	36.2
Passenger cars	5.4	8.3	8.2	7.0	6.3	8.6	10.0	8.7	7.9	2.9	2.7	6.9	14.7
Others	7.1	9.9	8.6	7.6	7.5	8.8	8.9	7.4	7.7	4.6	6.7	12.2	21.5
Intermediate goods	36.0	42.3	45.0	44.2	50.9	63.9	63.7	51.0	52.8	56.3	72.6	104.4	128.3
Raw materials	25.7	31.0	31.6	30.1	35.4	44.4	46.4	47.2	44.0	41.7	57.0	93.4	123.8
Fuel	10.3	11.3	13.4	14.1	15.5	19.5	17.3	3.8	8.8	14.6	15.6	11.0	4.5
Capital goods	45.8	50.6	55.1	53.2	52.5	80.1	98.2	106.2	76.1	66.6	85.9	155.6	228.8
Capital equipment	32.8	37.0	41.6	44.7	41.4	61.1	78.1	88.6	60.4	51.5	63.2	116.2	174.1
Transport equipment	13.0	13.6	13.5	8.5	11.1	19.0	20.1	17.6	15.7	15.1	22.7	39.4	54.7
Total imports	177.9	215.3	221.5	202.4	206.4	253.5	274.2	255.6	222.5	188.4	232.3	368.9	531.8

Source Federal Office of Statistics.

Table 17: EXTERNAL RESERVES, 1966–71

(millions of £N, end of period)

	1966	1967	1968[b]	1969[b]	1970	1971 March	1971 June	1971 September	1971 December
Central Bank	71.3	36.6	38.0	42.6	68.3	86.0	105.9	88.9	125.5
IMF position	3.0	3.0	3.0	4.1	4.1	4.1	4.1	4.1	4.1
SDRs	–	–	–	–	6.0	11.2	11.2	11.2	11.2
Federal Government	2.4	1.1	1.1	0.6	1.1	0.7	0.5	0.6	0.7
State governments	3.9	3.2	2.9	1.1	0.8	2.0	1.2	1.0	1.0
Marketing Boards	1.7	–	–	–	–	–	–	–	–
Others[a]	9.9	7.7	7.7	9.0	10.0	9.6	9.0	9.5	9.6
Total official and semi-official	92.2	51.6	52.7	57.4	90.3	113.6	131.9	115.3	152.0
Commercial banks (net)	-7.9	-12.7	-2.0	-0.1	-1.8	-8.3	-2.2	-2.6	-2.4
Total external reserves	84.3	38.9	50.7	57.3	88.5	105.5	129.7	112.7	149.6

[a]Includes local governments, statutory corporations and public institutions, universities and teaching hospitals.
[b]Exclude some parts of Eastern States.

Source: Central Bank of Nigeria.

Table 18: BALANCE OF PAYMENTS, 1960–71

(millions of £N)

	1960	1961	1962	1963	1964	1965	1966	1967	1968	1969	1970	1971[a]
Current account												
Exports: non-oil	160.8	159.6	148.1	165.1	178.2	196.9	188.9	166.8	171.4	181.5	187.1	182.0
oil	4.2	11.3	17.2	20.1	32.0	68.1	91.9	72.0	37.8	130.8	258.6	489.1
Imports: non-oil	-209.3	-214.6	-197.4	-197.0	-234.5	-254.0	-231.2	-200.9	-181.2	-216.2	-333.0	-504.4
oil	—	—	—	-4.2	-11.7	-13.5	-19.5	-17.5	-9.9	-12.7	-26.2	-25.3
Trade balance	-44.3	-43.7	-32.1	-16.0	-36.0	-2.5	30.1	20.4	18.1	83.4	86.5	141.4
Services (net)	-23.3	-14.2	-19.9	-36.8	-55.1	-108.4	-163.1	-108.1	-118.2	-222.0	-276.2	-330.3
Investment income: non-oil	-4.5	-3.9	-8.8	-16.8	-26.7	-38.2	-54.9	-20.6	-53.9	-55.0	-55.9	-55.0
oil[b]	—	—	—	-0.2	-1.0	-33.0	-57.2	-16.8	0.4	-73.9	-134.3	-196.5
Other service payments: non-oil	-18.8	-10.3	-11.1	-13.4	-15.1	-15.0	-11.5	-39.2	-36.5	-45.0	-37.5	-21.0
oil	—	—	—	-6.4	-12.3	-22.2	-39.5	-31.5	-28.2	-48.1	-48.5	-57.8
Transfers	-1.7	-3.8	-0.7	-2.7	-0.2	2.7	2.1	7.7	17.2	10.4	22.5	0.9
Private	-5.8	-6.4	-3.2	-5.2	-6.4	6.7	-6.7	-4.5	3.5	2.0	6.8	-0.6
Official	4.1	2.6	2.5	2.5	6.2	9.4	8.8	12.2	13.7	8.4	15.7	9.5
Balance on current account	-69.3	-61.7	-52.7	-55.5	-91.3	-108.2	-130.9	-80.0	-82.9	-128.2	-167.2	-188.0
Capital account												
Private direct investment: non-oil	19.0	25.0	21.7	32.8	45.0	24.6	20.5	-6.0	16.5	27.0	46.8	56.9
oil[b]	—	—	—	5.1	18.1	36.2	67.7	50.3	29.1	57.6	75.0	89.2
Other private long-term investments	5.9	3.4	2.2	5.5	4.2	14.6	13.2	9.9	14.4	-0.5	-3.5	1.6
Basic balance	-44.4	-33.3	-28.8	-12.1	-24.0	-32.8	-29.5	-25.8	-22.9	-44.1	-48.9	-40.3
Private short-term: non-oil	-0.4	—	3.5	2.6	0.9	7.2	-1.6	2.1	18.4	29.1	44.3	63.2
oil	—	—	—	—	—	—	—	7.8	-0.4	-0.4	2.0	-5.9
Official (net)	8.1	5.5	7.4	-2.2	11.9	17.9	-0.3	6.8	-1.5	-1.4	2.2	14.9
SDR allocation	—	—	—	—	—	—	—	—	—	—	6.0	5.2
Errors and omissions	4.7	2.0	-11.1	-29.6	-5.7	4.5	22.5	-18.4	16.6	21.6	23.7	22.7
Overall balance	-32.0	-25.8	29.0	-41.3	-16.9	-3.2	-8.9	-43.1	10.2	7.6	29.3	59.7

[a] Provisional.
[b] Mission estimates, see Table 46.

Source: Central Bank of Nigeria.

Table 19: ANALYSIS OF FOREIGN PRIVATE INVESTMENT

(millions of £N)

	1961	1962	1963	1964	1965	1966	1967	1968	1969	Cumulative through 1969
By type of activity										
Mining & quarrying	5.8	4.5	12.5	35.5	35.7	47.8	20.0	18.3	26.7	277.5
Manufacturing & processing	5.0	12.0	11.0	9.3	10.9	5.0	24.8	2.7	14.8	116.8
Agriculture, forestry & fishing	-0.9	-0.1	0.6	0.5	0.2	-0.8	0.7	0.3	0.8	6.6
Transport & communications	0.3	0.1	0.2	0.9	2.3	0.7	-1.7	1.0	0.9	6.7
Building & construction	0.5	2.8	2.4	1.4	7.8	-10.6	1.5	0.9	1.2	13.1
Trading & business service	12.3	-9.1	11.5	4.8	-8.4	13.0	4.8	13.0	14.1	137.7
Miscellaneous activities	—	0.2	-0.3	10.6	6.7	-5.7	-2.5	0.5	0.9	11.7
Total	23.0	10.4	37.9	63.0	55.2	49.4	47.6	36.7	59.4	570.1
By source of funds										
Unremitted profits	2.7	7.9	13.4	17.8	37.8	59.5	28.1	16.7	56.2	
Changes in foreign share & loan capital (net)	8.7	4.9	10.5	20.8	2.4	1.4	1.8	4.8	5.1	
Trade & suppliers' credit (net)	2.3	2.3	1.8	4.6	4.8	1.4	15.3	7.7	23.4	
Other foreign liabilities (net)	3.4	1.7	1.4	1.3	0.6	3.6	3.3	3.0	0.5	
Liabilities to head offices	10.2	0.9	10.8	18.5	9.6	-16.5	-0.9	4.5	-25.9	
Total	27.3	17.7	37.9	63.0	55.2	49.4	47.6	36.7	59.4	

Source: Central Bank of Nigeria.

Note: Totals by *type of activity* differ from the totals by *source of funds* in 1961 and 1962 due to revision of the latter.

Table 20: EXTERNAL PUBLIC DEBT OUTSTANDING[a]

(thousands of US$)

	Debt Outstanding December 31, 1970		
	Disbursed	Undisbursed	Total
Suppliers credits	48,364	15,249	63,613
of which:			
Belgium	259	1,003	1,262
France	3,041	–	3,041
Germany (Fed. Rep. of)	13,311	–	13,311
Israel	1,822	1,968	3,790
Netherlands	9,210	–	9,210
Sweden	9,758	823	10,581
Switzerland	1,190	–	1,190
United Kingdom	8,173	11,455	19,628
USA	1,600	–	1,600
Private banks	10,841	7,241	18,082
of which:			
Germany (Fed. Rep. of)	8,203	4,240	12,443
Netherlands	2,364	731	3,095
United Kingdom	274	2,270	2,544
Publicly issued bonds	14,640	–	14,640
of which:			
United Kingdom	14,640	–	14,640
Loan from international organizations	182,427	83,604	266,031
of which:			
IBRD	165,244	65,287	230,531
IDA	17,183	18,317	35,500
Loans from governments	207,326	113,737	321,063
of which:			
Canada	9,164	18,213	27,377
Germany (Fed. Rep. of)	29,973	14,534	44,507
Israel	190	–	190
Italy	23,520	–	23,526
Japan	3,500	24,000	27,500
Netherlands	8,286	–	8,286
United Kingdom	84,938	36,749	121,687
USA	47,749	20,241	67,990
Total external public debt[b]	463,598	219,831	683,429

[a]Debt with a maturity of over one year, repayable in foreign currency.
[b]Excludes an agreement of £5 million from Czechoslovakia under which no actual contract exists. Includes principal in arrears of $6.1 million.

Source: Economic Program Department, IBRD.

Table 21: ESTIMATED FUTURE SERVICE PAYMENTS ON EXTERNAL PUBLIC DEBT OUTSTANDING[a]

(thousands of US$)

Year	Debt Outstanding (Beginning of Period) Disbursed Only	Including Undisbursed	Commit-ments	Disburse-ments	Principal	Service Payments Interest	Total	Cancellations, Adjustments
1966	285,069	614,046	28,379	88,003	35,508	10,764	46,272	-4,392
1967	333,167	602,525	35,146	102,661	23,524	11,664	35,188	-17,875
1968	386,115	596,272	69,358	82,144	23,786	14,946	38,732	-3,368
1969	442,915	638,476	68,913	34,242	35,319	20,539	55,858	-5,098
1970	443,554	666,972	53,469	54,409	34,874	18,056	52,930	-8,262
1971	457,474	677,305	—	97,442	50,614	23,118	73,732	-105
1972	524,692	626,549	—	25,171	39,725	23,906	63,631	-107
1973	510,030	586,716	—	30,298	35,455	22,871	58,326	-114
1974	504,758	551,147	—	16,269	33,453	21,899	55,352	-121
1975	487,453	517,573	—	12,260	36,160	20,843	57,003	-127
1976	463,426	481,286	—	7,837	29,305	19,537	48,842	-134
1977	441,825	451,848	—	4,324	32,557	18,153	50,709	-185
1978	413,407	419,106	—	3,031	29,224	16,731	45,955	—
1979	387,214	389,882	—	2,346	29,075	15,388	44,462	—
1980	360,485	360,808	—	250	29,491	14,002	43,492	—
1981	331,244	331,317	—	69	28,721	12,521	41,242	—
1982	302,592	302,596	—	4	29,090	11,069	40,159	—
1983	273,501	273,501	—	—	26,860	9,610	36,470	—
1984	246,641	246,641	—	—	20,811	8,341	29,153	—
1985	225,824	225,824	—	—	17,285	7,448	24,733	—
1986	208,539	208,539	—	—	17,623	6,707	24,330	—
1987	190,916	190,916	—	—	17,742	5,950	23,692	—
1988	173,173	173,173	—	—	14,841	5,234	20,075	—
1989	158,332	158,332	—	—	13,350	4,672	18,022	—
1990	144,982	144,982	—	—	12,837	4,171	17,007	—

[a]Total External Public Debt Repayable in Foreign Currency, as of December 31, 1970. Includes service on all debt listed in Table 20 with the exception of the following for which repayment terms are not available:

Supplier Credits	1,766
Loans from Governments–Japan	24,000
Total	25,766

Source: Economic Program Department, IBRD.

Table 22: FEDERAL AND STATE (REGIONAL) REVENUES AND EXPENDITURE, 1961–1971/72

(millions of £N)

	Revenues Transferred to the States	Recurrent[e] Revenues	Recurrent Expenditures	Current Surplus (+)/ Deficit (-)	Capital Expenditures	Over-all Budget Deficit (-)
1971/72[a]						
Federal Government	126.0	349.8	218.6	+131.2	158.9	- 27.7
State governments		192.0	183.2	+ 8.8	131.3	-122.5
North-Central		17.0	16.9	+ 0.1	12.1	- 12.0
Benue-Plateau		9.7	9.3	+ 0.4	9.5	- 9.1
Kano		15.0	10.0	+ 5.0	12.6	- 7.6
North-Western		11.7	11.0	+ 0.7	11.0	- 10.3
North-Eastern		14.4	14.4	0.0	12.7	- 12.7
Kwara		7.5	7.4	+ 0.1	8.6	- 8.5
Western		27.5	27.4	+ 0.1	11.5	- 11.4
Lagos		17.1	16.8	+ 0.3	11.0	- 10.7
Mid-Western		22.7	16.5	+ 6.2	12.8	- 6.6
Rivers		13.9	14.0	- 0.1	15.3	- 15.4
South-Eastern		14.7	13.6	+ 1.1	14.2	- 13.1
East-Central		20.8	25.9	- 5.1	—	- 5.1
Total		541.8	401.2	+140.0	231.3	- 91.3
1970/71						
Federal Government	143.4	235.6	243.4	- 7.8	68.0	- 75.8
State governments[a]		154.2	163.0	- 8.8	121.6	-130.4
North-Central		10.2	10.1	+ 0.1	9.2	- 9.1
Benue-Plateau		7.7	7.9	- 0.2	5.7	- 5.9
Kano		12.5	12.4	+ 0.1	14.2	- 14.1
North-Western		8.8	8.8	0.0	9.7	- 9.7
North-Eastern		10.8	11.4	- 0.6	9.2	- 9.8
Kwara		5.3	5.9	- 0.6	5.5	- 6.1
Western		29.9	27.7	+ 2.2	13.5	- 11.3
Lagos		14.5	14.0	+ 0.5	4.6	- 4.1
Mid-Western		19.1	12.9	+ 6.2	9.2	- 3.0
Rivers		11.7	12.3	- 0.6	12.0	- 12.6
South-Eastern		9.7	10.2	- 0.5	12.4	- 12.9
East-Central		14.0	29.4	- 15.4	16.5	- 31.9
Total		389.8	406.4	- 16.6	173.2	-189.8
1969/70						
Federal Government	89.7	128.2	240.1	-111.9	87.5	-199.4
State governments[b]		125.8[g]	111.6	+ 14.2	41.7	- 27.5
North-Central		8.2	5.7	+ 2.5	1.7	+ 0.8
Benue-Plateau		6.6	5.7	+ 0.9	1.7	- 0.8
Kano		12.1	11.8	+ 0.3	4.0	- 3.7
North-Western		7.2	6.2	+ 1.0	3.1	- 2.1
North-Eastern		9.3	8.1	+ 1.2	3.9	- 2.7
Kwara		5.1	5.8	- 0.7	—	- 0.7
Western		24.0	24.6	- 0.6	9.6	- 10.2
Lagos		17.0	10.3	+ 6.7	0.5	+ 6.2
Mid-Western		13.5	12.3	+ 1.2	6.2	- 5.0
Rivers		4.4	9.7	- 5.3	—	- 5.3
South-Eastern		8.4	11.4	- 3.0	11.0	- 14.0
East Central		n.a.	n.a.	n.a.	n.a.	n.a.
Total		254.0	351.7	- 97.7	129.2	-226.9
1968/69						
Federal Government	53.0	96.9	129.3	- 32.4	69.4	-101.8
State governments[f]		80.9	75.4	+ 5.5	11.1	- 5.6
North-Central		5.6	4.9	+ 0.7	0.4	+ 0.3
Benue-Plateau		3.6	4.6	- 1.0	0.4	- 1.4
Kano		8.1	8.0	+ 0.1	0.7	- 0.6
North-Western		3.6	4.3	- 0.7	0.3	- 1.0
North-Eastern		4.3	5.4	- 1.1	0.4	- 1.5
Kwara		3.1	3.4	- 0.3	—	- 0.3
Western		21.3	21.1	+ 0.2	5.0	- 4.8
Lagos		13.1	6.8	+ 6.3	0.1	+ 6.2
Mid-Western		9.7	9.3	+ 0.4	3.8	- 3.4
Rivers		1.5	1.3	+ 0.2	—	+ 0.2
South-Eastern		2.5	6.3	- 3.8	—	- 3.8
East Central		3.0	n.a.	n.a.	n.a.	n.a.
Total		177.8	204.7	- 26.9	80.5	-107.4

Table 22: FEDERAL AND STATE (REGIONAL) REVENUES
AND EXPENDITURE, 1961−1971/72 (Cont'd)

(millions of £N)

	Revenues Transferred to the States	Recurrent[e] Revenues	Recurrent Expenditures	Current Surplus (+)/ Deficit (-)	Capital Expenditures	Over-all Budget Deficit (-)
1967/68						
Federal Government	61.4	88.7	92.3	- 3.6	68.9	- 72.5
State governments[c,d]		55.9	52.3	+ 3.6	12.1	- 8.5
Total		144.6	144.6	+ 0.0	81.0	- 81.0
1966/67						
Federal Government	68.6	101.0	94.2	+ 6.8	52.4	45.6
State governments[c,d]		58.9	63.5	- 4.6	25.4	- 30.0
Total		159.9	157.7	+ 2.2	77.8	75.6
1966						
Federal Government	60.7	92.5	88.6	+ 3.9	53.5	- 49.6
State governments		90.6	86.1	+ 4.5	32.0	- 27.5
Total		183.1	174.7	+ 8.4	85.5	- 77.1
1965						
Federal Government	65.4	95.1	78.3	+ 16.7	50.0	- 33.3
State governments		97.0	83.8	+ 13.2	30.5	- 17.3
Total		192.1	162.2	+ 29.9	80.5	- 50.6
1964						
Federal Government	56.5	82.3	71.3	+ 11.0	43.0	- 32.0
State governments		84.8	71.9	+ 12.9	31.3	- 18.4
Total		167.1	143.2	+ 23.9	74.3	- 50.4
1963						
Federal Government	37.8	86.7	59.8	+ 26.9	40.9	- 14.0
State governments		67.7	63.7	+ 4.0	27.8	- 23.8
Total		154.4	123.5	+ 30.9	68.7	- 37.8
1962						
Federal Government	36.0	83.4	51.8	+ 31.6	49.3	- 17.7
State governments		65.2	69.1	- 3.9	28.1	- 32.0
Total		148.6	120.9	+ 27.7	77.4	- 49.7
1961						
Federal Government	33.4	78.4	48.4	+ 30.0	38.0	- 8.0
State governments		58.6	57.8	+ 0.8	28.4	- 27.6
Total		137.0	106.2	+ 30.8	66.4	- 35.6

[a]Budget Estimates.
[b]Excluding East Central State.
[c]Calendar year.
[d]Excluding Eastern states.
[e]Federal revenues are net of transfers to states.
[f]Sum of individual items not equal to total because of inconsistencies between different sources.
[g]See Table 23 footnotes b and d.

Source: Central Bank of Nigeria, the Official Gazettes of the Federal Republic of Nigeria, and state government budgets.

Table 23: RECURRENT REVENUES OF STATE GOVERNMENTS, 1968/69–1971/72

(millions of £N)

States	Own Revenues				Federal Receipts				Total Recurrent Revenues			
	1968/69	1969/70	1970/71[a]	1971/72[a]	1968/69	1969/70	1970/71[a]	1971/72[a]	1968/69	1969/70	1970/71[a]	1971/72[a]
Lagos	7.2	10.0	8.4	11.3	5.9	7.0	6.1	5.8	13.1	17.0	14.5	17.1
Western	6.5	6.9	7.6	8.9	14.8	17.1	22.3	18.6	21.3	24.0	29.9	27.5
Mid-Western	3.4	4.3	3.7	7.3	6.3	9.2	15.4	15.4	9.7	13.5	19.1	22.7
Benue Plateau	1.0	1.1	0.9	1.9	2.6	5.5	6.8	7.8	3.6	6.6	7.7	9.7
Kano	2.5	2.5	3.2	3.6	5.6	9.6	9.3	11.4	8.1	12.1	12.5	15.0
Kwara	1.2	1.1	0.6	1.4	1.9	4.0	4.7	6.1	3.1	5.1	5.3	7.5
North Central	2.1	2.6	3.1	8.7	3.5	5.6	7.1	8.3	5.6	8.2	10.2	17.0
North Eastern	1.9	2.0	1.6	2.7	2.4	7.3	9.2	11.7	4.3	9.3	10.8	14.4
North Western	1.4	1.5	1.4	2.1	2.2	5.7	7.4	9.6	3.6	7.2	8.8	11.7
East Central	n.a.	n.a.	5.3	9.0	3.0	5.6	8.7	11.8	n.a.	n.a.	14.0	20.8
Rivers	—	0.4	2.3	3.2	1.5	4.0	9.4	10.7	1.5	4.4	11.7	13.9
South Eastern	0.7	3.7	2.6	5.8	1.8	4.7	7.1	8.9	2.5	8.4	9.7	14.7
Total	27.9	36.1	40.7	66.0	53.0[c]	89.7[b]	113.5	126.1	80.9	125.8[b,d]	154.2	192.0

[a]Budget estimates.
[b]Includes £4.5 million unapportioned mining royalties and rents.
[c]Official figure: sum of individual items shown total £N51.5 million.
[d]Includes transfers from Federal Government to East Central State.

Source: Central Bank of Nigeria.

Table 24: RECURRENT REVENUES OF FEDERAL GOVERNMENT, 1961–1972/73

(millions of £N)

	1961	1962	1963	1964	1965	1966	1966/67	1967/68	1968/69	1969/70	1970/71	1971/72 Rev. Estimates	1972/73 Budget
Import duties	60.2	59.0	61.3	75.8	84.8	58.5	56.9	53.6	58.2	80.7	115.5	126.9	128.4
Export duties	13.5	12.5	13.5	14.9	15.8	14.3	14.0	15.0	14.9	19.2	20.5	22.8	20.3
Excise duties	6.4	6.5	9.3	12.2	16.5	33.7	35.8	24.8	28.2	39.0	65.9	82.1	90.5
Corporation income tax	4.6	6.0	6.2	4.8	6.5	8.4	10.0	12.1	15.1	18.0	27.7	30.5	26.0
Petroleum profits tax	..	..	..	0.4	1.3	2.9	2.9	6.1	2.6	11.9	66.4	195.6	248.7
Mining rents and royalties	4.3	13.1	8.5	9.9	12.8	10.4	18.4	17.0	10.9	22.9	36.4	59.1	98.0
Other tax revenues	2.9	2.7	2.2	2.4	2.8	1.8	3.1	4.0	0.2	0.4	0.6	0.2	0.2
Other non-tax revenues	19.9	19.6	23.5	18.4	20.0	23.2	28.5	17.5	19.8	25.8	44.8	14.7	26.8
Total recurrent revenues	111.8	119.4	124.5	138.8	160.5	153.2	169.6	150.1	149.9	217.9	377.8	531.9	638.9
Less revenues transferred to states	33.4	36.0	37.8	56.5	65.4	60.7	68.6	61.4	53.0	89.7	143.4	143.4	174.7
Revenues retained by Federal Government	78.4	83.4	86.7	82.3	95.1	92.5	101.0	88.7	96.9	128.2	234.4	388.5	464.2

Source: Central Bank of Nigeria and Official Gazettes.

Table 25: COMPOSITION OF RECURRENT AND CAPITAL EXPENDITURE OF THE FEDERAL GOVERNMENT, 1961–1971/72

(millions of £N)

	General Administration			Defense & Internal Security			Social & Community Services			Economic Services			Public Debt Charges[a]	Other Transfers	Loans & Grants to States	Financial Obligations & Other Transfers	Total		
	Recurrent	Capital	Total	Recurrent	Capital	Total	Recurrent	Capital	Total	Recurrent	Capital	Total	Recurrent	Recurrent	Capital	Capital	Recurrent	Capital	Total
1961	10.8	1.8	12.6	9.6	3.3	12.9	11.1	5.7	16.8	7.1	19.8	26.9	5.1	4.7	4.5	2.9	48.4	38.0	86.4
1962	9.6	2.4	12.0	10.7	5.8	16.5	10.9	5.0	15.9	6.5	17.1	23.6	7.8	6.3	17.4	1.6	51.8	49.3	101.1
1963	11.7	5.7	17.4	11.1	4.5	15.6	10.6	4.1	14.7	6.0	16.8	22.8	15.5	4.9	9.0	0.8	59.8	40.9	100.7
1964	17.7	4.9	22.6	14.3	7.5	21.8	9.5	4.9	14.4	14.0	20.0	34.0	15.3	0.5	5.2	0.5	71.3	43.0	114.3
1965	16.7	4.5	21.2	15.8	7.0	22.8	10.0	4.7	14.7	16.9	21.8	38.7	18.4	0.5	10.2	1.8	78.3	50.0	128.3
1966	21.7	3.8	25.5	17.4	5.8	23.2	9.1	4.9	14.0	12.8	22.4	35.2	22.6	5.0	14.6	2.0	88.6	53.5	142.1
1966/67	19.7	2.6	22.3	18.2	5.6	23.8	9.5	3.0	12.5	11.3	22.3	33.6	31.6	3.9	16.9	2.0	94.2	52.4	146.6
1967/68	18.1	1.1	19.2	28.1	33.7	61.8	9.7	1.9	11.6	10.5	24.6	35.1	22.0	3.9	7.6		92.3	68.9	161.2
1968/69	17.4	1.4	18.8	59.4	32.1	91.5	5.5	0.9	6.4	10.6	18.3	28.9	32.6	3.9	12.0	4.7	129.3	69.4	198.8
1969/70	23.9	3.0	26.9	136.1	56.0	192.1	7.9	1.7	9.6	10.4	17.6	28.0	58.1	3.7	9.0	0.2	240.1	87.5	327.6
1970/71	26.9	3.2	30.1	144.8	28.0	172.8	9.0	1.2	10.2	12.9	20.4	33.3	45.9	3.9	8.4	6.8	243.4	68.0	311.7
1971/72 (Budget)	33.5	18.7	52.2	106.8	23.5	130.3	9.5	11.7	21.2	19.3	84.6	103.9	38.7	10.8	16.0	4.4	218.6	158.9	377.5

[a]Includes repayments.

Source: Central Bank of Nigeria and *Official Gazettes* of the Federal Republic of Nigeria.

Table 26: COMPOSITION OF RECURRENT AND CAPITAL EXPENDITURE OF THE STATE GOVERNMENTS, 1961–1971/72

(millions of £N)

	General Administration			Social Services			Economic Services			Others			Total		
	Recurrent	Capital	Total	Recurrent	Capital	Total	Recurrent	Capital	Total	Recurrent	Capital	Total	Recurrent	Capital	Total
1961	12.6	2.5	15.1	26.5	6.9	33.4	11.0	11.4	22.4	7.7	7.6	15.3	57.8	28.4	86.2
1962	13.5	2.8	16.3	25.6	6.3	31.9	11.0	14.5	25.5	19.0	4.5	23.5	69.1	28.1	97.2
1963	16.0	2.9	18.3	24.8	4.7	29.5	12.9	10.4	23.3	10.0	9.8	19.8	63.7	27.8	91.5
1964	17.1	2.5	19.6	31.8	7.5	39.3	14.6	15.2	29.8	8.4	6.1	14.5	71.9	31.3	103.2
1965	22.1	3.3	25.4	35.0	7.4	42.4	17.2	14.1	31.3	9.5	5.7	15.2	83.8	30.5	114.3
1966	18.1	1.4	19.5	40.3	8.1	48.4	18.1	18.8	36.9	9.6	3.7	13.3	86.1	32.0	118.1
1967	18.9	0.6	19.5	25.3	9.7	35.0	13.2	12.0	25.2	6.1	3.1	9.2	63.5	25.4	88.9
1968	12.2	1.3	13.5	24.3	3.2	27.5	12.0	5.9	17.9	3.8	1.7	5.5	52.3	12.1	64.4
1969[a]	12.8	1.5	14.3	38.9	5.8	44.7	16.5	9.9	26.4	18.4	4.1	22.5	86.6	21.3	107.9
1969/70[b]	23.9	n.a.	n.a.	46.0	n.a.	n.a.	23.1	n.a.	n.a.	18.6	n.a.	n.a.	111.6	41.7	153.3
1970/71[b]	34.5	n.a.	n.a.	72.4	n.a.	n.a.	33.9	n.a.	n.a.	22.2	n.a.	n.a.	163.0	121.6	284.6
1971/72[b]	n.a.	n.a.	n.a.	n.a.	n.a.	n.a.	n.a.	n.a.	n.a.	n.a.	n.a.	n.a.	183.2	131.3	314.5

[a]Excludes Benue Plateau, East Central and Rivers States for which data are not available.
[b]Based on Budget estimates and information provided by the Central Bank of Nigeria.

Source: Central Bank of Nigeria, *Economic and Financial Review*, 1970.

Table 27: FINANCING OF FEDERAL GOVERNMENT'S OVERALL DEFICIT, 1966/67–1970/71

(millions of £N)

	1966/67	1967/68	1968/69	1969/70	1970/71
Overall budget deficit	-45.6	-72.5	-101.8	-199.4	-75.8
Financed by:					
External borrowings (net)	21.4	13.8	1.8	1.7	0.2
External grants (net)	1.1	1.2	1.1	0.3	–
Internal borrowings (net)	23.1	57.5	98.9	197.4	75.6
Non-Bank (net)	(6.4)	7.9	20.0	57.0	11.7
Bank (net)	(16.7)	49.6	78.9	140.4	63.9

Source: Central Bank of Nigeria and the *Official Gazettes* of Federal Republic of Nigeria.

NIGERIA: OPTIONS FOR LONG-TERM DEVELOPMENT

Table 28: FINANCING OF THE STATE GOVERNMENTS' OVERALL DEFICIT, 1968/69–1971/72

(millions of £N)

States / Years	Benue-Plateau	East Central	Kano	Kwara	Lagos	Mid-Western	North Central	North Eastern	North Western	Rivers	South Eastern	Western
1968/69												
Overall Budget surplus (+)/Deficit (-)	-1.4	n.a.	-0.6	-0.3	+6.2	-3.4	+0.3	-1.5	-1.0	+0.2	-3.8	-4.8
Financed by:												
Loans from Federal Government	0.7		1.0	0.4	0.2	0.4	0.9	1.6	1.2	n.a.	n.a.	1.5
Loans from marketing boards	–	–	–	–	–	0.2	–	–	–	–	n.a.	5.6
Other financing (incl. gov't grants)	–		–	–	–	–	–	–	–	0.1	3.8	1.1
Change in cash balances (increase -)	0.7		-0.4	-0.1	-6.4	2.8	-1.2	-0.1	-0.2	–	n.a.	-3.4
1969/70												
Overall Budget surplus (+)/Deficit (-)	-0.8	n.a.	-3.7	-0.7	+6.2	-5.0	+0.8	-2.7	-2.1	-5.3	-14.0	-10.2
Financed by:												
Loans from Federal Government	0.7		0.8	0.2	0.2	0.3	0.8	0.5	0.6	0.7	0.8	0.2
Loans from marketing boards	–		–	–	–	0.3	–	n.a.	–	n.a.	n.a.	8.4
Other financing (incl. gov't grants)	0.5		–	0.4	–	0.4	–	2.5	0.4	2.0	12.1	0.6
Change in cash balance (increase -)	-0.4		+2.9	0.1	-6.4	+4.0	-1.6	n.a.	+1.0	n.a.	n.a.	-1.0
1970/71ᵃ												
Overall Budget surplus (+)/Deficit (-)	-5.9	-31.9	-14.1	-6.1	-4.1	-3.0	-9.1	-9.8	-9.7	-12.6	-12.9	-11.3
Financed by:												
Loans from Federal Government	2.2	n.a.	4.4	0.9	0.2	0.9	1.0	1.8	1.5	n.a.	2.8	0.8
Loans from marketing boards	–	n.a.	–	–	–	0.3	–	–	–	n.a.	1.0	7.5
Other financing (incl. gov't grants)	1.3	n.a.	1.8	3.3	–	0.3	1.1	2.5	1.4	n.a.	3.8	3.0
Change in cash balances (increase -)	2.4	n.a.	7.9	1.9	3.9	1.5	7.0	5.5	6.8	12.6	5.3	–
1971/72ᵃ												
Overall Budget surplus (+)/Deficit (-)	-9.1	-5.1	-7.6	-8.5	-10.7	-6.6	-12.0	-12.7	-10.3	-15.4	-13.1	-11.4

ᵃBudget estimates.

Source: Central Bank of Nigeria and state government budgets.

230

Table 29: FINANCIAL OPERATIONS OF MAJOR FEDERAL STATUTORY CORPORATIONS

(millions of £N)

	1960/61	1961/62	1962/63	1963/64	1964/65	1965/66	1966/67	1967/68	1968/69	1969/70	1970/71
Nigerian Railway Corporation											
Revenues	13.2	15.2	14.9	16.3	14.2	14.6	13.1	11.1	12.0	11.6	12.0
Operating expenses (including interest)	15.6	16.3	15.9	16.3	17.7	18.8	17.6	14.5	15.7	16.8	18.2
Operating profits (+)/losses (-)[a]	-2.4	-1.1	-1.0	—	-3.5	-4.2	-4.5	-3.4	-3.7	-5.2	-6.2
Electricity Corporation of Nigeria											
Revenues	5.7	6.9	8.1	9.6	11.1	12.6	14.0	11.1	12.3	14.6	18.5
Operating expenses (including interest)	4.5	6.0	7.3	9.1	10.0	12.2	13.9	14.2	16.0	19.9	20.2
Operating profits (+)/losses (-)[a]	+1.2	+0.9	+0.8	+0.5	+1.1	+0.4	+0.1	-3.1	-3.7	-5.3	-1.7
Nigeria Port Authority											
Revenues	6.9	7.7	7.7	8.9	10.6	12.3	10.4	8.5	9.5	13.6	22.7
Operating expenses (including interest)	n.a.	6.7	7.1	7.6	8.5	9.4	8.8	8.1	8.2	9.7	18.9
Operating profits (+)/losses (-)[a]	n.a.	+1.0	+0.8	+1.3	+2.1	+2.9	+1.6	+0.4	+1.3	+3.9	+3.7
Nigeria Airways Corporation											
Revenues	4.4	4.3	4.1	4.7	4.9	5.4	5.7	5.1	5.2	6.1	6.0
Operating expenses (including interest)	3.9	3.9	4.5	4.9	5.4	5.8	5.9	6.0	5.1	5.7	5.7
Operating profits (+)/losses (-)[a]	+0.5	+0.4	-0.4	-0.2	-0.5	-0.4	-0.2	-0.9	+0.1	+0.4	+0.3
Nigerian Coal Corporation											
Revenues	1.4	1.5	1.6	1.6	n.a.	n.a.	n.a.	n.a.	n.a.	n.a.	n.a.
Operating expenses (including interest)	1.6	1.6	1.7	1.7	n.a.	n.a.	n.a.	n.a.	n.a.	n.a.	n.a.
Operating profits (+)/losses (-)[a]	-0.2	-0.1	-0.1	-0.1	n.a.	n.a.	n.a.	n.a.	n.a.	n.a.	n.a.
Nigerian Dam Authority											
Revenues	—	—	(Neg)	(Neg)	—	0.7	—	1.8	—	5.2	n.a.
Operating expenses (including interest)	—	—	—	—	0.6	0.7	1.2	1.8	3.2	3.0	n.a.
Operating profits (+)/losses (-)[a]	—	—	—	—	-0.6	-0.7	-1.2	-1.8	-3.2	+2.2	n.a.
Posts & Telegraphs Department											
Revenues	4.4	4.7	5.2	5.3	6.1	6.8	7.9	5.8	.5.4	5.9	n.a.
Operating expenses (including interest)	5.0	5.3	5.7	5.6	6.3	6.8	8.5	6.6	6.2	6.9	n.a.
Operating profits (+)/losses (-)[a]	-0.6	-0.6	-0.5	-0.3	-0.2	—	-0.6	-0.8	-0.8	-1.0	n.a.
Nigeria External Telecommunication Ltd.											
Revenues	—	—	—	0.9	0.9	1.1	1.1	1.1	1.2	1.5	1.7
Operating expenses (including interest)	—	—	—	0.6	0.6	0.7	0.7	0.7	0.6	0.7	0.9
Operating profits (+)/losses (-)[a]	—	—	—	+0.3	+0.3	+0.4	+0.4	+0.4	+0.6	+0.8	+0.8
Nigerian Broadcasting Corporation											
Revenues	1.2	1.2	1.4	1.3	1.1	1.3	1.6	1.9	1.8	2.0	2.1
Operating expenses (including interest)	1.1	1.1	1.1	1.1	1.2	1.2	1.5	1.6	1.8	1.7	1.8
Operating profits (+)/losses (-)[a]	+0.1	+0.1	+0.3	+0.2	-0.1	+0.1	+0.1	+0.3	—	+0.3	+0.3

[a]Not accounting for depreciation.

Source: Central Bank of Nigeria.

Table 30: SUMMARY OF SECOND NATIONAL DEVELOPMENT PLAN PUBLIC SECTOR INVESTMENT PROGRAM, 1970/71–1973/74

	Total		Federal Government		State Governments	
	Amount (£N Million)	Share %	Amount (£N Million)	Share %	Amount (£N Million)	Share %
Economic						
Agriculture	107.7	10.5	30.8	5.5	76.8	16.3
Livestock, forestry and fishing	25.0	2.4	3.2	0.6	21.8	4.6
Mining	2.6	0.3	2.6	0.5	–	–
Industry	86.0	8.4	40.8	7.3	45.3	9.6
Commerce and finance	18.9	1.8	11.0	2.0	7.9	1.7
Fuel and power	45.3	4.4	45.3	8.2	–	–
Transport	242.6	23.7	167.1	30.1	75.5	16.1
Communications	42.6	4.2	42.6	7.7	–	–
Resettlement and rehabilitation	10.0	1.0	10.0	1.8	–	–
Sub-Total	580.8	56.7	353.5	63.7	227.3	48.3
Social						
Education	138.9	13.5	49.1	8.8	89.8	19.1
Health	53.8	5.2	10.1	1.8	43.7	9.3
Information	10.9	1.1	4.8	0.9	6.1	1.3
Labor and social welfare	10.0	1.2	3.0	0.5	9.0	1.9
Town and country planning	19.1	1.9	5.3	1.0	13.8	2.9
Water and sewerage	51.7	5.0	–	–	51.7	11.0
Sub-Total	286.4	27.9	72.3	13.0	214.1	45.5
Administration						
General administration	52.4	5.1	23.4	4.2	28.9	6.2
Defense and security	96.4	9.4	96.4	17.4	–	–
Sub-Total	148.7	14.5	119.8	21.6	28.9	6.2
Financial obligations	9.5	0.9	9.5	1.7	–	–
Nominal total	1,025.4	100.0	555.1	100.0	470.3	100.0
Less underspending	184.2	17.9	72.9	18.2	111.3	23.7
Less transfers	37.2	3.6	37.2	6.7	–	–
Net total	804.0	78.4	445.0	75.1	359.0	76.3

Source: Second National Development Plan 1970–74, Chapter 27.

Table 31: MONEY AND CREDIT, 1960–70

(Year-end outstanding, millions of £N)

	1960	1961	1962	1963	1964	1965	1966	1967[e]	1968	1969	1970
Liabilities of banking system[a]											
Currency	72.0	74.2	80.6	84.5	99.0	100.4	108.6	103.7	91.6[f]	126.3	171.2
Demand deposits[b]	41.2	42.6	47.7	48.2	58.5	62.7	66.9	54.8	74.2	93.2	147.6
Saving deposits[b]	18.4	21.2	24.2	28.2	34.1	40.0	44.3	25.2	37.2	47.1	64.9
Money supply	131.6	138.0	152.5	160.9	191.6	203.1	219.8	183.7	203.0	266.6	383.7
Time deposits[b]	9.0	14.1	17.4	19.0	21.7	28.9	38.0	37.1	50.2	59.7	100.7
Total	140.6	152.1	169.9	179.9	213.3	232.0	257.8	220.8	253.2	326.3	484.4
Assets of banking system											
Credit to public sector[c]	4.2	13.3	9.1	19.3	25.1	37.3	62.3	93.7	171.3	251.2	336.5
Credit to marketing boards[d]		–	10.5	14.6	16.6	3.1	7.6	9.9	34.1	40.7	58.7
Credit to private sector	55.0	55.7	73.2	85.8	118.0	130.6	145.8	135.0	109.8	117.3	178.4
Net foreign assets	75.5	82.3	78.3	66.8	60.9	76.1	61.7	15.5	29.7	42.0	63.0
Net unclass. assets & liab.	5.9	0.8	-1.2	-6.6	-7.3	-15.1	-19.6	-33.3	-91.7	-124.9	-152.2
Total	140.6	152.1	169.9	179.9	213.3	232.0	257.8	220.8	253.2	326.3	484.4
Money supply percent of GNP	11.0	10.9	10.9	10.9	12.2	12.2	12.7	12.5	13.0	13.8	16.2

[a] The banking system comprises the Central Bank and commercial banks but excludes the Post Office Savings Bank.

[b] Exclude holdings by Federal Government and non-residents.

[c] Comprising Federal, state and local governments and statutory corporations; net of Federal Government deposits with the Central Bank and commercial banks.

[d] Consists only of Central Bank advances and rediscounts. Commercial bank credit to marketing boards are included in credit to the private sector; they averaged approximately £ N25 million in 1963-67 and nil thereafter.

[e] From May 1967, figures are not available for Eastern states.

[f] Excludes old notes not yet redeemed.

Source: Data provided by the Central Bank of Nigeria.

Table 32: FEDERAL GOVERNMENT PUBLIC DEBT, 1959/60–1970/71

(millions of £ N, end of period)

	1959/60	1960/61	1961/62	1962/63	1963/64	1964/65	1965/66	1966/67	1967/68	1968/69	1969/70	1970/71	Sept. 1971
Internal	17.5	36.0	49.4	67.4	96.1	116.2	131.3	173.2	213.0	324.1	468.9	599.1	626.9
Treasury Bills	8.2	15.6	18.2	21.5	30.4	35.0	37.0	64.0	85.0	130.0	200.0	308.0	308.0
Treasury Certificates	–	–	–	–	–	–	–	–	–	50.0	106.0	128.0	128.0
Development stock	7.1	14.3	19.4	34.4	54.4	69.0	83.0	99.0	119.0	132.0	150.4	150.4	178.4
Unfunded loans (or loans from marketing boards)	2.4	6.1	11.8	11.5	11.3	12.2	11.3	10.2	8.7	8.0	7.5	6.9	6.6
National Reconstruction and Development Savings Scheme	–	–	–	–	–	–	–	–	0.3	4.1	5.1	5.8	6.0
External	24.9	34.8	42.9	46.2	40.8	46.5	63.0	70.2	84.0	85.8	88.3	88.9	88.0
Total	42.4	70.8	92.4	113.5	136.9	162.7	194.4	244.4	297.0	410.0	557.2	687.2	714.9
(Of which on-lent to regions/ states, and statutory corporations)	(18.7)	(22.9)	(35.1)	(42.3)	(52.3)	(61.9)	(76.9)	(97.3)	(104.3)	(100.0)	(110.7)	(117.3)	(128.7)
Public debt as a percent of GDP at factor cost (percent)	3.8	5.7	7.4	8.6	10.4	11.1	12.6	15.1	22.8	30.2	34.7	34.4	32.0

Source: Central Bank of Nigeria.

Table 33: INTERNAL PUBLIC DEBT BY HOLDERS 1963–71 (holdings as at 31 December)

Note on layout: The original is a single wide table with an upper block "(£N million) Assets of:" and a lower block "Percent held by", each spanning four instrument groups (Total Internal Debt, Development Stocks, Treasury Bills, Treasury Certificates). It is reproduced below as four instrument tables, each with its £N million and percent sub-blocks. Where the source groups several holders with a brace into a single value, that value is shown in a combined "Other holders" row (= Insurance companies + Other financial institutions + Statutory corporations + Companies + Individuals + Others). Braces combining Central Bank + Call money fund, or Federal Government + State & local govts, are noted.

Total Internal Debt

(£N million) Assets of:

Holder	1963	1964	1965	1966	1967	1968	1969	1970	1971[a]
Central Bank	18.2	20.3	31.5	50.2	78.8	45.2	50.3	88.4	⎱158.1
Call money fund	3.5	4.9	3.3	3.4	2.9	4.4	6.1	14.1	⎰
Federal Government	⎱1.9	6.5	5.0	6.3	5.9	–	–	1.3	50.6
State & local govts[b]	⎰	2.1	5.4	5.5	7.3	7.8	12.5	26.7	70.6
Nat'l provident fund	4.3	8.9	14.1	19.7	24.2	29.0	34.3	40.6	48.9
Commercial banks	1.7	5.9	7.0	13.7	16.7	109.2	169.2	253.8	158.0
Other holders (Insurance cos., other fin. insts., statutory corps., companies, individuals, others)	34.1	38.8	42.0	45.4	47.3	50.4	99.2	120.8	128.2
Total	63.7	87.3	108.2	144.1	183.0	246.1	371.5	545.5	614.4

Percent held by

Holder	1963	1964	1965	1966	1967	1968	1969	1970	1971[a]
Central Bank	28.6	23.3	29.1	34.8	43.0	18.4	13.5	16.2	⎱25.7
Call money fund	5.5	5.6	3.0	2.3	1.6	1.8	1.6	2.6	⎰
Federal Government	⎱2.9	7.5	4.7	4.4	3.2	–	–	0.2	8.2
State & local govts[b]	⎰	2.4	5.0	3.8	4.0	3.2	3.4	4.9	11.5
Nat'l provident fund	6.7	10.2	13.0	13.7	13.2	11.8	9.2	7.4	8.0
Commercial banks	2.7	6.8	6.5	9.5	9.1	44.4	45.5	46.5	25.7
Other holders	53.6	44.2	38.8	31.5	25.9	20.4	26.8	22.2	20.9
Total	100.0	100.0	100.0	100.0	100.0	100.0	100.0	100.0	100.0

Development Stocks

(£N million) Assets of:

Holder	1963	1964	1965	1966	1967	1968	1969	1970	1971[a]
Central Bank	2.5	13.7	19.0	21.2	31.3	40.9	38.6	37.1	52.0
Call money fund	–	–	–	–	–	–	–	–	–
Federal Government	–	–	–	–	5.1	3.6	6.6	9.5	10.0
State & local govts[b]	0.3	2.1	4.1	5.4	–	–	–	–	–
Nat'l provident fund	4.3	8.9	14.1	19.7	24.2	29.0	34.3	40.6	48.9
Commercial banks	0.6	0.5	0.6	2.4	2.4	1.7	1.9	3.6	5.1
Insurance companies	0.4	0.7	1.2	1.5	1.6	1.7	1.7	4.8	5.3
Other financial institutions	15.5	19.3	20.9	23.2	27.2	31.6	37.5	42.5	47.4
Statutory corporations	7.1	7.0	7.5	5.7	5.3	5.7	6.5	7.0	6.3
Companies	0.9	0.7	0.6	0.7	1.5	1.5	3.1	3.0	3.1
Individuals	0.2	0.2	0.3	0.3	0.3	0.3	0.3	0.4	0.4
Others	1.1	0.1	0.0	0.1	–	0.1	0.1	1.1	–
Total	33.7	53.3	68.2	80.1	99.0	116.1	130.5	149.5	178.4

Percent held by

Holder	1963	1964	1965	1966	1967	1968	1969	1970	1971[a]
Central Bank	7.5	25.8	27.9	26.4	31.7	35.3	29.6	24.8	29.1
Call money fund	–	–	–	–	–	–	–	–	–
Federal Government	–	–	–	–	5.2	3.1	5.1	6.3	5.5
State & local govts[b]	1.0	3.9	6.0	6.7	–	–	–	–	–
Nat'l provident fund	12.7	16.6	20.6	24.6	24.5	25.0	26.3	27.1	27.4
Commercial banks	1.6	1.0	0.8	3.1	2.4	1.4	1.5	2.4	2.8
Insurance companies	1.2	1.2	1.7	1.8	1.6	1.4	1.3	3.2	2.9
Other financial institutions	46.1	36.3	30.7	28.9	27.5	27.2	28.7	28.4	26.5
Statutory corporations	21.2	13.2	11.0	7.1	5.3	4.9	5.0	4.7	3.5
Companies	2.5	1.3	0.9	0.9	1.6	1.3	2.4	2.0	1.7
Individuals	0.7	0.4	0.4	0.3	0.3	0.2	0.2	0.2	0.2
Others	3.2	0.2	–	0.1	–	0.1	–	0.7	–
Total	100.0	100.0	100.0	100.0	100.0	100.0	100.0	100.0	100.0

Treasury Bills

(£N million) Assets of:

Holder	1963	1964	1965	1966	1967	1968	1969	1970	1971[a]
Central Bank	15.7	6.6	12.5	29.0	47.4	4.3	11.7	50.1	⎱104.0
Call money fund	3.5	4.9	3.3	3.4	2.9	4.4	6.1	14.1	⎰
Federal Government	⎱1.6	6.5	5.0	6.3	5.8	–	–	1.3	50.6
State & local govts[b]	⎰	–	–	0.2	2.2	4.2	5.8	17.2	60.7
Nat'l provident fund	–	–	1.3	–	–	–	–	–	–
Commercial banks	1.2	5.4	6.5	11.2	14.3	97.9	97.8	138.4	50.1
Other holders	8.1	10.7	11.5	13.9	11.4	9.3	48.6	56.9	42.8
Total	30.0	34.0	40.0	64.0	84.0	120.0	170.0	278.0	308.0

Percent held by

Holder	1963	1964	1965	1966	1967	1968	1969	1970	1971[a]
Central Bank	52.3	19.4	31.3	45.3	56.4	3.6	6.9	18.0	⎱33.8
Call money fund	11.6	14.4	8.3	5.3	3.5	3.7	3.6	5.1	⎰
Federal Government	⎱5.3	19.1	12.5	9.8	6.9	–	–	0.5	16.4
State & local govts[b]	⎰	–	–	0.3	2.6	3.5	3.4	6.2	19.7
Nat'l provident fund	–	–	3.3	–	–	–	–	–	–
Commercial banks	4.0	15.9	16.3	17.5	17.0	81.6	57.5	49.8	16.3
Other holders	27.0	31.5	28.8	21.7	13.6	7.8	28.6	20.5	13.9
Total	100.0	100.0	100.0	100.0	100.0	100.0	100.0	100.0	100.0

Treasury Certificates

(£N million) Assets of:

Holder	1968	1969	1970	1971[a]
Central Bank	–	–	1.1	2.2
Call money fund	–	–	–	22.5
Commercial banks	9.7	69.4	111.7	102.8
Other holders	0.3	1.6	5.2	0.6
Total	10.0	71.0	118.0	128.0

Percent held by

Holder	1968	1969	1970	1971[a]
Central Bank	–	–	0.9	1.7
Call money fund	–	–	–	17.6
Commercial banks	97.0	97.7	94.7	80.3
Other holders	3.0	2.3	4.4	0.5
Total	100.0	100.0	100.0	100.0

[a] End – October 1971.
[b] Local government holdings of Treasury Bills included in "other".

Source: Data provided by the Central Bank of Nigeria.

Table 34: COMMERCIAL BANK LOANS AND ADVANCES, BY CATEGORY OF BORROWER (Figures at End of Year)

(millions of £N)

	1958	1959	1960	1961	1962	1963	1964	1965	1966	1967[c]	1968	1969	1970	1971
Agriculture, forestry and fishing	0.154	0.956	0.562	0.430	0.651	0.815	0.661	1.593	2.423	1.851	1.924	2.200	3.496	4.636
Mining and quarrying	0.328	0.409	0.543	0.474	0.526	0.577	0.577	0.644	0.734	0.996	0.607	1.500	3.292	5.812
Manufacturing	1.836	1.649	2.429	3.296	5.857	8.933	13.131	14.500	19.560	19.802	18.516	21.000	38.194	59.858
Real estate and construction	2.471	3.068	3.595	5.541	5.185	6.444	5.760	6.469	12.767	11.182	9.932	8.800	12.978	18.698
Public utilities	0.148	–	0.522	0.102	0.178	0.980	0.779	1.644	0.579	1.743	1.192	0.800	0.339	1.821
Transportation and communication[a]	–	–	–	–	–	–	–	–	5.137	4.361	4.580	4.900	9.500	15.893
Exports	11.610	8.403	10.719	12.184	17.388	18.857	29.562	32.576	33.012	32.169	28.871	33.400	34.772	45.826
Imports and domestic trade	13.398	13.554	21.017	19.435	27.736	30.684	33.467	28.846	28.615	32.110	27.440	27.700	46.072	59.764
Bills discounted	–	0.606	1.271	1.117	3.098	7.444	15.052	21.030	30.057	18.192	2.557	2.200	2.927	5.012
Credit and financial institutions[b]	1.654	3.391	2.927	2.506	1.018	2.409	4.378	2.957	3.788	4.569	4.565	2.400	1.361	2.889
Governments	0.165	0.306	1.061	0.851	0.737	0.694	0.933	0.990	0.629	0.836	1.433	2.500	0.648	1.796
Personal and professional[a]	–	–	–	–	–	–	–	–	2.817	3.636	3.607	5.800	11.630	16.568
Miscellaneous	6.534	8.482	12.354	14.054	14.661	11.631	18.107	23.776	8.927	6.038	7.635	8.200	10.479	12.438
Total	38.298	40.824	57.000	59.990	77.035	89.468	122.407	135.025	149.045	137.485	112.859	121.400	175.679	251.011

Percentage Distribution

	1958	1959	1960	1961	1962	1963	1964	1965	1966	1967	1968	1969	1970	1971
Agriculture, forestry and fishing	0.4	2.3	1.0	0.7	0.8	0.9	0.5	1.2	1.6	1.4	1.7	1.8	2.0	1.8
Mining and quarrying	0.9	1.0	1.0	0.8	0.7	0.6	0.5	0.5	0.5	0.7	0.5	1.2	1.9	2.3
Manufacturing	4.8	4.0	4.3	5.5	7.6	10.0	10.8	10.7	13.1	14.4	16.4	17.3	21.7	23.8
Real estate and construction	6.5	7.5	6.3	9.2	6.7	7.2	4.7	4.8	8.6	8.2	8.8	7.3	7.4	7.4
Public utilities	0.4	–	0.9	0.2	0.2	1.1	0.6	1.2	0.4	1.3	1.1	0.7	0.2	0.7
Transportation and communication	–	–	–	–	–	–	–	–	3.5	3.2	4.1	4.0	5.4	6.3
Exports	30.3	20.6	18.8	20.3	22.6	21.1	24.2	24.1	22.2	23.4	25.5	27.5	19.8	18.3
Imports and domestic trade	35.0	33.2	36.9	32.4	36.0	34.3	27.4	21.4	19.2	23.3	24.3	22.8	26.2	23.8
Bills discounted	–	1.5	2.2	1.9	4.0	8.3	12.3	15.6	20.2	13.3	2.3	1.8	1.6	2.0
Credit and financial institutions	4.3	8.3	5.0	4.2	1.3	2.7	3.6	2.2	2.5	3.3	4.1	2.0	0.8	1.2
Governments	0.4	0.8	1.9	1.4	1.0	0.8	0.8	0.7	0.4	0.6	1.2	2.1	0.3	0.7
Personal and professional	–	–	–	–	–	–	–	–	1.9	2.7	3.2	4.8	6.6	6.6
Miscellaneous	17.0	20.8	21.6	23.4	19.1	13.0	14.6	17.6	5.9	4.2	6.8	6.7	6.1	5.0
Total	100.0	100.0	100.0	100.0	100.0	100.0	100.0	100.0	100.0	100.0	100.0	100.0	100.0	100.0

[a]Prior to 1966, this category was shown as miscellaneous.
[b]From 1966, this includes call money outside the Central Bank, previously shown as miscellaneous.
[c]From 1967, figures exclude the Eastern states.

Source: Central Bank of Nigeria.

Table 35: PRODUCTION OF MAJOR CROPS, 1959/60–1969/70

('000 long tons)

	1959/60	1960/61	1961/62	1962/63	1963/64	1964/65	1965/66	1966/67	1967/68	1968/69	1969/70
Rubber[a]	n.a.	57	61	65	74	70	72	49	54	58	67
Cocoa	149	186	191	186	216	294	165	263	234	180	218
Cowpeas	362	366	424	500	601	606	636	572	543	640	846
Cassava	6,771	6,575	7,282	7,478	7,675	7,872	8,069	8,266	8,462	8,679	8,895
Cocoyam	633	642	1,132	1,515	1,530	1,599	1,580	1,414	1,599	1,287	1,764
Yams	8,767	11,915	13,258	12,892	15,630	14,330	14,500	11,771	10,499	12,194	14,913
Millet	2,418	2,524	2,607	2,490	2,688	2,444	2,685	1,719	2,549	2,151	3,245
Sorghum	2,501	3,429	3,932	4,437	4,004	4,171	4,167	3,109	3,335	2,776	4,015
Wheat	16	16	16	16	20	20	20	20	20	20	20
Maize	990	1,091	977	1,150	1,191	1,141	1,115	1,082	1,039	1,561	1,560
Groundnuts (shelled)	533	446	619	686	787	679	978	1,026	684	764	634
Seed cotton	n.a.	149	83	144	129	129	127	146	76	166	272
Rice paddy	154	117	254	193	217	228	197	380	347	320	320
Palm oil[a]	n.a.	523	493	494	499	514	492	315	338	411	474
Palm kernels[a]		423	360	393	396	448	421	242	217	257	290
Sugar[a]	—	—	—	—	—	—	5	12	19	24	27

[a]Calendar years 1960 through 1970.

Source: NADC (National Agricultural Development Committee) except where indicated otherwise below. Rubber, Palm oil and Palm kernels – FAO. Groundnuts – *Annual Abstract of Statistics*, Nigeria. 1969.

Table 36: ACREAGE OF MAJOR CROPS, 1960–70

('000 ha)

	1960	1961	1962	1963	1964	1965	1966	1967	1968	1969
Rubber	n.a.	n.a.	n.a.	n.a.	n.a.	n.a.	n.a.	n.a.	n.a.	246
Cocoa	n.a.	n.a.	n.a.	n.a.	n.a.	n.a.	n.a.	n.a.	n.a.	615
Pulses (mainly cowpeas)	1,217	1,216	1,473	2,638	2,531	2,743	3,052	3,946	3,374	4,030
Cassava	n.a.	782	868	804	873	832	913	961	904	909
Cocoyam	n.a.	181	295	257	286	282	247	289	244	317
Yams	n.a.	1,416	1,303	1,566	1,627	1,534	1,348	1,376	1,704	1,296
Millet	n.a.	4,372	4,455	4,134	4,033	4,625	4,061	4,381	4,475	4,263
Sorghum	4,583	4,671	4,786	5,249	5,548	5,933	4,839	4,732	5,174	5,850
Wheat	n.a.	9	9	9	11	11	11	11	11	11
Maize	1,321	1,378	1,123	1,426	1,475	1,403	1,384	1,470	922	1,531
Groundnuts	1,467	1,488	1,501	1,992	2,000	2,245	2,262	2,256	1,925	1,821
Cotton	n.a.	662	535	489	438	463	310	765	484	709
Rice	135	150	219	162	180	189	140	263	236	259
Palm oil	n.a.	n.a.	n.a.	n.a.	n.a.	n.a.	n.a.	n.a.	n.a.	2,469

Source: FAO: IWP – Production/Utilization/Processing Account.

Note: n.a. = not available.

Table 37: YIELDS OF MAJOR CROPS, 1960–69

(Tons/ha)

	1960	1961	1962	1963	1964	1965	1966	1967	1968	1969
Rubber	n.a.	n.a.	n.a.	n.a.	n.a.	n.a.	n.a.	n.a.	n.a.	0.24
Cocoa	n.a.	n.a.	n.a.	n.a.	n.a.	n.a.	n.a.	n.a.	n.a.	0.35
Pulses	0.31	0.35	0.34	0.23	0.24	0.24	0.19	0.14	0.19	0.22
Cassava	n.a.	9.46	8.76	9.70	9.16	9.85	9.20	8.95	9.76	9.95
Cocoyam	n.a.	6.35	5.15	6.05	5.72	5.70	5.82	5.62	5.36	5.66
Yams	n.a.	9.52	10.06	10.14	8.95	9.61	8.87	7.75	7.17	11.69
Millet	n.a.	0.59	0.57	0.66	0.62	0.59	0.43	0.59	0.49	0.77
Sorghum	0.76	0.85	0.94	0.78	0.76	0.71	0.65	0.72	0.55	0.70
Wheat	n.a.	1.7	1.7	1.7	1.8	1.8	1.8	1.8	1.8	1.8
Maize	n.a.	0.80	0.88	0.81	0.82	0.83	0.82	0.75	1.15	1.04
Groundnuts (in shell)	1.28	1.34	1.68	1.26	1.18	1.13	0.96	0.89	0.56	0.85
Cotton Seed	n.a.	0.60	0.61	0.69	0.81	0.75	0.34	0.28	0.62	0.53
Paddy	1.16	0.79	1.18	1.21	1.23	1.23	1.43	1.47	1.50	1.25

Source: FAO:IWP – Production/Utilization/Processing Account.

Note: n.a. = not available.

Table 38: PRICES TO PRODUCERS OF MAJOR AGRICULTURAL COMMODITIES, 1960–71

(£N per long ton)

	Cocoa[a]	Rubber[b]	Palm Products[c]			Groundnuts[d]		Seed Cotton[e]		
			Palm Kernel	Special Palm Oil	Technical Palm Oil	e	f	NA1	NA2	NA3
1960	156	203	29	53	44	36. 8.3	45. 4.6	56.4	51.8	47.1
1961	108g	186	29	53	44	37. 8.3	46. 4.6	56.4	48.1	47.1
1962	96	189	25	40	34	33.13.3	43.11.6	49.9	32.7	n.a.
1963	101	158	25	40	34	30. 6.9	40. 5.0	44.8	51.3	n.a.
1964	106	165	27	41	35	30. 7.9	40. 5.0	44.8	48.1	n.a.
1965	116	165	27	41	35	32.13.3	42.14.6	46.7	41.1	36.4
1966	61	141	27	41	35	34. 3.3	43.11.3	47.6	42.0	37.4
1967	86	140	27	41	35	34. 4.3i	43.11.3j	45.8	40.2	35.5
1968	91h	160	27	41	35	29. 0.0k	38. 7.0k	43.0	37.4	32.7
1969	146	181	27	41	35	26. 0.0	40. 4.4	56.0	46.7	42.0
1970	151	148	29	41	35	28.18.0	40. 4.4	56.0	46.7	42.0
1971	n.a.	n.a.	30	44	37	33.16.0	40. 4.4	56.0	46.7	42.0

Sources: "Cocoa Marketing in Nigeria" by H.C. Kriesel, CSNRD-21, Jan. 1969. Report of the Study Group on Groundnuts, NADC (June 1971). Recast and Summary of Report of the Palm Committee appointed by the Federal Government of Nigeria. Report of the Study Group on Cotton and other Fibres, NADC (June 1971). "Cotton Marketing in Nigeria" by H.C. Kriesel, CSNRD, Dec. 1968.

Notes: [a]Average price paid by Western State Marketing Board after deduction of produce sales tax (£N 4/ton).
[b]Average world price CIF London, Nigerian rubber prices are not set by market boards.
[c]Minimum produce prices set by Western and Mid-Western states marketing boards after deduction of produce sales tax (£ N1 per ton).
[d]Standard Grade.
[e]Northern States Marketing Board net buying price after deducting produce sales tax per ton of shelled nuts at Kano buying station.
[f]Produce prices set by Northern States Marketing Board before deduction of produce sales tax.
[g]Reduced from £ N156 to £ N108, January 1961.
[h]Raised to £ N101 in mid season.
[i]Subgrade price for 1967 – 32.4.3
[j]Subgrade price for 1967 – 41.11.3
[k]Prices shown are for exportable grade.
[l]Produce prices paid by Northern State Marketing Board after deducting produce sales tax (0.15 pence/lb up to 1967/68 and 0.175/lb thereafter.

Table 39: MINERAL PRODUCTION

(In thousand tons unless otherwise specified)

	1960	1961	1962	1963	1964	1965	1966	1967	1968	1969	1970[a]	1971[a]
Natural gas (m.c.f.)	5.1	10.9	17.2	22.1	36.3	94.3	101.6	91.6	51.6	145.7	284.9	410.4
Refined tin	7.6	7.7	8.2	8.6	8.7	9.5	9.1	9.1	9.8	8.7	8.1	7.6
Columbite	2.0	2.3	2.3	2.0	2.3	2.5	2.2	1.9	1.1	1.5	1.6	1.2
Limestone	..	..	..	..	..	..	1,098.0	883.2	647.4	680.0	677.5	788.3
Coal	562.0	597.0	624.0	568.0	688.0	728.0	630.1	94.6	..	17.5	56.6	68.0
Gold (ounces)	974.0	679.0	411.0	315.0	244.0	79.0	45.0	39.0	214.0	299.0	124.0	..
Marble	..	..	..	..	..	..	1.0	1.0	0.5	1.2	1.8	3.8
Cassiterite	..	..	..	..	..	..	12.6	12.6	13.0	11.6	10.6	10.7

[a]Provisional.

Source: Federal Office of Statistics and Ministry of Mines and Power.

Table 40: DOMESTIC PRODUCTION OF SELECTED MANUFACTURES, 1963–70

	1963	1964	1965	1966	1967	1968	1969	1970	1970 Index (1963 = 100)	1970 Index (1965 = 100)
Beer ('000 gallons)	10,392	12,263	12,606	13,896	13,338	15,597	19,316	24,265	233.5	192.5
Soft Drinks ('000 gallons)	3,232	3,962	5,055	4,499	4,406	4,270	5,453	7,053	218.2	139.5
Cotton textiles ('000 sq. yards)	52,152	59,088	103,365	176,743	234,347	219,929	286,839	324,161	621.6	313.6
Cement ('000 tons)	518	650	967	985	722	565	557	575	111.0	59.5
Paints ('000 gallons)	444	650	897	1,080	1,023	920	1,475	2,379	535.8	265.2
Roofing Sheets (tons)	42,988	72,392	25,750	50,732	40,521	36,506	39,710	47,597	110.7	184.8
Footwear ('000 pairs)	5,028	6,521	5,350	9,322	11,031	10,743	14,551	21,157	420.7	395.5
Soap and detergents (tons)	29,104	27,969	36,613	41,240	37,972	27,157	27,499	29,861	102.6	81.6
Vehicle assembly (number)	3,892	5,231	4,896	3,712	4,643	4,128	6,213	7,425	190.7	151.7
Matches ('000 boxes)	n.a.	n.a.	n.a.	n.a.	105,257	94,168	139,832	187,356	n.a.	n.a.
Biscuits (cwts)	n.a.	n.a.	n.a.	169,000	172,713	89,956	132,326	233,362	n.a.	n.a.
Radio and TV assembly and changers (number)	n.a.	n.a.	79,148	107,795	123,215	118,818	193,765	269,387	n.a.	340.4
Sugar confectionary (cwts)	n.a.	n.a.	79,828	119,575	138,212	140,476	218,710	281,929	n.a.	353.2
Suitcases (number)	n.a.	n.a.	n.a.	224,169	329,448	311,528	509,716	944,926	n.a.	n.a.
Cigarettes (million sticks)	n.a.	n.a.	6,024	5,421	5,142	5,470	9,507	8,502	n.a.	141.1
Rubber products (tons)	43,076	46,608	41,576	39,411	36,994	35,717	37,821	43,309	100.5	104.2
Vegetable oil (tons) (groundnut oil and cake)	220,304	269,432	300,716	207,216	202,234	293,404	328,881	315,939	143.4	105.1
Sugar (refined) (tons)	—	—	4,880	12,000	20,900	23,000	25,000	27,000	—	553.0

Source: Federal Office of Statistics and Central Bank.

Table 41: DOMESTIC PRODUCTION AS PERCENTAGE OF TOTAL SUPPLY OF SELECTED COMMODITIES, 1963–70 [a]

	1963	1964	1965	1966	1967	1968	1969	1970
Beer	84.6	88.2	96.7	97.5	98.2	98.4	98.9	99.1
Soft drinks	99.0	98.4	98.7	98.1	98.5	99.3	99.1	98.8
Cotton textiles	20.2	22.1	32.4	54.4	44.4	63.2	61.6	68.4
Cement	63.6	78.5	85.0	86.7	84.3	86.3	84.4	55.6
Paints	77.9	69.6	50.6	82.4	81.2	80.9	70.3	84.6
Roofing sheets	58.1	80.8	86.9	96.5	96.8	94.9	90.4	76.6
Footwear	47.3	61.9	71.2	86.3	89.7	94.5	96.7	96.0
Soap and detergents	n.a.	n.a.	n.a.	95.4	88.4	90.1	93.2	91.4
Refined sugar	—	—	4.6	11.3	20.6	38.8	26.8	23.7
Biscuits	n.a.	n.a.	n.a.	94.4	93.1	95.7	98.5	98.8

[a]Ratio of domestic production to total supply is based on data expressed in volume.

Source: Federal Office of Statistics and Central Bank.

Table 42: PAID-UP CAPITAL BY SOURCE OF OWNERSHIP IN THE MANUFACTURING SECTOR, 1967

(thousands of £N)

	Private Nigerian	Public[a] Nigerian	Total Nigerian	Non Nigerian	Total	% Nigerian in Total
Food, beverages and tobacco	1,758	2,327	4,085	15,006	19,091	21.4
Vegetable oil milling	105	701	806	1,154	1,960	41.1
Textiles, footwear, apparel	1,494	3,438	4,932	8,057	12,989	38.0
Sawmilling and furniture	1,328	128	1,456	2,221	3,677	39.6
Printing and paper products	733	2,096	2,829	1,824	4,653	60.8
Chemicals, paints, plastics	89	37	126	3,791	3,917	3.3
Rubber products	353	375	728	1,313	2,041	55.4
Cement and glass products	267	783	1,050	1,999	3,049	34.4
Metal products and misc.	1,504	1,034	2,538	8,155	10,693	23.7
Motor vehicles repairs	1,011	556	1,567	1,445	3,012	52.0
Total	7,630	10,918	18,549	43,521[b]	62,070	29.9
% in total	12.3	17.6	29.9	70.1	100.0	

[a]Federal and regional governments.
[b]Including £2.5 million for the Commonwealth Development Corporation (CDC), i.e., mainly in sugar (£2.0 million), in rubber products and basic metals.

Source: Industrial Survey, 1967.

Table 43: GEOGRAPHICAL DISTRIBUTION OF GROSS OUTPUT, VALUE-ADDED AND EMPLOYMENT IN MANUFACTURING, 1963–67

In Value	Lagos	West[a]	Mid-West	North	Sub-Total	East	Total
Gross output (£N'000)							
1963	39,654	28,419	10,347	38,683	115,103	19,589	134,692
1967	67,827	61,304	8,002	82,113	219,246	n.a.	n.a.
Value-Added (£N'000)							
1963	13,371	17,023	4,706	10,762	45,862	9,060	54,922
1967	24,401	30,976	3,584	28,670	87,631	n.a.	n.a.
Employment (number)							
1963	15,379	12,021	10,190	15,784	53,374	12,425	65,799
1967	20,784	23,221	6,094	26,297	76,396	n.a.	n.a.
Percentages							
Gross output							
1963	34.5	24.6	9.0	31.9	100.0	17.0[b]	
1967	30.9	28.0	3.6	37.5	100.0	n.a.	
Value-Added							
1963	29.2	37.1	10.2	23.5	100.0	19.8[b]	
1967	27.8	35.3	4.1	32.8	100.0	n.a.	
Employment							
1963	28.8	22.5	19.0	29.7	100.0	23.3[b]	
1967	27.2	30.4	8.0	34.4	100.0	n.a.	

[a]Includes greater Lagos area.
[b]Percentage of total for other regions in Nigeria.

Source: Industrial Surveys, 1963 and 1967.

Table 44: CRUDE OIL PRODUCTION

Time Period	Average Daily Production (Thousands of barrels)		
	Onshore	Offshore	Total
1958	5.1	—	5.1
1959	11.2	—	11.2
1960	17.4	—	11.4
1961	46.0	—	46.0
1962	67.5	—	67.5
1963	76.5	—	76.5
1964	120.2	—	120.2
1965	245.7	26.5	272.2
1966	366.6	51.0	417.6
Jan-June 1967	517.9	53.7	571.7
July-Dec 1967	15.4	55.6	71.0
Jan-Sept 1968	—	79.8	79.8
Oct-Dec 1968	171.7	153.4	325.1
Jan-June 1969	351.1	187.9	539.0
July-Dec 1969	356.2	187.0	543.2
Jan-June 1970	663.7	245.9	909.6
July-Dec 1970	931.8	330.3	1,262.1
Jan-June 1971	1,149.3	348.2	1,497.5
July-Dec 1971	1,192.4	369.5	1,561.9
Jan-Mar 1972[a]	1,278.0	450.8	1,728.8
April 1972[a]	1,292.8	504.6	1,797.5

[a]Provisional.

Source: Federal Ministry of Mines and Power.

Table 45: COMPARATIVE COSTS OF CRUDE OIL LAID-DOWN AT ROTTERDAM AND NEW YORK

(US$ per barrel)

	Nigerian	Libyan	Iranian	Venezuelan
	(Low-Sulphur)		(High-Sulphur)	
January 1971				
Tax-paid cost	1.44	1.68	1.09	n.a.
Freight to Rotterdam	.61	.40	1.16	n.a.
Laid-down cost at Rotterdam	2.05	2.08	2.25	n.a.
Freight to New York	.68	.58	1.41	n.a.
Laid-down cost at New York	2.12	2.26	2.50	n.a.
July 1971				
Tax-paid cost	2.14	2.30	1.43	1.98
Freight to Rotterdam	.56	.39	1.10	.45
Laid-down cost at Rotterdam	2.70	2.69	2.53	2.43
Freight to New York	.62	.55	1.28	.26
Laid-down cost at New York	2.76	2.85	2.71	2.25

Source: Mission estimates.

Table 46: PETROLEUM SECTOR ACCOUNTS

(current £N millions)

	1963	1964	1965	1966	1967	1968	1969	1970	1971[a]
Volume of production (million barrels)	28	44	99	152	116	52	197	396	558
Contribution to Gross Domestic Product									
Gross proceeds	20.7	32.7	69.1	100.5	71.8	37.8	132.9	270.6	508.3
Exports	20.1	32.0	68.1	91.9	72.0	37.8	130.8	258.6	489.1
Local proceeds	0.6	0.7	1.0	8.6	-0.2	—	2.1	12.0	19.2
Intermediate inputs	12.8	16.1	18.0	19.2	23.1	19.1	26.0	35.8	45.0
Indirect taxes	0.2	0.9	2.2	2.7	1.4	1.6	4.0	7.5	9.0
Harbor dues and port charges	0.6	1.0	2.0	2.7	2.4	0.6	3.3	7.9	4.3
Value-added	7.1	14.7	46.9	75.9	44.9	16.5	99.6	219.4	450.0
Wages and salaries	2.0	2.3	2.7	2.7	2.5	1.8	2.8	4.4	6.0
Government income	4.8	11.4	11.2	16.0	25.6	15.1	22.9	80.7	247.5
Investment income[b]	0.2	1.0	33.0	57.2	16.8	-0.4	73.9	134.3	196.5
Balance of Payments									
Exports, f.o.b.	20.1	32.0	68.1	91.9	72.0	37.8	130.8	258.6	489.1
Imports, c.i.f.	-4.2	-11.7	-13.5	-19.5	-17.5	-9.9	-12.7	-26.2	-25.3
Trade balance	15.9	20.3	54.6	72.4	54.5	27.9	118.1	232.4	463.8
Non-factor service payments	-6.4	-12.3	-22.2	-39.5	-31.5	-28.2	-48.1	-48.5	-57.8
Investment income[b]	-0.2	-1.0	-33.0	-57.2	-16.8	0.4	-73.9	-134.3	-196.5
Current balance	9.3	7.0	-0.6	-24.3	6.2	0.1	-3.9	49.6	209.5
Direct investment	5.1	18.1	36.2	67.7	50.3	29.1	57.6	75.0	89.2
Short-term capital	—	—	—	—	-7.8	-0.4	-0.4	2.0	-5.9
Overall balance	14.3	25.1	35.6	43.4	48.7	28.8	53.3	126.6	292.8
Local Cash Transactions									
Payments to government	5.0	12.3	13.4	18.7	27.1	16.7	26.9	88.2	256.5
Other local payments	9.8	13.5	23.2	33.3	29.2	12.5	28.9	48.4	61.4
Less: local proceeds	-0.5	-0.7	-1.0	-8.6	0.2	—	-2.1	-12.0	-19.2
Variations in local cash balance	—	—	—	—	-7.8	-0.4	-0.4	2.0	-5.9
Net balance	14.3	25.1	35.6	43.4	48.7	28.8	53.3	126.6	292.8

[a]Provisional.

[b]Residual item.

Sources: Intermediate inputs, investment income and direct investment: mission estimates based on data provided by the Ministry of Finance and the research department of the Central Bank of Nigeria. Other items: Central Bank of Nigeria.

Table 47: PAYMENTS OF PETROLEUM EXPLORATION AND PRODUCTION COMPANIES TO GOVERNMENT

(thousands of £N)

	1958/59	1959/60	1960/61	1961/62	1962/63	1963/64	1964/65	1965/66	1966/67	1967/68	1968/69	1969/70	1970/71
Rentals	13	666	888	1,691	2,296	3,031	3,861	4,414	4,957	5,516	5,988	6,605	1,831
Royalties	48	222	338	1,186	1,768	1,998	3,346	7,767	10,516	9,065	7,999	15,412	29,926
Premium	–	–	–	5,657	4,404	–	635	42	500	–	18	50	21
Profits Tax	–	–	–	–	–	–	375	1,324	2,883	6,011	2,644	11,903	66,381
Oil pipeline fees	–	–	–	1	1	1	6	18	8	7	2	24	35
Total	61	888	1,226	8,535	8,469	5,030	8,223	13,565	18,864	20,599	16,651	33,994	98,194

Sources: 1958/59–1969/70: Reports of the Accountant-General of the Federation. 1970/71: *Recurrent Estimate of the Government of the Federal Republic of Nigeria, 1971–72.*

Table 48: CONSUMER PRICE INDEX,[a] 1960–71

	All Items		Food[b]		Non-Food	
	Index	% Change over Previous Year	Index	% Change over Previous Year	Index	% Change over Previous Year
1960	100.0	—	100.0	—	100.0	—
1961	106.4	6.4	109.8	9.8	103.6	3.6
1962	112.0	5.2	118.0	7.5	107.0	3.3
1963	108.9	-2.8	106.7	-9.6	110.7	3.5
1964	110.1	1.1	105.7	-0.9	113.8	2.7
1965	114.4	3.9	110.5	4.5	117.7	3.4
1966	125.5	9.7	133.1	20.5	119.2	1.3
1967	120.8	-3.8	119.3	-10.4	122.1	2.4
1968	120.3	-0.4	112.6	-5.6	126.7	3.8
1969	132.3	10.0	133.9	18.9	131.0	3.3
1970	150.6	13.8	164.5	22.9	139.0	6.1
1971[c]	173.3	15.1	208.9	27.1	143.6	3.3

Annual Average of Monthly Indices

Item	1969	1970	1971[c]	Percentage Change between:	
				1969 and 1970	1970 and 1971
Accommodation	126.1	129.7	132.0	+2.9	+1.8
Clothing	148.4	160.6	167.1	+8.2	+4.0
Drinks	137.5	140.1	145.8	+1.9	+4.1
Food	133.9	164.4	208.9	+23.5	+27.1
Fuel and light	132.5	144.9	157.6	+9.4	+8.8
Tobacco and kolanuts	92.2	97.1	99.1	+5.3	+2.1
Transport	132.0	143.4	143.3	+8.6	-0.1
Other purchases	134.8	151.5	157.3	+12.4	+3.8
Other services	121.3	125.7	126.3	+3.6	+0.5

[a]Compiled from urban price indices for consumers earning less than £N450 per annum in nine cities. Cities from Eastern states are not included for lack of data.

[b]Food items have 45.5 percent of the total weight in the all-items index.

[c]Provisional.

Source: Central Bank of Nigeria.

Table 49: ENROLLMENTS IN PRIMARY SCHOOLS BY GRADE AND STATE, 1970[a]

	Grade 1	Grade 2	Grade 3	Grade 4	Grade 5	Grade 6	Grade 7	Grade 8	Total Graduating Class (6, 7 or 8)	Percent Distribution	Total Primary School Enrollments	% Distribution	Total 1970 Population in Thous.	Primary School Enrollment as of Total Population
Lagos	45,514	39,847	38,267	34,233	30,840	26,494	15,704	9,936	9,936	3.6	240,835	6.5	1,799	13.4
Benue Plateau	30,279	28,043	25,485	23,330	19,536	16,283	14,171	—	14,171	5.1	157,127	4.2	4,760	3.3
Kano[b]	13,869	10,795	9,736	9,204	7,711	6,079	5,126	—	5,126	1.8	62,520	1.7	6,856	0.9
Kwara	22,758	21,715	19,761	17,929	15,364	13,896	13,265	—	13,265	4.7	124,688	3.4	2,848	4.4
North-Central	23,626	18,647	15,909	12,620	11,731	10,428	8,091	—	8,091	2.9	101,052	2.7	4,865	2.1
North-Eastern	25,664	22,419	20,146	18,643	16,191	15,113	13,164	—	13,164	4.7	131,340	3.6	9,252	1.4
North-Western	17,258	14,186	12,722	11,041	7,452	8,048	6,815	—	6,815	2.4	77,522	2.1	6,806	1.1
East-Central	392,612	237,858	183,239	128,749	79,162	67,398	—	—	67,398	24.0	1,089,018	29.5	8,580	12.7
Mid-Western	89,272	71,560	63,740	52,332	43,326	40,673	—	—	40,673	14.5	360,903	9.8	3,011	12.0
Rivers	57,329	34,717	24,816	15,663	10,659	7,816	—	—	7,816	2.8	151,000	4.1	1,833	8.2
South-Eastern	146,569	99,329	75,746	36,565	22,829	16,097	—	—	16,097	5.7	397,135	10.7	4,301	9.2
Western	206,788	160,925	140,627	118,362	97,910	77,922	—	—	77,922	27.8	802,534	21.7	11,263	7.1
Total Nigeria	1,071,538	760,041	630,194	478,671	362,711	306,247	76,336	9,936	280,474	100.0	3,695,674	100.0	66,174	5.6
Leaving school rate %	29.1	17.1	24.0	24.2	15.6	20.8[c]	36.7[d]							

[a] 1970 figures were available for all states except for Lagos, 1969, where a 4% annual increase was assumed, North-Central, 1969, (3%) and Mid-Western, 1969, (3%).

[b] Including unaided schools.

[c] Computed only for the states with Grade 7.

[d] Representing only Lagos state.

Source: UNESCO, Education in Nigeria, 1971, compiled from statistics supplied by state Ministries of Education.

Note: In comparing the total graduating class of 280,474 to the combined enrollment of the first grade of all post-primary schools (89,481) we find only 31.9% of primary school leavers continue post-primary levels.

Table 50: ENROLLMENTS IN ALL POST-PRIMARY LEVEL SCHOOLS, 1970[a] (National Totals)

Types of Post Primary Schools	Total Primary School Graduating Class	Combined Post-Primary Levels[b]					Total Post-Primary Levels
		I	II	III	IV	V	
Secondary Grammar Schools		62,797	55,902	47,931	36,233	27,815	230,678
Secondary Modern Schools		11,332	10,499	7,114	687	3,772[c]	33,404
Secondary Commercial Schools		8,041	6,171	3,868	2,535	1,283	21,898
Grade II Teacher Training Colleges (5-year post-primary and 2-year post-grade III or WASC)		7,311	5,671	3,513	5,794	4,646	26,935
Total post-primary levels	280,474	89,481	78,243	62,426	45,249	37,516[c]	312,915
leaving school rate %	68.1	12.6	20.2	27.5	20.1		

Source: UNESCO, Education in Nigeria, 1971, compiled from statistics supplied by state Ministries of Education.

[a]All enrollment figures were inflated so as to correspond to 1970 levels (when 1970 was not available), as in the following states: Benue-Plateau, Lagos, North-Central and South-Eastern. The assumed rate of growth was 3% p.a. in all states, except in Lagos where 4% p.a., was used.

[b]These post-primary levels were created for the purposes of this study. Although there are many differences between Grade I of Secondary Grammar and Secondary Commercial and Teacher Training Colleges, for this study those differences have been disregarded.

[c]Including in Grade V the total enrollment of a 3-year post-secondary modern school (Teachers' College), in the Western State which has the following attendance: Grade I, 1,560; II, 1,205; III, 1,007. For comparison purposes the real figure should be 36,148.

Notes:
Western State's Secondary Grammar and Commercial Schools statistics were combined. The breakdown was estimated by IBRD staff. Lagos State's Secondary Grammar School Grade VI is included in Grade V. Many Grade II Teachers' Colleges are planning to change their requirements to 5-year secondary grammar course plus teacher training. East-Central 2-year Teachers' College breakdown was estimated by IBRD staff.

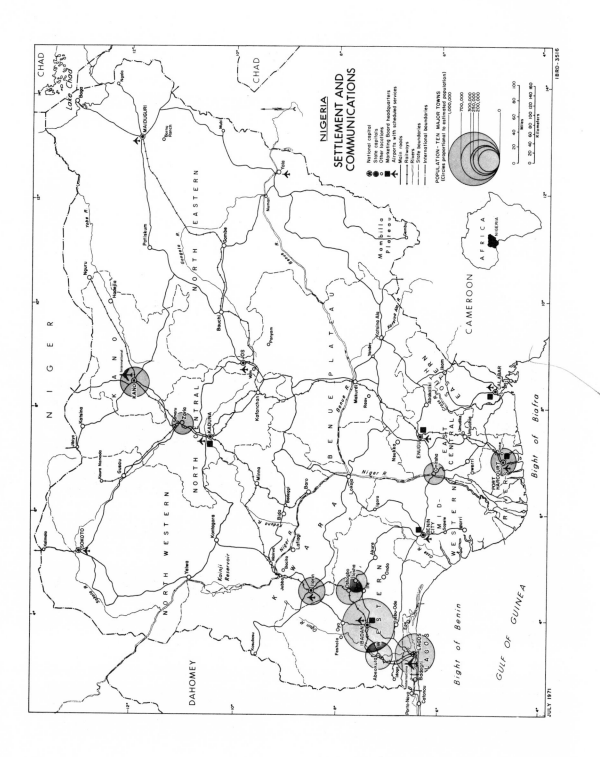

NIGERIA

SETTLEMENT AND
COMMUNICATIONS

National capital
State capitals
Other locations
Marketing Board headquarters
Airports with scheduled services
Main roads
Railways
Rivers
State boundaries
International boundaries

POPULATION – TEN MAJOR TOWNS
(Circles proportional to estimated population)

700,000
300,000
250,000
200,000

IBRD-3516

JULY 1971

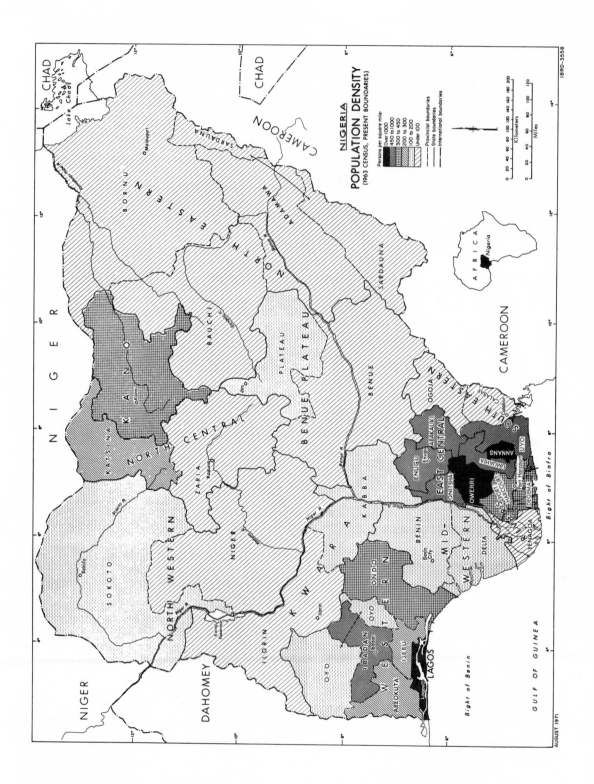

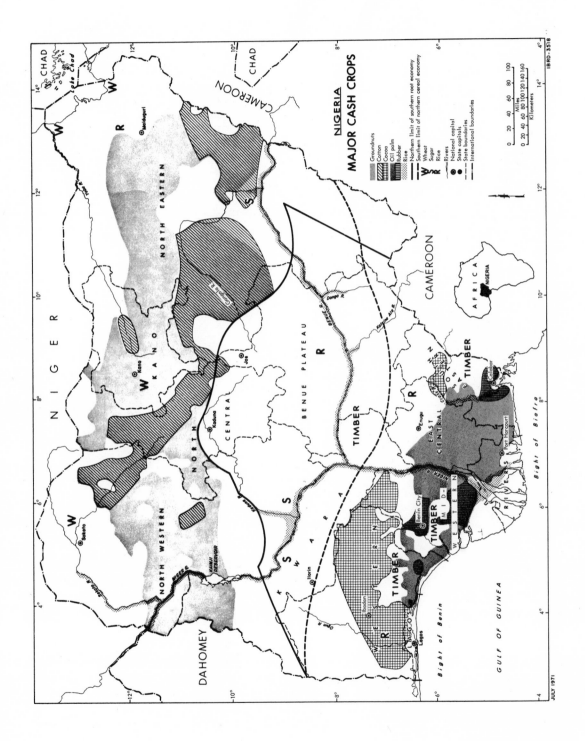

NIGERIA
MAJOR CASH CROPS

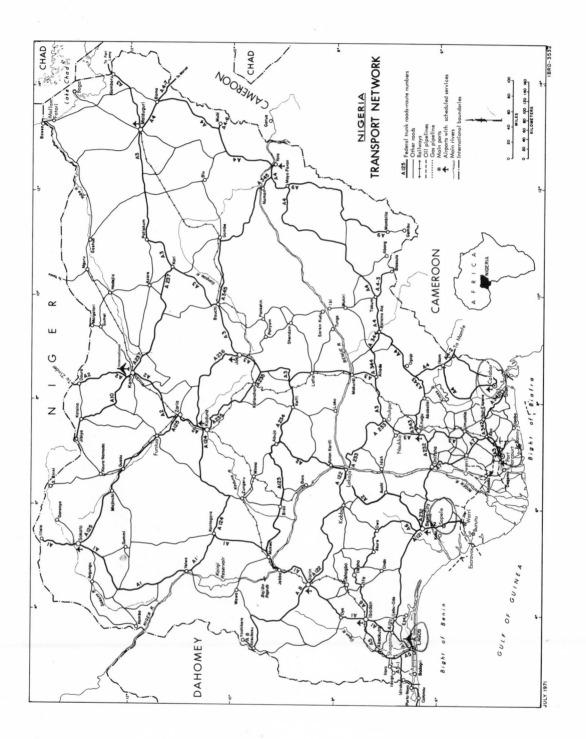